THE EMPEROR
AND THE
ROMAN ARMY
31 BC – AD 235

THE EMPEROR
AND THE
ROMAN ARMY

31 BC – AD 235

J.B. CAMPBELL

CLARENDON PRESS · OXFORD
1984

Oxford University Press, Walton Street, Oxford OX2 6DP

London Glasgow New York Toronto
Delhi Bombay Calcutta Madras Karachi
Kuala Lumpur Singapore Hong Kong Tokyo
Nairobi Dar es Salaam Cape Town
Melbourne Auckland

and associated companies in
Beirut Berlin Ibadan Mexico City Nicosia

Oxford is a trade mark of Oxford University Press

Published in the United States
by Oxford University Press, New York

British Library Cataloguing in Publication Data

Campbell, J.B.
  The emperor and the Roman army, 31BC–AD235.
  1. Roman emperors   2. Rome–Army–
  History
  I. Title
  354.37'0312   JC85.E/
  ISBN 0-19-814834-8

Library of Congress Cataloging in Publication Data
Campbell, J.B.
  The Emperor and the Roman Army, 31 BC–AD 235.
  Bibliography: p.
  Includes index.
  1. Rome–Politics and government--30 BC–284 AD.
  2. Rome. Army–Political activity. 3. Rome. Army–
  Organization. 4. Roman emperors–Duties. I. Title.
  DG276.5.C26 1984   322'.5'0937   83-19353
  ISBN 0-19-814834-8

Typeset by ROD-ART, Abingdon, Oxon.
Printed in Great Britain
at the University Press, Oxford.

TO
MY PARENTS

PREFACE

Ultimately the Roman emperor did not rely for survival on political parties, or the support of groups of senators and *equites*, or on mass popular support based on elections or assemblies, but on military strength and the personal loyalty of his army. Curiously, the theme of the political importance of the army and its relationship with the emperor who controlled it virtually as a personal mercenary force, has not received a coherent analysis, although the army of the imperial period has long been an attractive field of detailed study for scholars.

I first became interested in the relationship of emperor and army while studying the history of Septimius Severus and his dynasty, a period sometimes conveniently labelled as the 'military monarchy'. For it did not seem that the autocracy of Septimius Severus was much different from that of Augustus. Indeed Domitian, when mentioning a letter sent to some veterans by Augustus, could describe him as 'an emperor who was extremely attentive and benevolent towards his very own soldiers of the fourth legion' (*FIRA*² 1, no. 75). So I was led to ask precisely how all emperors persuaded the army to identify with them, how they secured themselves against military revolt, and in what sense if any the Roman empire could be described as a military monarchy.

My concern has been to examine this broad theme and emphasize the continuity and common factors in each emperor's personal relationship with the troops. Nevertheless, I also believe that the personality and character of individual emperors and the circumstances of their reigns were of great importance in influencing how they dealt with the traditional framework of relationships in Roman life and government. In this sense 'the emperor' did not exist. The means for promoting the identification of emperor and troops were not a coherent system; the army was not necessarily dominant in the thinking of all emperors. Tiberius, commenting on his position as emperor, used to say that he was 'holding a wolf by the ears'. I have tried to show what it was like to be a Roman emperor, primarily in his dealings with the army, but also in respect of his relations with other groups, especially the senatorial class, and to consider what was expected of an emperor in his military role.

I must emphasize that my intention is to place the picture produced by the ancient sources in as pure and clear a light as possible, and not suffuse it with lengthy reviews of secondary literature and discussion of points of detail. I am aware that in so doing I may have passed over much that requires further consideration, and that this picture may be one-sided, showing only what the upper classes thought it was like to be emperor, or what was notable about individual emperors. However, since most emperors themselves came from the higher orders, who also provided most of the chief administrators and the army commanders who executed the emperor's decisions, it seems to me that their point of view is the one that matters. The expectations which the upper classes had of an emperor in his military activities will have helped to influence his use of the army and his role as a military leader. This will have been specially true in the case of those emperors who sought to rule with the support of the senatorial class.

Furthermore, I believe that the Roman emperor and his army can best be understood in terms of the traditions and prejudices of Roman society and government. I have not, therefore, sought to compare the emperor with autocrats in diverse cultures and ages.

The chronological limit of this book is A.D. 235. However, material has been included from the reigns of Maximinus and Gordian III, where this throws fresh light on evidence from the earlier period. There was perhaps a case for carrying on the study to the reign of Constantine, but, apart from the technical problems of length, I decided that it was probably better to end before the relationship between emperor and army broke down in the mid-third century, and before the military reorganization of Diocletian and Constantine. Large sections of the text were complete by 1979/80, and I was unable subsequently to take consistent account of works not available to me at that time, unless they substantially affected my arguments. Furthermore, the study was abandoned for four years while I was teaching at the Royal Belfast Academical Institution, where my academic and cricket duties left little time for research. When I returned to it I found like Ovid that to amend a completed work 'animum lento curarum frigore laedit'. The production of a text for publication has been a long struggle, and it is with all the more gratitude that I remember those who have helped me. Professor Alan Astin introduced me to the study of Ancient History and has provided frequent assistance during my career; he also read large sections of the text in typescript and made many helpful suggestions. My colleagues at the Queen's University of Belfast, Dr. Richard Talbert and Dr. Raymond Davis, made numerous useful comments on the typescript; Dr. Davis, Mr. Philip Lomas, and my old friend Mr. Steven Jackson, most learned of schoolmasters, read the proofs with great diligence. Professor Zeev Rubin of the University of Tel Aviv kindly allowed me to consult and use material from his unpublished Oxford D. Phil. thesis. My pupils Keith Allen and Garry Corbett have ensured over a number of years that I have not become obsessed with Ancient History.

As is fitting, my greatest debt is to scholars in Oxford where the book began as a D. Phil. thesis, and where most of it was written. My examiners, Dr. John Matthews and Dr. Barbara Levick, made many perceptive and useful suggestions for improvement; my tutor at Worcester, Martin Frederiksen, gave me thoughtful and unfailing assistance, which is made all the more poignant by his premature death.

Professor Fergus Millar began the supervision of my thesis; his lively interest, patient advice, and continuing guidance are well known to all his students. One quality, however, should be singled out, and that is his ability to convince his pupils that they have something of importance to say and that they can make their own decisions in their research. A glance at the table of contents of this book will show how much I owe directly to the example of *The Emperor in the Roman World*. Professor Peter Brunt took over the supervision of my thesis at a critical stage and ever since has provided me with generous advice, guidance, and encouragement. His copious and penetrating comments on the entire text of the thesis have saved me from countless errors. Most stimulating has been his ability to recognize and expound all an argument's ramifications, which otherwise would have been only dimly discernible to me. Without the help of these two scholars this book would not have been completed. I hope that in some small way it is worthy of them.

I also wish to thank the Oxford University Press for the speed and patience with which they dealt with an untidy typescript.

This final paragraph must stand as an expression of everything I feel for K.H.

Belfast
8 December, 1983   J.B.C.

ACKNOWLEDGEMENTS

The translation on p. 365 is reprinted by permission of Penguin Books Ltd. from Machiavelli: *The Prince,* translated by G. Bull (Penguin Classics, revised edition 1981), p. 53.

The translation on p. 423 is reprinted by permission of the University of Columbia Press from *Roman Civilization II: The Empire,* edited by N. Lewis and M. Reinhold (Harper Torchbooks, 1966), p. 530.

Certain passages on pp. 227-8, 235, 333, and 345 are reprinted by permission of the Council of the Society for the Promotion of Roman Studies from my articles, 'Who were the *Viri Militares?' JRS* LXV (1975), 11 and 'The Marriage of Soldiers under the Empire', *JRS* LXVIII (1978), 153.

CONTENTS

PART TWO

THE SOLDIER AND THE LAW

PART THREE

THE ORGANIZATION OF MILITARY COMMANDS

ABBREVIATIONS

This list contains the full title of a number of works frequently cited in the footnotes in a shortened form:

Abbott and Johnson — F.F. Abbott and A.C. Johnson, *Municipal Administration in the Roman Empire*, Princeton (1926).

ANRW II.1 etc. — *Aufstieg und Niedergang der römischen Welt : Principat* (ed. Temporini), Berlin (1974).

Birley, *Septimius Severus* — A.R. Birley, *Septimius Severus, the African Emperor*, London (1971).

Brunt, 'Pay and Superannuation' — P.A. Brunt, 'Pay and Superannuation in the Roman Army', *PSBR* 18, N.S. 5 (1950), 50.

Buckland, *Text-Book* — W.W. Buckland, *A Text-Book of Roman Law from Augustus to Justinian* (3rd. edition by P. Stein with bibliography), Cambridge (1975).

Campbell, *JRS* 1975 — J.B. Campbell, 'Who were the *viri militares?*', *JRS* 65 (1975), 11.

Campbell, *JRS* 1978 — J.B. Campbell, 'The Marriage of Roman Soldiers under the Empire', *JRS* 68 (1978), 153.

Caprino, *La Colonna* — C. Caprino, *La Colonna di Marco Aurelio* Rome (1955).

Cheesman, *Auxilia* — G.L. Cheesman, *The Auxilia of the Roman Imperial Army*, Oxford (1914).

CJ — *Codex Iustinianus*, ed. P. Krüger (1877).

Crook, *Law and Life* — J.A. Crook, *Law and Life of Rome*, London (1967).

D — *Digesta Iustiniani Augusti*, ed. T. Mommsen (1877).

*FIRA*²	S. Riccobono, J. Baviera, C. Ferrini, J. Furlani, V. Arangio-Ruiz, *Fontes Iuris Romani Anteiustiniani*² (I–III), Florence (1940-3).
Florescu, *Trajanssäule*	F.B. Florescu, *Die Trajanssäule*, Bonn (1969).
Forni, *Il Reclutamento*	G. Forni, *Il Reclutamento delle legioni da Augusto a Diocleziano*, Rome (1953).
Harmand, *L'Armée*	J. Harmand, *L'Armée et le Soldat à Rome 105-57* BC, Paris (1967).
Honoré, *JRS* 1979	A.M. Honoré, 'Imperial Rescripts AD 193-305: Authorship and Authenticity', *JRS* 69 (1979), 51.
Kraft, *Rekrutierung*	E. Kraft, *Zur Rekrutierung von Alen und Kohorten an Rhein und Donau*, Bern (1951).
MacMullen, *Soldier and Civilian*	R. MacMullen, *Soldier and Civilian in the Later Roman Empire*, Harvard (1963).
Millar, *Cassius Dio*	F. Millar, *A Study of Cassius Dio*, Oxford (1964).
Millar, *ERW*	F. Millar, *The Emperor in the Roman World (31 BC-AD 337)*, London (1977).
Pflaum, *Carrières*	H.G. Pflaum, *Les Carrières procuratoriennes équestres*, Paris (1960-1).
Rostovtzeff, *SEHRE*²	M. Rostovtzeff, *Social and Economic History of the Roman Empire*² (ed. P.M. Fraser), Oxford (1957).
Williams, *JRS* 1974	W. Williams, 'The *Libellus* Procedure and the Severan Papyri', *JRS* 64 (1974), 86.
Williams, *JRS* 1976	W. Williams, 'Individuality in the Imperial Constitutions, Hadrian and the Antonines', *JRS* 66 (1976), 67.

EMPERORS FROM AUGUSTUS TO GORDIAN III

This list gives the name by which each emperor is referred to in the main text, and, in brackets, his official nomenclature.

Augustus (Imperator Caesar Augustus)	27 BC–AD 14
Tiberius (Ti. Caesar Augustus)	AD 14–37
Gaius (C. Caesar Augustus Germanicus)	37–41
Claudius (Ti. Claudius Caesar Augustus Germanicus)	41–54
Nero (Imperator Nero Claudius Caesar Augustus Germanicus)	54–68
Galba (Ser. Sulpicius Galba Imperator Caesar Augustus)	68–69
Otho (Imperator M. Otho Caesar Augustus)	69
Vitellius (A. Vitellius Augustus Germanicus Imperator)	69
Vespasian (Imperator Caesar Vespasianus Augustus)	69–79
Titus (Imperator Titus Caesar Vespasianus Augustus)	79–81
Domitian (Imperator Caesar Domitianus Augustus)	81–96
Nerva (Imperator Caesar Nerva Augustus)	96–98
Trajan (Imperator Caesar Nerva Traianus Augustus)	98–117
Hadrian (Imperator Caesar Traianus Hadrianus Augustus)	117–138
Antoninus Pius (Imperator Caesar T. Aelius Hadrianus Antoninus Augustus Pius)	138–161
Marcus Aurelius (Imperator Caesar M. Aurelius Antoninus Augustus)	161–180
Lucius Verus (Imperator Caesar L. Aurelius Verus Augustus)	161–169
Commodus (Imperator Caesar M. Aurelius Commodus Antoninus Augustus)	176–192
Pertinax (Imperator Caesar P. Helvius Pertinax Augustus)	193
Didius Julianus (Imperator Caesar M. Didius Severus Julianus Augustus)	193
Septimius Severus (Imperator Caesar L. Septimius Severus Pertinax Augustus)	193–211

PROLOGUE

I

THE ROMAN SOLDIER

Flavius Arrianus, during his governorship of Cappadocia
c. AD 132, made a trip to inspect the Roman forts and outposts protecting the Black Sea coast. He wrote reports in
Latin to Hadrian about his findings, and also produced in
Greek a summary of the topographical and antiquarian
interest of the area:

Arrianus greeting to Imperator Caesar Traianus Hadrianus Augustus.

Before midday we came more than about sixty miles to Apsarus
where five units are stationed. I gave the soldiers their pay, and
inspected their weapons, the fortifications, the ditch, the sick, and the
existing supply of food. The opinion I formed on these matters is
written down in my Latin report.

Arrian then describes another inspection:

The guard post there [near the river Phasis], where four hundred
picked soldiers are stationed, was in my opinion very strong because of
the nature of the terrain, and very suitable for the protection of those
sailing in the area. . . . In a word, everything is organized in such a way
as to discourage any of the savages from approaching it; and there is
no danger that those on guard in it will be put under siege. Since the
harbour needed to be secure for ships, and the surrounding territory
inhabited by veteran soldiers and other people engaged in trade had to
be made safe, I decided to build, starting from the second ditch which
surrounds the wall, another ditch down to the river; this will protect
the harbour and the homes outside the wall.[1]

---

[1] Arrian, *Periplous* 6; 9; cf. 3.1; 10.3.

These extracts illustrate several themes of importance and interest for the place of the Roman army in relation to the emperor, its commanders, and the local community.

At the death of Augustus there were twenty-five legions in service; this figure fluctuated over the next two centuries, and Septimius Severus brought the total to thirty-three by recruiting three new legions. At the legion's paper strength this meant that about 180,000 Roman citizens were under arms. In addition, by the second century AD the *auxilia*, specialist infantry and cavalry units largely comprising noncitizens, may have numbered about 220,000.[2] *Numeri*, consisting of un-Romanized barbarian troops outside the formal structure of the *auxilia*, and the imperial fleets stationed at Ravenna and Misenum, with detached squadrons on the Rhine, Danube, Black Sea, in Britain, Egypt, Mauretania, and Syria, made up the total of the armed forces.[3] In Rome itself the emperor's personal force, the Praetorian Guard, numbered ten cohorts from the time of Domitian, with probably one thousand men in each. The Urban Cohorts, commanded by the Praefectus Urbi, consisted of four thousand men, and finally there were seven thousand freedmen, *Vigiles*, commanded by the *Prafectus Vigilum*, to deal with fires in the city. Therefore, the professional army at the disposal of the Roman emperor in the second century contained some 450,000 troops, larger than any other army until comparatively recent times.

The main body of troops was spread round the provinces of the empire, and before Marcus Aurelius, at least fifteen provinces had a permanent legionary garrison: Britain(3); Hispania Tarraconensis(1); Upper Germany(2); Lower Germany(2); Upper Pannonia(3); Lower Pannonia(1); Dacia(2); Upper Moesia(2); Lower Moesia(2); Cappadocia(2); Syria(3); Judaea(1); Numidia(1); Arabia(1); Egypt(2). There were about twenty-three provinces without a permanent legionary garrison, although from time to time auxiliary

---

[2] Cheesman, *Auxilia*, 53 ff.; E. Kraft, *Rekrutierung* 21–68; 140 ff.; *RE* Suppl. IX (1962), cols. 617-24.

[3] For the *numeri*, see J.C. Mann, 'A Note on the Numeri', *Hermes* 82 (1954), 501; for the fleets, C.G. Starr, *The Roman Imperial Navy 31 BC–AD 324*[2] (1960).

troops were stationed in these areas.[4] Many provinces, however, will have experienced smaller outposts, and all of course were liable to have soldiers passing through them. Nevertheless, with the exception of Spain and Syria, the provinces with the biggest concentration of troops in them were the less civilized parts of the empire. The obvious difficulty for the emperor was how to keep track of a large number of soldiers scattered round a vast empire – how to maintain their loyalty and discipline, how to make himself known to them and impress them with his concern for them, and of course how to pay them. The payment of troops was one of the purposes of Arrian's expedition round the Black Sea. Furthermore, soldiers stationed in small outposts like those described by Arrian were for most of the time far removed from the supervision of the governor, and were in close proximity to the local community. Their behaviour, good or bad, was more likely to have an immediate and persistent impact on the civilian inhabitants than if they had been stationed in formal barracks under closer control. Yet these soldiers performed a vital function in protecting local trade routes and shipping; the army's role was not just to fight spectacular battles.[5]

Nevertheless, the security and defence of the empire against outside attack were the first responsibility of the emperor and his soldiers. If anything went wrong, the

[4] e.g. *Bithynia*: cf. Pliny, *Ep.* 10. 19; 20; 21; 22; 27; 28; 52; 53; 77; 78; 100; 101; 106; 107; *IGR* 3.59 – *Cornicularius*. *Africa*: after Gaius took the command of the *III Augusta* away from the proconsul and appointed a separate legate, it seems that the proconsul retained some troops for his own use – Tac., *H* 4.48; *ILS* 2487. *Baetica*: cf. Pliny, *Ep.* 3.9.17; a military tribune in the province in an official capacity implies the presence of soldiers. *Lugdunum*: there was a garrison of some of the Urban Cohorts from Rome, at least in the winter – Tac., *H* 1.64. *Carthage* appears to have had a military garrison – *ILS* 2118; 2120. For garrisons in the 'provinciae inermes' in the East, see R.K. Sherk, *AJP* 76 (1955), 400 ff. Arrian mentions five military garrisons round the southern coast of the Black Sea: *Periplous* 3; 6.1; 9.3; 10.3; 17.2. *Macedonia*: cf. Cheesman, *Auxilia*, 159. And it is worth quoting Tertullian's general comment (*Apol.* 2.8): 'latronibus vestigandis per universas provincias militaris statio sortitur'.

[5] For the role of the soldiers as police in the empire and in local guard duties, see MacMullen, *Soldier and Civilian*, Chap. III; *RE* VII. 1, s.v. 'frumentarii'; Baillie Reynolds, *JRS* 13 (1923), 168 ff.; G. Lopuszanski, 'La Police romaine et les chrétiens', *L'Antiquité classique* 20 (1951), 5 ff.; R.W. Davies, 'The Daily Life of the Roman Soldier under the Principate', *ANRW* II.1, 299.

emperor would incur the blame since in practice he controlled the army personally, provided its emoluments, appointed its commanders, and was the embodiment of the military *virtus* of the Roman state. Military disaster could lead to instability and lack of confidence in an emperor's capacity to rule, and loss of support among the rank and file soldiers. A conscientious emperor like Hadrian would want to keep an eye on the training of the troops and the fortifications of their bases. Arrian clearly expects that Hadrian would be interested in his meticulous inspections and special reports. Hadrian was of course exceptional in his travels round the empire and his dedicated inspections of the army, but it was in the interests of every emperor to keep in as close touch with his army as he could manage, and thus ensure its efficiency and readiness for action.

For this, if he chose not to travel widely, he must rely on his governors. In the period under consideration, the provinces containing legionary troops were governed exclusively by senators, except for Egypt, which was in the hands of an *eques*. These men could raise revolts with their armies, and therefore their selection and supervision were of paramount importance for every emperor. But they were also responsible for training and leading the armies and protecting the Roman state; and so although every emperor would want to prevent the development of any military hierarchy, he also needed competent commanders who would be respected by the troops.

Arrian himself is a particularly interesting example of a consular governor. He was a Greek from Nicomedia, a historian of Alexander, and a prolific writer on a variety of subjects. But he also wrote a treatise on military tactics and an account of the expedition he conducted while governor of Cappadocia against a marauding tribe, the Alani.[6] Arrian was no professional soldier, but he was prepared to serve the state in whatever capacity it demanded, and had adopted his own native customs to the Roman traditions of office holding and the importance of military *virtus*. His *Periplous* and *Ectaxis contra Alanos* illustrate the kind of role a senatorial commander could hope for in the imperial period. It

[6] See pp. 354 f.

consisted in the main of loyalty to his emperor, the diligent
training and inspection of the troops and army ordnance, and
the rare chance to lead a limited campaign. Perhaps many
wanted no ˙more than this. For others, because the emperor
dominated his army and eclipsed his commanders in military
glory and prestige, the governorship of an armed province
may have lacked some of the savour it once had.

Augustus established an autocracy backed ultimately by
military force, and the ruler's relations with the troops were
of the first importance. But how could this relationship be
translated into real terms, when the huge army was so dis-
parate and the emperor a remote figure who might never see
most of his men? An ideal element of the relationship had to
be built up. The military oath symbolized the bond between
emperor and soldier and was sanctified by religious ties and
the Roman military tradition; it also emphasized the *personal*
connection between ruler and army; in this context the
emperor was the *res publica*. The effectiveness of such oaths
would depend to some extent on the real affection among
the officers and the rank and file for the recipient of the
oath. To this end it was expedient for an emperor to be seen
to identify himself with his troops, and perhaps adapt his life
style and demeanour to theirs when he was present in the
camps or on campaign. In his absence he must impress his
agents and officials with a similar concern, so that this could
be seen to come from the emperor's initiative. Arrian is careful to report to Hadrian his solicitude for the sick soldiers
and the protection of veterans. When in 119 Hadrian wrote
to the Prefect of Egypt about the provision of certain legal
privileges for soldiers, he thought it worth pointing out,
either sincerely or not, that his intention was not merely to
gain the good will of his men: 'You should make this benefaction of mine well known to the soldiers and the veterans,
not so that I may be well thought of by them, but so that
they may make use of it if they are ignorant of it'.[7]

Furthermore, in an age of poor communications nomenclature is very important. The *praenomen imperatoris* ('forename of commander') and acclamation as *imperator*, with

[7] *BGU* 140 = *Select Papyri* (*Loeb,* ed. A.S. Hunt and C.C. Edgar, 1934) II,
no. 213.

their connotations of military excellence, will have made the
emperor seem more impressive to his troops. He also had at
his disposal a monopoly of honorary *cognomina* and the
celebration of a full-scale triumph, although both these
honours were more than mere formalities and generally
required some military activity on his part. An accumulation
of military honours could increase his prestige, make his titulature still more impressive, and raise him far above any
other senators, for whose military success recognition was
now very restricted.

But arguably the most effective way to cement affection
and loyalty was by the provision of emoluments and benefits.
This involved prompt payment of regular wages, booty or
donatives, and a discharge bonus. In the Republic the Senate
had failed to assume responsibility for discharge payments to
veteran soldiers; instead the military leaders had striven to
secure these bonuses for their men, whose political support
they could then rely upon for the future. Now, however,
there was no question of a major role for the Senate. The
payment and maintenance of the army was solely the
emperor's responsibility and it became one of the 'secrets of
ruling' ('arcana imperii').[8]

Although conditions were harsh for the ordinary soldier
at the start of the imperial period, they improved steadily,
and the troops were much better off in a variety of ways than
most civilians who came from the same class in society. This
improvement was assisted by the development of several
privileges, particularly in the operation of the law and its
application to soldiers, which not only made military life
easier, but also gave the common soldier an advantaged
position normally enjoyed by men of wealth and high social
standing. In the imperial period the army could act as a social
catalyst for men of low degree, who otherwise would have
had few prospects in life, and about whom the imperial
government would have cared little.

What type of man made up the army with which every

---

[8] Tacitus uses the following phrase to describe the effect on imperial politics
of the events of 68–9: 'evulgato imperii arcano posse principem alibi quam Romae
fieri' (*H* 1.4).

Roman emperor had to deal? There can be little doubt that most of the recruits were poor men.

And indeed *equites* should also be admitted to the Senate even if they have been centurions in the citizen legions, though not those who have served as rank and file soldiers. For it is a shameful disgrace that men of this type, who have acted as porters and carried charcoal, should be found among the membership of the Senate. On the other hand, there is nothing to prevent the most distinguished of those *equites* who began their military service as centurions from being members of the Senate.[9]

This advice, which, according to Cassius Dio, Maecenas gave to Augustus in 29 BC, presumably reflects Dio's own views and upper-class opinion about the composition of the army in the late second century AD. Since Dio also recommends that men most in need of a livelihood should be enlisted and trained as soldiers,[10] the speech suggests an awareness that few men of property or settled occupation served as common soldiers. In AD 23 Tiberius complained that there was a shortage of volunteers for the army and that if they did appear in sufficient numbers, they did not conduct themselves with the usual bravery and discipline; generally men of no substance and vagrants volunteered for military service.[11]

Early in the imperial period conditions of service were not such as to attract men of property and good family to enlist. Much of the limited evidence showing that soldiers had wealth and property of various kinds[12] can be explained on the hypothesis of enrichment through life in the army as the terms of service improved, or by illegal exactions. Furthermore, well-off people with dubious records may have enlisted to escape the law; perhaps others received inheritances they had no reason to expect when they joined up. Conscripts might be men of some means, but it is plausible to suppose that the wealthy could escape military service by their influence or by bribing the recruiting officer or by paying substitutes to take their place. Most of the men in the

[9] Dio, 52.25.6.
[10] 52.27.4.
[11] Tac., *A* 4.4.
[12] Forni, *Il Reclutamento*, 119 ff.; the same author has surveyed recent evidence in 'Estrazione etnica e sociale dei soldati delle legioni nei primi tre secoli dell'impero', *ANRW* II. 1, 339 ff.

legions, although Roman citizens, were probably of low
social class, and poor education; they will have had little
political consciousness or understanding of the prerogatives
of the senatorial class. This would be even more true of the
auxiliaries, most of whom were nòt Roman citizens, and who
frequently came from the less civilized parts of the empire.
Since the Praetorians had superior conditions of service
and generally acted as an élite corps in Rome, it may be that
service in the Guard attracted men from a slightly better
social class. What is more, up to the time of Septimius
Severus the Guard was predominantly Italian. But the
behaviour of the Guard, especially in 68–9, does not suggest
that its members were any more 'respectable' than the legionaries. And Dio tells us that after Severus had barred recruitment in the Guard to Italians, brigandage and disorder
increased in Italy,[13] which suggests that the men affected
were not from the propertied classes. The new Praetorian
Guard recruited by Severus in 193 from the Danubian legionaries will have been little better: 'He filled the city with a
motley crowd of soldiers who were ferocious in appearance,
terrifying in manner of speech, and uncultivated in conversation.'[14] Dio despised these soldiers as uneducated, low-class
fellows with whom he could have no affinity or contact and
who should not be allowed to rise above their true station in
life.[15] It seems likely that in this Dio is representative of his
class. Tacitus too, in his account of the mutinies in AD 14,
and the civil wars of 68–9, implies contempt for the common
soldiers and their low social origins.

It is interesting that senators apparently despised the rank
and file troops, since most of these men continued to be
commanded by senators until well into the third century, and
military expertise was held in high esteem. Indeed since
most emperors themselves came from the upper classes and
shared their upbringing, education, and conservative outlook,
it is reasonable to suppose that they too would feel little in
common with the mass of the troops, on whom their position
ultimately depended and whose support they needed to win.

[13] 75.2.5.
[14] 75.2.6.
[15] Cf. 68.7.5, where Dio praises Trajan because he did not allow the troops
to become overbearing or arrogant during the long campaigns in his reign.

In the closing years of the Republic Italians formed the bulk of the large number of legions enlisted by the competing military commanders. In 43 BC up to 270,000 Italians were under arms; at the campaign of Actium Octavian and Antony probably had about 200,000 Italians serving in their armies, although Antony was also forced to recruit provincials in the East to make up his depleted forces.[16] It has been conclusively shown that in the first century of the imperial period there was a gradual and steady decline in the number of Italians in the legions and that in their place Roman citizens were recruited from the provinces.[17] The *auxilia* were recruited almost entirely from provincials. By the time of Hadrian very few Italians served as legionary soldiers, although the Praetorian Guard continued to be recruited mainly from Italians until the time of Septimius Severus.[18]

The slow decline in the numbers of Italians in the legions can best be explained on the supposition that they were increasingly reluctant to serve far from their homeland in remote and savage parts of the empire.[19] It seems that at first the provincial recruits came from the more civilized and Romanized areas, far from the military camps.[20] Presumably these troops also were reluctant to be detained far from their homes. But by the second century it had become common practice for the legionaries to be recruited in or near the areas in which they were stationed. Hence a recruit had a chance of serving near his home. This of course could never be a certainty, since a military crisis might require his legion or a detachment of it to be transferred to another part of the empire, temporarily or permanently.[21]

In the early empire at least, many auxiliary regiments were

[16] P.A. Brunt, *Italian Manpower* (1971), 498–512.

[17] Forni, *Il Reclutamento*, 65 ff.

[18] See M. Durry, *Les Cohortes Prétoriennes* (1938), 239 ff.; see also A. Passerini, *Le Coorti Pretorie* (1939). For the recruitment of new legions in Italy, see J.C. Mann, 'The Raising of New Legions during the Principate', *Hermes* 91 (1963), 483 ff.

[19] P.A. Brunt, 'Conscription and Volunteering in the Roman Imperial Army', *Scripta Classica Israelica* 1 (1974), 90, especially 99 ff., supporting and developing a suggestion by Forni, *Il Reclutamento*, chapter 5.

[20] Forni, *Il Reclutamento,* 55 ff.; 76 ff.; 159 ff.

[21] For an analysis of one area of the empire, see B. Dobson and J.C. Mann, 'The Roman Army in Britain and Britons in the Roman Army', *Britannia* 4 (1973), 191.

recruited in districts far distant from those in which they eventually came to serve. But the Roman government had no policy of deliberately distributing the contingents of each recruiting district over as wide an area as possible, except in particular circumstances, for example after revolts or disturbances amongst mutinous auxiliary regiments.[22] Indeed from the first many cohorts on the Rhine and the Danube formed a kind of local militia.[23] Under Tiberius there was a serious revolt in Thrace because Thracian auxiliaries suspected that they were to be included in the Roman army as regular units and transferred to districts far away.[24] This is a useful indication of how service in distant lands was hated.

By the second century the *auxilia,* just like the legions, were in the main recruited in the provinces where they were stationed, or those adjacent.[25] But, once again, *auxilia* were always likely to be moved in an emergency and there was no guarantee that a recruit would serve near his home. In addition, specialized units recruited men who had the necessary skill, who then might be required to serve anywhere in the empire.[26] There can be no doubt that the possibility of serving for long periods far from home was one of the main rigours of military life. One of the complaints of the mutineers in AD 14 was that they spent their life amid savage tribes and could see the enemy from their quarters; the Praetorians could return to their own homes after sixteen years, whereas the legionary would serve for thirty or even forty years and then might receive infertile land in a remote country as his discharge bounty.[27]

It is commonly held that at least up to the Severan age most recruits were volunteers. Naturally the government would wish to have as many volunteers as possible, since it is reasonable to suppose that volunteers would make more enthusiastic and efficient soldiers than unwilling conscripts. But it has recently been contended that conscription in the

[22] Cheesman, *Auxilia,* 67 ff.; special circumstances, 70 ff.

[23] Kraft, *Rekrutierung,* 21 ff.; 43 ff.

[24] Kraft, op. cit., 35 ff.; Tac., *A* 4.46.

[25] Cheesman, *Auxilia,* 79 ff. Dacia provides an example of soldiers who had to serve in a province adjacent to their homeland. Its large auxiliary garrison was supplemented by levies from the nearest recruiting grounds in Moesia and Thrace.

[26] Kraft, *Rekrutierung,* 26 ff.; Brunt (n. 19), 105 ff.

[27] Tac., *A* 1.17.

first two centuries of the empire was much more prevalent than has hitherto been supposed and that the evidence for the principle of voluntary enlistment relates mainly to the Severan period. If the argument that it was in the Severan period that conscription fell out of common use is accepted, then this development may be connected with the improved emoluments for military service granted by Septimius Severus, and indeed the general improvement in the conditions of service in the second century.[28] In any event, it is not possible to assume that the grant of privileges to the army in the first two centuries was *primarily* designed to promote the flow of volunteers. For it was essential for the emperors to do what they could to ensure the contentment and loyalty of their troops, however and wherever they had enlisted.

Even the Italian peasants who had made up the legions in the late Republic had seldom displayed any devotion to the 'state'. At best they were loyal because of either affection for or hope of reward from − or both − individual commanders. Romanized or semi-Romanized provincials were still less likely to display any form of traditional patriotism. And even when local recruitment was the common practice, it did not necessarily follow that a soldier would be conscious of defending his own homeland and his 'kith and kin'. It was up to the emperor to inspire his troops with devotion to himself, and through himself the state.

However, the Roman emperor did not have a free hand to give the army everything it wanted. Prudent management of the empire's financial affairs, the equitable government of the provinces, and the protection of the civilian population from abuse and corruption, imposed restraints. Moreover, it was surely desirable for the emperor to have the support of the upper classes, who provided the vital assistance he needed in the administration of the empire. In particular, Senators commanded most of his armies; with the good will and loyalty of the leading men the holder of the supreme authority did not need to rely so openly on his troops; he would be under less pressure and would have more choice in dealing with the problems the army created. For he could hope to

[28] Brunt (n. 19), 109 ff.

dispose of mutinous soldiers if they could find no leaders of note to give effective expression to their discontent. But to win the goodwill of senators and *equites* an emperor would have to show his honourable intentions by his demeanour, consistency, willingness to reward merit, and his conduct towards the Senate. He could not therefore seek the affection of the army by methods that were offensive to the upper classes, but only through those means which were sanctified by tradition and habit.

The legacy of Augustus was a delicate balance. On the one hand there was the autocrat controlling his mercenary army; on the other the *princeps*, first among equals in a pampered aristocracy, operating within the framework of the old Republic with all its conventions and traditions. It is the purpose of this study to examine this broad theme and the general trends associated with it, and also to mark the changes and developments inspired by individuals or dynasties. For the character of individual emperors and the circumstances of each reign dictated how the ruler's relationship with the army and the upper classes developed. In this way some explanation can be found, free from modern preconceptions and anachronisms, of what 'military monarchy' meant in the Roman context.

PART ONE

THE ASSOCIATION OF EMPEROR AND ARMY

II

THE EMPEROR WITH HIS TROOPS

1. INTRODUCTION

In his biography of Gaius Marius, Plutarch describes how Marius won the affection of the soldiers he commanded by showing that he could live as hard as they did and endure as much. He continues:

What a Roman soldier enjoys most is the sight of his commanding officer eating in the open the same food as the rest of the troops, or sleeping on a cheap bed, or sharing the toil of digging a ditch or building a palisade. The soldiers have more respect for those commanders who share their work and danger than for those who distribute honours and money; they have more affection for those who are willing to join in their toils than for those who allow them to lead an easy life.[1]

The generalization is perhaps extreme, but there is no reason to doubt Plutarch's judgement on the importance of a commander's personal association with his troops. And he seems to project this relationship into his own day, into the first and early second century AD.

The military dynasts exploited the loyalty of their armies in order to overthrow the Republic, and so everything that contributed to the bond of affection and devotion between commander and soldiers was encouraged. Political skill and financial influence, though not eclipsed, now contended with military power, and in the end it was military strength that was decisive. Octavian triumphed in the political struggle because he proved the best leader with the strongest forces.

[1] 7.4-5.

Although he brought peace and order, he found it impossible to distance himself entirely from the army. Even in times of peace, the origins of political power in military strength would be remembered. Furthermore, in the early principate there was much fighting against foreign foes, with either the emperor himself or a member of the imperial family present in person. So the military connotations of the principate and the idea of the *princeps* as 'fellow-soldier' (*commilito*) had scope to develop. It was unrealistic of Tiberius to hope that he would be merely *imperator* of the troops.[2]

The problem for each emperor was to combine the role of an impressive *imperator*, acceptable to the upper classes, with a close association with the ordinary soldiers. Furthermore, it was bound to be difficult to sustain the idea of military comradeship which had been fostered in the last years of the Republic by leaders who commanded relatively small armies and who were frequently or constantly with their soldiers. An emperor had a wide range of responsibilities and duties to the Senate and the upper classes and the other elements that contributed to his tenure of power. Rome was the vital centre of the empire which it might be dangerous to leave. Tiberius, for example, considered it right 'not to leave the centre of affairs and put himself and the state at risk'.[3]

Despite these difficulties, emperors did make a definite attempt to win the affection of the army. By emphasizing their role as 'fellow-soldier' and by making speeches to the army, they attempted to translate into real terms the ideal relationship symbolized by the military oath. Various ploys could be used to identify army with imperial house: legionary titles, imperial portraits in the camps, and religious observances in the Roman military calendar. It is necessary to evaluate these in relation to the other factors which contributed to the army's loyalty: the pedigree and personal reputation of the ruler, material emoluments, and other privileges conferred on the troops.

---

[2] Dio, 57.8.2.
[3] Tac., *A* 1.47.

2. THE MILITARY OATH TO THE EMPEROR

The Republic

After 216 BC, according to Livy, a formal oath was imposed on Roman soldiers by the military tribunes.[1] The terminology used (*ius iurandum*) signifies the religious sanction and legal obligation imposed by this oath (*foedus ac legitima iuris iurandi adactio*), and this idea remained in the word widely used subsequently to describe the military oath (*sacramentum*).[2] Although the exact text of the oath cannot be recovered, the main ideas are illustrated by Livy and Polybius.[3] The soldiers swore that they would assemble on the consul's orders and not leave their military service without his instructions, or desert in battle; they also undertook to be obedient and carry out the orders of their officers to the best of their ability. If large numbers of troops were being sworn in, one man repeated the text in full and each of the rest swore that he would do the same as the first, perhaps using the words 'idem in me'. Servius (*ad Aen.* 8.1) adds one detail: 'they swore that they would act on behalf of the State'. This is the only specific mention of the State in the various accounts of the *sacramentum* of the Republic.

The character of the oath will have been changed by the retention of legions in service for several years together with changing commanders, a practice which went back perhaps as far as the third century BC. Furthermore, after Marius' enlistment of previously ineligible men, there was a greatly increased number of soldiers who were willing to serve on a long term basis, under several commanders. But there is no reason to suppose that the basic elements of the *sacramentum* were altered, in particular the personal tie between troops and army leader. The soldiers were bound in loyalty and obedience to the consul or the magistrate appointed to command them, and they were to follow wherever he might lead and carry out his orders. They will have sworn their oath

---

[1] 22.38

[2] *Sacramentum* originally perhaps referred to the preliminary enlistment of new recruits.

[3] See S. Tondo, *Studia et Documenta Historiae et Iuris* XXIX (1963), 1 ff.; R.E. Smith, *Service in the Post-Marian Roman Army* 31 ff.; Harmand, *L'Armée*, 299 ff.; G.R. Watson, *The Roman Soldier*, 44 ff.

to each successive commander. And, in the opinion of Dionysius of Halicarnassus, the Romans observed the military oath beyond all others (11.43).

After Sulla used his army in 88 BC to march on Rome and arrange the political situation to suit his own interests, a new dimension was added to this personal relationship between commander and army. When he returned to Italy in 84 BC, Sulla bound his troops to him by a personal oath, according to Plutarch (*Sull.* 27.4). The military oath's insistence on loyalty and obedience to the commander 'wherever he might lead' now had a much wider and potentially sinister relevance. The consul might order his troops against the government of the State; and yet, if Servius is right, the soldiers also swore to protect the *res publica* itself.

In the turbulent political climate of the last century of the Republic the personal loyalty of the troops to a commander, and his acceptance of responsibility for their rewards and superannuation, increasingly became the avenue to political power for ambitious dynasts. By comparison the *res publica* was a feeble concept, though it is legitimate to suppose that military leaders might include reference to the 'State' in the oaths they employed, as useful political propaganda.[4] No doubt the traditional formula of the *sacramentum* was adapted as the circumstances demanded. In this way Cinna invoked a personal *sacramentum* in a time of political crisis.[5] Addressing army officers and a few senators at Capua he complained that the Senate had taken his consular authority away. At once the military tribunes 'swore the military oath to Cinna, and each one swore in the soldiers under his command'. This military oath was clearly in Cinna's name and bound the troops to support him not only militarily, but also politically in whatever he decided to do.[6]

In Spain in 49 BC the Pompeian leader Petreius, suspecting that many of his legionaries were planning to go over to

---

[4] Caesar was alleged to have remarked: 'nihil esse rem publicam, appellationem modo sine corpore ac specie' (Suet., *Caes.* 77). Cf. Caesar, *BC* 3.91, where a centurion mentions the fight for 'libertas', which was closely associated with the *res publica.*

[5] Appian, *BC* 1.66.

[6] There is also an echo of the *sacramentum* in the statement of the army officers to Cinna that he was consul and could lead them wherever he wanted.

Caesar, made a tour of the camp and demanded an oath from the troops that they would not desert the army and their leaders, would stay loyal, and adopt no policy individually that had not been agreed by all.[7] The oath was exacted in the traditional way and was clearly a *sacramentum*, adapted to suit the immediate crisis. It again shows the oath as an expression of personal loyalty and devotion between commander and troops, emphasized by the fact that Petreius bound himself with the oath.

Because of the added significance of the bond between commander and troops expressed by the *sacramentum* at the end of the Republic, it is plausible to suppose that the oath was exacted again in the name of each new commander who took charge of the troops. This was all the more likely in civil war when the troops passed from the control of one faction into that of another. When Caesar's general Curio addressed his troops in Africa, he paid special attention to those soldiers who had joined Caesar's army after serving under the Pompeian L. Domitius at Corfinium. 'Can a man hold you under his oath when he has been deprived of his *fasces* and power and reduced to private station; when he has himself been captured, and come under the power of another?'[8] The old obligation had in this case been replaced by a new one in the name of Caesar himself.[9] There are several examples of this process in the civil wars.[10]

In the evidence discussed above, there is no reason to doubt that the sources are consistently referring to the *sacramentum*, the oath of military service. Von Premerstein wished to distinguish between this oath and the general oath of allegiance imposed by some leaders on the civilian population and possibly soldiers also, and based in his opinion on the concept of *clientela*.[11] However, in the oaths exacted by Cinna, Petreius, Curio, and Caesar the context is purely military and no civilians are involved. The manner of exacting the oath was the traditional method for the *sacramentum*,

[7] Caesar, *BC* 1.76.
[8] *BC* 2.32.8 f.
[9] *BC* 1.23.5; 2.32.10.
[10] e.g. Appian, *BC* 4.62; 116.
[11] A. Von Premerstein, *Vom Werden und Wesen des Prinzipats* (1937), 22 ff.; 73 ff.

taken to the commanding officer and his subordinates.[12] The *sacramentum*, with its emphasis on *military* loyalty and obedience, was best suited for soldiers and it is hard to believe that a military leader would not bind his troops to him with this oath, which was sanctified by Roman military tradition and could be enforced by military law according to ancestral custom. This is illustrated by Caesar's speech to his mutinous legions at Placentia.[13] He reminded them of the advantages he had brought them and that they had sworn an oath to him for the whole war and not just part of it. This is surely the *sacramentum*, since Caesar spoke of the men's obligations to obey their officers (this was part of the military oath), and planned to punish the defaulters with the military penalty of decimation. It looks as if Caesar had adapted the *sacramentum* and bound these soldiers to him anew at the start of the civil wars, an appropriate time to remind them of their personal obligations to their commander.

But this is not to say that soldiers, when they happened to be present, did not join in any general oath of loyalty taken by the civilian population, and indeed it would be foolish for a commander to exclude his soldiers from such oaths. The general oath of allegiance imposed quasi-military obligations of a kind that had certainly not existed between patron and client in orderly times, and these would indeed have infringed the rule of law, were it not that the beneficiary of the oath was also, from Augustus onwards, the legal ruler. The evidence is best explained by the hypothesis that the oath of allegiance as it was in the imperial period had arisen through the development of the *sacramentum* in the chaos of the late Republic, and its extension to include the military leader's civil following.[14] It may seem odd that soldiers should bind themselves by both the *sacramentum* and the general oath of allegiance. But eagerness for tangible expressions of loyalty can explain this.

Wars against fellow Romans, frequent changes of allegi-

---

[12] e.g. Caesar, *BC* 2.28 — L. Domitius had included his quaestor in the oath.

[13] Appian, *BC* 2.47. This speech was presumably invented; but it is important that Appian or his sources, when they came to consider Caesar's oath, from their knowledge of this period thought in terms of a *sacramentum*; cf. 2.140.

[14] P. Herrmann, *Der römische Kaisereid* (1968), 64 ff; 119 ff.

ance, and the repetition of the solemn demands of the *sacramentum* presumably did much to discredit the solemnity and awe of the traditional formulae and hence the value of the oath as an effective expression of loyalty.[15] However, it clearly retained some force, and it is significant indeed that commanders continued to think it worthwhile to bind the troops to them with an oath. Caesar's *Commentaries* on his campaigns in the civil wars were intended to some extent to win the support of his readers and we may suppose that they reflect attitudes commonly held among the upper classes. In several places he stresses the importance generally ascribed to the *sacramentum*. Curio needed to make a lengthy justification to those of his troops who had switched their allegiance from L. Domitius (*BC* 2.32.8 f.). The word *religio* is used to describe the bond of the oath, implying a religious sanction: defaulters would be perjurors. Moreover, Caesar remarks that the troops of Petreius were strengthened in their resolve to fight by 'the fear instilled in them by their leaders, and punishments, and the new sanction of the oath ('nova religio iuris iurandi' – *BC* 1.76.5).

The Imperial Period

There is little specific evidence about the exact wording of the *sacramentum* in the imperial period.[16] Vegetius (*c.* AD 383) mentions the military oath in the *Epitoma Rei Militaris*, but it is doubtful how much can be made of this evidence. The *Epitoma* is a rambling antiquarian collection of chronologically unsorted material from all periods of Roman history.[17] However at least part of the oath he describes belongs to the late empire; the soldiers swear 'by God, Christ, the Holy Spirit, and the majesty of the emperor . . . to carry out all the emperor's commands energetically, never desert their military service or shirk death on behalf of the Roman

---

[15] For the importance of the oath see Harmand, *L'Armée*, 301; P.A. Brunt, 'The Army and the Land in the Roman Revolution', *JRS* 52 (1962), 77.

[16] Servius, *ad Aen.* 7.614; 8.1, and Isidorus, *Etym.* 9.3.53, although they appear to be referring to the military oath of the Republic, may have in mind the oath used during the empire. For example, Isidorus refers to the length of military service as twenty-five years, and this would not be appropriate in the Republic.

[17] See D. Schenk, *Die Quellen der Epitoma Rei Militaris, Klio, Beiheft* XXII (1930).

State' (2.5). The oath has been arranged to suit an empire and army that were now officially Christian. Presumably, therefore, the oath was still considered to be of some importance and worth adapting to changing circumstances. It is interesting that the emperor was still mentioned by name and that the troops still swore to do whatever he ordered. The phrase 'on behalf of the Roman State' is curious, and it may have been added in the later empire to emphasize loyalty to Rome, when perhaps many of the soldiers employed had only a nominal connection with the Roman State and when emperors were frequently transient. But, since Servius mentioned a similar obligation, this may have been inherited from the Republic and included in the *sacramentum* from the start of the imperial period.

The philosopher Epictetus (*c*.AD 55-135) provides further evidence. He urges philosophers to swear an oath to god, 'just like the soldiers to the emperor', and proceeds: 'For the soldiers, when they enter military service, swear an oath to value the safety of the emperor above everything.'[18] Epictetus must then be referring to the oath taken when the recruits entered upon military service, the *sacramentum*.[19] The context of Epictetus' account is purely military and he implies that the oath he mentions refers only to soldiers; he is in fact comparing one group (philosophers) with another identifiable group (soldiers) who swear a specific oath.

Epictetus does not mention the *res publica*, and although his description of the military oath may be selective, it is notable that it occurred to him as a familiar example of an oath embodying a personal bond, in this case between emperor and soldier. Probably the traditional elements of the *sacramentum* of the Republic remained, and the soldiers will have sworn the military obligations of discipline, and

---

[18] 1.14.15: ἀλλ' ἐκεῖνοι μὲν τὴν μισθοφορίαν λαμβάνοντες ὀμνύουσιν πάντων προτιμήσειν τὴν τοῦ Καίσαρος σωτηρίαν.

[19] μισθοφορία means 'a period of service for wages', it does not normally mean 'pay' itself: Liddell and Scott, s.v. μισθοφορία; E.A. Sophocles, *Lexicon of Roman and Byzantine Periods* (1914); Stephanus, *Thesaurus*, V, p. 1090 C. I cannot therefore accept Von Premerstein's translation of τὴν μισθοφορίαν λαμβάνοντες as 'when receiving pay'. He ascribes this to 1 January, and claims that the passage refers only to the general oath of allegiance taken on that date.

obedience to commands. There is a hint of this in Epictetus, who goes on to say that the philosopher should swear 'that he will never disobey at any time'. At this point he still seems to have in mind the military oath.[20] If, in the passage discussed above, Epictetus is indeed talking about the traditional *sacramentum*, sworn when the recruits joined up, then the clause to value the emperor's safety above all seems odd, for it is closer in idea to the general oath of allegiance taken by the civilian population.[21] Since it was obviously desirable for soldiers also to swear the oath of allegiance, perhaps this latter oath was incorporated with the *sacramentum*.

To sum up, in the first two centuries of the imperial period the *sacramentum* mentioned the emperor by name and bound the soldiers to him by ties of personal loyalty and obedience to his instructions. The oath may have included a further undertaking of personal allegiance, to hold the emperor's safety to be of paramount importance. Possibly the oath also exhorted the troops to act bravely on behalf of the *res publica*. This was presumably an attempt to preserve the fiction that the army was the army of the Roman people, just as Tiberius proclaimed: 'the legions are not mine, but the State's.'[22] But the real importance of the *sacramentum* lay in the soldiers' bond of personal loyalty to the emperor; and this was secured by ties of *religio* and sanctified by Roman military tradition.

Since the *sacramentum* mentioned the name of the reigning emperor, *a priori* each new emperor would be obliged to exact the oath anew at his accession. This was all the more desirable if that accession was accompanied by violence and civil war. There is much evidence in Tacitus' account in the *Histories* of the civil wars in 68-9, where he frequently refers to the swearing in of soldiers. But what does Tacitus mean by the word *sacramentum*? If the *sacramentum* included a clause stating a general oath of allegiance, as suggested above, Tacitus may have thought it

[20] Cf. 1.14.17.
[21] For the texts of these oaths, see Herrmann (n. 14), 122 ff.
[22] Dio, 57.2.3. The German legions who briefly swore allegiance to Senate and people in 69 (Tac., *H* 1.56) must have used some formulation invoking the interests of the *res publica.*

unnecessary always to distinguish consistently between the two in the terminology he employed. Because of the close proximity of the two obligations in the eyes of the soldiers and others, the word *sacramentum*, which can mean either (more commonly) the military oath, or simply an oath, could be used to express both the enlistment and allegiance oath. But it would be odd for Tacitus to use *sacramentum* solely to mean the oath of allegiance, especially in contexts where it could be confused with the more usual meaning of the word. In fact in the *Histories* Tacitus consistently employs *sacramentum* in a military context, in reference only to the oath taken by soldiers.[23] The one exception involves the use of *sacramentum* in a metaphorical sense (*H*.2.81): 'All Syria was on Vespasian's side.' It may be concluded, therefore, that when Tacitus employed the term *sacramentum*, he had in mind primarily the traditional military oath, and the oath of allegiance as it applied to soldiers was assumed to be part of this.

To illustrate this we may note the events in 69 when Cerialis accepted for service under Vespasian the Vitellian legions that had sided with Civilis. He said to the soldiers, 'You must consider this as the first day of your military service and your military oath'.[24] The use here of the phrase 'primus dies' implies that this is the first day of a completely new period of military service, indicated by the start of their pay, and that the *sacramentum* was consequently a new enlistment oath, exacted in the name of a new master. Many other incidents in these years show that it was usual for the *sacramentum* to be imposed again on the troops when a new emperor took control.[25]

Although soldiers may on some occasions have joined with civilians to swear the oath to a new emperor, there is no reason to think that they swore *only* the general oath of allegiance and not the *sacramentum*.[26] Tacitus' statement that after the death of Augustus, 'the Senate, soldiers, and

[23] *H.* 1.12, 36, 53, 55-6, 76; 2.6, 64, 79; 4.31, 37, 46, 58, 59, 72. Tacitus occasionally used the phrase 'ius iurandum' or 'in verba adigere': 1.76; 2.14, 79, 80; 3.13; 4.31, 57, 60; cf. *A* 1.8.

[24] Tac., *H* 4.72: 'primum illum stipendiorum et sacramenti diem haberent'.

[25] See n. 23.

Footnote 26 at foot of page 27.

people' swore an oath to Tiberius[27] merely shows that the entire citizen body took an oath to the emperor, not that they swore together or in precisely the same terms. Dio, however, comments that Tiberius won the troops in Italy over to his side by oaths established by Augustus.[28] Dio *may* be referring to the oath taken by 'tota Italia' in 32 BC, which of course embraced Octavian's civil following and cannot have been a military *sacramentum*. But it is possible that Dio was thinking of a military oath established or adapted by Augustus for the Praetorian Guard and other troops. In AD 192 there appears to have been a united oath of plebs and soldiers at the accession of Pertinax. But not much can be made of Herodian's confused account; we do not know exactly what went on at this meeting, and the circumstances may have been exceptional, in that the troops were outnumbered and intimidated by the people and consented to the acceptance of Pertinax only with a bad grace.[29]

It seems best to conclude that the soldiers' military oath, incorporating the oath of allegiance, was exacted in the name of every new emperor, and in normal circumstances was sworn immediately by the soldiers alone in the camps. The oath taken by the civilian population or their representatives was less significant and was doubtless completed as soon as possible, and sometimes perhaps simultaneously with the swearing in of the soldiers.[30]

On the anniversary of an emperor's accession this oath was renewed. No doubt the soldiers swore to be loyal to their previous oath and, informally at least, this will have included the *sacramentum* as well. Certainly the soldiers will have seen it that way. Where there were small numbers of troops in a province, the civilian representatives could join with them for

---

[26] As argued by Von Premerstein, 75 ff., citing in addition to the passages in the text: Tac., *A* 1.34, 37; 14.11, *H* 1.36; 2.80, 81; Plut., *Galb.* 26.1. The evidence he discusses shows only that soldiers and civilians swore the oath at an emperor's accession at about the same time (this seems entirely reasonable), not that they swore together or that the texts of the oaths were exactly the same. The passages discussed in the text seem to be the most plausible of Von Premerstein's *testimonia*.

[27] *A* 1.7.

[28] 57.3.2.

[29] 2.2.10 f.

[30] Cf. the accession of Nero: Tac., *A* 12.69; Dio, 61.3.

the ceremonial renewal of the oath, just as Pliny organized the event in Bithynia.[31] But the importance of what the two groups swore was radically different. When there were large concentrations of troops the oath will have been exacted in the military camp in a purely military ceremony.

What were the advantages of including the troops in a general oath of allegiance? An emperor far removed from his soldiers, whom he perhaps did not often see, might consider frequent expressions of loyalty desirable. It built up the idea of a personal tie between soldiers and commander. In the extant formulae, the oath of allegiance was taken to an individual as such, not to a person who is expressly described as having certain legal, constitutional, or representative powers. What is more, the oath of allegiance, in all the formulae but that of the community of Aritium in Lusitania, bound the takers to the descendants or the *oikos* of the emperor. It is plausible to suggest that a ruler with a dynastic policy would wish to cement by oath the loyalty of the troops to his dynasty, which the *sacramentum* by itself failed to do. For example, if Gaius introduced his sisters into the oath of allegiance, he would surely wish his soldiers also to be bound to them. However, for the mass of the population any oath was a formality; their behaviour and actions were of less significance, and it is not even clear how many of them took the oath of allegiance.[32] But the troops had the power to make their loyalty effective: a soldier might have to die for his emperor. And it was easy to ensure that every soldier took the oath personally. The man to whom the ordinary soldier swore loyalty was the source of his pay and rewards, and the oath was as much a guarantee of his own security as that of the emperor. It is no accident that in his account of the civil wars in 68–9, Tacitus is almost exclusively concerned with the oaths sworn by soldiers.[33] He saw the truth: in contests of political intrigue and violence, the army's loyalty was paramount; the allegiance of the rest of the population could wait.

[31] *Ep.* 10.52. Trajan apparently changed the renewal of the oath ceremony from 3 January to the *dies imperii*; see A.N. Sherwin-White, *The Letters of Pliny*, 633.

[32] Presumably the representatives of the local communities received the oath.

[33] See n. 23.

It remains to be considered if the *sacramentum* and the oath of allegiance had any effect in practical terms in ensuring the loyalty of the army. Emperors continued to impose the oath on the army at their accession and to renew it annually. The strength of Roman military tradition may help to account for this persistence, but it cannot be the whole answer. Emperors surely believed that the *sacramentum* and the oath of allegiance had some value, even if only to give an impression of united support in the army.

The nature of the obligations imposed by the oaths taken by the soldiers was religious, in that the takers of the oath would invoke the vengeance of Jupiter on themselves in the event of perjury. The question of the efficacy of the oath is therefore one of the strength of religious sentiment in the empire, and this is notoriously hard to assess. Contemporaries, however, believed that the oath had some religious power. Seneca thought that it was a *nefas* — that is, something contrary to divine law, — to desert from the army.[34] Apollonius of Tyana describes the difficulties faced by a governor planning a revolt against an emperor: 'If he intends to use force against the man who appointed him to his command and in whose best interests he swore to give advice and to act, he first of all must prove to the gods that he is breaking his oath without any impiety.'[35] Although Apollonius is cynical, he implies that at least a charge of impiety would be made against an oath-breaker. When Hordeonius Flaccus attempted to administer an oath for Vespasian to his reluctant troops, they accepted it but mumbled Vespasian's name or passed over it in silence. This was surely an attempt to guard against the charge of oath-breaking. They could say that they had not sworn specifically to Vespasian. Indeed the soldiers could even assuage their conscience by supposing that the gods' chief concern was to protect Rome and that by transferring their allegiance they were fulfilling the divine will by giving the state a better human protector. In this context omens that purported to show that a usurper was destined by the gods to rule might

[34] Seneca, *Ep.* 95.35.
[35] Philostratus, *Vit. Ap.* 5.35.5. Note the tendency of usurpers to argue that the empire needs to be saved: Tac., *H* 1.38; Herodian, 2.10.2; 8.2–3.

be important in winning over the troops. For instance, it seems that omens portending Vespasian's destiny to rule were publicized before his proclamation.[36]

Dio records that Septimius Severus in AD 193 made a bitter speech to the Praetorians who had murdered Pertinax, accusing them of lawlessness (παρανομία).[37] He presumably refers to the soldiers' breach of the law in that the emperor was entitled to fidelity as representative of the *res publica*. But this also involved·a disgraceful breach of their military oath, as Herodian points out explicitly. No doubt Severus considered this good propaganda to justify his revolt against a reigning emperor. He could argue that the man who had profited from the lawless infidelity of the Praetorian Guard was not a suitable defender of the state. Apparently he expected the charge of oath-breaking and the need to avenge it to have some validity. Herodian indeed uses emotive language to describe the act of breaking the military oath to an emperor, which he describes as an act of impiety (ἀσεβεία).[38] Moreover, in an invented speech, put into the mouth of Pupienus in 238, he describes the oath as a 'holy secret' (σεμνὸν μυστήριον), something that demands respect for the gods and loyalty to the recipient.[39]

In general the soldiers came from the lower classes and were men of little education or sophistication. Possibly a simple-minded piety persuaded them to have some respect for the oaths they swore to the emperor. Scribonianus' rebellion against Claudius lasted only five days, '. . . since the legions that had changed their allegiance were turned from their purpose by superstitious fear; for when the order was given to march to their new commander, by some providential chance the eagles could not be adorned nor the standards pulled up and moved.'[40] Religious awe induced by strange portents apparently caused the troops to repent of their broken oath. The persuasion of officers loyal to

[36] *H* 4.31; cf. 4.41. For the omens, *H* 2.78.
[37] 75.1.1 ff.; cf. Herodian, 2.13.5 ff.
[38] 2.13.8.
[39] 8.7.4 ff.
[40] Suet., *Cl.* 13.2. It is worth noting that the mutineers in Pannonia in AD 14 were discouraged by an eclipse of the moon, and feared divine disfavour of their crimes (Tac., *A* 1.28).

Claudius may also have played a part and in this case the omens supported the idea that the ruling emperor was the gods' chosen defender of the State. The omens may have been manufactured, but the incident shows that it was believed that soldiers could be persuaded by the religious power of their obligations.

It is difficult to believe that in the civil wars of 68-9 anyone placed much reliance on the power of an oath to sustain an army's loyalty. Tacitus commented, 'There was no fidelity or affectionate loyalty.'[41] Nevertheless, even in these years there are signs of loyalty to the oath: 'The soldiers in Rome were imbued with a long tradition of sworn loyalty to the [Julio-Claudian] emperors.'[42] This suggests that by habit and familiarity with one dynasty the oath could acquire an important influence in the minds of the troops. Furthermore, in 69 the legions at Vetera refused the oath to Vespasian and proclaimed that Vitellius was their emperor and that for him they would retain their loyalty (*fides*) and fight until the last breath.[43] After the battle of Bedriacum, Otho's army, that 'fidissimus exercitus', showed remarkable loyalty to the defeated emperor.[44] At this stage there was little else other than their sworn oath and personal affection to sustain such loyalty and devotion. To the soldiers the personal oath was an integral part of military service and had to be sworn to a man of standing and prestige, for the oath also stood as a symbol and guarantee of the troops' own security. Hence in AD 14 loyal soldiers undermined the position of the mutineers partly by asking, 'Are we really going to swear an oath to men like Percennius and Vibulenus?'[45] There may also be some significance in the fact that commanders seeking to restore or confirm an army's loyalty often reminded the soldiers of the obligations of their oath.[46]

The oath did, after all, symbolize the ideal relationship between emperor and army, and, as an expression of personal

---

[41] Tac., *H* 1.76.
[42] *H* 1.5; cf. 1.30. And note *A* 2.76; Calpurnius Piso's son speaks of the legions in Syria as having 'penitus infixus in Caesares amor'.
[43] *H* 4.21.
[44] 2.46.
[45] *A* 1.28.
[46] e.g. Appian, BC 5.529; Tac., *A* 1.43; *H* 1.30; Herodian, 2.5.6.

loyalty and devotion, it might be made very effective by an emperor of charismatic character who could inspire the troops. Other emperors, of course, could not. And so the oath was always unpredictable as a means of retaining military loyalty. That would depend on the army's morale, its relationship with the emperor, satisfaction with the emoluments and other benefits of military service, the attitude of the officers, and perhaps a judicious manipulation of suitable omens and signs of divine approval. If all or some of these factors were against an emperor, it was unlikely that the *sacramentum* and the allegiance oath could long sustain the troops' loyalty if leaders of a revolt could be found. Yet, in the case of the rebellion of Scribonianus, the oath apparently did just this. The oaths taken by soldiers were always a boost to imperial morale, and a symbolic warning to the ambitious and discontented that the emperor was fully in control of the most effective source of political power in the State.

3. THE EMPEROR AS 'FELLOW-SOLDIER'

The Roman emperor was also commander-in-chief since his *legati*, who from the end of Augustus' reign had virtually all the military forces under their command, operated under his auspices, and in practice he could take charge of military activities wherever and whenever he chose. The role of the mighty *imperator*[1] was hardly compatible with the life-style and duties of the ordinary soldier.[2] Nevertheless, Roman emperors referred to their troops as 'fellow-soldiers' (*commilitones*) and to some extent tried to live up to the implications of this claim.

In the civil wars of the Republic, the military dynasts could not afford to be over-scrupulous about the methods they employed to acquire the vital loyalty and devotion of the army. It was not only Plutarch who observed the new demands on a commander, the closeness of his association with his troops, and the deleterious consequences for

---

[1] Cicero (*De. Imp. Pomp.* 10.28) analysed the essential qualities of a commander as knowledge of military affairs, courage, authority, and good luck.

[2] Cic., *Tusc.* 2.62.

discipline.[3] Appian believed that serious and long term damage had been done to the balance between commander and army by the unusual pressure upon generals in the civil wars:

'. . . the soldiers did not serve the interests of the state, but only of those who had recruited them; and they gave their support to these people not because of the compulsion of the law, but because of personal inducements; and they fought not against the enemies of Rome but against private adversaries, not against foreigners, but against fellow citizens, men just like themselves. All these factors contributed to a breakdown of military discipline; the soldiers believed that they were not so much serving in an army as helping out, through their personal decision and favour, leaders who found their assistance essential for private ends.'[4]

It is no surprise in these circumstances that Caesar, in his speeches to his army, deliberately preferred to call his men 'fellow-soldiers' (*commilitones*) rather than *milites*, because they enjoyed this rather more flattering term ('blandius nomen'). Caesar's flattering concern for his soldiers was one of the reasons for their extreme devotion to him.[5] Appian's history of the civil wars indicates that it was probably normal for a commander to address his troops as *commilitones*.[6]

After the conflict however, Augustus refused to call the soldiers *commilitones* in a speech or an edict and forbade any member of his family with *imperium* to do so: 'He thought that it would be rather more ostentatious, ('ambitiosius') than military discipline, or the peaceful nature of the age, or his own majesty and that of his house required'.[7] Suetonius attributed the word 'ambitiosius' to Augustus himself, and it is possible that the biographer had got hold of a private memorandum circulated by Augustus among the members of the imperial family. The language is interesting. In the comparative normality after 31 BC, it was expedient to

---

[3] *Mar.* 7.4–5.
[4] *BC* 5.17.
[5] Suet., *Caes.* 67.2; 68.1.
[6] *BC* 2.72; 3.65; 4.90, 117; 5.39; Cf. 2.73 — Caesar calls his men φίλοι on this occasion.
[7] Suet., *Aug.* 25.1: 'ambitiosius id existimans, quam aut ratio militaris aut temporum quies aut sua domusque suae maiestas postularet'.

avoid too open a flattery of the troops. The new regime was to be peaceful and ordered, bringing an end to the excesses of commanders and armies which were so detrimental to the State. Augustus therefore wished to avoid on public occasions the word *commilitones* with its taint of association with the armies which had held the balance in the Roman State. It was all a façade. Little had changed. The military usurper ruled the Roman empire backed by the personal loyalty of his mercenary army, but now inside an apparently respectable framework of constitutional government. Nevertheless, the façade was important for preventing the troops from finding out that the emperor was at their mercy and in assuring the upper classes that the emperor was capable of maintaining a stable regime.

The spirit of military comradeship fostered in the civil wars continued, and Augustus wished it to be so, but in a limited context. In private conversation the emperor still used the expression 'fellow-soldier'. When confronted with an unreasonable request from a soldier, he replied, 'I will no more do what you request, fellow-soldier . . . '.[8] In 9 BC Augustus appeared in court on behalf of a veteran soldier of his. At first he asked a friend to speak on the soldier's behalf, but the soldier objected: 'Whenever you needed help, I did not send some one else to you but endured dangers myself everywhere on your behalf.'[9] Augustus then pleaded the case personally. The story seems to refer to an ordinary soldier from the ranks and illustrates the obligations that could be imposed by service and military comradeship. In this case at least Augustus was willing to respond, and on another occasion he invited to dinner a man who had been one of his bodyguards and in whose villa he used to stay.[10] Furthermore, twenty-eight military colonies of his veterans in Italy, apparently thickly populated in Augustus' day, and others spread round the empire, were a strong support to his rule (*RG* 28).

Tiberius professed that he was '*imperator*' of the troops.[11] However, when mutiny broke out among the Pannonian

[8] Quint., *Inst. Or.* 6.3.95: 'Non magis . . . faciam, commilito, quod petis . . .'.
[9] Suet., *Aug.* 56.4; Dio 55.4.2 (probably the same case).
[10] Suet., *Aug.* 74.　　　[11] Dio, 57.8.2.

legions in AD 14, he wrote to the troops that 'he himself had an oustanding concern for the very brave legions with whom he had endured numerous campaigns'.[12] Similarly, when Germanicus confronted the mutinous German legions, he reminded them that they were no ordinary troops. The first legion had received its standards from Tiberius, the twentieth had shared many battles with him ('tot proeliorum socia') and received his rewards. Was rebellion really the kind of gratitude they wished to display to their old commander? What would Tiberius think when he heard that 'his very own recruits, his very own veterans' were behaving like this?[13] In both cases there is an appeal to the idea of military comradeship. Tiberius, like a good 'fellow-soldier', had endured much with his troops in the toils of campaign and had rewarded them well. He hoped to exploit the prestige he had obtained as a successful and sympathetic commander to confirm the army's loyalty.

But there is no sign that Tiberius, Germanicus, or Drusus addressed the soldiers as *commilitones*, and it is not possible to decide when this expression was employed again officially in public documents and speeches.[14] We know that the term *commilitones* was commonly in use by 68 (see below), and its introduction can probably be attributed to Gaius or Claudius. Gaius adopted unique and grandiose titles – 'Son of the Camp' ('Castorum filius') and 'Father of the Armies' ('pater exercituum')[15] – proclaiming his identification with the armies. He also displayed an enthusiastic if erratic interest in the art of generalship and presented himself as a vigorous and energetic commander.[16] For the first time in over fifty years an emperor took personal command of an army. Furthermore, under Gaius there appears on coinage the first known representation of an imperial speech to the army.[17] The accumulation of evidence shows an emperor who ostentatiously emphasized his connection with the army.

[12] *A* 1.25.

[13] *A* 1.42. For speeches in Tacitus, see R. Syme, *Tacitus,* 191-3; 316-21.

[14] Valerius Maximus, who wrote in the reign of Tiberius, in his account of the civil wars uses the word 'commilitones' casually in various contexts (1.8.9; cf. 3.2.20; 3.2.23; 3.2. Ext., 3,5). But this need not imply that the term was in common use in his day; he may have been influenced by his sources for republican history.

[15] Suet., *Cal.* 22.1.   [16] Suet., *Cal.* 43-47.   [17] *BMC* I, Caligula, no. 33.

The circumstances of his accession thrust Claudius into close association with the Praetorian Guard.[18] Two extraordinary and unique coins show Claudius shaking hands with a guardsman in the Praetorian camp, one with the legend 'Imperator Receptus' (The Acceptance of the Emperor'), the other with 'Praet [orianus] Receptus' ('The Acceptance of the Praetorians').[19] These coins are so unusual that it is plausible to suppose that Claudius himself was responsible for the message they convey. They proclaim the comradely spirit between emperor and soldiers and mutual recognition of each other's power. Claudius' special dependence on the troops may well have been expressed in his addressing them as *commilitones*. His sensitivity about the Praetorians can be seen in his decision to forbid by senatorial decree any soldier from entering the house of a senator to greet him. There is hardly any evidence for Claudius' speeches to the Guard, but some fragments preserved by Suetonius may indicate that the severe style of the public speech laid down by Augustus had disappeared.[20]

Possibly, then, the word 'fellow-soldier' was in use on official occasions before the civil wars of 68–9, when it was clearly the usual form of address to soldiers. Both Tacitus and Plutarch employ the term consistently in speeches attributed to emperors and usurpers.[21] This is unlikely to be anachronistic, since Tacitus understood the period very well and his use of *commilitones* is part of his careful exposition of the relationship between emperor and army in the crisis.[22] Furthermore, two apparently verbatim statements from Galba are preserved. To a soldier who claimed to have killed Otho he said, 'Fellow-soldier . . . who gave the order?'[23] This was certainly not casual conversation, rather

[18] Suet., *Cl.* 10.2 f.; Dio, 60.1.4; Josephus, *BJ* 2.206 ff.; *AJ* 19.229 ff.

[19] *BMC* I, Claudius, nos. 5, 8. For Claudius' military pretensions, see p.41.

[20] Prohibition on soldiers visiting senators: Suet., *Cl.* 25.1; *Cl.* 26.2 records that Claudius spoke to the Guard in intimate terms about his marriage relationship.

[21] Tac., *H* 1.29–30; 37–8; 83; Plut., *Galb.* 27.3; *Otho* 15.3.

[22] Note the carefully balanced speeches he attributes to Piso and Otho in 69 (*H* 1.29; 37).

[23] Tac., *H* 1.35. Plutarch, giving the same quotation, omits 'fellow-soldier' (*Galb.* 26.2). Although it is possible that 'commilito' was not part of the original quotation, it is preferable to follow Tacitus on this point.

the formal interrogation of a soldier by his commander. One tradition records Galba's last words as he was murdered by his soldiers: 'What are you doing, fellow-soldiers?'[24] In these turbulent years those who aspired to the purple were compelled to identify themselves closely with the troops who supported them. Even Galba, who had a reputation as a strict disciplinarian, could not escape the implications of this: 'I am yours and you are mine' ('ego vester sum et vos mei').[25]

After 69 there is no evidence for the use and development of *commilito* before the reign of Trajan. However, his *mandata* to provincial governors on military wills provide the first known example of *commilito* in a public document: 'In response to the justness of my feelings for my excellent and most loyal fellow-soldiers' ('optimos fidelissimosque commilitones').[26] It if significant that Trajan, the 'Optimus Princeps', chose to describe his relationship with the army in this way. The flattering and indeed rather emotional language perhaps reflects the fact that the emperor is trying to grant the troops something that they had no good right to.[27] When writing officially to Pliny, the governor of Bithynia, Trajan employs *commilitones* and *milites* in the same letter regarding the use of soldiers to guard the prisons in Bithynia.[28] He probably used *commilitones* once at the start of the letter to establish the tone and then resorted to *milites* so as not to reduce the colour and impact of the more flattering term by over-use. Elsewhere when writing to Pliny, Trajan employs 'fellow-soldiers' when he refers to the anniversary of his accession and the *vota* for his safety; in two other letters about the routine duties of soldiers he uses only *milites*.[29] Presumably Trajan thought it suitable to call the troops 'fellow-soldiers' in an emotional context like the renewal of their oath of loyalty, or when the term was not ambiguous, that is, when the troops could not be the 'fellow-

---

[24] Suet., *Galb.* 20.1; Tacitus found that there were several accounts of Galba's last words (*H* 1.41).

[25] Suet., *Galb.* 20.1.

[26] *Dig.* 29.1.1: 'Secutus animi mei integritudinem erga optimos fidelissimosque commilitones . . .'

[27] See below, pp. 216f.

[28] Pliny, *Ep.* 10.20.

[29] 10.53, 101, 103 (*commilitones*); 22, 28 (*milites*).

soldiers' of some one else. In the same way, when Pliny wrote to Trajan, he spoke of *milites* except when he recorded the loyal oaths and *vota* of the troops.[30] However, Pliny did understand the ideal of military comradeship between Trajan and his troops. In his *Panegyric* in honour of the emperor, he describes Trajan as a good 'fellow-soldier': 'For how many are there to whom you have not been a 'fellow-soldier' before a commander?'[31] This is the first known example where the term *commilito* is formally attributed to an emperor, and it is interesting that it should have been done so by a senator in the Senate house. Clearly the idea of the emperor as a comrade of his troops had been well established by the second century and was presumably not offensive to senators.

For the second and third centuries an abundance of evidence in the literary sources shows that *commilitones* was a very common form of address in the formal speech to the army; indeed it virtually became a synonym for *milites*.[32] It is notable that Dio attributes συστρατιῶται three times to Marcus Aurelius in an invented speech in which he appeals to the soldiers for support against the rebellious Avidius Cassius.[33] It has been observed that this speech of Marcus is at least in character;[34] Dio obviously expected that Marcus would have addressed the troops in this way.

The word *commilito* is not registered, after Trajan's *mandata* about military wills, in any extant public documents until a speech by Constantine in the early fourth century.[35] This is hardly significant. Firstly, even in the second and third centuries there is a paucity of relevant evidence. Secondly, if the word was not to lose its special impact, emperors could use it only on special occasions when they wished particularly to impress the troops. In this context *commilito* was perhaps most often employed in speeches to the Praetorian Guard or the legions.

---

[30] 10.19, 27, 106 (*milites*); 52, 100 (*commilitones*).
[31] 15.5; 19.3: 'quotus enim quisque cuius tu non ante commilito quam imperator'.
[32] Dio, 71.24.1; 72.9.3; Herodian, 1.5.1 f.; 2.11.2; 4.7.6, 14.4; 6.3.3.
[33] 71.24.1; 25.1; 26.1.
[34] See P.A. Brunt, *JRS* 64 (1974), 13.
[35] *Cod. Theod.* 7.20.2 (320 or 326) — 'conveterani'.

At this point we need to ask in what ways an emperor could truly represent himself as comrade in arms of the troops. For it seems that the term *commilito* was more than a desirable and conventional flattery, and that some emperors at least followed a definable pattern of behaviour in their role as 'comrade'.

The Julio-Claudians

Julius Caesar was famous for his exceptional relationship with his troops. Antony was quick to learn; strong of body, genial and open-handed in manner, he used to stand in the mess line, sharing the rough jokes of his men.[36] In 35–33 BC Octavian campaigned in person in Illyricum and once even risked his life as he intervened at a critical part of the battle.[37] Secure in power, Augustus was less daring. Nevertheless he took personal command of the war in north-west Spain from 26–25 BC; although he fell ill and achieved only limited success, he felt sufficiently proud of his exploits there to recount them in his autobiography.[38] After 8 BC Augustus did not leave Italy. Perhaps he thought that he had done enough to win his laurels; yet despite his public restraint, he maintained a close relationship with his men (p.34). Other members of the imperial family, Tiberius, Drusus (until his death in 9 BC), and Germanicus, were frequently with the armies in these years. When Augustus died there was a strong military element to his funeral, which he had organized himself. When the funeral pyre had been built in the *Campus Martius* the Praetorian Guard ran round it and those soldiers who had received decorations from Augustus threw them on it. Then the pyre was lit by centurions of the Guard.[39] The military elements of the funeral may well have been modelled on that of Sulla.[40]

Tiberius was a popular and hard-working commander. He often spent the night in the open, rode in the saddle all day, sat at the table to eat his meals instead of reclining, or even

[36] Plut., *Ant.* 4.2; 6.5.
[37] Florus, 2.23.
[38] Ibid. 2.33; Orosius, 6.21.1–11. See in general, R. Syme, *Roman Papers* (1979), 825 ff.
[39] Dio, 56.33, 34, 42.
[40] Appian, *BC* 1.105–6.

took them on the bare turf; he was careful to look after the sick and preserved his soldiers from unnecessary losses in battle. In fact Tiberius behaved as a bold *commilito* and the joy of his troops when he returned to command them was doubtless genuine.[41] Tiberius won such a great reputation under Augustus that he perhaps felt it unnecessary to go on campaign when he became emperor himself, and indeed he had little occasion to do so. This reputation was certainly a help in quelling the mutiny of the legions in Germany and Pannonia in AD 14.[42]

Germanicus' conduct with his army after AD 14 was ostentatiously that of the *commilito*. His attitude towards the ordinary soldier was characterised by kindness (*comitas*): after the army had been mauled by the Germans in AD 15, he distributed his own money among the troops to compensate them for what they had lost, went round the wounded personally praising the exploits of each man, and so developed their personal loyalty and discipline.[43] His wife Agrippina stood at the bridge over the Rhine to greet and thank the returning soldiers; she handed out clothes to the needy and herself tended the wounded.[44] What is more, Gaius, the young son of Germanicus, was dressed in miniature military uniform and brought up in the camps, where he received the nickname Caligula. His parents intended him to be a youthful *commilito* of the army, and the object was to win the support of the soldiers.[45] Suetonius remarks that Gaius won the devotion of these troops because he was brought up with them ('per hanc nutrimentorum consuetudinem').[46] Tiberius thought that Germanicus went too far to gain the good will of the troops, and, echoing the words of Augustus, considered that it was 'nimium ambitiose'. However, it is clear that in the early principate it was firmly established that a commander should work hard for his success, show concern for the troops, and as far as possible share the rigours of the campaign; furthermore, this could be politically important.

It is no surprise therefore that Gaius, when he became emperor, not only adopted the title 'Father of the Armies',

---

[41] Velleius, 2.104.3–4.   [43] Tac., *A* 1.71; cf. 2.26.   [45] 1.41; cf. 69.
[42] See above, p.35.   [44] 1.69.   [46] *Cal.* 9.

but also tried to appear as an active commander. It is difficult to get a clear picture of Gaius' plans for military expeditions in Germany and Britain since the hostile sources have
presented his projects as ludicrous failures. However, his
behaviour in Gaul and Germany, though unpredictable, does
show that he sought the reputation of a tough *commilito*
sharing the rigours of military exercises and campaigns.[47] His
father's reputation, his own youth spent sojourning with the
troops, and the conspiracy of Lentulus Gaetulicus, the
governor of Upper Germany, will have suggested a more
active participation with the army.

After his undignified elevation to the purple with the help
of the Praetorian Guard, Claudius was eager for prestige,
and especially among the soldiers. His token appearance at
the invasion of Britain is quite remarkable. Claudius was
elderly and sickly and of a scholarly disposition; it would be
hard to imagine a more unmilitary figure. Yet he made the
long and difficult journey to Britain and returned in six
months for a splendid triumph. It seems clear from Dio's
account that Claudius had arranged with Aulus Plautius, the
commander of the invasion forces, that he should be
summoned to appear at a critical part of the campaign.[48] He
then could preside at a decisive battle and receive the capitu-
lation of numerous tribes. Two reasons lie behind Claudius'
conduct. He wanted a triumph, and that required the
personal participation of the commander.[49] Secondly, his
appearance on the campaign would help to sustain the idea
of military comradeship propagated by some of the coins of
his reign, in that he would appear to share the rigours of war
and show his concern for his troops. It is plausible to suppose
that the decision to invade Britain was governed mainly by
the emperor's desire for military acclaim.[50] Furthermore,
Claudius scrupulously observed the tradition that the
emperor himself gave the password to the tribune of the
detachment of the Praetorian Guard on duty at the palace.[51]

[47] Ibid. 43–7; *Galb.* 6.3; for an explanation of Gaius' conduct, see J.P.V.D.
Balsdon, *The Emperor Gaius* (1934), 58. See also above, p.35. Not since
Augustus' Spanish campaign in 26–25 BC had a Roman emperor taken the field
with his troops.

[48] Suet., *Cl.* 17.1; Dio, 60.21.   [50] See below, pp.140–1.
[49] See below, pp. 133ff.   [51] Suet., *Cl.* 42.1; Dio. 60.16.7.

'It did not require the fate of a Nero to remind Domitian that his own security and the peace of the world demanded at the very least that an emperor should know and be known by his troops.'[52] It is an easy assumption that an emperor who ignored his army, did not identify himself with it, and was uninterested in military affairs could inspire no devotion and so fall a prey to military revolt and usurpation. Caution is necessary. Nero ruled untroubled for fourteen years and the legions were slow to desert him. Vindex, who began the rebellion, had no Roman troops at his command. Indeed the Praetorian Guard was inspired by its long tradition of allegiance to the dynasty and at first had no desire of its own to revolt.[53] Yet although Nero vigorously tried to organize distant armies to deal with the revolt, he was deserted by nearly everyone. It is difficult to say how big a part the attitude of the soldiers played in his fall. If it is true that he allowed the army's pay to fall into arrears and refused to pension soldiers off at the proper time, and that this happened often, then he can hardly have been popular. Some news of his extravagant and ridiculous exploits may have filtered through to the army in the provinces from centurions and tribunes who had served in Rome. One of the Praetorian tribunes implicated in the conspiracy of Piso told Nero, 'I started to hate you after you turned out to be the murderer of your mother and your wife, a charioteer, actor, and arsonist.' The officers who felt this way could have worked on their men. On the other hand, it is doubtful if the rank and file soldiers were much influenced by the emperor's personal conduct, at least while it was kept at a distance; and although Nero entrusted his wars to others and had no military inclinations, the Parthian war and the reception of Tiridates could be represented as great achievements, and there were military plans for the future.[54] Nevertheless, Nero was something of a contrast to the emperors after

[52] Syme, *CAH* XI, 162.

[53] Tac., *H* 1.5.

[54] In general see P.A. Brunt, 'The Revolt of Vindex and the Fall of Nero', *Latomus* 18 (1959), 534–43; *contra*, R.J.A. Talbert, 'Some Causes of Disorder in AD 68–9', *American Journal of Ancient History* 2 (1977), 69. Cf Dio, 63.3.4 (the reception of Tiridates); 63.8 (planned expedition to Caucasus and creation of 'Alexander's Phalanx').

Augustus. Tiberius had a great military reputation before he became emperor; Gaius was popular because of his family background, and at least appeared with his men on the frontiers. Claudius was an unmilitary figure, but he kept the troops well paid and was briefly present on a campaign that added a new province to the empire. The troops may have been indifferent to the fate of Nero, and that was important since the upper classes, who certainly hated him, were prepared to provide leaders for rebellion. Nero had lost contact with his army and its commanders and perhaps did not have the confidence to put the matter to the ultimate test. In the end the deluded man could only dream wildly of appearing before the troops and weeping silently.

In any event, there is no doubt that Nero's removal, and the subsequent success of various military commanders in seizing power for themselves, will have served as a further warning about the importance of military strength in the imperial position, and the imperative need to retain the army's approval. The ordered peace of a great dynasty had been upset. Rome and the Praetorian Guard could no longer be the main centre of attention: 'One of the secrets of ruling had been revealed: an emperor could be created outside Rome'.[55]

The Civil Wars (68-9); The Flavians

Four of the five emperors who ruled between 68 and 81 had previously commanded armies, and it is likely that it was in this period that the military overtones of the imperial position developed. Galba, though old, had a distinguished reputation, and he is said to have marched from Spain wearing a huge sword at his side, although this provoked only amusement, according to Dio.[56] Otho, despite his inclination towards the soft life, donned a steel breastplate and, unkempt and ill-shaven, led his men out of Rome in person for the campaign of Bedriacum. Even the lazy Vitellius showed a comradely and indulgent attitude when he took up the governorship of Upper Germany.[57] More significantly, Vespasian and Titus acquired from the Judaean war a repu-

---

[55] Tac., *H* 1.4.   [56] 64.3.4.   [57] Tac., *H* 2.11; 1.52 (Vitellius).

tation for sharing the toils of the army and identifying themselves with the ordinary soldier. Vespasian was an excellent
soldier: he led the line in person, selected camp sites, pursued
the enemy day and night and would even engage in personal
combat if necessary; he accepted whatever food was available and in dress and appearance was much the same as a
private soldier.[58] Titus also showed himself to be a fine figure
of a man and displayed enterprise in arms; he achieved the
perfect combination of the *commilito* and the general.[59]
When his father was on the way to Italy to secure the purple,
Titus will certainly have been anxious to associate himself
with the troops remaining in Judaea since their loyalty was
also vital. It is curious that Vespasian's conduct in the East
as commander and *commilito* was remembered in such detail;
perhaps his previous reputation was extensively propagated
when he became emperor.

Domitian undoubtedly profited from the excellent
military reputation of his predecessors in the dynasty. But he
acquired a reputation of his own and followed the policy that
wherever possible he should take personal charge of military
campaigns. He was absent from Rome in 83 to fight the
Chatti, in 85-6 against the Dacians, and in 89 to deal with
the rebellion of Saturninus and to chastise the Chatti; in this
year he also visited Pannonia, and in 92 he returned to the
Danube to fight the Sarmatians. It has been suggested that
Domitian was an efficient and intelligent commander who
employed the military strength of the empire wisely. The
state of the evidence, however, does not allow a firm conclusion on how far Domitian was responsible for either the
disasters or successes of his reign, although the hostile
senatorial class clearly believed that Roman arms reached a
low ebb at this time.[60] This does not alter the fact that
Domitian built up an excellent rapport with his men: several
of the coins of the reign show the emperor shaking hands
with a soldier across a lighted altar, symbolising the
comradely association of ruler and army.[61] This was

---

[58] *H* 2.5.

[59] (ibid.) 'Titus by his polite and friendly behaviour won good will and support. In routine duties and on the march he often associated with the common
soldiers, while maintaining the respect to which a commanding officer was
entitled.'

[60] R. Syme, *CAH* XI, 158-77.   [61] *BMC* II, Domitian, pp. 304, 372-9, 381.

cemented by the pay rise granted by Domitian.[62] This rapport may have contributed to the fact that when Saturninus, the governor of Upper Germany, did dare to revolt in 89, the rebellion was short-lived and easily crushed. Indeed the Praetorians were greatly incensed at Domitian's assassination and demanded retribution against the murderers.[63] It is possible that whereas Vespasian strove to preserve discipline without paying the troops too much, and to revive the policy of Augustus, Domitian far more openly based his power on military support.

Nerva; Trajan; Hadrian

When, in the chaos after the murder of Domitian in 96, the Senate chose Nerva to be emperor, he must have seemed an uninspiring choice. He was sixty-one years old and in failing health.[64] How could he control and guide the legions and their commanders and so ensure stability? It is no surprise that he adopted, as his son, Trajan, the governor of Upper Germany, a man of apparently exceptional military experience and well known to several of the legions through his long sojourns as military tribune and his legionary legateship in Spain when he had intervened to assist Domitian against Saturninus. Perhaps his adoption was a veiled *coup d'état*. The running of the vast empire, it could be argued, needed a man of influence and experience and one who could be respected by the troops, whom therefore he could effectively control.

Trajan was just such a man and indeed the 'Optimus Princeps' was a prime example of the active 'fellow-soldier'. According to Pliny, Trajan joined in the military exercises, sharing the heat and thirst of his men and comforting the tired and the sick. 'It was your custom not to enter your tent until you had inspected your fellow-soldiers' quarters, and to retire to bed only after every one else.' He spent long nights in the open, and by sharing his soldiers' labours was both 'a praiser of and witness to' their courage.[65] By this behaviour Trajan won the admiration of his soldiers and succeeded in finding the right blend between the role of commander and

[62] See p.185.
[63] Dio, 68.3.3.

[64] 68.1.3. See Syme, *Tacitus*, 1.
[65] *Pan.* 13.1 ff.; 15.3–5; 19.3.

comrade-in-arms: 'You were therefore equally well liked by those of high degree and humble men, and in this way you combined the duties of *imperator* and fellow-soldier so well that on the one hand you encouraged the eager toil of everyone like· a superintendent, and on the other lightened it like a comrade and ally.'[66] Of course Pliny's *Panegyric* contains much that derives from a literary *topos*, and there is exaggeration.[67] But this need not mean that it had no applicability in contemporary life. It is true that Pliny may have said what Trajan wanted to hear, but the speech would have to be based on the emperor's known opinions and actions, if it were not to appear insulting or ridiculous. In any event, further evidence confirms the main outline of what Pliny says.

Dio of Prusa, speaking in front of Trajan, observed that the good king loved his soldiers. For if he rarely visited those who toiled for the empire, then he would be like a shepherd who did not know the men who assisted him in guarding the flock and who did not stay awake with them.[68] Dio was no doubt well briefed on Trajan's interest in his army and his identification with the troops in the performance of their duties. Cassius Dio remarks that Trajan marched with the army on foot, made military dispositions in person, and took great care to honour fallen soldiers.[69] Trajan's prolonged campaigns in Dacia and against the Parthians gave him plenty of opportunity to perform the role of the energetic *commilito*. There are indeed curious anecdotes that Trajan tore up his own clothing for bandages for wounded soldiers in the Dacian wars and that he knew many soldiers by name, or even nickname.[70] It is possible that these stories derive from the gossip and memoirs of soldiers who had been on one of

[66] 19.3.
[67] 15.5 — Trajan knows all the troops by name.
[68] 1.28-9. See in general, C.P. Jones, *The Roman World of Dio Chrysostom* (1978), 115-23.
[69] 68. 8.2. The altar and mausoleum at Adamklissi may be of Traianic date. The mausoleum bears the names of four thousand Roman soldiers who fell in a Dacian war. For a Traianic date: Gr. R. Tocilescu, *Le Mausolée d'Adamklissi* in *Fouilles et Recherches en Roumanie* (1900), 66-70; F.B. Florescu, *Das Siegesdenkmal von Adamklissi* (1965), 17-18. For a Domitianic date: G. Dorçitiu, *Dacia* NS 5 (1961), 345.
[70] Dio, 68.8.2; Fronto, ed. Haines (*Loeb*), vol II, p. 204; Pliny, *Pan.* 15.5.

Trajan's campaigns and had perhaps actually encountered the emperor, but they probably reflect the kind of impression that Trajan made generally on the army. Even if he spoke to only one or two soldiers by name, rumours of this could easily spread and be magnified.

Trajan's own view is perhaps expressed in the mighty column whose sculpture provides a picture of the Dacian wars in a series of carefully chosen vignettes.[71] It is likely that a monument of this size and scale would convey what was acceptable to the emperor and depict activities that it was at least possible for contemporaries to imagine that he might engage in.[72] Trajan's column shows how he conducted a major campaign, and his duties and responsibilities with the hard working troops. The main theme is that Trajan undertook a full share of the difficulties and trouble of a campaign, by leading the army in person, by supervising routine military tasks, by addressing the troops at critical stages of the war, and by being present in person at the major battles.[73] In Trajan's case the role of *commilito* was far from being an empty convention, and the emperor's conduct with his troops was consistent with the flattering language he used in his *mandata*. By his energy, participation, and concern he earned the respect of his 'excellent and most loyal fellow-soldiers', and preserved discipline and readiness for war.[74] Trajan was, of course, much interested in military affairs and an enthusiastic commander of the army, and may not be entirely typical. However the evidence shows that Trajan's behaviour was not unique and that emperors did try with varying degrees of enthusiasm to live up to the ideal of military comradeship.

Hadrian carried out his predecessor's policy in this respect even though he eschewed grandiose military ventures. He travelled round all the provinces and visited the legions, visits which were celebrated in a remarkable and unique series

[71] See I.A. Richmond, *PBSR* 1935, 1; Florescu, *Trajanssäule*; L. Rossi, *Trajan's Column and the Dacian Wars* (1971).

[72] See below, pp. 146ff.

[73] Florescu, Taf. 8,9; 10; 12; 14; 43; 52; 84; 87.

[74] Note the comments of Dio (68.7.5): 'Nor did the result which normally occurs in such circumstances — pride and arrogance on the part of the soldiers — ever appear during his reign; so firmly did he rule them.'

of coins.[75] He inspected all the forts, living quarters, weapons and siege equipment, and the personal records of the soldiers, hoping to achieve fairness and reduce luxury. He personally drilled the troops, commending or reproving where necessary. And he was always ready to set an example himself; he led a rigorous life and either walked or rode on horseback on all occasions; indeed it was said that he would walk twenty miles in armour. The emperor went about bare-headed even in scorching heat or bitter cold. He preferred simple military dress, visited sick soldiers, ate simple camp fare of bacon and cheese, and drank coarse wine, like Trajan and the great commanders of the past.[76]

Antoninus Pius; Lucius Verus; Marcus Aurelius; Commodus

After his adoption by Hadrian in 138 Antoninus Pius never left Italy or saw an army, and it seems that he had little interest in military affairs. He in turn adopted Lucius Verus and his nephew Marcus Aurelius, and they also had no experience in military matters. Antoninus Pius cannot have presented himself to the army as an active *commilito*. Nevertheless, a series of coins minted under Pius shows the emperor in military dress advancing at the head of a file of soldiers carrying standards.[77] This may be an example of the continuation of a conventional formula by those in charge of the mint, but it does help to illustrate that an emperor's military associations were never far in the background, even if his personal inclinations were quite different.

Lucius Verus, who ruled jointly with Marcus Aurelius from 161-9, commanded in person during the war against the Parthians (162-6); he marched bare-headed in front of his troops, was satisfied with the plain fare of the camp, inspected the soldiers in the field, and made the rounds of the sick, returning to bed after everyone else for his hard-earned rest.[78] Fronto's *Principia Historiae* is virtually panegyric, but it was intended seriously[79] and cannot be

---

[75] *BMC* III, pp. 497 ff.
[76] Dio, 69.9.1 ff.; Fronto (*Loeb*), II, p. 206; *HA, Vit. Had.* 10.2 ff.
[77] *BMC* IV, p. 270, no. 1675.
[78] Fronto (*Loeb*), II, p. 208 f.
[79] Verus had directed the commanders in the war to provide commentaries of their part in the campaign, and offered to send one of his own to Fronto.

pure invention. Verus, though he was at times impetuous and ostentatious, probably genuinely wanted to do his duty as commander, and Trajan and Hadrian had recently established a clear pattern of what this involved. Rhetoric may have coloured the details of Fronto's account and much of what he says may seem like a traditional cliché, but that cliché is itself revealing for what Roman emperors might encourage people to think of them.

Marcus Aurelius faced frequent foreign wars during his reign. Although Marcus preferred intellectual and philosophical pursuits, had no military experience, and was often ill, he insisted on going to the scene of the action in person. Dio stresses his personal leadership, courage, and endurance.[80] Like Trajan, Marcus had his exploits on the Danube frontier recorded on a sculptured column. The reliefs depict the emperor in military dress sharing the rigours of the campaign with his toiling soldiers.[81] Marcus no doubt had a strong sense of his duty to supervise the defence of the frontiers of the empire in time of crisis. However he will not have been unaware that it was necessary to preserve the good will of the army and cement their loyalty and discipline. This was especially important at this time since it seemed that the empire must face a succession of difficult foreign wars, and even Marcus was not immune from rebellion. Although the insurrection in 175 of the governor of Syria, Avidius Cassius, was easily crushed, Marcus visited Syria and Egypt to reassert his position there.

Marcus' son, Commodus, joined his father at Sirmium in 175 where he assumed the *toga virilis*. From 177 to 180 he accompanied Marcus on the Danube frontier, while holding *tribunicia potestas* and the title of Augustus, and was introduced to the troops. His popularity and prestige with at least some of the troops helped him when he assumed sole control in 180, though he was never to command in person during the rest of his reign. The speech that Herodian puts into the mouth of Commodus at his accession is interesting. There are three main themes. Firstly, the young emperor had been brought up as the comrade of the troops: Marcus used to call

[80] 71.6.3; 24.4.
[81] Caprino, *La Colonna*, figs. 10; 22; 28; 43; 48–9; 59; 98; 112; 131.

Commodus 'fellow-soldier' rather than 'son' and had an equal affection for the soldiers and his offspring; Commodus had not pretended to be better than the soldiers and had been entrusted to their care; Commodus expected the complete loyalty of the troops since they were fellow pupils in arms and because Marcus had loved them all alike. Secondly, Commodus had un-impeachable claims to legitimacy, being born to the purple. Thirdly, emperor and soldiers should work together for the well being of the empire, and military victory would increase Commodus' prestige and authority.[82]

It is important that Herodian gives such prominence to Commodus' role as *commilito*, and to the significance of this idea for confirming the allegiance of the army. It is impossible to say how much, if any, of this speech was actually made by Commodus. The historical background seems to be accurate. A coin dated 171/2 shows Commodus being presented to the troops by Marcus.[83] If this coin was minted to pay the troops a donative distributed on this occasion, it indicates an attempt to identify Commodus with the army at an early age.[84] However, it is not possible to show the authenticity of a speech by the fact that it mentions demonstrably real events. It is the history of Commodus' reign that provides some justification for Herodian's view. Despite his cruelty and irresponsibility, Commodus displayed personal bravery and deeds of prowess in his performances as a gladiator.[85] In addition, he spoke personally with a deputation of ordinary soldiers from Britain, and addressed them as 'fellow-soldiers'.[86] It was rumoured that he intended to call the legions 'Commodiana' and distribute to the soldiers the property of the rich.[87] These stories may be hostile propaganda (only a few legions bear the name 'Commodiana', and this may have been taken unofficially), but they indicate that contemporaries believed that the emperor sought a very

[82] 1.5.3 ff. See E. Hohl, *Sitzungsberichte der Deut. Akad.* (1954), 3, 10 ff.; F. Grosso, *La Lotta Politica al tempo di Commodo* (1964), 30 ff.; R. Whittaker, *Loeb*, vol. I, 1viii ff.

[83] *RIC* III, p. 296, no. 1046. Cf. an inscription dedicated 'pro salute et reditu', which mentions the children of Marcus — G. Barbieri, *Kokalos* 7 (1961), 15.

[84] See p. 187.

[85] Herodian, 1.13.8; 15.1 f.; 15.7-8; 17.12.

[86] Dio, 72.9.3.

[87] Herodian, 1.17.2.

close relationship with the soldiers. It is indeed significant that, after the murder of Commodus, Pertinax and Laetus had to tell the Praetorian Guard that he had died from natural causes.[88] Herodian may well represent the view of contemporary observers that towards the end of the second century the worthiness of an emperor as *commilito* was an important factor in his acceptance by the troops and their loyalty to him.

The Severan Dynasty

Neither Pertinax nor Didius Julianus had any chance to build up a rapport with the troops and their short reigns were followed by prolonged civil wars from 193 to 197, when Septimius Severus emerged in undisputed control and founded a dynasty which lasted, with one short break under Macrinus, until the death of Severus Alexander in 235. Military might was clearly pre-eminent again, the loyalty of the armies vital to political survival. After 193 there were three foreign wars and two civil wars in all of which Severus campaigned in person. Although he was present at only one of the three battles that confirmed his sovereignty,[89] there was much scope for the development of the emperor's active role as *commilito*. During the rapid march from Pannonia to Rome, Severus shared the toils of his men, used a cheap tent, and ate and drank only what was available to everyone. He avoided any display of imperial luxury. And so he was respected and very popular among his 'fellow-soldiers'.[90] Similarly, in the campaign against Clodius Albinus, Severus marched at the front of his men, bare-headed in the rain and snow, and set the troops an example of determination and bravery: 'So he made them endure their hardships not only by instilling a fear of breaking military rules and discipline, but also by encouraging them to emulate their emperor.'[91] Dio confirms the idea of Severus' personal leadership and association with the troops, and he recounts a story of Severus' campaigns in the East. When the army was suffering

[88] 2.2.5–6. For legions named 'Commodiana' or 'Commoda', see *RE* XII 1–2, s.v. 'legio' cols. 1505; 1663; 1820.

[89] Dio, 75.6.1.

[90] Dio, 74.15.3; Herodian, 2.11.2; 3.6.10.

[91] 3.6.10.

from thirst and was reluctant to drink dirty water from a desert well, he set the example by ostentatiously draining a cup in full view of all.[92]

Severus' son Caracalla, who was particularly anxious to win the support of the army after he had murdered his brother Geta, carried the idea of the emperor as *commilito* to new lengths. He was adored by the soldiers, partly because he shared their duties and was the first to carry out menial tasks done by the ordinary soldiers. He used wooden utensils for eating and drinking, ate the bread available locally, and sometimes even baked his own. He avoided extravagance and used only the cheapest articles available to the poorest of his men. The emperor marched on foot, neither bathing nor changing his clothes, and occasionally carried the same equipment as the troops. In particular, despite his small stature, Caracalla even carried the legionary standards himself, although they were so heavy that the strongest soldiers had difficulty in bearing them. Herodian, although generally hostile to Caracalla, praises his performance in the role of *commilito*.[93] Dio also agrees that the emperor scrupulously performed all routine duties on terms of equality with the soldiers, though he sneers at Caracalla's ability as a commander.[94] Caracalla differed from his predecessors in that he not only called the soldiers *commilitones*, but said that he loved being called 'fellow-soldier' instead of emperor by them.[95] This is a significant development and shows how far Caracalla was prepared to go to encourage the soldiers to identify themselves with him. As soon as he entered the Praetorian camp in 211 after the murder of his brother, he proclaimed, 'Rejoice, fellow-soldiers, for now I can benefit you.' And he went on to say, 'I am one of you, for you alone do I wish to live so that I can confer many favours on you.' Caracalla professed his wish to live with the soldiers, and, if not, at least to die with them. He espoused the military ideal; death had no fears for him, and he desired to perish in battle.[96] That these effusive utterances, which combined an appeal to military comradeship with the promise of great

[92] 75.2.2.
[93] Herodian, 4.7.4–7; 12.2.
[94] 77.13.1–2.
[95] Herodian, 4.7.6.
[96] Dio, 77.3.2 ff.

financial rewards, were more than the product of impetuous enthusiasm and relief after the murder, is shown by the emperor's behaviour on campaign and an official inscription which describes him as 'Father of the Soldiers'.[97]

Caracalla may have enjoyed the life of a *miles gregarius* and the rigours and excitement of military action. But he was also fearful, for not all the army had approved of the murder of Geta.[98] The emperor was certainly not blind to the political benefits that would accrue if he built up a devoted and unassailable relationship with the army. He chose to do this partly by developing and exploiting his role as *commilito*, and of course through material emoluments. Then, completely confident in his 'comrades', the emperor could ignore or debase others who thought that they should have some influence in the government of the empire. He openly gloated in a letter to the Senate: 'I am well aware that what I am doing does not please you; but that is why I have weapons and soldiers, so that I may disregard those who are talking about me.'[99] And when he wrote to commend one of his *commilitones,* he added that he was not ashamed at feeling more gratitude to him than to the soldiers in general, and that he considered them in turn to be better than the senators.[100] In winter quarters at Nicomedia he kept senators waiting all day while he mixed and passed round wine to the soldiers guarding him.[101] Fortunately Caracalla did not always treat the Senate as badly as his impetuous comments threatened, and this kind of incident may have been the exception rather than the rule.[102] The significance is that, whether he meant it or not, the emperor could so openly boast of his total dependence on the army and contempt for the other institutions of the state. The reality of the ultimate dependence on military power remained unaltered as it had done from the late Republic, but the façade of constitutional government established by Augustus and Tiberius had worn

[97] *ILS* 454.
[98] The legion stationed at Alba at first apparently refused to admit Caracalla (*HA, Vit. Car.* 2.7).
[99] Dio, 77.20.2.
[100] 77.13.6.
[101] 77.17.4.
[102] See below, pp. 412f.

thin. In seeking the political support of the army in this way, Caracalla was in danger of giving military excellence and comradeship too much weight in the imperial position, and indeed corrupting military discipline. Ironically Caracalla was murdered in the midst of the troops he loved so much. Dio was baffled by this.[103] But no ruler then, or now, could be entirely safe. And the more an emperor staked his survival on his reputation with the troops, in one sense the more vulnerable he became. He might be killed in war, or the army might find a better general.

Macrinus the Praetorian prefect, who inherited Caracalla's war against the Parthians, was unable to control a soldiery incensed at the murder of their comrade, and used to extravagant rewards; he was soon murdered in turn. Elagabalus, who can hardly have seemed like a *commilito*, may have won the support of the troops against Macrinus partly by donatives and partly by the claim that he was the natural son of Caracalla. However, once in Rome he devoted himself to the worship of the Sun-God, of which he was a priest, and avoided the rigours of military life. He was persuaded to adopt his cousin Severus Alexander and was subsequently murdered in 222 by a palace conspiracy of those who feared that he intended to dispose of Alexander.

Severus Alexander was only thirteen when he became emperor, and was much under the influence of his mother. It is generally agreed that Herodian gives a misleadingly favourable view of the reign.[104] But even Herodian is forced to concede that there was general discontent among the troops at the way in which the eastern campaign against the Persians was conducted. Although Severus Alexander may have gained some success, the war was costly in men and materials and there was no spectacular achievement; the army's morale and the emperor's reputation sank.[105] The discontent was intensified by the personal loss suffered by soldiers from the northern legions who were serving in the East, when their homes were overrun by invaders attacking across the Rhine and Danube.[106] Alexander hastened to the

---

[103] 78.4.1.
[104] R. Syme, *Emperors and Biography* (1971), 146 ff.
[105] Herodian, 6.6.3; 7.10.
[106] 6.7.2 f.; and see Whittaker, ad loc.

German frontier and took personal charge of the campaign. But he had lost the confidence and affection of the army and Maximinus exploited this. In fact, Severus Alexander was the first emperor to be overthrown by specifically military discontent on a wide scale.

Maximinus, who was in charge of training recruits, played upon the troops' anger at Alexander's alleged incompetence and cowardice in the conduct of his campaigns. His supporters said that Alexander was no soldier and taunted him as a 'mean little girl' and a 'timid little child entirely the slave of his mother.[107] Maximinus on the other hand was a brave fellow soldier devoted to a life of military action. He was a συσκῆνος (sharer of the same tent) as well as a συστρατιώτης (fellow-soldier), and because of his skill and courage was ideally suited to lead the army in its present campaign.[108]

Maximinus

As a serving soldier Maximinus was closely in touch with the troops, and when he became emperor he actually fought in battle — a virtually unprecedented action.[109] He spent all his time with the army, never visiting Rome or the Senate. Instead he arranged for a large picture showing his deeds of martial prowess to be exhibited outside the senate house.[110] Although Herodian is very hostile to Maximinus, and the emperor was probably unavoidably detained outside Italy by the pressure of the military situation,[111] it is likely that Maximinus did indeed trust only his troops and wish to live among them like a man inhabiting a fortress.[112] It is clear that the emperor's personal behaviour with the troops and his ability to direct a campaign and appear a good soldier were now uncomfortably important factors in the ability of an emperor to maintain the support of the army. In the reign

[107] 6.8.3; 9.5.
[108] 6.9.5; 8.4.
[109] See below, p. 68.
[110] Herodian, 7.2.8.
[111] See Herodian 7.1.6, where he says that Maximinus invaded Germany to prove his military reputation to the troops. There may be something in this, but it is also true that a major conflict was threatening when Alexander was murdered.
[112] 7.1.3.

of Maximinus the idea of *commilitium* had developed into the almost total identification of the warrior-emperor and his army.[113] But in the end the soldiers abandoned Maximinus at Aquileia, partly because of his failure to pursue the siege successfully despite his previous victories and personal bravery. An emperor who consciously based his position largely on military might could find the soldiers fickle and dangerous supporters, especially if he could find no backing elsewhere in society.

It has been suggested that Pliny's *Panegyric* to Trajan expresses the concept that an emperor could find recognition among the soldiers only if he were first one of them and undertook to prove himself a *commilito* in the future.[114] This view is too extreme. The Roman empire was not a military monarchy, in the sense that the emperor was rarely an experienced and skilled commander and never, at least before the reign of Maximinus, a warrior-leader. He did not spend all or even, in many cases, much of his time with the army and was not compelled to conduct campaigns in person. Emperors shared the outlook and education of the upper classes and many were doubtless not enthusiastic about their association with the ordinary soldier. The Roman emperor can be firmly placed in the tradition of the distinguished senator of the Republic, versed in the skills of civil government and law, and all the accomplishments of a man of the upper classes, but also capable of accepting the duties and learning the skills of an *imperator*, which he might be called upon to be. All should be able to cope, though some might have a preference for one type of activity. It was much the same for the Roman emperor, except that his security and survival might depend on his relationship with the army.

Although emperors generally exercised effective supervision of the conduct of a military campaign when they were present, up to the early third century their role as comrade of the troops did not require them to fight personally in battle.[115] Furthermore, the qualities of the *commilito* were

---

[113] Propaganda against Gordian also alleged that he was a feeble old man with no army (Herodian, 7.8.5).

[114] H.U. Instinsky, *Gymnasium* 63 (1956), 267.

[115] See below, pp. 59ff.

of course in no sense a formal routine. The behaviour of individual emperors as 'fellow-soldier' was conditioned by their personality and perhaps the circumstances of their reign. Some doubtless viewed it as a tedious convention, but others certainly took it very seriously.

From the reign of Domitian onwards the number of campaigns where the emperor commanded in person increased significantly. After the war in Spain (26–25 BC) Augustus does not seem to have directed campaigns himself. And with the exception of Gaius' abortive campaign in Germany and Claudius' brief appearance in Britain, no Julio-Claudian emperor campaigned personally. But between AD 81 and 192 only two emperors, Nerva, whose reign was very brief, and Antoninus Pius, did not campaign or visit the armies in the provinces. After 193, up to the death of Maximinus in 238, only Elagabalus did not campaign in person. Furthermore, on the imperial coinage virtually every emperor after Gaius is portrayed in some context with the soldiers.[116] In these types the emperor usually appears in military dress, the traditional garb of the Roman *imperator*, with all its martial associations.

It is unlikely that the increase in participation by emperors in campaigns was accidental. The civil wars of 68–9 had highlighted again the importance of military loyalty. It would not be surprising if emperors sought a closer relationship with the troops: to display generalship, to share the rigours of a campaign, or visit the soldiers in their camps will have seemed the most direct kind of contact. And it was expedient not to allow a senatorial commander the military prestige of a successful campaign, and the affection to be gained by a long sojourn alone with the troops: 'The quality of a good general was the emperor's virtue.'[117] Most emperors, therefore, would seek to be present on campaigns where major operations were planned, since that would bring them greater glory. Hadrian's peregrinations to inspect and supervise the army in its routine labours were unique. But the presence of the emperor with the troops in the provinces for any reason will have made his role as *commilito* more effective and con-

---

[116] See below, pp. 142 ff.
[117] Tacitus attributes the thought to Domitian — *Ag.* 39.2.

vincing. This indeed was the weakness of the concept of the emperor as military comrade. It could make a major impression only among those armies where he appeared in person. This should be contrasted with the financial emoluments, which were always effective whether the emperor was present or not.

However, the identification of the emperor with his soldiers, inherent in the idea of *commilitium*, could certainly help to establish an extra bond of affection and loyalty in addition to the persuasion of material benefits. An emperor who did succeed in uniting his troops behind him in this way had created another barrier which the potential usurper would have to overcome; mere grants of money might not always be enough.

Unfortunately there is no direct evidence for what the ordinary soldiers thought about the various emperors in their role as 'fellow-soldier'. But ancient observers certainly believed that the soldiers would offer outstanding loyalty to the man with whom they could identify. Plutarch indeed believed that a display of military comradeship could be a more important inducement than money.[118] Tacitus and Velleius had no doubts that the great bond of affection Tiberius established with the German legions was partly due to his personal presence and noted concern for the troops.[119] Much of this may have disappeared by AD 14 when these very soldiers mutinied against Tiberius, but who can say that the residual ties of affection did not help to quell a potentially more serious outbreak? Dio believed that Hadrian led a rigorous life with the troops so that they should benefit from watching him, and that he succeeded in organizing and training the army through his own example and instructions.[120] It was said that the troops of Septimius Severus did everything enthusiastically because they saw him labouring with them.[121] The army mourned Caracalla as a fellow-soldier and a man who shared their lives, and insisted that he be enrolled among the demi-gods.[122] His successor Macrinus,

[118] See n. 3.
[119] Vell., 2.104.4; 115.5; Tac., *A* 1.25; 42.
[120] Dio, 69.9.4.
[121] Herodian, 2.11.2.
[122] Dio, 78.9.2 f.; Herodian, 4.7.4-7, 13.7, 14.4-5; 5.2.5.

on the other hand, was reviled by the troops because his luxurious way of life on campaign contrasted with the privations they suffered.[123] No doubt a variety of factors influenced the attitude of the soldiers to a particular emperor: money, birth, ancestry, the support and leadership of important men. But there is no reason to doubt the insistence by the ancient sources that the troops much appreciated an emperor who made some attempt to identify himself with them, appeared personally on campaign, and shared some of the rigorous life they faced. The funeral inscription of an ordinary sailor in the imperial fleet goes some way towards illustrating the emotions of dignity and honour felt by humble men who served 'at the side of the emperor', even though they may have seen their emperor only in the distance, or not at all: 'I was born in extreme poverty, and then served as a soldier of the fleet at the side of the emperor for seventeen years during which I incurred no displeasure and committed no offence, and received an honourable discharge.'[124]

4. THE EMPEROR AS MILITARY LEADER

Once the classical Greek hoplite phalanx had been committed to battle, there was little the commander could do to influence the outcome of the struggle, and so it was customary for him to fight in the ranks. When a more flexible form of the phalanx developed with a wider use of cavalry and other types of troops, it became necessary for the commander to stay outside the press of battle in order to review his tactics and consider when troops were to be committed.[1] The Roman military system involved the employment of cavalry and light-armed troops along with the heavy infantry, and particularly the use of reserves. The disposition of forces and the strategic siting of available reserves were vital elements of generalship that required the commander to be in a position from where he could see the entire battle.[2] It

[123] 5.2.5.
[124] *ILS* 2905.

[1] F.E. Adcock, *The Greek and Macedonian Art of War* (1962), 89 ff.
[2] Caesar, *BG* 2.20-2, implying what the usual practice was.

could therefore be dangerous for him to commit himself too early to the battle-line.

But, at a critical stage of the conflict a leader might still choose to intervene personally in battle to rally and inspire his men. And if all were lost, a glorious death might be preferable to ignominious retreat and the subsequent recriminations. At Lake Trasimene, the consul Flaminius entered the battle wherever he saw his troops being hard pressed and actually perished in hand-to-hand combat.[3] That personal intervention in battle was not considered incompatible with the demands of generalship can be seen from Caesar's praise of his officer Cotta for fulfilling the duties of a commander and fighting in the ranks as a common soldier.[4] It has indeed been suggested that in the period after Marius, Roman commanders tended to fight personally in the ranks.[5] Doubtless on many occasions this was necessary because the commander's troops were in imminent danger of defeat,[6] but it is plausible to suppose that some of the ambitious military leaders were anxious to cut a fine figure with their men and develop a greater rapport with the troops. It is no surprise that stories of personal valour in battle are most frequently told about Caesar and Pompey.[7] Caesar inspired his men by his distributions of rewards and honours, but also by his own conduct:

. . . he was willing to undergo any danger and did not shrink from any hard work. His soldiers were not surprised at his love of taking risks since they knew his ambition for distinction. What did astonish them was his ability to endure physical toils which appeared to be beyond the strength of his body.

When Pompey addressed his soldiers in Greece, he said, 'I have not yet failed, nor shall I ever fail to fight along with you and for you. I offer you my services both as a soldier and a commander.'[8]

[3] Livy, 22.6.1 ff.; cf. Paulus at Cannae (22.49.6 ff.).
[4] *BG* 5.33.
[5] Harmand, *L'Armée*, 397 ff.
[6] e.g. Plut., *Sulla* 21.2; 29.5; *Sert.* 21.2; Appian, *BC* 1.58; Caes., *BG* 2.25.
[7] Plut., *Pomp.* 7.2; 19.2; 35.3; *Caes.* 17; Caesar, *BG* 1.52; 7.17; 7.88; *Bell. Afr.* 83; Appian, *BC* 2.51; 62; 104.
[8] Caesar — Plut., *Caes.* 17; Pompey — Appian, *BC* 2.51.

After the battle of Philippi, Marcus Antonius had the reputation of being invincible in war.[9] The esteem to be gained
from this was useful propaganda, and could be exploited in
the struggle for political supremacy. By contrast, Octavian
did not distinguish himself at the first battle of Mutina, and
Antony wrote that he had run away and appeared only two
days later without his horse or his general's cloak. Octavian,
eager to reassert himself, apparently performed deeds of
prowess in the second battle: when the standard bearer was
wounded the commander took the eagle and carried it himself, or so his propaganda alleged.[10] Then, at Philippi,
Octavian's forces were routed and when the camp was
captured he was found to be absent. A dream had warned
him to beware that day, so he wrote in his memoirs.[11]
There is no doubt that down to 31 BC Octavian lagged
behind Antony in his reputation as a courageous military
leader. The Illyrian campaign of 35-33 BC did something
to build up his prestige; here it was said that he led his
hesitating soldiers across a river, and then, stranded on the
other side by the collapse of a bridge, fought courageously
though wounded several times.[12] The proliferation and exploitation of this kind of story in these years indicate the
importance of a reputation for personal bravery in battle. It
was another way of building up the devotion and loyalty of
the troops. It was naturally expected that a commander
knew, or could learn from textbooks available (pp. 325f.), the
basic art of generalship. Now he might have to prove that he
was a brave soldier as well.

Our sources indicate that it was normal for the emperor to
assume responsibility for the overall direction of the strategy
of a campaign; this involved the choice of combat plan, the
disposition and organization of available forces, transport,
and diplomacy with the enemy. For example, Florus
describes Augustus' operations in Spain in 26-25 BC in the
following terms: 'He himself came to Segisama, pitched
camp, and from there, having divided the army into three
sections, he surrounded all Cantabria and enclosed that

[9] *BC* 5.58; cf. 4.111.   [11] Appian, *BC* 4.110.
[10] Suet., *Aug.* 10.4.   [12] Florus, 2.23.7.

savage race like a wild beast in a net.'[13] Similarly, Germanicus personally directed the advance across the Rhine in the reign of Tiberius: 'Germanicus divided the eager legions into four groups so that they could devastate a wider area, and the land for fifty miles around was pillaged and burnt'.[14] Trajan's leadership was equally impressive in the campaign against the Parthians: 'He always marched on foot with the ordinary soldiers; he was responsible for the disposition of the troops on the entire march and sometimes drew them up in one order, sometimes in another.'[15]

It may well have been difficult to get precise information concerning imperial campaigns. Dio was worried by the secrecy of much of political life in the imperial period and went on to say:

Moreover, the very size of the empire and the number of events taking place make it extremely difficult to obtain an accurate account. For in Rome itself there is a great deal of activity and also much in the provinces. In addition, as regards hostile peoples there is always something happening, indeed every day. No one except the participants can easily get clear information on these activities; most people in fact do not even hear that they have taken place.[16]

Presumably the historian had to rely on the emperor's despatches to the Senate, letters, campaign histories or personal memoirs. It is natural therefore that much of the history of imperial campaigns is episodic, anecdotal, and lacking in military detail. Dio illustrates the problem of the source material in commenting on the campaign of Caracalla in Parthia. After a vague introduction he confesses, 'I have found nothing of especial interest to record concerning the incidents of that campaign except the following anecdote.' And he proceeds to tell a story about two soldiers who brought their personal dispute before the emperor.[17] In the absence of definite details, the sources perhaps assumed that the emperor took personal charge of a campaign, and underestimated the contribution of others. But that assumption was surely plausible. Doubtless an emperor took advice from

13 2.33.48.   16 53.19.3 ff.
14 Tac., A 1.50–1; 55.   17 78.1, 3.
15 Dio, 68.23.

his senior commanders, and indeed the execution of part of the plan of campaign was often entrusted to the senatorial commanders who accompanied the imperial party.[18] But there is no reason to doubt that the ultimate direction and responsibility were in the hands of the emperor and that all major decisions on strategy emanated from him. Indeed very few substantial military operations were entrusted to the direct control of senators. Aulus Plautius during the conquest of Britain, except for the short period when Claudius was present in person, Corbulo in the East (55-66), Agricola in Britain (78-84), had limited freedom to organize the campaign, but major decisions probably came from the emperor, although his absence from the scene will have extended a greater scope to the initiative of the man on the spot.[19]

Control of the general strategy of a campaign should be distinguished from the direction of tactics in battle. Once again precise and detailed evidence for the role played by the emperors in this respect is lacking. However it seems clear that frequently a prince or emperor worked out and executed battle tactics, presumably with the appropriate advice. In AD 16 Germanicus directed the battle against Arminius.

Germanicus knew all about these arrangements; he was aware of their plans, dispositions, their secret and open preparations; he exploited the enemy's ambush to bring about their own destruction. He gave the command of the cavalry and the responsibility for the level ground to his officer Seius Tubero. He divided the infantry into two parts, one of which was to enter the wood along the level ground while the other attacked the rampart. Germanicus took the more difficult task himself and delegated the rest to his officers.[20]

Claudius, according to Dio, was at least present at the decisive battle against the British near the river Thames,[21] though it is difficult to believe that Aulus Plautius did not

[18] See pp. 355 ff.
[19] For senators in independent commands, see pp. 352-4. In this category could also be included Hadrian's appointment of Julius Severus to deal with the Jewish revolt, though Hadrian probably himself attended the scene of the conflict at some time.
[20] Tac., *A* 2.16 ff.; especially 20.
[21] 60.21.2 ff.

make the dispositions himself. Titus personally conducted the siege of Jerusalem, where his valour won renown.[22] Trajan too acquired a reputation for bravery and generalship (στρατηγία and ἀνδρία) in his Dacian campaigns.[23] The emperor was not afraid to risk his life and later in the Parthian War was nearly wounded while organizing the cavalry attack on the walls of Hatra. The rigours and anxieties of the campaign may well have undermined his health.[24] The sculptor of Trajan's column, who depicts the emperor and his senior advisers present in person at all major operations and battles in the campaign, was expressing an ideal of imperial control of military affairs that was well established by the second century.[25] Septimius Severus was not present at two of the battles in the civil wars, but he took the field at Lugdunum against Clodius Albinus and apparently intervened with the Praetorians at a decisive stage.[26] Later, in his campaign against the Parthians, he directed the siege of Hatra from a high tribunal and it was his decision to withdraw the troops from the assault at the crucial moment that contributed to the failure of the siege.[27]

When an emperor went on campaign he assumed an active role as commander-in-chief of the army, directed strategy and tactics, and appeared in the military dress of the Roman *imperator*. But at the same time he was also the 'fellow-soldier' of his troops, and might be expected to share the dangers they endured in battle. Now, it may have been acceptable for the tough *imperator* of old, or the military dynasts of the late Republic, with power and glory still to win, to risk their lives in combat and deeds of valour. But once a man had secured the purple, it would be foolish to risk his life merely to enhance his reputation as *commilito*. He could hope to win the respect of the soldiers by his successful conduct of the war and his performance of the other duties of the *commilito*. The troops could be told that the emperor was needed to supervise all the operations on the field of battle and was displaying his courage, interest, and concern for them by his presence at the scene of the action.

[22] Josephus, *BJ* 5.56 ff.; 81 ff.

[23] Dio, 68.14.

[24] 68.31-2.

[25] See pp. 146-8.

[26] Dio, 75.6.6.

[27] 75.12.

Although emperors often displayed courage in their military duties, there is little evidence that they fought in the battle line. And in this case the silence of the sources seems conclusive, for a story of the courageous part played by an emperor in battle was just the kind of anecdotal material that they used. No act of personal valour of Augustus as emperor or Tiberius as prince is recorded, though Tiberius' long campaigns are well chronicled and the effusive Velleius was unlikely to miss an opportunity for glorifying the reputation of his hero. However, during Tiberius' reign Germanicus displayed personal bravery. Tacitus emphasizes that in the battle against Arminius, 'Germanicus himself led the charge of the Praetorian cohorts into the wood when the rampart had been taken; there hand-to-hand fighting took place'.[28] As the enemy fell back, Germanicus tore off his helmet so as to be recognized and urged his men forward. Perhaps because he was relatively inexperienced Germanicus felt that he still had a reputation to win as the noble *imperator* in the service of the state; and there was the example of Tiberius' long service on the Rhine and the Danube in the reign of Augustus. In much the same way, after Vespasian had secured the purple, his son Titus performed outstanding deeds of prowess at the siege of Jerusalem, often rallying his men by personal example.[29]

Emperors, on the other hand, were more circumspect. Gaius indulged in exciting forays during his manoeuvres in Germany, but at no risk to his person. Although Claudius was present at one battle in Britain to acquire some military glory and earn his triumph, it is inconceivable that he participated in the conflict, and no source asserts this. Domitian, despite his close relationship with the troops, his willingness to campaign in person, and his desire for military renown, does not seem to have ventured into the battle line.

It is perhaps in Trajan that we should most expect to see the embodiment of the warrior-emperor. Dio says that Trajan was most notable for his justice, his bravery, and the simplicity of his habits.[30] He does not define further what he

---

[28] *A* 2.20-1; cf. the activities of Gaius Caesar, *ILS* 140.
[29] n. 22; Dio, 65.5.1; Tac., *H* 5.1 ff.; Suetonius, *Titus* 5.2 Contrast Frontinus, *Strat.* 2.3.23 (Domitian).   [30] 68.6.3.

means by 'bravery', but elsewhere he emphasizes the emperor's courage in the Dacian wars.[31] There is no hint that Trajan engaged in actual fighting and Dio probably means no more than that he did not shirk personal danger when making troop dispositions and organizing the army. At the siege of Hatra, Trajan, while riding past the city, just missed being struck by a missile hurled from the walls, even though he had removed his imperial clothing to avoid recognition.[32] This in itself implies that he did not intend to get personally involved in the battle, and at the time of the incident he was involved in directing the siege operations. Furthermore, Aurelius Victor and the author of the *Epitome*, although both are very favourable to Trajan, do not mention prowess in battle. The statement that an emperor should display 'bravery in arms', corresponding to 'integrity in home affairs', merely means that he must ensure the efficient conduct of the military business of the empire.[33] Finally, Trajan's own propaganda, the great column depicting the Dacian wars, gives no hint that the emperor entered the battle-line, although he is present at the scene of the action to direct tactics. Trajan appears in military dress, but is not seen with helmet, sword, or spear, the weapons necessary for battle. It is true that one coin type portrays Trajan on horseback spearing a fallen foe. But this and other similar coins are more likely to be a stylized, conventional representation of the military *virtus* of the emperor than a reference to any particular event, and may have been designed primarily to make an impact on the troops.[34]

Pliny alone claims that Trajan fought in person. In his *Panegyric* he envisages what the emperor's triumph will be like. In front of his chariot will be borne the enemy shields pierced by Trajan himself. And he would have won the *spolia opima* (awarded for the slaying of an enemy leader in

---

[31] See n. 23.
[32] 68.31.3.
[33] Aurelius Victor, *De Caes*. 13; *Epit.* 13.4.
[34] Examples of this coin type are known for: Vespasian (*BMC* II, p. 136, no. 622); Titus (II, p. 140, no. 634); Domitian (II, p. 371, no. 339); Trajan (III, p. 65, no. 245); L. Verus (IV, p. 438, no. 390); Commodus (IV, p. 760, no. 376); Septimius Severus (V, p. 179, no. 142); Caracalla (V, p. 256, no. 506). Note that neither Vespasian nor Commodus campaigned in person while emperor.

personal combat) if any other king had dared to fight him.[35] If Pliny's revision of his speech for publication took place after Trajan's campaigns against the Dacians, he at least had some evidence for the emperor's interest in the martial arts; and of course Trajan's exploits as military tribune and legionary legate will have been well known. The *Panegyric* contains flights of fancy and exaggeration, and it is plausible to suppose that Pliny, without being ridiculous, could develop the theme of the emperor's military background and interests to include a suggestion of deeds of prowess in battle. In any event the passage is skilfully worded to imply a dream or a vision in the writer's imagination. The reality is clear: Trajan did not fight in the battle line.

Fronto claims that Lucius Verus left his head unprotected even against missiles. However, this may mean no more than that Verus appeared on the battlefield to supervise the dis-, position and organization of the troops.[36] It is significant that the emperor, who was certainly proud of his achievements, in a letter to Fronto setting out what he wished him to include in his history of the Parthian war, does not mention any deeds of valour of his own. Instead he asks Fronto to consider his plans ('consilia'), his speeches to the Senate and to the army, and his negotiations with the enemy.[37] Marcus Aurelius was present in person at most of the major campaigns during his reign, but there is no suggestion that he fought in person. Just like the column of Trajan, the monument celebrating Marcus' campaigns shows the emperor closely engaged in the direction of the war, but not in combat.[38]

Septimius Severus was well thought of by his troops as a leader who shared their toils. At the battle of Lugdunum, according to Dio, in a moment of crisis for his army when he had lost his horse, he tore off his cloak, drew his sword and inspired his men by plunging into battle.[39] Herodian, however, rebukes his predecessors, claiming that those historians who wrote the truth and not to gain favour said that

[35] 17.2-3.
[36] Fronto (Haines, *Loeb*), vol. II, p. 210. Cf. Dio, 71.2.2.
[37] Fronto, II, p. 194.
[38] See above, p. 49.
[39] 75.6.7.

Severus decamped ignominiously, was knocked off his horse, and tore off his cloak to escape recognition.[40] Dio's version looks like Severan propaganda designed to enhance the reputation of the emperor as a military man. Even if the story is true, it shows only the spontaneous intervention of a man whose life depended on the successful outcome of the battle. No other act of valour by Septimius Severus in his foreign wars can be adduced. And during the expedition to Britain he was carried on a covered litter for most of the way because he was suffering from gout.[41] His son Caracalla proclaimed that only in battle should a man die.[42] On campaign he often sent messages to enemy leaders and challenged them to single combat.[43] Caracalla was impetuous and eagerly enthusiastic about his duties as *commilito*, in addition he revered the memory of Alexander the Great.[44] It is easy to suppose that in the heat of the moment he would expose himself to danger in battle. But no source records any deed of valour, although there is a detailed account of his exploits on campaign. Perhaps he had no opportunity to involve himself in battle, or perhaps he realised that it was not necessary to go quite so far to prove himself an excellent comrade to his men.

The reign of Maximinus seems to mark a decisive change. He displayed great bravery in battle against the Gemans. While the Roman troops hesitated to follow the enemy into a swamp, the emperor plunged into the water on horseback and killed many of the Germans. Herodian in general is hostile to Maximinus, and so this favourable account of his courageous military activity is likely to be true. Maximinus reported his distinguished part in the battle in a despatch to Senate and people and ordered large pictures of it to be painted and displayed in front of the senate house.[45] The emphasis and publicity given to Maximinus' action suggest that it was unusual and unexpected, and untypical of his predecessors. This is easily explicable. The emperor's role as 'fellow-soldier' had been taken to new lengths by Caracalla, yet it possibly still lacked something if the emperor avoided

[40] 3.7.3.
[41] Dio, 76.13.4.
[42] 77.3.2.
[43] 77.13.2.
[44] 77.7.
[45] Herodian, 7.2.6 ff.

the actual fighting. A true *commilito*, it could be argued, should be seen in the forefront of the battle. And Maximinus had added reason to display his soldierly prowess since he had overthrown Severus Alexander by harping on his own military excellence in contrast to that feeble coward. Alexander indeed chose to follow the advice of his mother, that it was the responsibility of other people to take risks for him; he must not get involved in battle.[46] This idea became more difficult to sustain, and in the critical wars of the late third century the emperor was more likely to intervene personally in the battle where necessary.

For an upper-class Roman, life revolved round a series of elaborate conventions, in politics, administration, military affairs, and in the family. Most emperors came from the upper classes, and wished to follow these conventions. Every emperor, whatever his personal abilities or inclinations, was expected to be a good defender of the empire and to be capable of directing armies and organizing military operations. Incompetence in military affairs, or pretentious celebrations of feeble successes that had not been fully earned, would incur criticism among men of note. But it seems clear that Romans did not expect their emperors to fight personally in battle. Although he should look the part and appear in the military dress of an *imperator*, and be personally responsible for his army, the emperor was not expected to risk his life. This was not considered to be inconsistent with his role as 'fellow-soldier'. At least up to the reign of Maximinus, the idea of a 'warrior-' or 'soldier-' emperor is completely out of place. Indeed after it, in 238, the soldiers were prepared to acclaim a child, Gordian III as emperor.

5. IMPERIAL SPEECHES TO THE ARMY

In the absence of means of widespread communication, the ability to speak in public and persuade a large audience was of great importance in the ancient world. Senators in public life were expected to be able to adapt their eloquence to suit either the political and forensic debate of the forum, or the

---

[46] 6.5.9.

military camp. It was said of Lucullus that he appeared to be
equally intelligent and clever at speaking in the forum and
the military camps.[1] The army commander had to explain
the military situation to his men and encourage them to
deeds of valour. Before the conflict at Pharsalus, Caesar,
'following the custom of war, made a speech of encouragement to battle'.[2] But Caesar went on to explain his political
position and justify his decision to go to war against his
political enemies. Once the full significance of the political
support of the army was recognized, the camp tribunal had
also become the platform upon which appeals for support in
the commander's personal political career were made to the
troops. A new tradition of military eloquence grew up. When
Sulla addressed the soldiers assembled for the war against
Mithridates in 88 BC, he spoke of the indignity he had suffered at the hands of Sulpicius and Marius and urged them to
be ready to obey his orders. The response was enthusiastic
and the troops told him to lead them to Rome.[3] From
then on, the formal speech to the troops was frequently used
by the ambitious army commander to justify his political
actions, revile opponents, test the army's loyalty, and
promise rewards.[4]

It is clear that this formal address to the troops (*adlocutio*)
remained a prominent feature of the emperor's relationship
with the army, and that an emperor was expected to be
capable of eloquence both in the forum and in the military
camp. It was observed that Nero was the first ruler who
needed to borrow the eloquence of others.[5] All his predecessors had displayed rhetorical talents of various sorts. Nero
apparently declined to address the troops except through
written orders, or had someone else read out the speech for
him, in order to protect his delicate singing voice.[6] The story

[1] Plut., *Luc.* 33.3.
[2] Caesar, *BC* 3.90.1; *BG* 2.20.3; 5.33.2; *Bell. Alex.* 10; Livy, 21.40; 25.38.3 f.;
in general, see Harmand, *L'Armée*, 303 ff.
[3] Appian, *BC* 1.57.
[4] Caesar, *BC* 1.7.1 f.; Appian, *BC* 2.50; 65; 72-3; 90 f. And cf. Livy, 3.50.4
f. L. Verginius' speech here is surely anachronistic and probably reflects the
appeals for political support made to the legions in the last years of the Republic.
For the lack of historicity in the story, see R.M. Ogilvie, *Commentary on Livy
I-V* (1965), 476 ff.
[5] Tac., *A* 13.3.   [6] Suet., *Ner.* 25.3.

suggests that speeches to the army were fairly common. Indeed when Augustus decided that no member of his family should use the words 'fellow-soldiers' in speeches to the army,[7] he clearly thought that the *adlocutio* was going to be quite a regular occurrence in his reign. Furthermore, from the reign of Gaius the speech to the troops was frequently portrayed on coinage.[8] In fact between AD 68 and 235, only Vespasian, Antoninus Pius, and Didius Julianus lack attestation for a speech to the soldiers, and at least in the first two cases this is surely an accident of the evidence.

These speeches were perhaps merely routine, the continuation of an old military tradition. Indeed, how many soldiers could an emperor actually speak to during his reign? It is difficult to estimate what impact imperial speeches made and what importance can be attached to them with regard to the political relationship between emperor and army. However, as I discussed above, it was important for an emperor to meet his soldiers, be seen by them and show his interest. The formal address to the soldiers was a traditional part of the *imperator*'s duties, which might also serve to bring the emperor closer to the army. What is more, when conceived and staged with all the Romans' skill for a grandiose and impressive display, it was a good demonstration of an emperor's military excellence and his command over the troops.

It is not true to say that only the Praetorian Guard would benefit from imperial eloquence. Naturally the emperor tended to address them most often because of their proximity in Rome. But this was reasonable since the Praetorians were the major military force at the centre of power and their support could be immediately important to an emperor's position. Just as they enjoyed better pay and conditions than the rest of the army, so they also saw more of their emperor. In any event, from the late first century there were more opportunities to address the men of the legions and *auxilia*. Hadrian was exceptionally diligent in

[7] Suet., *Aug.* 25.1.
[8] e.g. Gaius, *BMC* I, p. 151, no. 33; Nero, II, p. 128, no. 122; Nerva, III, p. 14; Trajan, III, p. 155; Hadrian, III, pp. 497 ff.; Marcus Aurelius, IV, p. 613, no. 1371; Lucius Verus, IV, p. 556; Caracalla, V, p. 481, no. 264; Macrinus (?), V, p. 518; Severus Alexander, VI, p. 181, no. 672.

speaking to virtually all the armies in the provinces. His speech to the *III Augusta* in the camp at Lambaesis in Africa illustrates the procedure by which an emperor could speak to as many soldiers as possible of the army he was with. For Hadrian spoke knowledgeably to many different units of the legion, although his general theme of concentration on training, practice, and organization was the same. It is plausible to suppose that an emperor on campaign could even repeat his speech until most of the troops had seen him and heard at least some of his words. A man speaking in the open in the right kind of physical setting could perhaps make himself audible to several thousand men in a brief address. Of course this kind of personal contact with a large number of soldiers depended on an emperor's willingness and opportunity to visit the provinces. It is however possible that an emperor could circulate to the provincial governors the text of the message he wished to convey, and have them read it out in the military camps.

By these means it will have been possible for emperors to communicate in some way with a reasonably large number of soldiers. This is all the more significant in that the *adlocutio* was not only a military exhortation to discipline and bravery; the speech to the troops could also be a way of getting the army's support for particular items of an emperor's policy, or his general political position. And in time of political crisis the more quickly and effectively the ruler's point of view was impressed on the soldiers and accepted, the less chance there was for a usurper to build up military support.

The Formal Setting of the 'Adlocutio'

The setting for the formal *adlocutio* was solemn and majestic and obviously designed to create the right impression of imperial grandeur and military prestige. The emperor usually spoke from a lofty tribunal. Hyginus remarks that the platform was part of the equipment of the marching camp: 'on the left hand side a platform was built so that he might climb up and address the army'.[9] This suggests that a properly constructed platform was carried round with the army's baggage and perhaps dismantled when not in use. Plutarch's

[9] *De Munit. Cast.* 11 (ed. Gemoll, 1879).

description of a speech by Pompey indicates that it was unusual for a commander not to have a constructed tribunal from which to speak:

There was no regular platform and not even the usual substitute made by the soldiers (they construct this by cutting large sods of earth and piling them on top of one another). Because of the excitement of the occasion and their enthusiasm they dragged together the saddles of the pack animals and raised them into a kind of platform.[10]

Representations of the *adlocutio* on coins, the columns of Trajan and Marcus Aurelius, and triumphal arches show the emperor standing on a structure probably constructed of blocks or planks of wood and secured by nails and bolts. Access was provided by means of steps built at the back of the platform; sometimes the tribunal was elaborately carved.[11] When Maximinus addressed his troops at Aquileia he used a daïs specially constructed for him.[12] Probably there was a permanent tribunal in the main army camps and when an emperor went on campaign a special structure was carried with the army and erected or dismantled as required.[13] If there was no time for this, or the emperor had to address the troops outside the camp, then the traditional Roman military expedient of piling up clods of earth could be used.[14] Hadrian indeed appears sometimes to have addressed his troops from horseback. The care taken over the provision of the tribunal and the prominence of its position and construction show the frequency and importance of the formal speech to the troops.

The emperor's speeches on campaign presented a great opportunity to show himself as the efficient *imperator* and build up his reputation with the troops. And so the emperor usually wore military dress: body armour, military cloak (*paludamentum*), and military boots.[15] Weapons were

[10] *Pomp.* 41.2.
[11] See n.8. For the column of Trajan, see Florescu, *Trajanssaüle*, taf. 9, 20, 34, 41, 60, 89, 105, 111. For the column of Marcus Aurelius, see Caprino, *La Colonna*, figs. 10, 11, 69, 103, 106, 115, 119.
[12] Herodian, 8.7.3; cf. 2.8.1.
[13] 1.5.2.
[14] Dio, 62.2.3.
[15] See the evidence cited at nn. 8 and 11.

not normally carried at the *adlocutio*, and although Marcus Aurelius is depicted with a spear, this may be intended as a symbol of his sovereignty.[16] One scene from Trajan's column shows the emperor speaking while wearing the toga, and the troops too are without their armour and weapons.[17] This is unusual and the intention was probably to symbolize the end of the First Dacian War and the establishment of peaceful conditions. In Rome, however, the tradition was apparently that the emperor should address the Praetorians clad in his toga. Coins show Gaius, Nero, and Nerva with the legend 'The Speech [*adlocutio*] of the Emperor'.[18] This may have begun as a concession to tradition, and a desire by Augustus not to demonstrate ostentatiously his military backing. In the Republic regular troops were not usually stationed in Rome. Emperors may not have wished to wear military dress in Rome and appear as the great military leader. But a coin of AD 119 depicts Hadrian addressing the Praetorian Guard in military dress.[19] Presumably by this time it was normal for the emperor to wear military dress while reviewing the Guard in Rome; or it may have been worn on special occasions.

In all the scenes of an *adlocutio* on the columns of Trajan and Marcus Aurelius, the emperor has with him on the tribunal other men in military dress. They must be his senior advisers, friends, and commanders. When Commodus addressed the troops after the death of Marcus Aurelius, he was flanked on the platform by his father's advisers.[20] All this will have added to the dignity and impressiveness of the occasion.

However the audience was naturally an important element of the *adlocutio*. In virtually all the portrayals of these speeches the soldiers appear in full armour with shields and weapons.[21] They are grouped round the emperor and listen respectfully. The military standards are prominently displayed, either on the platform itself with the emperor, or

[16] e.g. Marcus, *BMC* IV, p. 613, no. 1371. And see A. Alföldi, *AJA* second series, 63 (1959), 1.
[17] Florescu, *Trajanssäule* taf. 65.
[18] See n. 8.
[19] *BMC*, III, p. 497.
[20] Herodian, 1.5.2.
[21] For the exceptions, see nn. 8 and 17.

among the front ranks of the soldiers. Before Germanicus addressed the recalcitrant German legions during the mutiny of AD 14, he ordered them to form up in small groups and bring the cohort standards to the front, to distinguish each cohort.[22] The troops' disorder and disruption of this usually dignified and solemn occasion provided another indication of their mutinous attitude.

It is not clear what response, if any, was expected from the audience. When the emperor and his companions had taken their places on the tribunal the soldiers were expected to fall respectfully silent. When Drusus got up to address the mutinous Pannonian legions he was greeted by a bad tempered roar. But the sight of the prince unnerved the soldiers and intermittent yelling soon gave way to a sullen silence.[23] This was unusual and disrespectful conduct towards a member of the imperial family. Normally, it must have been the duty of the centurions and other officers to organize the troops and bring them to silence. The response of the troops to the emperor's speech naturally depended on the type of occasion. A military exhortation would require an expression of an enthusiastic eagerness to fight. Furthermore, it is likely that some of the acclamations of the emperor as *imperator* on the field of battle took place at the imperial *adlocutio*. Trajan is seen addressing his army at the end of the First Dacian War, and since the soldiers raise their hands in salute, this may be the occasion of his third salutation as *imperator*.[24] This was hardly spontaneous and will have been organized in advance by the officers on the instructions of the emperor. On the other hand, in completely different circumstances in AD 48 Claudius, threatened by the conspiracy of his wife, Messalina, and Gaius Silius, appealed directly to the Praetorian Guard. Narcissus made a preliminary statement, presumably to explain the situation, and then Claudius addressed the troops. Either spontaneously or at the instigation of their officers, he got an immediate response: 'The Guardsmen roared again and again that the guilty should be named and punished.'[25]

[22] Tac., *A* 1.34–5.
[23] *A* 1.25.
[24] Florescu, taf. 65.
[25] Tac., *A* 11.35.

Failure to applaud at an *adlocutio* might be a sign of disapproval of what was said. Galba's announcement of his adoption of Piso was greeted enthusiastically by the officers and front ranks, but the rest remained sullenly silent.[26] It was particularly outrageous if the soldiers interrupted a speech and shouted hostile comment.[27] In AD 43 Claudius apparently sent Narcissus to help persuade the reluctant troops to embark for the invasion of Britain. But as soon as he mounted the tribunal of the commander, Aulus Plautius, the soldiers shouted in unison 'Io Saturnalia', in mockery of the slave origins of Narcissus, and refused to let him speak.[28]

Normally, the *adlocutio* was an effective demonstration of order, discipline, and military splendour in a dignified and formal setting which was dominated by the majestic position of the emperor in his role as the great *imperator*, master of his army.[29]

Regular Occasions for the 'adlocutio'

The formal speech to the soldiers by the emperor was delivered only on a restricted number of occasions. The context was originally military and speeches dealing with aspects of military life appear to have been common. Campaigns demanded that the emperor's eloquence be expended in the traditional manner of the *imperator* in the encouragement of his troops. Josephus liked to think that Titus' stirring words gave heart to his troops in the siege of Jerusalem. The prince believed that the fervour of the troops in battle was best roused by hope and encouraging words, and that exhortations and promises often made men forget danger.[30] This ideal is expressed by the sculptured vignettes of military life on the columns of Trajan and Marcus Aurelius. On campaign the emperor sought to encourage the army to the routine tasks of war, to urge them on to battle, and to reward them and receive their congratulations at the

---

[26] *H* 1.18.

[27] As, for example, happened to Drusus (*A* 1.26) and Germanicus (1.35).

[28] Dio, 60.19.2.

[29] See R. Brilliant, *Gesture and Rank in Roman Art (1963)*, 107 ff.

[30] *BJ* 3.472 ff.; 6.33 ff.; 7.2ff.

close of the campaign.[31] The theme is that by his presence, example, and speeches of encouragement, the emperor had a major influence in the success of the Roman army. This noble idea was well parodied by Dio in his description of Gaius' escapades. The emperor built a bridge of boats across the bay of Naples and drove across accompanied by the entire Praetorian Guard. 'Of course, while on such a campaign and after so magnificent a victory he had to deliver a speech; so he climbed onto a platform which had been erected on the ships near the centre of the bridge.' Gaius then praised the soldiers as men who had undergone great hardships and dangers, since they had actually crossed the sea on foot.[32] This story at least illustrates how it was expected that an emperor would address his troops. The importance of such speeches by emperors can be seen in Lucius Verus' request that Fronto should include in his history of the Parthian war Lucius' addresses to the army.[33]

Military life did not often consist of the glamour and excitement of campaigns and eloquent exhortations to battle. There were parades and much routine training, and the other preparations needed to achieve battle readiness. A vigilant emperor could show his interest and knowledge here. A unique series of coins testifies to Hadrian's diligence in visiting and speaking to the soldiers in the provinces.[34] Part of his speech in AD 128 to the *III Augusta* stationed at Lambaesis in Africa survives.[35] Hadrian made appropriate comments to various elements of the army, and in the surviving part of the inscription he addresses the chief centurions, the cavalry of the legion, a cavalry cohort, the first company of Pannonians, and the cavalry of the sixth cohort of Commagenians. This was a way of communicating with large numbers of troops and making himself known to the entire legion and the auxiliary forces. In his orations Hadrian spoke in a brief, forceful, and direct style in which he frequently employed adverbs, words of action, courage,

---

[31] See n. 11.
[32] 59.17.6.
[33] Haines (*Loeb*), II, p. 196.
[34] *BMC* III, p. 497 ff.; and see J.M.C. Toynbee, *The Hadrianic School* (1934), 5 ff.
[35] *ILS* 2487; 9133-5.

and discipline, and technical military vocabulary.[36] He must have hoped that much of this would be comprehensible to the troops, many of whom would not have appreciated sophisticated eloquence. The emperor expressed encouragement, generous approval of the soldiers' performance in the exercises, and offered a donative as a reward, though he was willing to chastise where necessary.

In all this Hadrian gives the impression that he knows what he is talking about. He shows a detailed knowledge of the various units and their capabilities, military procedure and training, in wall building, cavalry exercises, and missile throwing.

Military exercises have, in my opinion, their own rules, and if anything is added to or taken away from these, then the exercise becomes either of no value or too difficult. The more elaborate it becomes, the less pleasing a show it makes. But you have performed the most difficult of all military exercises, in that you have thrown javelins while clad in armour. Furthermore, I praise your spirit.

To the cavalry cohort he said:

You have completed in a single day fortifications which others take several days to finish. You have built a wall which normally requires much work and is suitable for permanent winter quarters, in a time not much longer than that usually required to build one of turf. For turf is cut to a regulation size and is easy to carry and work with, and the construction of the wall causes no trouble since the turf is by its nature soft and level. But you have built a wall of huge, heavy stones of all sizes which are difficult for anyone to carry or lift or fit in position unless the irregularities happen to stick together. You have dug a straight ditch through rough and coarse gravel and then evened it off by smoothing it. When your work had been approved you entered the camp quickly and collected your rations and weapons, and then followed the cavalry which had been sent out. . . . I congratulate my commander for having introduced to you this military exercise which resembled a real battle and which has trained you so effectively that I am able to congratulate you. Cornelianus, your prefect, has carried

---

[36] *Agiliter, velociter, non ineleganter, sollicite, strenue, expedite, raptim, recte, ordo, cura, agiles, fortes, animus* (= spirit), *exercitatio, dimicatio, discursus.* Verbs of violent action: *perago, exstruo, vehor, tracto, struo, attollo, percutio, rado, ingredior, capio, iaculor, sequor, exerceo, congredior, concurro, vado, mitto* (= throw), *confligo, salio.*

out his duties satisfactorily. However, the cavalry advance did not entirely please me. . . . The cavalryman should ride out from his hiding place and display caution when pursuing. For if he does not see where he is going and cannot check his horse whenever he wants to, he will certainly be exposed to hidden traps.

There is a note of experience and authority in Hadrian's declaration to the first company of Pannonians:

You have done everything in an organized fashion. You have filled the plain with your manoeuvres; you have thrown the javelin with a certain degree of grace, although you used short and stiff javelins. A good number of you threw your lances with equal skill. Just now you mounted your horses with great agility and yesterday you did so speedily. If anything had been lacking I would have noticed it; if anything had been below standard, I would have pointed it out; but you have pleased me uniformly in the entire exercise. Catullinus, my legate, *vir clarissimus*, displays equal interest in all the tasks of which he is in charge . . . your prefect also seems to look after you carefully. I grant you a largess.

Hadrian did not omit to praise the officers, and in particular the legate of the legion, Q.Fabius Catullinus, who probably joined the emperor on the tribunal for his speech. It was important that the emperor kept his senatorial commanders happy and did not undermine the respect they had from the troops. His tours of inspection doubtless inspired them to see some point in the diligent training of the men under their command. Hadrian was apparently pleased with Catullinus, who became *consul ordinarius* in 130.

Furthermore, the emperor was well informed about the recent history of the *III Augusta* and the problems it had faced.

Your commander has, on your behalf, told me all the details which should excuse you in my eyes; namely, one cohort is absent, since every year one is sent in turn for duty with the proconsul; and two years ago you contributed a cohort and four men from each of the centuries to make up the numbers of the third legion; in addition, many widely scattered guard duties keep you apart; and I myself remember that you have not only changed camp twice, but have even built new ones. For all these reasons I would have pardoned you if the legion had been careless in its training for any length of time. But in fact you have not been lax in your training. . . . The chief centurions and the other centurions were as agile and brave as usual.

Hadrian's address to the Commagenian cavalry cohort illustrates the kind of interest in military affairs for which, according to Dio, he was famous.

It is difficult for the cavalry of the cohorts to give a satisfactory performance even on their own, and it is even more difficult for them to avoid performing unsatisfactorily after an exercise conducted by the auxiliary cavalry. For they cover a larger area of the plain, they have a larger number of men throwing the javelin, they can wheel to the right in close array, they perform the Cantabrian manoeuvre in close ranks, and the beauty of their horses and the elegance of their armour match the level of their pay. But by your energy you have avoided causing any annoyance to the spectators, and by doing enthusiastically what had to be done. Furthermore, you fired stones from slings and fought with missiles. Everywhere you mounted your horses speedily. The outstanding diligence of my legate Catullinus, *vir clarissimus*, is clear from the fact that he has men of your calibre under his command.

The knowledgeable interest on the part of the emperor and his convincing attention to detail will have added more authority and effect to his declarations of personal approval for the soldiers' operations. Hadrian's supervision of the exercises and his speeches to the army must have taken at least two days, since one speech was delivered on 1 July and another on some date between the Kalends and the Ides of July. No doubt the successful visit of an emperor would serve to boost morale of officers and soldiers, and promote the association of emperor and army. It is notable that Hadrian's speeches to the *III Augusta* were recorded and commemorated at length, and that in the inscription the legion was described as 'legio sua' ('his very own legion').

Apart from military occasions, the formal *adlocutio* took place most often when a new emperor assumed the purple. After the death of Augustus, Tiberius 'sent letters to the armies as though he was already emperor'.[37] Perhaps the army commanders had instructions to read out the message

[37] Tac., *A* 1.7.

to the soldiers; it presumably informed them of the death of Augustus and that Tiberius had taken control. Tiberius also gave the watchword to the Praetorian Guard and was escorted by soldiers in the forum and the senate house. However there is no evidence that Tiberius addressed the Praetorian Guard formally, though it is plausible that he did speak to the various detachments. It rapidly became the regular practice for the new emperor to approach the entire Praetorian Guard. Gaius may have been the first to do so. Dio remarks that just after Tiberius' death Gaius, in the company of the senators, inspected the Praetorians at drill and distributed to them the money bequeathed by Tiberius, and a donative of his own.[38] A coin struck in AD 37/8, showing the emperor addressing the Guard,[39] suggests that Gaius did make a formal *adlocutio* on this occasion.

The events surrounding the accession of Claudius were unique: after the death of Gaius he was conveyed by Praetorian guardsmen to their camp. The sequel is obscure, but it is clear that Claudius was not the helpless puppet of the troops. He negotiated with a hostile Senate through king Agrippa, apparently to persuade them to grant the customary powers without conflict. His proclamation by the soldiers took place either on the day of the murder of Gaius or on the following day, but all sources agree that it preceded the Senate's grant of powers.[40] Claudius addressed the troops, administered the oath, and bestowed a large donative.[41] In this case the *adlocutio*, where Claudius presumably expressed his willingness to assume the purple and consolidated the support of the Praetorians, formed a vital part of the public demonstration of Claudius' military support, which in turn was a major justification of his position. Doubtless the emperor's words and financial promises will have been conveyed rapidly to the rest of the army.[42] The united support of the Praetorians was still an excellent lead for the rest of the armed forces in the empire.

[38] 59.2.

[39] *BMC* I, p. 151, no. 33.

[40] See in general, A. Garzetti, *From Tiberius to the Antonines* (1974), 106 ff; Suet., *Cl.* 10.4; Dio, 60.1.1 f.; Josephus, *BJ* 2.204 ff.; *AJ* 19.212 ff.

[41] For the donative, see below, pp. 166-8.

[42] See Jos., *AJ* 19.247.

This pattern was followed by Nero. Escorted by Burrus, the Praetorian prefect, he was saluted on the palace steps by those guardsmen on duty and conveyed at once to the camp. There he made a speech, apparently composed by Seneca. 'Nero was brought into the camp where he made a speech appropriate to the occasion; he promised a donative, following the precedent of his father's generosity, and was saluted *imperator*. The vote of the Senate followed the decision of the soldiers, and there was no hesitation in the provinces of the empire.'[43] Nero probably announced Claudius' death, expressed his right to the purple, and requested the support of his loyal troops, for which they would be well rewarded. By this time approval of the Praetorian Guard after the prospective emperor's *adlocutio*, and by implication the approval of the rest of the army, constituted a very important part of the process by which a new emperor emerged.[44]

It is a plausible assumption that in the settled times after 69 the formal *adlocutio* to the troops they were with remained an important part of the accession of emperors, even when there is a lack of specific evidence. We know that Marcus Aurelius apparently addressed the troops on behalf of himself and Lucius Verus before his powers had been conferred by the Senate.[45] Herodian, writing about the speech delivered by Commodus and his grant of a donative, commented that this was normal at the accession of an emperor.[46]

Princes were frequently given command of armies or accompanied an emperor on campaign.[47] In this way they

[43] Tac., *A* 12.69; Suet., *Ner.* 8; Dio, 61.3.1.

[44] For this theme, see below, p. 126.

[45] *HA, Vit. Ver.* 4.3. For the general reliability of the *Vita Veri*, see T.D. Barnes, *JRS* 57 (1967), 65. There is little reason why the biographer should invent a detail like this, which seems to come in a reliable context. Cf. the accession of Domitian (Dio, 66.26.3), Caracalla (77.3), Severus Alexander (Herodian, 5.8.10). See in general, M. Hammond, 'The Transmission of the Powers of the Roman Emperor', *MAAR* 24 (1956), 63.

[46] 1.5.1.

[47] Gaius and Lucius Caesar under Augustus; Tiberius, his brother Drusus, and Germanicus also under Augustus; Germanicus and Drusus in the reign of Tiberius; Titus in the reign of Vespasian; L. Aelius Commodus under Hadrian; Commodus under Marcus Aurelius; Caracalla and Geta accompanied Septimius Severus on some of his campaigns.

obtained experience of their imperial responsibilities, and they might be considered more reliable than senatorial commanders.[48] Nevertheless, a major motive will have been to make the princes known to the troops as possible heirs and win their approval. Thus Tiberius sent Drusus to Illyricum 'to get used to military life and to win the favour of the troops'.[49] Claudius often took his infant son Britannicus in his arms and commended him to meetings of the soldiers, presumably the Praetorian Guard.[50] All this is an indication of the importance attributed to a personal appearance before the troops. Indeed the adoption and presentation of an heir could be announced through the *adlocutio*. In 69 the aged Galba decided to adopt Piso to establish a focus of loyalty for the wavering legions. Should the adoption be proclaimed at the *rostra*, the Senate, or the Praetorian camp? Galba decided on the camp, because this would be a tribute to the army, whose support and favour he badly needed.[51] The announcement was to be made in an *adlocutio*, which Galba and Piso believed would flatter and please the troops. Galba spoke in the clipped tones suitable to a supreme commander; the adoption of Piso, he claimed, was in accordance with the precedent of Augustus and the military practice by which one man co-opted another. He went on to quash rumours of discontent elsewhere in the army.[52] The speech was unsuccessful in winning support because he refused to offer a donative, according to Tacitus. But the idea was sound enough and if properly executed could produce an assurance of dynastic policy. A coin of Marcus Aurelius, struck in 171/2, shows the emperor and his son Commodus both in military garb addressing a group of soldiers.[53] The coin was clearly intended to celebrate Marcus' introduction of Commodus to the troops, and the legend 'providentia' may suggest his foresight for the succession, and the safety of the Roman world.

[48] Tacitus comments on Tiberius' policy: 'seque tutiorem rebatur utroque filio legiones obtinente' (*A* 2.44).
[49] Ibid.
[50] Suet., *Cl* 27.2.
[51] Tac., *H* 1.17.
[52] 1.18.
[53] *BMC* IV, p. 624, nos. 1425–6.

The same theme appears on a coin issued by Septimius Severus, which shows the emperor and his two sons addressing the army. It is dated to AD 210.[54] As coins depicting an *adlocutio* are relatively infrequent and seem to refer to particular occasions, this coin probably depicts a speech on the British expedition. In fact Severus died in 211, and Dio tells us that he was very ill before leaving Rome and did not expect to return.[55] Severus presumably used this *adlocutio* to display his sons to the legions and announce his plans for the dynasty as his own life drew to its close. It seems probable that the practice of introducing the chosen heir to as many troops as possible, or at least to the Praetorian Guard in Rome, by the formal *adlocutio* was consistently employed in the second century.

Indeed there were probably many more speeches to the army than we know about, and not all speeches need have been as formal as those described above. It can be surmised that the emperor addressed the troops he was with, on his birthday, the anniversary of his coming to power, and on the presentation of donatives. And of course the *adlocutio* would be used for the announcement of important information relevant to the soldiers. There survives part of a speech delivered by Marcus Aurelius in the Praetorian camp in 168.[56] He is talking about privileges which would ultimately benefit Praetorian veterans, and it is worth noting that Marcus took the trouble to bring this matter before the troops himself: 'In order that our veterans may more easily find fathers-in-law, we shall tempt them also with a new privilege, namely that a grandfather whose grandchildren have been born to a veteran of the Praetorian Guard shall enjoy the same advantages in their name as he would enjoy if he had the grandchildren from his own son.' The main point of the emperor's speech must have been to attract the soldiers' attention with words like 'novo privilegio' and 'sollicitabimus' (which has the connotation of 'seduce with gifts'), and to associate himself with them in the phrase 'veterani nostri'.

---

[54] *BMC* V, p. 395, no. 192.
[55] 76.11.1; 13.4; 14.3; 16.1.
[56] *Fragmenta Vaticana* no. 195 (*FIRA*[2] II, p. 503).

The 'Adlocutio' in Exceptional Circumstances

The army was usually the first to hear from the emperor in times of political turmoil. The *adlocutio* gave him direct contact with a fairly large group of troops on the spot; he could test their loyalty personally without relying on the statements of the officers, or other advisers. This was useful even if the emperor communicated with only the Praetorian Guard, which might give a lead to the other military forces. When Claudius recognized the seriousness of the conspiracy of Messalina and C.Silius, on the advice of Narcissus he hastened at once to appeal to the Guard.[57] Even Nero in 68 thought of making a personal appearance before his troops. He would go before the troops unarmed and weep, and having won them over in this way would sing to them.[58] When Avidius Cassius revolted, Marcus Aurelius immediately went before his soldiers at Sirmium on the Danube frontier, since they had been disturbed by reports of the revolt, and explained the situation to them.[59] Coins issued by Commodus in 185/6 show the emperor addressing the troops, with the legend 'fides exerc[ituum]' (the loyalty of the armies').[60] It is likely that these speeches were made as a result of a serious mutiny in Britain in 185 after the fall of Perennis.[61] After the murder of Geta, Caracalla hurried off to the Praetorian camp and made an impassioned speech.[62]

What did an emperor say when he appealed directly to the troops on these occasions? For this we have to rely on the literary sources, and the speeches they provide are generally invented. But the ancient historiographers probably express at least what an emperor was expected to say when he confronted the troops.[63] As examples I have chosen the speech Tacitus attributed to Piso in 69, and that attributed by Dio to Marcus Aurelius during the revolt of Avidius Cassius in

[57] Tac., *A* 11.35.
[58] Suet., *Ner.* 43.2.
[59] Dio, 71.24.1 ff.
[60] *BMC* IV, p. 805, no. 577 (185/6); cf. p. 718, no. 160.
[61] For a discussion of the mutiny in Britain, see P.A. Brunt, *CQ* 23 (1973), 172.
[62] Dio, 77.3.1.
[63] See Quintilian, 10.1.101; Cf. Lucian, *How to Write History*, 58; Thucydides, 1.22.1.

175.[64] Piso attempted to cement the loyalty of the Praetorian Guard, wavering because of the schemes of Otho, by appealing to the righteousness and justice of his cause (29.2); the criminal and deleterious vices of his opponent (30.1); his widespread support — 'consensus generis humani' (30.2); the previous loyalty of the troops and their responsibility to the whole empire (30.2-3); the necessity of their loyalty and the fact that they stand or fall together (30.3).

Marcus Aurelius announced the fact of an impending civil war to his troops (24.1); criticised his opponent for his disloyalty and evil plot (24.2); emphasized that the struggle was not on his behalf alone but for the entire Roman State, and that it touched them all equally (24.4); depreciated the strength of the eastern legions who were no match for his men, who also had better leaders (25.1-2); expressed his desire to settle the war without bloodshed if possible and even to spare Avidius Cassius (26.1 ff.). All this of course was an indication of Marcus' own righteousness. The themes of these two speeches are plausible and simple enough to be comprehensible to the average soldier, who will not have been interested in political subtleties.

Naturally the reaction of the soldiers on the spot to this kind of political speech could be decisive and their example might influence the conduct of others. As soon as Claudius appealed to the Guard during the conspiracy of C.Silius and Messalina, they roared that the offenders should be punished. Silius and other conspirators were immediately dragged onto the tribunal and disposed of.[65] Dio says that a chance remark made by Pertinax in 192 in a speech to the Guardsmen aroused their suspicions that he was about to remove some of their privileges. They never trusted the emperor and later murdered him.[66] After Caracalla had explained the murder of Geta to the Praetorians, he spent the night in the camp temple. Then, filled with confidence at their response, he proceeded to the senate house.[67] For the usurper in particular the *adlocutio* could be vital as a demonstration of the

[64] Tac., *H* 1.29 f.; Dio, 71.24.1 ff. And cf. Tac., *H* 1.37-8; Herodian, 2.6.1; 8.1; 10.2.

[65] *A* 11.35.

[66] 74.1.3.

[67] Herodian, 4.4.5 f.

soldiers' approval. After Pescennius Niger's appeal to the Syrian legions, they proclaimed him emperor enthusiastically.[68] Similarly, in the case of Septimius Severus the initial, favourable response of the troops was all-important for the confidence of the man who intended to risk everything to gain power.[69]

In conclusion, it is difficult to discover what it was like to be emperor and go before a large group of soldiers and make a speech, especially when the audience was in general poorly educated and uncultivated. Perhaps it was often an anxious moment. The fact that emperors addressed the troops regularly tells us something about their hopes and fears and the inherent pressures of being emperor. The emperor could not in fact do what he liked; he had to comply with various conventions and consequences of a rule based ultimately on military force. It seems clear that emperors thought it important to address the troops in person at some time, even if they encountered only a limited number of them, and consolidate their relationship with the army. The successful *adlocutio* served to emphasize their role as commander-in-chief, extended the range of their contact with the ordinary soldier, and was a useful demonstration of loyalty gained by other devices. It was taken seriously, and was organized deliberately to be a grand and prestigious military display, which usually took place on specific and important military and dynastic occasions. No emperor could neglect to communicate his hopes, wishes, and ideas to the army by the most direct means he could manage. The more frequent his appearances and the more often he expressed his views to the soldiers, the less likely it was that a rival could make an impression on them. Indeed any unauthorized attempt by a senator to address the troops could be viewed as tantamount to treason. In Vespasian's reign Titus, in his capacity as Praetorian prefect, had the consular Aulus Caecina executed; he had attempted to corrupt the soldiers, and Titus had gained possession of a signed copy of a speech that Caecina had intended to deliver to the troops.[70]

[68] 2.8.6.
[69] 2.10.9.
[70] Suet., *Tit.* 6.2; Dio, 65.16.3.

The thoughts of the soldiers about the *adlocutio* are virtually impossible to discern. Perhaps they considered it to be boring and stereotyped. On the other hand, the number of formal speeches was probably limited and so the personal appearance of the emperor would be sufficiently unusual to have an impact. For simple men the break in the humdrum tedium of the normal duties of a soldier was no doubt welcome, regardless of what the emperor actually said. And the *adlocutio* was a majestic occasion when military pride and *esprit de corps* could reign supreme. This may be reflected in the long inscription set up by the *III Augusta* celebrating Hadrian's visit and speeches to the troops in Africa; though advice from their officers doubtless played a part here. More illuminating is the unfortunate experience of Narcissus when he tried to address the troops assembled for the invasion of Britain. Perhaps the soldiers were annoyed not so much by the slave origins of the imperial envoy as by the fact that they expected to be addressed by a man of accepted status and prestige, either the emperor himself, or his consular legate. For them the formal *adlocutio* was an important occasion.

6. LEGIONARY TITLES, 'PRAENOMEN IMPERATORIS', IMPERIAL PORTRAITS ON THE MILITARY STANDARDS, THE ROMAN MILITARY CALENDAR

Legionary Titles

In the late Republic several of the legions bore their own title or nickname. These *cognomina* were generally not associated with individual commanders, but celebrated instead a legion's place of origin, special circumstances of its foundation, a god particularly associated with it, or any unusual characteristics.[1] During the civil wars the rival military leaders apparently did not bestow on the legions *cognomina* based on their own names, although this practice would have been a way of claiming ownership over particular legions. The eighteenth legion may at one stage have been called 'Cornelius Spinter', after the governor of Cilicia of that

---

[1] H.M.D. Parker, *The Roman Legions* (1928), 264 f.; *RE* XII. 1-2, s.v. 'legio', and supplements; A. Passerini, *Dizionario Epigrafico*, s.v. 'legio' (1950).

name.[2] But this was presumably temporary and since the title appears in only one inscription, it may reflect what an individual soldier or centurion thought, and not official nomenclature. The third legion had served with Caesar in Gaul and then saw service with Octavian at Mutina. In one inscription a soldier describes himself as 'miles de l[egione] III p[aterna]'.[3] Similarly, in 27 BC Caesar's old twelfth legion bore the *cognomen* 'paterna'.[4] Later it was renamed 'fulminata'. These may be attempts by Octavian to develop the official nomenclature in order to remind the veteran troops of the legions' earlier association with his 'father', Julius Caesar. But the evidence is very slight and may again represent the notions of individual soldiers rather than official policy. Indeed it seems clear that Octavian and the other military leaders did not systematically claim proprietorship over the legions they enlisted or employed by bestowing their name on them. In the confusion of the civil wars donatives and other material inducements were likely to occupy the commander's attention most.

A desire to play down the open association between the *princeps* and the army may have dissuaded Augustus, once secure in power, from bestowing his name on the legions; he may also have considered that it was untraditional, and ostentatious for Roman legions to receive a *cognomen* derived from their commander's name. Of the twenty-eight legions in service up to AD 9, only three, the II, III, and VIII, bore the title *Augusta*, while the *XV Apollinaris* had the name of his protecting deity.[5] The reason for the special honour accorded to these legions evades enquiry.[6] Furthermore the *XX Valeria Victrix*, originally enlisted by Augustus between 41 and 31 BC, seems to have acquired its honorific titles from the exploits of Valerius Messalinus who was governor of Illyricum and its immediate commander during the

[2] *RE* col. 1768.
[3] *CIL* X 3884; *RE* col. 16141
[4] *CIL* XI 1058; *RE* col. 1705
[5] *RE* col. 1747; cf. Propertius, 4.6.3 f.
[6] It may be surmised that Augustus honoured the veteran legions of Caesar in this way. However, *X Fretensis, XII Fulminata, IV* and *V Macedonica* had Caesarian origins and were not so honoured. Also, *legio VII*, Caesar's old seventh legion, had no *cognomen*.

Pannonian revolt in AD 6.[7] Valerius received triumphal ornaments for his timely success, but to have the legion named
after him was a unique honour and perhaps reflects the relief
felt by the emperor at a crucial victory. But the gesture was
probably safe enough since it involved just one legion and
Valerius would be in command for a limited period only.

With these exceptions Augustus followed the practice of
the Republic in the naming of his legions. Indeed this is true
in general of the emperors up to the reign of Caracalla. Therefore the appearance of special *cognomina* associated with a
reigning emperor has a particular significance. They occur
most commonly in circumstances where the loyalty of some
legions had been in doubt. Claudius gave the titles 'Claudia
Pia Fidelis' (Claudian, Loyal, True') to the two legions in
Dalmatia that had refused to follow Scribonianus in his
rebellion.[8] It is interesting that Claudius did this by vote of
the Senate. The titles were unusual and he may have wished
to associate the senators with them in an attempt to avoid
criticism of an action which, by honouring the political
loyalty of the legions to an individual, openly emphasized
the emperor's association with the army. Inscriptional
evidence shows that Domitian honoured the legions of Lower
Germany, which remained loyal during the revolt of
Saturninus in the upper province, with the titles 'Pia Fidelis
Domitiana'.[9] In the reign of Commodus the *VIII Augusta* in
Upper Germany is styled 'Pia Fidelis Constans Commodiana'.
The date, between 185 and 187, suggests that this had something to do with the fall of Perennis and the military unrest
in Britain.[10] Indeed, according to Dio, Commodus had the
intention of calling all the legions 'Commodiana'.[11]

Occasionally, titles commemorating a legion's loyalty were
granted without the inclusion of the emperor's name. Marcus
Aurelius was sufficiently worried by the revolt of Avidius

[7] *RE* col. 1170 f.; Vell. 2.112.2.
[8] Dio 55.23.4; 60.15.4; *RE* col. 1614 f.; 1690.
[9] *RE* col. 1603; *CIL* XIII 8071.
[10] *CIL* XI 6053; XIII 11757. For the view that the mutiny in Britain involved
soldiers and not just their officers, see P.A. Brunt, *CQ* 23 (1973), 172. The
V Macedonica in Moesia also received the titles 'Pia Fidelis' — *RE* col. 1580.
[11] 73.15.2. Inscriptional evidence indicates that the emperor did not systematically name the legions in this way see p. 51, n. 88.

Cassius in Syria to attribute special *cognomina* to the legions of Martius Verus, governor of Cappadocia, who helped to put down the rebellion. The *XV Apollinaris* is called 'Loyal and True', the *XII Fulminata* 'Sure and Steadfast'.[12] No emperor was free from the fear of revolt and the need to employ devices to flatter and pacify troops whose loyalty was suddenly put to the test.

In civil war the emperor tended to identify himself very closely with his troops. In 68 the legion Galba raised in Spain bore the designation 'Galbiana'.[13] Clodius Macer, legate of the *III Augusta* in Africa in 68, made an ephemeral attempt to seize power. His coinage shows that his newly recruited legion was called the 'First Legion of Macer, the Liberator',[14] by which he proclaimed his ownership of the legion and the emotive intention of freeing Rome from tyranny. Septimius Severus issued a series of coins in 193/4 celebrating those legions in the northern provinces that had supported his attempt to gain power for himself. The reverse of each type shows the legion's number, its standards, and some of the emperor's titles: 'Tr[ibunicia] P[otestas] Co[n]s[ul]'.[15] Severus distributed various honorary *cognomina* to certain legions that had particularly assisted his cause. The *III Augusta* in Africa received the title 'Loyal Avenger'; it had refused to join Pescennius Niger in 193.[16] The *VII Gemina* in Spain was named 'Loyal and Lucky' in 197.[17] The precise circumstances of this are not clear, but Novius Rufus, the governor of Spain, was executed after the defeat of Clodius Albinus,[18] and it may be that he declared for Albinus but failed to carry his army with him. The *II Italica* in Raetia and the *XXX Ulpia* became 'Loyal and True' in 197, presumably for their support for Severus against Clodius

---

[12] *CIL* XIII 1680; *RE* col. 1755; *CIL* III 6768; *Rhein. Mus.* 59 (1904), 196 f.

[13] Tacitus (*H* 2.11) speaks of the legion 'septima a Galba conscripta', which seems to mean that he recruited a new legion. It was presumably this and not the *VII Gemina* which was called 'Galbiana'; cf. *H* 2.86; 3.7, 10, 21.

[14] *BMC* I, p. 286; *RE* col. 1417 f.; R. Cagnat, *L'Armée romaine d'Afrique* (1913), 141-6, argues convincingly that the legion referred to by Tacitus is distinct from the *III Augusta*

[15] *BMC* V, pp. 21 ff.

[16] *RE* col. 1500.

[17] *RE* col. 1314.

[18] *Vit. Sev.* 13.7.

Albinus.[19] In general, the development of legionary nomenclature to include a reference to a legion's loyalty to an individual emphasized the personal relationship between leader and soldiers, and provided a public demonstration of the value of this association.

On rare occasions newly recruited legions were named after the emperor who founded them. Vespasian founded the *IV Flavia Felix* and the *XVI Flavia Firma*, probably in AD 70. The *II Adiutrix*, also founded *c*.70, was called 'Loyal and True'.[20] Vespasian was presumably eager to establish his personal connection with these new legions which had helped him confirm his control of the Roman world. It is worth mentioning that a host of auxiliary units also bear the Flavian *cognomen*.[21] In the second century several auxiliary units bear the name 'Nerviana' and 'Aelia', probably because they had been established in the reigns of Nerva and Hadrian respectively.[22] Two legions newly recruited under Trajan were called *II Traiana Fortis* (Second Traianic Courageous) and *XXX Ulpia Victrix* (Thirtieth Ulpian Victorious).[23] This may reflect Trajan's interest in the army and military affairs, and the stout service of these troops in the Dacian wars.[24] But it remained unusual in the second century for legions to be honoured with the emperor's name. The two legions established in the 160s by Marcus Aurelius were called 'Italica'.[25] Septimius Severus termed each of his three new legions 'Parthica' to celebrate his Parthian victories, although soldiers who served in them occasionally add the title 'Severiana', presumably on their own initiative.[26]

This conservatism in the nomenclature of the Roman legions persisted until the reign of Caracalla. The dramatic

---

[19] *RE* col. 1472; 1826. The *VI Ferrata* received the title 'Fidelis Constans' — *RE* col. 1313. It is not clear why this legion was honoured in this way; cf. J. Hasebroek, *Untersuchungen zur Geschichte des Kaisers Septimius Severus* (1921), 70-2.

[20] Dio 55.24.3; *RE* col. 1540; 1765 f.; *CIL* III p. 849.

[21] *CIL* XVI, nos. 20, 23, 29, 35, 40, 47, 56, 61, 73, 75.

[22] *CIL* XVI, no. 56 — 'I Nerviana Aug. Fidelis'; 16, 76, 93, 96 — 'Aelia'.

[23] See *RE*, ad loc. For Traianic *auxilia, CIL* XVI, nos. 69, 76, 77, 106, 160.

[24] Pliny praised Trajan for increasing the number of Rome's soldiers — *Pan.* 26.3.

[25] *RE* cols. 1468-1532.

[26] *CIL* VIII 2877; VI 3403; *RE* col. 1436.

change brought about by this emperor is therefore all the more significant. He bestowed his name on all the legions and *auxilia* units. During his reign twenty-two legions are attested with the title 'Antoniniana'.[27] This ties in with his ostentatious behaviour as 'fellow-soldier' and his effusive gestures of good will to the soldiers. Once again this emperor was prepared to recognize overtly his dependence on the army. It seems that his successors followed this policy. For example, the *I Minervia* is referred to successively on inscriptions as 'I Mincrvia Antoniniana', 'I Minervia Severiana Alexandriana', and 'I Minervia Gordiana'.[28]

These titles certainly increased the identification of emperor and army, though in the first two centuries the comparative rarity of imperial *cognomina* for legions, or titles honouring loyalty and devotion, indicates that these were not held to be a very significant element in building up the army's loyalty. Furthermore, once special legionary titles had been bestowed, they tended to remain under succeeding emperors. They became a mark of honour to a legion and lost any particular connotation of associattion with an individual emperor. The appellation 'Loyal and True' had a timeless quality that would make it constantly acceptable.

'Praenomen Imperatoris'

Emperors celebrated their military excellence in a variety of ways, particularly by taking acclamations as *imperator* into their titulature, and by adopting *cognomina* celebrating victory over certain peoples or kingdoms.[29] Imperial titulature was important as an expression of an emperor's powers, prowess, dynastic and family aspirations, and as an indication of what he wanted people to think of him and his administration. It is notable, therefore, that in the titles and names adopted by most emperors there are few indications of their close connection with the army. It is plausible to suppose that since the emperor's titles were widely publicized and often encountered by the upper classes, it was thought

[27] Legions:— *RE* cols. 1404, 1434, 1435, 1456, 1483, 1493, 1505, 1517, 1531, 1539, 1586, 1613, 1628, 1642, 1663, 1678, 1690, 1727, 1747, 1781, 1820, 1829. For the *auxilia*, see Cheesman, *Auxilia*, 47.
[28] *CIL* XIII 8038; 8728; 8041.
[29] See below, pp. 120-33.

expedient to keep them in line with republican precedent as much as possible.

The *praenomen* was usually a man's first name, coming before his family name. The *praenomen imperatoris* ('forename of commander') meant that the first name was 'Commander' or 'General' and represented an emperor's claim to outstanding power and glory. It suggested his association with the troops as their commander, the military basis of his position, and had connotations of military glory through its association with the *imperator* acclamation. This is the significance of the formulation adopted by Augustus, 'Imperator Caesar Augustus'.[30] In the early years of his reign Augustus needed to distinguish himself in some way as the leading man in a state that had recently seen a profusion of military leaders. But the *praenomen imperatoris* was born in the violence of the Republic and in nomenclature was revolutionary.[31] This must be why Tiberius and Claudius publicly refused the name. Suetonius places both decisions in the context of an attempt to refuse excessive honours and adopt conduct that was unassuming.[32] Tiberius was doubtless reluctant to accept nomenclature that was so out of keeping with republican practice and his own concept of how the state should be run.[33] However, despite Tiberius' wishes, a number of inscriptions refer to him as 'imperator', notably one set up by L.Nonius Asprenas, proconsul of Africa in AD 14.[34] This illustrates how much high-ranking officials associated the name with the imperial family.

Although Nero took the *praenomen imperatoris* in the last year of his reign,[35] the civil wars of 68–9 undoubtedly provided a major impetus towards the regular adoption of this name. 'Imperator Caesar Vespasianus Augustus' becomes the prototype for imperial titulature in the future.[36] In time of

---

[30] See R. Syme, *Hist.* 7 (1958), 172 = *Roman Papers*, 361.; R. Combès, *Imperator* (1966), 121 f.

[31] Syme, op. cit.

[32] *Tib.* 26.2; *Cl.* 12.1 – 'In enhancing his own dignity, he was restrained and unassuming, and refrained from adopting the *praenomen imperatoris*'.

[33] Claudius, who elsewhere chose to emphasize his military achievements, perhaps sought the approval of the senatorial class by this gesture.

[34] *ILS* 151

[35] *ILS* 233 f.

[36] *RE* IX col. 1150.

political conflict, men who sought and obtained power by
violence and armed revolt needed some claim to military pre-
dominance among the contending factions.

There are few other recorded titles proclaiming association
with the army. Gaius assumed the appellations 'Son of the
Camp' ('castrorum filius'), and 'Father of the Armies' ('pater
exercituum').[37] Suetonius relates this among Gaius'
misdeeds, and the extravagant gesture perhaps owed much to
the young emperor's upbringing in the military camps and his
enthusiastic adoption of the commander's duties. It was not
repeated by his successors. However Faustina, the wife of
Marcus Aurelius, enjoyed the title 'Mother of the Camp'
('mater castrorum').[38] This is the first known appearance of
such a title and it was extensively propagated on a series of
coins showing the empress sacrificing surrounded by
standards.[39] It is curious that Marcus Aurelius, who is not
usually associated with flattery of the troops, should have
allowed his wife to adopt this title. Its introduction cannot
be securely dated, but it is tempting to speculate that it was
connected with Marcus' reaction to the revolt of Avidius
Cassius. There was a rumour that Faustina had been in some
way implicated in the plot, though this is hard to believe.[40]
The *Historia Augusta* alleges that Marcus bestowed the title
because he had Faustina with him in his summer camp.[41] But
this seems merely a suitable opportunity for granting the
title, not an adequate motive. Possibly, because Marcus'
family had spent some time with him at the front, he thought
it useful to emphasize the army's connection with the whole
imperial family, and, by implication, the dynasty.

'Mater castrorum' was a popular title in the reign of
Septimius Severus, who also had intentions to establish a
dynasty. Iulia Domna, the wife of Severus, is regularly
termed 'Mater Castrorum' in inscriptions dating from
197-215.[42] Indeed Iulia is sometimes referred to as 'Mother

[37] Suet., *Cal.* 22.1.
[38] Dio 71.10.5; *Vit. Marc. Ant. Phil.* 26.8; *CIL* XIV 40.
[39] *BMC* IV, p. 534; 929 f. (date 161–76).
[40] See Dio 71.22.3.   [41] 26.8.
[42] *ILS* 324, 426, 427, 433, 442, 443, 450, 2163, 2186, 2354, 2371, 2397,
2398, 2484, 3366, 4134, 4283, 4312, 6178, 6488, 9096, 9097. Cf. *BMC* V,
p. 164.

of the Emperor, of the Camp, of the Senate, and of the Country'.[43] Iulia Mammaea, mother of Severus Alexander, is honoured with the same formula, with the addition of the phrase 'Mother of the Whole Human Race'.[44] No doubt this kind of title owed something to the concept of universal motherhood associated with the goddess Cybele. Iulia Domna was also known as 'Mother of the Gods' ('mater deorum').[45] Nevertheless, the adoption of titles like 'Mother of the Camp' meant that the association of emperor and imperial family with the army was now more openly proclaimed.

The titles employed by emperors themselves continued to show great restraint. The extravagant appellations of Gaius found no imitator before Caracalla. In an official inscription on a Spanish milestone dated to 217, the emperor describes himself as 'Father of the Soldiers' ('pater militum').[46] Although he may have been influenced by the adoption of 'mater castrorum' by female members of the imperial family, there is little doubt that Caracalla took a different attitude from his predecessors to the army and his public association with it. But no trend was created and, so far as we know, even the warlike Maximinus employed no unusual military titles.[47]

Imperial Portraits on the Military Standards

Literary references and artistic representations together make it clear that the Praetorian Guard carried the reigning emperor's portrait on their standards.[48] But, unlike the Praetorians, the legions and auxiliaries have *imaginiferi* ('portrait carriers') and no portraits of the emperor appear on representations of the legionary or auxiliary *signa*.[49] It may be, therefore, that in these units the *imago imperatoris* was carried on a separate pole. There is no clear artistic

---

[43] *ILS* 4484.
[44] e.g. *ILS* 485.
[45] *BMC* V, p. 163. For the importance of 'Magna Mater' in the Severan age, see J. Ferguson, *The Religions of the Roman Empire* (1970), 26-31.
[46] *ILS* 454.
[47] *ILS* 487 ff.
[48] Tac., *H* 1.41.1; Herodian, 8.5.9; 2.6.11. See in general, A. Von Domaszewski, *Die Fahnen im römischen Heere* (1895), 56 ff., reprinted in *Aufsätze zur römischen Heeresgeschichte* (1972), 56 ff.
[49] Domaszewski, op. cit, 69 ff.

representation of this and the evidence makes it impossible to decide in precisely what form the emperor's image was carried by the legions and *auxilia*.[50] But it remains clear that all units of the army did have the imperial portrait with them, and that it was closely associated with the military standards, which the Romans held in high regard. They received religious observances of a kind and it was considered a disgrace for them to be lost in battle to the enemy.[51] Tertullian thought that the soldier 'venerated the standards, swore by the standards, set the standards before all the gods'.[52] There may be some exaggeration here, but other writers too noticed the reverence the Romans had for their military standards.[53] In his campaign against the Cherusci, Germanicus, according to Tacitus, took the appearance of eagles as a good omen, 'the legions' own special guiding spirits'.[54] The standards were kept in the camp temple, and with them and sharing their honour were the portraits and statues of the reigning emperor.[55] It was a mark of signal honour if anyone outside the imperial family had an image placed in the camp temple. Tiberius was especially pleased with the legions in Syria because they alone had not established and worshipped a statue of Sejanus among the military standards.[56] No doubt in the eyes of the soldiers and casual observers the emperor's portrait was virtually a military standard.

The use of portraits of an autocrat to remind the troops and also the people of their loyalty and devotion to an individual is still current in the modern age. Perhaps the imperial *imagines* and statues in the camps, as well as boosting imperial dignity and prestige, had a symbolic significance in that they demonstrated an emperor's ownership of his soldiers and his association with them. A portrait or statue might represent an emperor who could rarely be present in

[50] op. cit., 71-3; E. Neuffer, *Festshrift für Auguste Oxè* (1938), pp. 191-6.

[51] Domaszewski (n. 48), 1 ff; and see *Die Religion des römischen Heeres* (1895) 12-14; = *Aufsätze*, 92-5; A.S. Hoey, *HThR* 30 (1937), 15.

[52] *Apol.* 16.8.

[53] Josephus, *BJ* 6.316; Dio, 40.18.

[54] *A* 2.17: 'sequerentur Romanas avis, propria legionum numina'.

[55] Tac., *A* 1.39; *CIL* 3.3526; Herodian, 4.4.5. See also the interesting comments in K. Hopkins, *Conquerors and Slaves*, 219-24.

[56] Suet., *Tib.* 48.2.

person with the army. When Artabanus, the Parthian king, sought the friendship of Rome, he came to a conference with Vitellius the governor of Syria and did obeisance to the Roman eagles and standards and the statues of the emperors.[57] In Nero's reign Tiridates promised that he would present himself before the emperor's standards and statues and inaugurate his reign before the Roman army. And later he laid his diadem at the feet of Nero's statue and said that he would take it again only from the hand of the emperor himself.[58]

Septimius Severus used the standards of his Praetorian Guard to express his ambitions for his dynasty. On the arch of the *Argentarii* in Rome a praetorian standard is depicted with portraits of Severus and his two sons, Caracalla and Geta.[59] And the incident over the introduction of the *imagines imperatoris* into Jerusalem by Pontius Pilate shows how such portraits might be viewed.[60] Earlier procurators had avoided giving offence to the Jews, who regarded the iconic standards as symbols of the imperial cult and objects of worship to the troops.[61]

When the reigning emperor's portrait was torn down from the standards, it was a sign of revolution. The soldiers who surrendered to Civilis in 69 encountered supreme disgrace because 'the portraits of the emperors had been torn down and the standards disgraced'.[62] When the Vitellian commander Caecina succeeded in winning over some of his army to the cause of Vespasian while the rest were away on military duties, the troops signified the change by tearing down the portraits of Vitellius and taking an oath to Vespasian.[63] But when the rest of the soldiers returned and saw that Vitellius' portraits had been torn down and Vespasian's name written up, they were stunned.[64] The

---

[57] *Cal.* 14.3.
[58] Tac., *A* 15.24; 29.
[59] Domaszewski (n. 48), p. 64, fig. 80.
[60] Josephus, *AJ* 18.55 ff.; *BJ* 2.169 ff.
[61] See E.M. Smallwood, *The Jews under Roman Rule* (1976), 160 ff. Of course the Jews' objection to 'graven images' was much deeper than their immediate dislike of emperor worship.
[62] Tac., *H* 4.62.
[63] Dio 64.10.3.
[64] Tac., *H* 3.13.

soldiers were perplexed because the presence of the imperial portrait was a sign of normality and loyalty and that all was well in the camp. Once they realized what had happened, they set up Vitellius' portraits again. Indeed in 68-9 the frequent changes of allegiance were characterized by the destruction of the *imagines* of the emperor from whom the troops revolted.[65]

The significance of the imperial portraits among the military standards was largely symbolic and pyschological. They helped to keep an emperor's name and face in constant view of the troops and perhaps remind them of their loyalty and devotion. That loyalty of course depended on other factors, but those who aimed to secure or retain the imperial power could neglect no means of maintaining their connection with the troops. To smash or tear down the imperial *imagines* was not casual vandalism, but a gesture of political and military disloyalty to the reigning emperor, and indeed almost a formal indication of revolt.

The Roman Military Calendar

The main evidence for the military calendar is the *Feriale Duranum*, a list of festivals celebrated by the *Cohors XX Palmyrenorum* stationed at Dura-Europus, in the reign of Severus Alexander.[66] It may be inferred that other units of the army celebrated the same festivals. The striking feature is the large number of festivals devoted to the reigning emperor and his deified ancestors. It may be true that this does not necessarily indicate the close association between emperor and army, but rather the predominant position the imperial cult had acquired at the expense of the other gods in the state religion in general.[67] Nevertheless, the point is the number of occasions on which the emperor's name was

[65] See *H* 1.36.1, 41.1, 55.2; 2.85.1; 3.12.2, 13.1, 31.2; Dio 63.25.1; Herodian, 8.5.9. Note that the crime of *maiestas* committed by defacing statues or portraits was held to be much worse when done by soldiers — *D* 48.4.7.4.

[66] *Dura Final Report: The Parchments and Papyri* V.1 (1959), 197 ff. A.D. Nock, 'The Roman Army and the Roman Religious Year', *HThR* 45 (1953), 187, especially 189 ff. (reprinted in *Essays on Religion and the Ancient World* (1972), 736 ff.); see too A.S. Hoey, *YCS* 7 (1940), 173; J. Gilliam, *HThR* 47 (1954), 182; K. Hopkins, *Conquerors and Slaves*, 207-8.

[67] Hoey, op. cit., 173.

brought before the troops in religious festivals. If these rites had any effect at all on the mind of the ordinary citizen, it is likely that they had most effect on the soldiers. For the army formed the largest and most coherent single group of those expressing devotion to the emperor in this way. The soldiers were aware from whom their benefits came, and in a way they shared a community of interest with the emperor. Even if the soldiers were not much interested in religious activities, frequent festivals in an emperor's name would remind them of their connection with him.

It is plausible to suppose that emperors recognized and deliberately exploited the fact that the calendar brought their name before the troops. The calendar was presumably revised by each new emperor and his advisers, who could suggest particular changes if they felt strongly enough. In the calendar of Dura-Europus Severus Alexander has pride of place. The soldiers made vows for his safety, which was equivalent to the eternity of the empire;[68] they sacrificed for his acclamation as *imperator* by the army;[69] for his *dies imperii*; for the granting of the titles *Augustus, Pater Patriae*, and *Pontifex Maximus;*[70] for his proclamation as Caesar and adoption of the toga of manhood;[71] for his first designation as consul.[72] The birthdays of his grandmother and his mother were also celebrated.[73]

The troops in addition celebrated the day on which discharges were granted and pay counted out;[74] and there were observances connected with the standards.[75] Various entries celebrating the Parthian victories of Trajan and Septimius Severus, and the appearance of Julius Caesar and Germanicus on the calendar, were probably designed to emphasize imperial military prowess.[76] There are, however, entries in the calendar celebrating several rulers and princes, and also

[68] col. i, lines 1 f. 3 January. Note that out of forty-one festivals recorded on the calendar, twenty-seven are associated with the imperial cult.

[69] col. i, lines 22–5. 13 March.

[70] col. i, lines 27 f. – 14 March.

[71] col. ii, line 16. – 26 January.

[72] col. ii, line 17. – 1 July.

[73] col. ii, line 26. – 14/29 Aug.; col. ii, line 7.

[74] col. i, lines 6 f.

[75] See *YCS* (1940), pp. 115 ff.

imperial women, who had nothing to do with the Severan dynasty.[77] What vitality could these celebrations and those in honour of Julius Caesar and Germanicus have had by this time? Perhaps many of the festivals were casually observed in a routine manner. It may not have been considered proper to remove a festival if it did no harm to leave it. Therefore the importance of the calendar should not be overestimated. Its special military elements are not many and it is difficult to understand what impact the frequent festivals in honour of the reigning emperor made on the troops. Furthermore, although the military calendar may have developed originally from a special directive of Augustus, it seems unlikely that it was intended deliberately to promote the Romanization of the army.[78] Nevertheless, many of the festivals were celebrated with an animal sacrifice, and doubtless involved feasting and a welcome break from routine duties. In general, the calendar found at Dura-Europus is a good example of the thoroughness with which an emperor attempted to foster his relationship with the army and focus attention on himself and his family.

Though the emperor was in Rome, the armies of the provinces were reminded by his *praenomen* that he was their commander; they gazed upon his portrait, prayed for his safety and success, and celebrated his victories in politics and war. It may not be wrong to suppose that some soldiers prayed fervently, since the man for whom they prayed was their protector and benefactor, and seemed to dominate their life wherever they looked.

7. THE ROLE OF THE CENTURIONS

Promotion to legionary centurionates was open to men from the legions and from the ranks of the Praetorian Guard. After sixteen years of service men from the Guard could be promoted to a centurionate in Rome. In addition, men from outside the army could be directly commissioned to

[76] col. i, lines 14 ff.
[77] See *YCS* pp. 202 ff.
[78] Nock, (n.66).

legionary centurionates; it was possible for such men to be transferred subsequently to urban and praetorian centurionates.[1] Once he had become a centurion the way was open for a man to be advanced to the *primi ordines* and thence to the post of *primuspilus*, the highest ranking centurion in the legion. From here the *primuspilus* could proceed to the tribunates of the *vigiles*, Urban Cohorts, and Praetorian Guard, and thence to the prestigious post of *primuspilus bis* or *iterum*. A very few went on to equestrian procuratorships and prefectures.[2] All posts in the centurionate brought substantial financial benefits. In the reign of Augustus the ordinary centurion received five times the pay of a Praetorian Guardsman, while the *primuspilus* received twenty times.[3] Furthermore, although specific evidence is lacking, it may be assumed that centurions received donatives and discharge bonuses along with the other troops, at a proportionately higher rate. The vastly higher pay-scales for centurions separated them from the rest of the troops, and provided a lucrative post which was in theory open to any legionary from the ranks. It is also clear that the centurions shared the legal privileges of the rest of the army, and perhaps even had special consideration.[4]

It has been estimated that ninety posts as legionary centurion and seven posts as centurion in Rome became available every year. Although evidence on the origins of centurions is inconclusive, it has been suggested that about seventy of these new centurions were recruited from serving legionaries, about ten were directly commissioned, and about seventeen came from the Praetorians.[5]

It is plausible to assume that those serving soldiers, either

---

[1] B. Dobson, *Die Primipilares* (1978); 'The Significance of the Centurion and 'Primipilaris' in the Roman Army and Administration', *ANRW* II.1, 392; D.J. Breeze, 'The Career Structure below the Centurionate during the Principate', ibid., 435; G.R. Watson, *The Roman Soldier* (1969), 86 ff.; E. Birley, *Roman Britain and the Roman Army* (1953), 104 ff.; H.G. Pflaum, *Les Procurateurs équestres* (1950).

[2] Dobson, *ANRW* II.1, pp. 401 ff.

[3] Ibid., p. 408; and see further below, pp. 161–2.

[4] Nesselhauf, *Hist.* 8 (1959), 434. He argues that when the auxiliaries lost the privilege of citizenship for children born in service, *auxilia* decurions and centurions retained this right for their children.

[5] Dobson, *ANRW*, II.1, 427 ff.

in the legions or the Praetorian Guard, who were promoted to the centurionate were distinguished by their education, competence, and general ability. Those who were directly commissioned presumably had influence in the right places and this in turn suggests that they were men of some standing and education. According to Suetonius, Marcus Probus of Berytus, the grammarian, spent a long time looking for a centurionate post before, finally, he tired of waiting and devoted himself to scholarly pursuits.[6] Pertinax in his early career took up the profession of a grammarian and then, because he found it unprofitable, sought the post of centurion with the help of Lollianus Avitus, a man of consular rank who was his father's patron.[7] Apparently he was unsuccessful, but these two stories show that men of education and influence could expect to apply directly for a centurionate. This theme is further illustrated by a letter of Pliny. He relates how he obtained a centurion's post for a fellow townsman, Metilius Crispus. The man clearly had no military experience since Pliny provided him with money to buy the necessary equipment and dress. Yet Crispus was a man of some status, for he knew Pliny and was rich enough to own slaves.[8]

In the speech he provides for Maecenas in 29 BC, which in part presumably reflects his own view of the army in the second century AD, Dio is anxious that ordinary soldiers should not rise to membership of the Senate. He continues, 'On the other hand there is nothing to prevent the most distinguished of those *equites* who began their military service as centurions from being members of the Senate.'[9] Dio apparently believes that men of respectable social status and sound means might enter the army as centurions. Indeed several inscriptions attest that men of equestrian rank sought and obtained the post of centurion.[10] Doubtless such men had a variety of motives; some will have enjoyed the military style of life; others perhaps sought to escape from family

---

[6] *De Gram.* 24.
[7] *HA, Vit. Pert.* 1.4-5; Birley, *Septimius Severus*, 106 ff.
[8] *Ep.* 6.25.
[9] 52.25.7.
[10] e.g. *ILS* 2654-6.

troubles, crime, or social stigma at home; many were possibly facing financial anxieties, and promotion to higher grades of centurion would mean a steady and high rate of pay. In this context it is worth noting a passage of Juvenal, in which he imagines a greedy father urging his son to seek a centurionate with a written petition ('vitem posce libello') in order to become rich.[11] Vespasian once discovered that a young man of good family and no military ability had received a high post in the centurionate because of the poverty of his household. The emperor bestowed a sum of money on the young man and dismissed him from the service honourably.[12]

The responsibilities and importance of the post of centurion were recognized in the high pay and emoluments. Emperors could hope that centurions, being in general the more able of the troops, or occasionally men of some standing, would appreciate that their position and promotion prospects raised them far above the ordinary soldier; there could be little identification of interests with the troops, for the centurion had too much to lose. These factors will have helped to make the centurions a closely knit, élite group of officers, enjoying a lucrative career and sometimes high hopes of future advancement. It is plausible therefore, to suppose that centurions were a stongly conservative force, tending to be loyal to the reigning emperor so as not to risk their emoluments and careers by undisciplined or seditious conduct.

Indeed it has been suggested that the emperor was ultimately responsible for the promotion of centurions.[13] This may have been true in theory since the emperor was commander-in-chief, and no doubt a centurion's appointment was recorded in Rome. But in general it seems unlikely that emperors will have had time to concern themselves personally with the promotion of every centurion in the Roman army. The story about Vespasian quoted above (n. 12) could perhaps be interpreted to show that Vespasian scrutinized all appointments himself and did not want people like the young man who had no aptitude for military life. But Frontinus

[11] 14. 193-9.
[12] Frontinus, *Strat.* 4.6.4.
[13] E.B. Birley, *Carnuntum Jahrbuch* (1963), 21 ff. For auxiliary centurions, see J.F. Gilliam, *TAPA* 88 (1957), 164.

puts the story under the heading 'On Good Will and Moderation', and it is more likely that this was a special case, brought to the emperor's notice because a young man of good family was being forced into a career he disliked. In any event, the story shows that Vespasian cannot have been consulted about the appointment before it took place. This may well be the truth of the matter. Normally promotions to the centurionate will have been suggested by the immediate commanding officer and then enacted in a routine fashion.[14] Only in cases involving special circumstances or difficulty would the emperor be consulted or take the initiative.[15] Other literary evidence does not disprove this idea.[16] For example Caracalla, who was especially fond of Macedonians, commended a Macedonian tribune on the skill with which he jumped from his horse, and when he found that his father's name was Philip, he personally promoted him through the remaining grades of the military career and eventually made him a senator.[17]

A few inscriptions illustrate how the career of some soldiers was personally advanced by an emperor. Claudius Maximus, the captor of Decebalus, is the most notable example. The wording of his funeral inscription suggests that Maximus was promoted on three occasions in auxiliary units by Trajan himself.[18] It has been pointed out that Maximus was not an outstanding soldier; his promotion was slow and he did not reach the top of his career. It is difficult to see why Trajan took such a personal interest. The last promotion can be explained by the exceptional circumstances in which Maximus brought the head of Decebalus, the emperor's arch-foe, to Trajan. Perhaps Maximus owed his previous two promotions to the fact that he distinguished himself in battle and Trajan, who happened to be present on campaign, was prepared to honour this by personal intervention.

Maximus seems to have been exceptionally favoured in the extent of Trajan's intervention in his career. However other

[14] See M. Speidel, 'The Captor of Decebalus', *JRS* 60 (1970), 146.

[15] e.g. Hadrian was noted for his wide interest in military affairs: Dio 69.9.

[16] Dio 75.10.2; Herodian, 6.8.1 ff.; R. Syme, *Emperors and Biography* (1971), 179 ff.

[17] Dio 77.8.1 ff.

[18] Speidel, *JRS*, 1970, p. 149.

soldiers too who distinguished themselves in the performance of their duties or in battle received promotion from an emperor: 'In honour of Sextus Aetrius Ferox, centurion of the Second Traianic Courageous legion; he was the first to be promoted from the post of *cornicularius* of the prefect of the *Vigiles* to the rank of centurion in Alexandria by the emperor Caesar Antoninus Pius, Father of his Country, because he conducted himself so diligently in the various military ranks.'[19] A certain Flavinus was marked out for promotion by Caracalla because of his bravery: 'T. Aurelius Flavinus, *primuspilus* . . . was honoured by the divine Magnus Antoninus with 75,000 sesterces and promotion because of his dashing bravery against the enemy forces of the Carpi and an action successfully and courageously accomplished.'[20] Such examples are unusual and we do not know what other factors were involved. For example, Ferox, who was promoted by Antoninus Pius, appears to have had influence with the emperor, since he prevailed upon him to accede to the petition of his local town about the reduction of a road tax.

In general, it was probably rare for an emperor to intervene personally in a soldier's career and it is unlikely that there was any deliberate attempt by emperors to get particular types of men into the centurionate and promote them systematically. It remains true that centurions were an important group who had a vital role to play in maintaining the discipline and organization of the army and providing continuity of command. They also constituted a direct channel of access to the soldiers and could therefore have a significant part to play in testing and sustaining the loyalty of the army.

An emperor could perhaps expect to rely on their

[19] *ILS* 2666: Sex. Aetrio Sex. f. Ouf. Feroci centurioni leg. II Traianae fortis; huic primo omnium ex cornicul. praef. vigil. imp. Caesar Antoninus Aug. Pius p.p. ordinem Alexandriae dedit, quod per gradus militiae suae tam industrie se administraverit, dec. dec. et consensu plebis ob merita eius. Cf. 2643; 2080.

[20] *ILS* 7178: T. Aurelio T. fil. Papir. Flavino primipilari et principi ordinis col. Oesc., et buleutae civitatum Tyranorum Dionysiopol. Marcianopol. Tungrorum et Aquincensium, patrono collegi fabr., honorato a divo Magno Antonino Aug. HS L milia n. et XXV et gradum promotionis ob alacritatem virtutis adversus hostes Carpos et res prospere et valide gestas.

stabilizing influence. There is little evidence to test this generalization except for the years AD 68-9, which can hardly be described as normal. Even if the centurions stood for loyalty and discipline, they might be powerless in the face of the determination and hostility of their men, who might find leaders among their own ranks[21] or the junior officers, or be incited by their senatorial commander. Indeed the centurions might be most influenced by their immediate commander and his promises of success. The emperor by contrast was remote and a man could hope that questionable actions would be concealed in the general chaos of civil war. And so for reasons of self-interest or personal survival, centurions perhaps tended to fall in with the views of the troops, and in this the rivalry between various legions and armies no doubt played a part.

In 68-9 some centurions honourably did their duty and stood for discipline and loyalty to the military oath. In 69 Piso found some support from two *primipili*, and the tribunes and centurions of the Praetorian Guard apparently did nothing to encourage the troops to revolt.[22] Piso himself was heroically protected by the centurion of the detachment of Praetorians assigned to watch over his safety.[23] But only four centurions protected the portraits of Galba during the revolt of the legions in Upper Germany against their emperor.[24] When the Praetorians, suspecting a plot against the new emperor Otho, began a riot, only the tribunes and the strictest centurions offered any resistance.[25] When the soldiers in the Flavian army attempted to march straight on the town of Cremona in 69, it was the centurions and the tribunes who first tried to prevent them, though unsuccessfully.[26]

It is equally clear that other centurions were prepared to fall in with the views of their men when they did not themselves instigate them. As the revolt against Galba spread in the Praetorian camp, 'the other tribunes and the centurions

[21] Cf. the mutinies of AD 14: Tac., *A* 1.20; 23; 28; 29; 31; 32; 44.
[22] Tac., *H* 1.31; 38.
[23] 1.43.
[24] 1.56; cf. 59.
[25] 1.80.
[26] 3.19.

chose their immediate advantage rather than the honourable but dangerous course of action'.[27] Tacitus comments on the failure of the four centurions of the twenty-second legion to prevent the revolt of the army of Upper Germany against Galba: 'No one cared anything about loyalty or remembered the ties of the military oath. The mutiny went the way all mutinies go — the wishes of the majority became the view of everyone.'[28] This commonplace may well represent the reality of the centurion's position in civil war. When the troops of the Othonian general Spurinna marched off without orders, there was nothing the centurions could do about it.[29] Again, the Flavian commander Antonius Primus allowed the troops to fill vacant commissions with men of their own choice; the most unruly candidates were selected and 'the soldiers were not guided by the decisions of the commanders, but the commanders by the violence of their soldiers'.[30] When in 69 Tutor and Classicus deserted to the enemy, Vocula's legions decided to join them and centurions openly joined their men in disloyalty to Rome.[31]

Furthermore, on some occasions in 68-9 centurions attempted to persuade their men to revolt, though it is not clear how much influence they had. We hear of a Silian cavalry unit which was persuaded to declare for Vitellius entirely at the instigation of its officers.[32] While the Flavians were planning to make their bid for the purple they were careful to win over the tribunes and centurions, who no doubt worked on the soldiers.[33] But it is clear that they found a very willing audience.[34] In 69, when the Vitellian commander Caecina decided to desert to the side of Vespasian, he enlisted the help of the senior centurions and Vitellius' portraits were torn down. However the centurions had no influence with their men on this occasion; the troops refused to accept the change of allegiance, replaced Vitellius' portraits and put Caecina under arrest.[35] Apparently some pro-Vitellian centurions in Britain caused unrest among the troops after Vespasian's victory, but it seems that nothing

[27] 1.28.
[28] 1.56.
[29] 2.18.
[30] 3.49.
[31] 4.57.

[32] 1.70.
[33] 2.5; cf. 81.
[34] 2.6-7.
[35] 3.13-14.

came of it and we may assume that here again the centurions lacked real influence with the men.[36] In the Vitellian camp at Interamna the tribunes and centurions were the first to defect to Vespasian as his troops marched on Rome; the ordinary soldiers, on the other hand, remained loyal until the last moment.[37] Indeed, throughout the events leading to the revolt of Civilis it appears that the senior officers of the army of Upper Germany favoured Vespasian, while the rank and file continued in their loyalty to Vitellius.[38] The 'gregarii milites' were to have the final say.

In the confused events of 68-9 a variety of factors influenced the behaviour of the legions. Although it is difficult to say who was responsible for the revolt of individual legions or units, the evidence presented by Tacitus tends to suggest that the influence of the cenuturions alone was not decisive either in preventing a mutiny when the soldiers were determined to revolt, or in instigating insurrection against an emperor to whom the soldiers wished to remain loyal. The value of the centurions in preserving the loyalty and discipline of the army should not be overestimated. For an emperor the aim must still be to win the widespread affection of the legions and *auxilia*, and the loyalty and good will of the senators who commanded the armies.

8. THE PRAETORIAN GUARD AND THE PERSONAL SECURITY OF THE EMPEROR.

The Roman emperor faced the same problems of personal security as most modern rulers. He was expected to appear in public at the games, in processions, in the senate house, and in the streets of Rome. A conscientious emperor might also meet delegations and receive petitions in person. Quite apart from the danger of military revolt, the emperor was always liable to assassination attempts by the disaffected, a lunatic, or a fanatic. Domitian observed with some justice that the lot of emperors was a very unhappy one because when they discovered a conspiracy, no one believed them

---

[36] 3.44.
[37] 3.61.
[38] 4.27.

until they had actually been killed.[1] The Praetorian Guard had the major responsibility for protecting the person of the emperor from such attacks.

The Guard was clearly distinguished from the rest of the army. The most striking difference was pay. The Guardsman in the time of Augustus received more than three times as much as the legionary.[2] Clearly, from the start Augustus intended the Praetorians to be an élite force. This was maintained by his successors, and in Caracalla's reign, the legionary received 3,000 sesterces a year while the Praetorian got 10,000. The Praetorians also received a bigger discharge bonus, 20,000 sesterces under Augustus.[3] They were much better treated in the distribution of donatives; in proportion they received more per man and some donatives were distributed to the Praetorians alone.[4] In addition the Guard was best placed to receive special gifts from the emperor. For example, after the conspiracy of Piso in AD 65, Nero bestowed a donative on the Guardsmen and also granted free corn as a special concession; previously they had had to pay the market price.[5]

Furthermore the Praetorian Guard enjoyed better conditions of service than the legions and *auxilia*. They served for only sixteen years, and service in Rome could be more pleasant than military duties in a remote province ·close to the enemy.[6] The recruit to the Praetorian Guard could look forward to the status of an élite corps close to the emperor, a distinctive and grand uniform, superior pay and conditions, and enhanced prospects of promotion.[7] The special relationship of the Praetorians with the emperor is emphasized by their discharge *diplomata*. In contrast to the legionaries who got none, and the auxiliaries and sailors of the fleet who got

---

[1] Suet., *Dom.* 21.

[2] Brunt, 'Pay and Superannuation', 50–61. G.R. Watson, *Hist.* 5 (1956), 332; D. Breeze, 'Pay Grades and Ranks below the Centurionate', *JRS* 61 (1971), 130.

[3] See below, pp. 161–2.

[4] See below, pp. 165ff. and 182ff.

[5] Tac., *A* 15.72.

[6] Note the complaints of the mutineers in Tac., *A* 1.17.

[7] M. Durry, *Les Cohortes Prétoriennes* (1938), 195 ff.; A. Passerini, *Le Coorti Pretorie* (1939), 41 ff. Millan, *ERW*, 61 ff.; For promotion prospects, see above, p. 102. Note also, M. Speidel, *Die Equites Singulares Augusti* (1965).

less elaborately worded *diplomata*, the Praetorians were addressed by the emperor in the first person ('I have granted' — 'tribui'). In the other *diplomata*, although the emperor also granted the *beneficia*, the third person was used ('imperator . . . dedit'). Furthermore, in the Praetorian *diplomata* the phrase 'to those soldiers who have bravely and loyally completed their service' was inserted, and this can only be for honorific purposes. It may also be that the Praetorians received more privileges than other troops on discharge.[8] It is relevant that Italians continued to think that the Praetorian Guard was a desirable unit to get into long after their recruitment to the legions had begun to decline.[9] Doubtless service near home in Italy, the higher pay and status, and possibilities of advancement influenced young Italians.

The elevated position of the Praetorian Guard depended in part on its special function of protecting the emperor's person. It had a vital responsibility of permanent vigilance, not regularly enjoined upon the rest of the army, since some part of the Guard was always on duty. But this was not the only reason for the privileges of the Praetorian Guard. Augustus will also have considered the political implications of the only military force (along with the Urban Cohorts, who also received more money than the legions) at the centre of power. Not only did they preserve peace and stability in the capital, but also they were instrumental in the emperor's political survival. If the troops in Rome were suborned, then the armies in the provinces, though loyal, might be powerless to prevent his overthrow. Politically, it was necessary to make especially sure that the Guard was contented. The special relationship between Augustus and his Praetorians was symbolized by the acts of devotion they performed at his funeral pyre (p.39).

In AD 32 Tiberius, in rejecting the offer of a bodyguard of senators, proclaimed the ideal, 'If I have to protect my life with weapons, it does not seem worth having.'[10] Tiberius

---

[8] See *ILS* 2008 for an example of a Praetorian *diploma*. In these *diplomata* the Praetorian prefect is not even mentioned. For Praetorian privileges, see Appendix 3.

[9] Durry, 239 ff.; Passerini, 141 ff.; Forni, *Il Reclutamento*, 65 ff.; *ANRW* II 1, 339 ff.

[10] Tac., *A* 6.2.

may have been sincere in this hope, but there was little chance of its being realized. In the nature of things an autocrat backed by a strong army would acquire enemies, and the duty of administering the empire was often invidious, as Tiberius recognized: 'People will do more than adequate honour to my memory if they believe that I was worthy of my ancestors, provident in looking after your interests, firm in time of danger, and courageous in accepting hostility incurred in service of the state.'[11] From the start of his reign he was accompanied in the forum and the senate house by Praetorian Guardsmen.[12] Of course the emperor's residence was continuously guarded by a detachment of Praetorians, to whom the emperor himself gave the password.[13] In AD 14 Quintus Haterius discovered their vigilance. He went to the palace to apologize to Tiberius for comments made in the Senate. As Haterius grovelled at Tiberius' feet, the emperor fell to the ground and the unfortunate senator was almost killed by the Guardsmen who dashed up to protect their master.[14] The role of the Praetorians as personal bodyguards was certainly organized by Augustus, who had no illusions about the enemies he had made in his revolutionary career. During his reign there were frequent conspiracies and plots, though they were generally detected early on.[15]

Furthermore, in the public streets of Rome and at the games and ceremonies where his presence was expected, the emperor was open to abuse and even assault from the ordinary people, particularly over the price of grain. In AD 32 during the games there were abusive demonstrations against the absent Tiberius.[16] In 51 Claudius was surrounded by a hostile mob as he sat in judgement; he was driven to the edge of the forum, jostled, abused, and pelted with stale crusts, until a detachment of the Guard arrived and bundled him away into the palace through a back door.[17] Again,

[11] 4.38.
[12] 1.7.
[13] See Durry, p. 274.
[14] Tac., A 1.13.
[15] Suet., Aug. 19; Vell., 2.88; 2.91.2; Dio 54.3.4 ff.; 55.14; 55.15.1; R. Syme, The Roman Revolution (1939), 426–32.
[16] Tac., A 6.13.
[17] 12.43; Suet., Cl. 18–19.

unpopular political or legal decisions could provoke a reaction against an emperor. In 61, when Secundus, the city prefect, was murdered by one of his slaves, there was widespread popular opposition to the implementation of the ancient custom requiring every slave in his household to be executed. Nero was forced to use troops to secure the route along which the slaves were to be taken to execution.[18] After Nero's divorce of Octavia in favour of Poppaea, there were popular demonstrations in favour of the first wife. Rumours that Octavia was to be reinstated sitrred up the feelings of the people and a crowd broke into the palace. But they were clubbed down by the Guardsmen and forced back at sword point.[19]

The character of each emperor and his relationship with the various elements in Roman society will have helped determine how much the Praetorian Guard was in evidence in Rome. It may not be right to suggest from a few examples that each emperor was accompanied everywhere by troops.[20] Nevertheless, apart from the permanent guard at the palace, it was probably normal for the Praetorians to accompany the emperor in the streets, to the Senate and on other public business, and to be present at public games and ceremonies. However, perhaps as a concession to senatorial opinion the Guardsmen may not always have worn full armour and uniform in Rome.[21]

The Praetorian Guard will hopefully have acted as a deterrent against those who plotted to overthrow an emperor. Gaius, Domitian, and Commodus were all assassinated as a result of intrigue, and in all three cases the murder took place inside the palace at a time and place where the emperor was unprotected, and was organized by intimates of the emperor who presumably knew palace routine. The prefects of the Guard were also implicated, and they will have ensured that the Guardsmen were kept out of the way. Indeed the murder of these emperors appears to have been resented by the rank and file members of the Praetorian Guard.[22] Against the

---

[18] Tac., *A* 14.45. [20] Durry, pp. 274 f.
[19] 14.61; cf. 14.8. [21] Durry, 276 ff.
[22] Suet., *Cal.* 58; Dio 59.29.30; Suet., *Dom.* 17; Dio, 67.15; 78.22; Herodian, 1.16.4 ff.; 2.2.4 ff.

well-timed attack based on inside information, even the protection of the Guard could achieve nothing. Similarly
Caracalla was murdered in the midst of the troops he loved
so much, by a centurion of his escort and two tribunes of
the Guard suborned by Macrinus the Praetorian prefect.[23] He
had gone apart from the rest of his escort to urinate, and was
therefore left alone.

Although the primary function of the Praetorian Guard
was to protect the emperor and provide appropriate military
ceremonial in the capital, at least part of the Guard
accompanied the emperor when he journeyed to the
provinces on campaign. But there is no sign that the
Praetorians were developed to be an élite strategic striking
force. Even in the field of battle they remained the emperor's
bodyguard and seem to have had no decisive impact on
military tactics. The Praetorian prefects, so far as we can tell,
were not professional military men, any more than were the
senators who commanded the legions.[24] Up to the reign of
Marcus Aurelius, the Praetorian prefect took the field only in
exceptional circumstances and, as in the case of Fuscus under
Domitian, the results were not always encouraging. The role
of the Praetorian prefect on campaign depended on the
emperor's opinion of him and the capability of the other
commanders available. Naturally, a greater responsibility for
military affairs was thrust upon the prefects in the reign of
Marcus Aurelius since that emperor was often on campaign
and faced a succession of difficult battles.[25]

It has been suggested that the Praetorian prefects were
formally in command of all the troops in the provinces of
the empire, but this seems unlikely, even for the first half of
the third century.[26] Indeed it is hard to see what legal authority there could be for this since the *legati Augusti* had their
imperium delegated directly from the emperor. The
suggestion depends on a statement in Zosimus that the pre-

[23] Dio 79.5.2 f.; Herodian, 4.13.1 ff.
[24] See R. Syme, 'Guard Prefects of Trajan and Hadrian' *JRS* 70 (1980), 64;
Roman Papers (1979), 552 f.
[25] Cf. the role played by Furius Victorinus, Bassaeus Rufus, Macrinius Vindex,
Tarrutienus Paternus.
[26] Howe, *The Praetorian Prefect from Commodus to Diocletian* (1942),
21 ff., appears to espouse this view, though with certain qualifications.

fects before Constantine were in command not only of the imperial bodyguards but of all the troops in Italy and on the frontiers.[27] Not much weight can be placed on such a generalization in a late source; Zosimus has completely misunderstood the role of the prefect. However, in the speech attributed to Maecenas, Dio states that the Praetorian prefect should be commander of the troops in Italy, apparently with the exception of the Urban Cohorts.[28] Perhaps Dio wished to imply that the Praetorian prefects had too much power and that their command extended beyond Italy, to the armies in the provinces.[29] Nevertheless, he is simply describing the situation of his own time, when two legions were stationed in Italy by Severus, commanded by equestrians and no doubt under the general control of the Praetorian prefects, who traditionally commanded military forces in Italy. Dio's description of the fall of Perennis, Praetorian prefect under Commodus, is also relevant. He notes that 1,500 soldiers arrived from Britain to demand the surrender of the prefect and that Commodus 'handed over the prefect to those very soldiers whose commander he was, and did not dare to ignore 1,500 men, although he had many times that number of Praetorians'.[30] What Dio means here is surely that although Commodus could have deployed the Guard against the soldiers from Britain, he chose to believe them and arranged for Perennis to be killed by the Praetorians whose commander he was.[31] In any event, Perennis was an exceptional case. As Dio points out, he was looking after the civil administration and military affairs since Commodus was negligent and indolent. This does not mean that it was normal for a Praetorian prefect in this period to exercise such power or that it became common practice in the future;

---

[27] 2.32.2.
[28] 52.24.3 ff.
[29] This is the view of Howe, 21 ff. His inference that Dio in his description of the Praetorian Prefects in the speech of Maecenas cannot be describing the situation in his own day seems unwarranted.
[30] 72.9.3 f.
[31] The Greek reads:— καὶ ἐξέδωκε τὸν ἔπαρχον τοῖς στρατιώταις ὧν ἦρχεν, οὐδὲ ἐτόλμησε καταφρονῆσαι χιλίους καὶ πεντακοσίους, πολλαπλασίους αὐτῶν δορυφόρους ἔχων. There is no need to accept Howe's contention (p. 25, n. 17) that the phrase 'the soldiers whose commander he was' cannot refer to the Praetorians, because the Praetorians are mentioned immediately afterwards.

it merely indicates that under weak and incompetent rulers their advisers and confidants acquired positions of unusual power and prestige.

What sort of man was chosen to fill the post of Praetorian prefect? Obviously an emperor sought to appoint a man whose friendship and loyalty could be trusted, who had a general competence, who could command the respect of the Guardsmen, and who was willing to serve the emperor energetically and help in the day to day matters of administration and government. Hadrian's prefect Marcius Turbo seems to have come close to this ideal. No mean soldier, he could be found holding court in the early hours of the morning, and proclaimed that a Praetorian prefect should die on his feet.[32] There were no plans or schemes of promotion for future Praetorian prefects; an emperor chose the man who suited him best, according to his own character and inclinations. 'Chance and personalities prevail when Caesar selects his deputy and companion'.[33]

In no sense however was the Praetorian prefect the formal deputy of the emperor. Originally he will simply have looked after the administration of the Guard. But since he was present in Rome the emperor no doubt found it convenient to delegate informally whatever he wanted to him. And so in time the Prefect acquired a range of activities unconnected with his duties as a corps commander, and it was accepted that he should perform them.[34] How much an individual Praetorian prefect did, depended on his ability and the character and diligence of the emperor. Some prefects, like Sejanus and Perennis, acquired an influence and control far beyond the formal powers of their office. But the position of Praetorian prefect was always likely to be influential as the principate developed because he was close to the emperor and commanded the largest group of troops at the centre of power. Augustus recognized this when he appointed two

[32] Dio, 69.18.
[33] R. Syme, *JRS* 1980, p. 77. Note also Millar, *ERW*, 122 ff.; For further discussion of the nature of the equestrian career, see P.A. Brunt, 'The Administrators of Roman Egypt', *JRS* 65 (1975), 124; R.P. Saller, 'Promotion and Patronage in Equestrian Careers' *JRS* 70 (1980), 44.
[34] For the powers acquired by the Praetorian prefect, see Howe, 32 ff.

Praetorian prefects, a security measure to reduce the potential political influence of the prefects.

The prefects were also *equites*. Augustus may have thought that such men would not aspire to the purple. But he was probably more influenced by the difficulty of asking a senator to serve in a post which was not an elected magistracy, for which there was little precedent, and where he would be a personal subordinate of the emperor. Did Augustus succeed in incorporating the Praetorians and their commanders into the fabric of his regime, or did they eventually acquire any special political power corresponding to their superior emoluments and privileges, and their special relationship with the emperor? By its position in Rome and its reaction to a new ruler the Guard could sometimes have a more immediate impact on the destination of the purple than armies in the provinces. This may be why Augustus intended to keep the Guard out of Rome by quartering it in various Italian communities. But Tiberius, at the instigation of Sejanus, who probably aimed to increase his own power, concentrated the troops in Rome. Although rebellion among the Praetorians need not be fatal, the murder of Pertinax showed the practical power of the Praetorian Guard for deciding the fate of an emperor. However, the majority of successful usurpations came from army commanders in the provinces — Galba, Vitellius, Vespasian, Septimius Severus. In these cases the Guard was powerless to prevent the nominee of the provincial armies from being imposed upon it.

It seems likely that the Praetorians shared the other soldiers' complete lack of political principles and consciousness; their actions were almost always guided by lucre and the desire to maintain the system that assured their benefits and privileged position. Therefore, in general they supported the reigning emperor regardless of his conduct towards others, and regardless of the opinion of the upper classes. They revolted only if they were persuaded that they would benefit more from a change of ruler. Long familiarity with one dynasty also helped to breed the habit of loyalty.[35] Generally, it seems that the officers would fall in with the

---

[35] Tac., *H* 1.5; *A* 14.7.

views of their men, unless they had been suborned by discontented members of the upper classes, ambitious adventurers like Otho, or the Praetorian prefect himself. The Guardsmen bitterly resented the murder of Domitian, who had indeed granted a pay rise, and later demanded and obtained from Nerva the execution of the murderers. But without leaders the Praetorians, just like the other troops, could do nothing more. Had they persisted in their mutinous discontent, they would have run the risk of provoking the intervention of a provincial army commander who might seek to exploit the consequent disorder and instability and have little sympathy with their interests. Severus disbanded the Praetorian Guard in 193 because he needed to make an example of the troops who had murdered one emperor and deserted another, and because he needed to reward his own troops.

In practice, despite its position in Rome, the Praetorian Guard had little more say in who ruled the Roman empire than the troops in the provincial armies. In normal circumstances the new emperor approached the Guard first to seek its approval and acclamation, but he had to ensure the approval of the rest of the army. There was no question of the Guard's being able to impose an emperor on an unwilling army. If the new emperor was resented and leaders could be found, there was little the Praetorians could do to protect him, as the fate of Otho and Didius Julianus showed.

Furthermore, it is certainly incorrect to think that the Praetorian Guard actually 'chose' emperors. In AD 41 the leaderless Praetorians, shocked by the murder of Gaius, desperately desired someone to perpetuate a system that was very lucrative to them. Therefore they willingly supported Claudius, who was a member of the imperial family and who, as the evidence suggests, was ready to negotiate and exploit this support as a bargaining counter with the Senate. Their initial support was nevertheless vital and this is shown by the special coin types issued and the huge donative offered.[36]

The discipline of the Praetorians declined towards the end of the second century. They were allowed to do virtually what they wanted under Commodus and when it seemed that his successor Pertinax was less generous and more likely to

[36] See pp. 166-7.

enforce a stricter discipline, they murdered him.[37] Then followed the so-called 'auction' of the empire, which had a traumatic effect on contemporaries. Didius Julianus received the purple from the Praetorians because he promised a larger donative than his rival Sulpicianus. Dio describes this as 'a most shameful deed'. Herodian comments that it was disgraceful and outrageous.[38] The amount of the donative promised was unprecedented, but Herodian shows extraordinary political naïvety in saying that this was the first time that the soldiers' characters had been corrupted with a cash donative. The same thing might have happened in AD 41 if there had been a rival to Claudius willing to try his luck. Perhaps, however, in 193 the soldiers played more of an initiating role. Herodian claims that the soldiers offered the empire for sale from the walls of the camp, promising their support for the highest bidder.[39] But his account in general seems rather careless,[40] and this detail should probably be rejected in favour of Dio's less dramatic account which does not mention any such offer from the Guard and indicates that the two senators approached the soldiers on their own initiative.[41] As there were two claimants and both were prepared to offer money, the troops naturally waited for the highest offer. Even here the initiative lay with the senators. Only after several bids did the sum reach 20,000 sesterces — the same amount as paid by Marcus Aurelius. Dio seems to think that 20,000 would have won the Guard's support, had not Julianus raised it by 5,000, — probably to discourage Sulpicianus.[42] Clearly the senators were not the helpless slaves of the soldiers' greed. In such a situation ambitious men could exploit the natural tendency of the Guardsmen to seek the most lucrative rewards for themselves. They had no

[37] Dio, 74.8.1 ff.
[38] 74.11.2; Herodian, 2.6.5.
[39] 2.6.4.
[40] He implies (6.3) that several days elapsed between the fall of Pertinax and the accession of Julianus. This can hardly be right and runs counter to Dio's account. As we know that Dio was present in Rome, and is in general more reliable than Herodian, and as there is no reason why he should distort this detail, his account should be preferred.
[41] 74.11.1-2. Julianus went to the camp when he heard of the death of Pertinax.
[42] 11.5.

political motives and this was the only occasion since 68 on which the Guard obtruded itself forcibly into the political life of the empire. Septimius Severus disbanded the Guard for personal political reasons, and his new Praetorians, recruited largely from his loyal Danubian legions and with few Italians, constituted the same sort of élite force in Rome, subject to the same influences and dangers.

And so the Praetorian Guard had no distinctive position of political power corresponding to its special relationship with the emperor. At times, because of its place in Rome, circumstances could combine to give it a degree of immediate influence not shared by the other troops, but it did not have the power or the political awareness to exploit or sustain this. Like all the other troops it needed prompting and leadership from above; without this it could achieve nothing except mutinous disruption and disorder. In general the Praetorians remained quiescent and loyal to the reigning emperor whether he was a conscientious ruler or a rogue, and, with the exception of the civil wars in 68-9 and the events of 193, they had little direct impact on imperial politics. Nevertheless, the Praetorian Guard stood as a powerful, visible symbol of an emperor's command of his armies, and hence its loyalty and discipline were an important element in the stability of his rule.

9. IMPERIAL MILITARY HONOURS AND THE IMPORTANCE OF MILITARY PROPAGANDA

The Roman emperors were far more directly in control of their troops than a modern constitutional president or sovereign. Increasingly they tended to take the field in person on major campaigns, and this emphasized their responsibility for the efficiency and deployment of the Roman army, and its military success or failure. Most emperors probably desired to find acceptance for their abilities and policies from the upper classes, many of whose interests they shared, from the people, and also from the army. Naturally enough there was a conscious attempt to direct public opinion and that of the army, and build up the image of the efficient commander interested in military affairs, who defended the empire successfully and was also a worthy 'fellow-soldier'. It is undeniable that in the Republic military success could increase a family's political standing. Pliny (*NH* 35.23) tells us how Mancinus, commander of the Roman fleet in the Third Punic War and first to enter Carthage, exhibited in the forum pictures showing the battle, and himself recounted details to the spectators. This good propaganda helped him to the consulship for the following year. An emperor too could hope to profit politically from a good military reputation.

In the ancient world the means of providing information to large numbers of people were strictly limited. In this context imperial titulature was important since it was encountered frequently by the upper classes, by the people, and in the military camps, and was used to express an emperor's achievements and honours. In the same way the great public ceremonies of triumphs and the reception of foreign kings provided a splendid display, emphasized the emperor's successful actions on behalf of the empire, and brought to everyone an occasion they could enjoy; an emperor could therefore hope that it would generally enhance his prestige and dignity. Coins perhaps reached the widest audience, and martial themes and the celebration of military victories in particular might find some favourable response, since many coins were in the first place distributed to soldiers. On the other hand, the triumphal arches and the columns of Trajan and Marcus Aurelius, erected to celebrate military victories, can have been intended only to make a general impression of splendid achievement. Yet although soldiers and common people were doubtless most impressed by grand displays and pictorial representations, the upper classes might be more difficult to convince. Here a more sophisticated approach was necessary to create a certain impression of what was happening, and to persuade the more educated members of society in Rome and the provinces that the emperor's actions were worthy of support. Imperial despatches and reports to the Senate, the encouragement of writers who understood and supported the emperor's policy and wishes, and even autobiography all had a part to play. And the dissemination to the provincial communities of news of imperial military activities and successes could not be neglected.

(a) Acclamations as Imperator

Imperator acclamations, which emperors added to their titles, were quite distinct from the *praenomen imperatoris* ('forename of commander').[1] In the Republic the successful commander was occasionally acclaimed by his soldiers on the field of battle for a great victory, and added the honour to his name, for example, 'L.Mummius L.f. imp[erator]'.[2]

These acclamations were much more common in the imperial period. From the reign of Augustus up to 235 every emperor who ruled for more than one year took at least one *imperator* acclamation, with the exception of Elagabalus and Severus Alexander.[3] There was still some idea that the *acclamatio* should take place on the field of battle after a great victory. In his *Panegyric* Pliny compares Trajan to the leaders of old 'on whom battlefields covered with the slain and seas filled with victory conferred the name *imperator*'.[4] Dio comments sarcastically on Gaius because he was acclaimed *imperator* seven times on the German expedition although he had killed no foe and fought no battle,[5] and implies criticism of the adoption of *imperator* by Augustus and Tiberius for what he thinks were minor campaigns against the Germans.[6] Then, in describing Trajan's meeting with Parthamasiris, the nephew of the Parthian king, Dio

---

[1] See above, pp. 93-5.

[2] *CIL* II, 1119.

[3] Evidence for emperors who ruled for more than one year: *Augustus* – De Ruggiero, *Dizionario Epigrafico* (1961-), I pp. 915-22; T.D. Barnes, 'The Victories of Augustus', JRS 64 (1974), 21; *Tiberius* – RE X.1, cols. 478 ff.; *Gaius* – De Ruggiero, II.1 pp. 36-7; RE X.1, cols. 381 ff.; *Claudius* – De Ruggiero, II.1, pp. 298-300; *Nero* – RE Suppl. III, col. 391; *Vespasian* – RE VI.2, cols. 2643-72; *Titus* – RE VI.2, cols. 2710-22; *Domitian* – De Ruggiero, II.3 pp. 2035-6; *Nerva* – RE IV.1, col. 142; *Trajan* – F. Lepper, *Trajan's Parthian War* (see n.15); *Hadrian* – De Ruggiero, III p. 167; *Antoninus Pius* – De Ruggiero, I pp. 506-7; *Marcus Aurelius* – De Ruggiero, I pp. 943-4; A.R. Birley, *Marcus Aurelius* (1966), 284; *Lucius Verus* – Birley, op. cit., 201-2; *Commodus* – De Ruggiero, II.1 pp. 554-6; *Septimius Severus* – A.R. Birley, *Septimius Severus*, 252, n. 1; *Caracalla* – De Ruggiero, II.1 pp. 107-9; *Elagabalus* – De Ruggiero, III pp. 668-9; *Severus Alexander* – De Ruggiero, I pp. 397-8. See also, R. Cagnat, *Cours d'Epigraphie* (1914), 177 ff.

[4] 12.1.   [5] 59.22.2.   [6] 55.28.5.

appears to suggest that a victory that was without a significant achievement and bloodless should not bring an *imperator* acclamation.[7] Claudius is criticised because he was acclaimed *imperator* in Britain several times, and precedent demanded that a commander be acclaimed only once for the same war.[8]

It is impossible to say how many *imperator* acclamations were genuinely earned by emperors on these criteria. Some clearly were. Both Trajan and Septimius Severus were acclaimed *imperator* in Ctesiphon, the Parthian capital, after its capture. Marcus Aurelius was hailed *imperator* for the seventh time after a successful battle against the Quadi.[9] But from the time of Augustus it was recognized that acclamations need have little to do with military action on the part of the emperor. The idea of spontaneous acclamation by the troops moved into the background, and emperors frequently received the title *imperator* for campaigns directed by others, even if they were not present in person. Augustus accepted an acclamation for victories won by Tiberius, other members of the imperial family, and senatorial legates.[10] This determined normal practice thereafter.[11] After a battle directed by Germanicus, 'the soldiers on the battlefield saluted Tiberius as *imperator*'.[12] Indeed Dio could say that Claudius received the well-merited title of *imperator* for the achievements of his commander Gabinius, who defeated the Chauci and recaptured the one remaining eagle lost by Varus.[13] Everything was decided by the emperor, and when in 11 BC his troops proclaimed Drusus *imperator*, Augustus did not allow him to accept the title, but took it for himself.[14]

Increasingly acclamations ceased to be connected with substantial military success and any formal demonstration by the troops. Indeed the proliferation of *imperator* acclam-

---

[7] 68.19.3–4.
[8] 60.21.4.
[9] 68.28.2 (Trajan); Herodian, 3.9.12 (Severus), and see Whittaker, ad loc; Dio, 71.10.5 (Marcus). Contrary to his usual practice, Marcus accepted the acclamation before it had been voted by the Senate.
[10] 51.25.2; 53.26.4; 54.33.5; 55.6.4, 10a.6, 28.5.
[11] e.g. Claudius (60.8.7); Titus (66.20.3); Marcus (71.33.3).
[12] Tac., *A* 2.18.
[13] 60.8.7.
[14] 54.33.5; cf. 55.6.4.

ations for some emperors points to political difficulties rather than outstanding military achievement. Augustus received 21, Tiberius 8, Gaius 7 (Dio, 59.22.2), Claudius 27, Nero at least 12, Vespasian 20, Titus 17, Domitian 22, Nerva 2, Trajan 13,[15] Hadrian 2, Antoninus Pius 2, Marcus Aurelius 10, Lucius Verus 5, Commodus 8, Septimius Severus 11, Caracalla 3, Elagabalus 0, and Severus Alexander 0 (?).[16] Significantly Claudius holds more acclamations than any other emperor before Constantine. This can hardly be justified by the level of military activity in his reign and suggests an attempt by an unsure emperor to build up his prestige by creating a great military reputation. There was no major military activity in Vespasian's reign after 70, except perhaps in Britain. Yet Vespasian received twenty salutations and Titus seventeen. These acclamations probably served the same purpose as the frequent consulships the Flavians held; they added dignity and honour to an imperial dynasty that originally owed its position to being the victor in a civil war. Domitian, who held twenty-two acclamations, fully exploited his father's methods. In fact he took one more *imperator* acclamation than Augustus, and this may have been a deliberate attempt to show that he had surpassed Augustus' military glory. The twenty-one acclamations enjoyed by Augustus were not entirely the product of military success. He too needed to dignify his house and back up his claim to be the outstanding military leader, inherent in his adoption of the *praenomen imperatoris*. In this context the Severans provide something of a paradox. Septimius Severus himself had only eleven salutations in a seventeen-year reign, Caracalla held only three and none is recorded on the inscriptions of Severus Alexander. Yet all these emperors conducted long military campaigns which would have provided the ostensible justification for the exploitation of military honour. In par-

---

[15] See Cagnat, op. cit. *ILS* 303 (from 117) gives *imp. XVIII*, but Dessau (ad loc.) doubts this figure. Cf. F. Lepper, *Trajan's Parthian War*, 135–6; 208–9. It is possible however that Trajan received a large number of acclamations in the last year of the Parthian war.

[16] No inscription of either emperor mentions any acclamations. Yet Severus Alexander celebrated a triumph and it is difficult to believe that he was not acclaimed then. There is no convincing explanation of the silence of the inscriptions.

ticular, it is curious that Caracalla, who posed enthusiastically as the 'fellow-soldier' of his troops, has so few salutations. Perhaps he wished to emphasize his personal relationship with the troops rather than the more formal connotations of *imperator*. Severus may have thought that any military honours he adopted would be inevitably associated with the prolonged civil wars he had fought against Pescennius Niger and Clodius Albinus.

The political significance of the *imperator* salutation can also be seen in its use to mark out and distinguish intended heirs. Tacitus thought that Augustus had conferred on his stepsons Tiberius and Drusus the *imperator* acclamation as part of his dynastic plans, in order to boost their prestige and standing.[17] He may be mistaken in the details since it seems that Drusus received his acclamation only posthumously, and Tiberius was acclaimed for the first time on the death of Drusus.[18] Indeed in 11 BC, when Drusus' soldiers conferred the *imperator* title on their commander, Augustus refused to allow him to accept it, and himself accepted acclamations for the exploits of both Drusus and Tiberius.[19] The emperor had to be careful not to diminish his own glory; however Tacitus is probably right to think that the bestowal of an *imperator* acclamation became an important part of the means used by Augustus to bring members of the imperial family into the limelight of public life.[20] In 8–7 BC, Tiberius' second *imperator* acclamation was associated with another consulate and a triumph, and can be seen as part of an attempt to show his worthiness for high office.[21] In fact Tiberius received seven of his eight acclamations in Augustus' reign. Germanicus received two acclamations, in AD 13 or 14 and 15.[22] As Germanicus was the emperor's adopted son and likely successor, and as he was granted a triumph in AD 17, a consulate with Tiberius in AD 18, and *maius imperium*

---

[17] *A* 1.3.

[18] See Barnes, *JRS* 1974, 22.

[19] Dio, 54. 31.4; 33.5.

[20] Note that Gaius Caesar was hailed *imperator* in AD 3 for a minor exploit in Syria (Dio 55.10a.6).

[21] Dio, 55.6.4; cf. *ILS* 95.

[22] Tac., *A* 1.58. On the question of the acclamations of Germanicus, see now P.A. Brunt, *Zeitschrift für Papyrologie und Epigraphik* 13 (1974), 176 ff.

over all the East, it seems likely that the salutation was partly intended to show that Germanicus was worthy of his military responsibilities, and to strengthen his dynastic claims.

Titus received fifteen of his seventeen salutations during his father's reign.[23] The intention was to raise him to virtually the same degree of honour as his father and therefore provide him with adequate military and political standing for an incontestable succession. Similarly he held seven ordinary consulships between 70 and 79, always with his father. On the other hand Domitian held only one ordinary consulship in his father's reign and was not acclaimed *imperator*.[24] The intention may have been to keep Domitian in an obviously subordinate position. Furthermore, Commodus received three salutations during his joint reign with Marcus Aurelius (177-80).[25] And Caracalla received his second acclamation during his father's reign.[26]

In the Augustan system it was impossible formally to designate a successor. The person intended to succeed had to be raised above all others to a position where the transfer of power could not be disputed. In this context the honour of the *imperator* acclamation was a useful extra boost to a man's military standing. Tiberius and Germanicus, when princes, had at least done something to earn their honour. Increasingly these salutations had less and less to do with military accomplishments and were granted to intended heirs purely as an honour for political reasons. The reigning emperor safeguarded his own position by ensuring that he had more acclamations than the prospective heir, and by taking an acclamation for himself when the honour was conferred on the heir.[27] The political importance of the acclamation is highlighted by the fact that from the time of Gaius emperors apparently considered their acceptance by the army as their first salutation. Indeed, from this time part of the accession ceremony of a new emperor was perhaps carried

---

[23] Cagnat, (n.3), p. 190.
[24] He held five suffect consulships.
[25] Cagnat, pp. 202 ff.
[26] He is *imp. II* by 208; cf. *CIL* III, p. 890; *ILS* 437.
[27] Cf. Augustus (Dio, 55.6.4; 10a. 6); for Marcus and Commodus, see Cagnat, pp. 202-4.

out in the form of an acclamation.[28] In any case, from the reign of Gaius onwards it was normal for the emperor to address the Praetorian Guard at his accession, and it may be conjectured that the men expressed their approval by acclaiming him *imperator*. That could be construed as the first imperial acclamation and might eventually be expressed in the *praenomen imperatoris,* for which it may even have been seen as a justification. This perhaps explains why from Vespasian's reign onwards, when all emperors regularly adopted the *praenomen imperatoris*, the titles *imperator I* or *imperator* do not appear. When an emperor had received one or more acclamations, he would use *imperator II* and so on in his titulature in order to show his special military honour.[29]

The *imperator* acclamation became the prerogative of the imperial family early in the reign of Augustus. In 29 BC Crassus, proconsul of Macedonia, was granted a triumph for his defeat of the Moesians. But, as Dio emphasizes, Augustus alone received the *imperator* acclamation.[30] As Crassus was not operating under his own auspices, technically he was not entitled to be acclaimed imperator,[31] and Augustus could not afford to be magnanimous since the *imperator* salutation was too closely connected with his own name and titles, which must suggest his surpassing military excellence. The few occasions on which the emperor did allow senators to accept an acclamation show that it was no longer a right earned by military success, but a personal concession by Augustus, usually granted to close friends.[32] Augustus coveted this military honour for his family and first of all for himself: 'I celebrated two ovations and three curule triumphs and I was twenty-one times saluted as *imperator*.'[33] AD 22 saw the last award of an *imperator* acclamation to a senator. It was

---

[28] *RE* IX.I col. 1149, citing *CIL* VI, p. 417 from the *Acta Arvalium* for 18 March, AD 38 (the ceremony would also have taken place in 37) — 'quod hoc die C. Caesar Augustus Germanicus a senatu imperator appellatus est'.

[29] See in general, M. Hammond, *The Antonine Monarchy* (1959), 59 ff.; 76 ff.

[30] 51.25.2.

[31] 24.2. See further below, pp. 349–51.

[32] Tac., *A* 3.74.

[33] *RG* 4.

a concession by Tiberius to Junius Blaesus, and the circumstances were exceptional — he was the uncle of Sejanus.[34]
From the start the *imperator* acclamation was one of the
important titles that distinguished the military bearing and
excellence of the emperor. In the imperial titulature the
imperator acclamations usually appear after the statement of
the priestly and tribunician powers, but before the consulship and *pater patriae*: 'The Emperor Caesar Nerva Trajan
Augustus, the most Excellent, son of the divine Nerva,
Conqueror of the Germans, Conqueror of the Dacians,
Conqueror of the Parthians, Chief Priest, holding the
Tribunician power for the eighteenth year, Victor for the
seventh time, Consul for the sixth time, Father of the Fatherland'.[35]

It is difficult to estimate what impact this kind of propaganda had on the soldiers. However, at least when the
emperor was present in person, the *imperator* acclamation
provided an occasion for emphasizing imperial military glory.
The acclamation of Trajan at his meeting with Parthamasiris
is a striking example. Trajan, surrounded by his troops, sat
on a high tribunal in his camp. When Parthamasiris laid his
diadem at Trajan's feet, the soldiers, clearly on a prearranged
plan, saluted the emperor with a great shout.[36] The solemn
and formal nature of these occasions can be seen from a
representation on Trajan's column. Trajan addresses the
troops at the end of the First Dacian War; the emperor
is accomapnied by his officers and the soldiers are grouped
round with their standards as at an *adlocutio*. They raise
their right arms aloft to acclaim the emperor.[37]

(b) Imperial Cognomina

Of the nineteen emperors between Augustus and Severus
Alexander who ruled for more than one year, eleven bore
a *cognomen* suggesting military honour. Gaius, Claudius, and
Nero, however, had the name *Germanicus* in their titulature
because of their family connection with the elder Drusus,

[34] Tac., *A* 3.74.
[35] *ILS* 297.
[36] Dio, 68.19.3-4.
[37] Florescu, *Taf.* 65.

who had been voted *Germanicus* for himself and his descendants. The honorific *cognomen* was usually taken by emperors
only when they themselves had participated in the campaign
that had earned the title. Commodus was an exception
since in 184 he accepted the title *Britannicus* apparently
for successes won in Britain by Ulpius Marcellus.[38] Furthermore, the adoption of *Germanicus* by Vitellius and Nerva
has obvious political connotations.[39] It is true that Marcus
Aurelius adopted *Armeniacus* in 164 and *Parthicus Maximus*
and *Medicus* in 166 for the victories of Lucius Verus, who
had taken these titles in 163, 165, and 166 respectively.[40]
But as Marcus and Lucius were joint emperors, political
expediency demanded that the outward marks of their power
were exactly parallel. It is notable, however, that Marcus
hesitated before accepting these titles and at first refused
them. The *Historia Augusta* ascribes the motive to modesty
('verecundia') and this may be true, since, after the death
of Lucius, Marcus dropped the titles and used only
Germanicus 'because he had won this title in his own war'.[41]

Cognomina were usually accepted for campaigns that
represented a genuine military achievement, involving a
decisive victory over the people referred to in the title. Dio
says that when Trajan took Ctesiphon 'he established his
right to the title of Parthicus'.[42] Pliny also comments on the
fact that Trajan earned his military glory.[43] By contrast
Domitian, according to the hostile senatorial sources,
received widespread honours for insignificant military activities.[44] In this context it is worth noting that in 178

[38] The eleven emperors: Gaius, Claudius, Nero, Domitian, Nerva, Trajan,
Marcus Aurelius, Lucius Verus, Commodus, Septimius Severus, Caracalla. See
in general, P. Kneissl *Die Siegestitulatur der römischen Kaiser* (1969), 186 ff.; 27
ff. The descendants of Drusus — Suet., *Cl.* 1.3. Commodus — Dio, 72.8; *ILS* 393;
396.

[39] See below, p. 132.

[40] *Armeniacus* — *RIC* III, p. 321, nos. 1360 ff. (Verus, AD 163); cf. pp.
281-3, nos. 861-8 (Marcus, AD 164); *Parthicus Maximus* — *RIC* III, p. 320,
nos. 1429 ff. (Verus, AD 165); cf. pp. 285-6, nos. 915, 926 (Marcus, AD 166);
Kneissl, 200-201; cf. *Vit. Ver.* 7.1 ff.; *Vit. M. Ant. Phil.* 9.1 ff.; *Medicus* —
Kneissl, 201 ff.

[41] Ibid. 12.9.

[42] 68.8.2.

[43] Pliny, *Pan.* 14.1.

[44] Dio, 67.4.1; cf. Frontinus, *Strat.* 2.11.7. Domitian adopted the title
Germanicus — Kneissl, 43 ff.

Germanicus and *Sarmaticus* disappear from the coins of Marcus Aurelius. It may be that the deteriorating military situation showed that further campaigns were necessary and Marcus thought that the titles were unjustified if he had to return to fight the same enemy.[45]

The *cognomen* was regarded as the personal possession of the emperor to whom it had been granted and was not normally taken in their nomenclature by his heirs and relatives, although Trajan apparently inherited *Germanicus* from Nerva. A few inscriptions show Hadrian with Trajan's *cognomina*, and Antoninus Pius is found once with *Germanicus* and *Dacicus*.[46] But these were probably mistakes made by over-enthusiastic local officials. A new emperor might, after his accession, continue to hold *cognomina* granted to him in his father's reign. But he did not assume those that had been his father's sole preserve. Hence Caracalla retained *Parthicus* and *Britannicus Maximus*, which had been granted to him by Severus, but did not take *Arabicus* and *Adiabenicus,* which had been adopted by Severus alone.[47]

The honorary *cognomen*, being part of an emperor's nomenclature, followed his personal and family names, and preceded his various posts, powers, and other attributes: 'The Emperor Caesar Domitian Augustus, son of the divine Vespasian, Conqueror of the Germans, Chief Priest, holding Tribunician Power for the eight year, Victor for the twenty-first time, consul for the fifteenth, Censor without limit'.[48] This is the usual pattern,[49] although there are a few exceptions.[50]

Naturally emperors reserved this signal military honour for themselves. Some families with names of high distinction from the remote past were left undisturbed.[51] But there are only two examples of senators who won such an honour under the principate, namely Cossus Cornelius Lentulus

[45] See A.R. Birley, *Marcus Aurelius* (1966), 281.
[46] *ILS* 345.
[47] e.g. *ILS* 452.
[48] *ILS* 269.
[49] *ILS* 279 (Nerva), 286 (Trajan), 373 (Marcus), 393 (Commodus), 418 (Septimius Severus), 452 (Caracalla).
[50] Cf. *ILS* 417 (Septimius Severus); 399 (Commodus). And note *ILS* 293.
[51] e.g. the Torquati.

under Augustus (his son Cnaeus Lentulus Gaetulicus inherited his father's title), and Publius Gabinius Chaucicus under Claudius.[52] We can only guess why these men received such signal honour. The Lentuli were apparently well trusted by Augustus and Tiberius.[53] Gabinius, in his campaign against the Chauci, managed to recapture the one remaining eagle lost by Varus in AD 9.[54]

Imperial titulature was long and complicated, being in itself awe-inspiring and majestic. It served to proclaim the strength of a firmly established position by listing powers, attributes and achievements. The military *cognomina* added a new dimension to the emperor's surpassing military might. Apart from the *imperator* acclamations, this was the only way an emperor could indicate in his titles that he had won great victories. Since the emperor's name and titles were much in evidence in the camps, the troops could see proof of his military achievement in the campaigns he had shared with them. Therefore, there was perhaps some truth in the assertion of an inscription set up in honour of Probus in 280 that the emperor was 'famous by the names of all his victories'.[55]

What is more, several emperors accepted more than one *cognomen*. Trajan had three, Lucius Verus three, Marcus during the course of his reign five, Commodus three, Septimius Severus four, Caracalla three.[56] From the reign of Marcus Aurelius and Lucius Verus, the term *Maximus* appears, and becomes more common from the end of the century onwards.[57] The title suggests a desire to surpass other emperors and appear as the greatest conqueror. There is no reason to think that it indicated any special success; it was a conventional expression of the supposedly unique

---

[52] See below, pp. 361-2.
[53] R. Syme, *The Roman Revolution*, 436 ff.
[54] See above, n. 13.
[55] *ILS* 597.
[56] Trajan — *Germanicus, Dacicus, Parthicus;* L. Verus — *Armeniacus, Medicus, Parthicus Maximus;* Marcus Aurelius — same as Verus, and *Germanicus, Sarmaticus;* Commodus — *Germanicus Maximus, Sarmaticus, Britannicus;* Septimius Severus — *Arabicus, Adiabenicus, Parthicus Maximus, Britannicus Maximus;* Caracalla — *Parthicus Maximus, Britannicus Maximus, Germanicus Maximus.* For the evidence, see Kneissl, 189 ff.
[57] e.g. *ILS* 437, 454, 489; Kneissl, 201 ff.

military valour of the emperor. The frequent use of *Maximus* may indicate a cheapening of the value of *cognomina* in general, and the need to find new ways to boost the idea of imperial military success. Nevertheless the accumulation of titles and superlatives was no doubt impressive – 'The Emperor Caesar L.Septimius Severus Pius Pertinax Augustus, Conqueror of the Arabians, Conqueror of the Adiabeni, Greatest Conqueror of the Parthians, Greatest Conqueror of the Britons'.[58] And emperors who faced new and great dangers could legitimately claim that their achievements were more significant than any before. In an inscription set up in honour of Marcus Aurelius, the Senate and people congratulate the emperor because he 'surpassed all the glorious achievements of even the greatest emperors who had gone before him, by destroying or subduing exceptionally warlike peoples'.[59]

Cognomina could be used to associate an emperor more closely with the soldiers. Vitellius' adoption of the *cognomen* *Germanicus* is interesting.[60] Militarily he had done nothing to deserve a title that was intended to identify him more closely with the German legions, his chief supporters. It was a purely political move and this is confirmed by the fact that Vitellius also conferred the title on his six-year old son.[61] Nerva took the *cognomen* *Germanicus* for a minor military operation by one of his legates.[62] This was perhaps intended to increase his prestige with the army, some of which resented the fall of Domitian. Furthermore, these military *cognomina* were exploited in the same way as *imperator* acclamations to strengthen the political position of an emperor's intended successor. Marcus Aurelius bestowed the titles *Germanicus* and *Sarmaticus* on Commodus when he accepted these honours himself. Caracalla and Geta shared several of the military *cognomina* taken by Septimius Severus.[63] These traditional honours did not reflect any

---

[58] *ILS* 432.   [59] *ILS* 374.
[60] Tac., *H* 1.62; 2.64; cf. *ILS* 241, lines 76 ff.
[61] Dio, 65.1.2a. Vitellius perhaps also wished to exploit the name of Germanicus, who had been very popular.
[62] R. Syme, *Tacitus* (1958), 13 and 222; *ILS* 277.
[63] *ILS* 375 (Commodus); 429, 434, 437 (Caracalla); Cohen, IV, p. 267, nos. 138–9 (Geta).

military achievement on the part of the intended successors (although they were present on the campaigns); they served to increase their prestige and standing.

A conscientious emperor who desired a good relationship with the senatorial class could allow the Senate formally to vote the *cognomen* to him: 'The Senate, on learning of his [Claudius'] achievement, gave him the title of Britannicus and granted him permission to celebrate a triumph.'[64] This, of course, was a concession to the Senate and not a right. The senators presumably acted on receiving a despatch or statement from the emperor, intimating that he was willing to accept a particular honour. The process is illustrated by Trajan's adoption of *Parthicus* in 116: 'On 20 February a despatch decked with laurel was sent to the Senate by the emperor Trajan Augustus; for this reason he was named Conqueror of the Parthians, and for his safe deliverance a decree of the Senate was passed, offerings were made at all the shrines, and games were carried on.'[65]

(c) Imperial Triumphs and Military Ceremonies

The triumph was the most direct expression of an emperor's military glory and must have seemed particularly attractive since it retained many of the respected traditions of the Republic. The association of the triumph with Jupiter Optimus Maximus, the triumphal dress, the route, and the traditional customs of the ceremony were all maintained as far as possible by emperors.[66] The Senate continued to vote triumphs, presumably on the suggestion of the emperor. Nominally at least this emphasized the Senate's responsibility and associated it with the military affairs of the empire.

The triumph was a splendid public occasion which involved senators, plebs, and soldiers, and highlighted the emperor's personal military glory. Claudius brought the

---

[64] Dio, 60.22.1; cf. 68.10.2. Claudius declined the title *Britannicus*, but adopted it on behalf of his son — see Kneissl, 35-6.

[65] *Fasti Ostienses AE* 1936.97.

[66] Tac., *H* 4.58; Suet., *Ner.* 25.1; Dio, 60.23.1; 63.20.3; Josephus, *BJ* 7.128-31; 153; 155; Tert. *Apol.* 33.4. See in general, *RE Zweite Reihe* VII 1, s.v. 'triumphus', cols. 493 ff.; A. Alföldi, *Die Monarchische Repräsentation im römische Kaiserreiche* (1971), 143; 147-8.

provincial governors back to Rome specifically to see his triumph.[67] Vespasian addressed the senators and *equites* before his triumphal procession and conducted the traditional prayers with them.[68] For the people the personal appearance of the emperor was very important. Vespasian and Titus deliberately picked a route that would let more people see them.[69] The crowds were organized to get the best view and the festivities might last for days.[70] The procession itself, with its succession of spoils, captives, soldiers, divine images, and pictorial stages showing scenes from the war,[71] was calculated to inspire a large crowd with mass emotion and excitement. Everything led up to the climax of the appearance of the emperor riding in his triumphal chariot, and clad in his purple cloak and star bespangled toga. Tertullian thought that the Roman emperor 'in that most exalted chariot' was at the very height of his glory.[72] Philostratos too was impressed by the golden triumphal chariot.[73]

Naturally the military elements of the triumph were prominent: the special breakfast for the soldiers and the imperial speech; the full parade of the troops and the acclamation of the emperor; the parade of the spoils of war; the pictorial account of the campaign; the public execution of the enemy leader. The triumph associated emperor and soldiers in their most acceptable function of waging war for the empire. It was good for the morale and prestige of the army and it presented the emperor to his soldiers as a great military leader, the directing force of the campaign.

The same exploitation of military glory can be seen in several other ceremonies of which we have a record. Claudius organized two special occasions on which were exhibited foreign kings captured in war — Mithridates of the Bosphorus, and the British king Caratacus.[74] The appearance of the latter was more spectacular, and according to Tacitus he was a

[67] Suet., *Cl.* 17.
[68] Jos, *BJ* 7.125.
[69] Ibid. 131.
[70] Dio, 51.21.5; cf. Nero's ceremonial entry into the city after the murder of Agrippina (Tac., *A* 14.13).
[71] Josephus, *BJ* 7.130 ff.
[72] *Apol.* 33.4.
[73] *VS* 488.
[74] Tac., *A* 12.21; 36–7; Dio, 60.33.3c.

figure who inspired the interest of contemporaries. The people were summoned 'as if to a remarkable spectacle', the Praetorian Guard paraded in full armour, and at the climax Caratacus and his family were brought in. Claudius presided in military dress, and having tried the king on a high tribunal, displayed his magnanimity by pardoning him. The emperor got what he wanted: everybody was talking about him and the capture of Caratacus, the senators were suitably impressed, and his prestige was enhanced.[75]

Equally inspiring was the visit of Tiridates to Rome in 66 to be crowned king of Armenia by Nero.[76] The occasion was organized to create the best impression of Roman power and imperial prestige. The people were drawn up in ranks; the soldiers appeared in full armour with their standards. Nero himself entered in triumphal dress accompanied by the Senate and the Praetorian Guard. To the spectators it must have seemed that Tiridates was humiliated. He was led in between lines of heavily armed soldiers and did obeisance before the emperor, who was acclaimed *imperator* with such a great roar that Tiridates was terrified. Finally, he sat beneath the feet of Nero, who placed the crown on his head, with the following words:

You have done well in coming here yourself so that you may receive my beneficence from me personally. For I bestow upon you what neither your father left you nor your brothers gave and preserved for you. I declare you king of Armenia, so that both you and they may realise that I have the power to grant and take away kingdoms.

The effect of this ceremony was immense. Dio, although he used sources very hostile to Nero, referred to the occasion as 'a most splendid event'. Suetonius placed it among the emperor's commendable actions. The ordinary people who thronged the rooftops no doubt enjoyed the spectacle and accompanying games and could participate in the great shout of *imperator*.[77] The soldiers had a chance to parade with their emperor in full armour and accept the plaudits of the

[75] *A.* 12.36 — 'et Caesar dum suum decus extollit, addidit gloriam victo'.
[76] Dio, 63.1.2; Suet., *Ner.* 13.
[77] Note that a man of praetorian rank was appointed to translate for the crowd Tiridates' words of supplication — *Ner.* 13.2.

crowd. Even the senators, who probably despised the emperor, may have enjoyed being the centre of attention along with Nero, and the echo of the Senate's traditional responsibilities for the foreign policy of the Roman state. The military aura of the occasion could help to increase Nero's prestige with the army and emphasize his ultimate responsibility for the humiliation of Tiridates. This was important since Nero did not visit the armies in the provinces.

The arrival of Septimius Severus in Rome in 195 was also the occasion for a grand display. Severus donned the toga at the gates of the city since it was not permitted for a commander to enter the *pomerium* in military dress, and proceeded on foot with his entire army. The city was decorated with flowers; incense and torches blazed. According to Dio, senators walked about in state while the crowds wore their best clothing and shouted good omens. Everyone strove to see Severus himself. Even if fear was also one of the emotions on this day, it is clear that the entry of the army made a vivid impression on the onlookers.[78]

How did emperors use the triumph to increase their personal prestige? In general the triumph was treated with respect and was relatively rare, being reserved for those campaigns where the emperor directed at least some of the operations in person. Augustus held three triumphs, Claudius triumphed for his campaign in Britain, Vespasian and Titus for the defeat of the Jewish revolt, Domitian for campaigns against the Chatti and again jointly over the Chatti and the Dacians, Trajan for the defeat of the Dacians, and posthumously for the Parthian war, Marcus Aurelius and Lucius Verus for the defeat of Parthia, Marcus and Commodus in 176 for victories over the Sarmatians, Commodus himself in 180 for the conclusion of the northern wars, and Severus Alexander for his victory over the Persians. Between 31 BC AD 235 there were only thirteen triumphs in all, and nine emperors held the honour, four holding more than one

---

[78] Dio, 75.1.3. Herodian (2.14.1 ff.) says that fear rather than joy was the dominant emotion of the people and gives the impression that Severus entered the city fully armed. I prefer to follow Dio, who is in general more reliable than Herodian and who was present in person. For the formal arrival in, and departure from, Rome, see n. 123.

triumph.[79] There were long periods without any celebration,[80] and it is clear that this ceremony was not
excessively exploited. In popular conception the triumph
could not be separated from the person who had earned its
glory[81] as can be seen from the macabre episode of Trajan's
posthumous triumph. Hadrian, having declined to conduct
himself the triumph voted in Trajan's name, arranged that a
statue of the dead emperor should ride in the triumphal
chariot.[82]

Most of these triumphs could be justified on the grounds
of the emperor's personal presence and the ultimate success
of the campaign, although there are some suspicious cases.[83]
In general the respectability and dignity of the triumph were
maintained. Certain informal conventions were observed. In
AD 21 it was proposed in the Senate that Tiberius should
receive the lesser honour of the *ovatio* after he had written
to announce the defeat of the rebellion of Florus and
Sacrovir and his intention to go to the scene in person. This
drew a withering rebuke from the emperor. After defeating
the most savage nations, and declining or holding so many
triumphs in his youth, he was not so devoid of glory that he
sought this empty honour for a trip round the suburbs in
his old age.[84] For a proper triumph (*iustus triumphus*) the
criteria were much more strict. Claudius refused the Senate's
offer of triumphal ornaments for some minor campaigns in
Mauretania conducted by his legates and pronounced that
only Britain could bring a proper triumph; for the conquest
of Britain would bring new territory to the empire.[85] He
returned to this theme in 50 when he decided the fate of

[79] Augustus, Domitian, Trajan, Marcus Aurelius, Commodus. Note that between 252 and 53 BC there had been 70 triumphs.

[80] Between Augustus (in 29 BC) and the triumph of Claudius, between the
reigns of Hadrian and Marcus Aurelius, and between the reigns of Commodus and
Severus Alexander.

[81] Marcus' triumph with L. Verus for the latter's victory in the East can be
justified on the grounds of their joint rule, which would demand that all responsibilities and honours be shared alike. So too the triumph of Commodus, which
apparently celebrated victories gained under his joint rule with Marcus — *Vit.
Comm.* 3.6; *ILS* 1420.

[82] *Vit. Had.* 6.3.

[83] See below, pp. 140–2.

[84] Tac., *A* 3.47; cf. Aulus Gellius, 5.6.21.

[85] Suet., *Cl.* 17.1.

Mithridates, king of the Bosphorus: he thought that triumphs were acquired over unconquered peoples and kingdoms.[86] He must have been referring to nations untouched before, that is to say outside the Roman sphere of influence, whose conquest would add more territory to the empire.[87] However, the idea that a triumph could be claimed *only* if new territory had been added to the empire was not republican and was not adhered to in the empire.[88] Only Augustus, Claudius, Trajan, Septimius Severus and perhaps Domitian could legitimately claim to have extended the empire. Nevertheless, it seems to have been accepted that a triumph should normally follow a decisive victory which contributed to the successful outcome of a campaign. There was a strong belief that triumphs should not be held for victories in a civil war. Tacitus alleges that triumphal ornaments were given to Mucianus in 69 because of his activites in the civil wars, 'but they made a campaign against the Sarmatians the excuse'.[89] The *Historia Augusta* asserts that Septimius Severus refused a triumph in 195 'in case it seemed that he was triumphing for a victory in a civil war'.[90] This indeed seems a plausible explanation of the strange fact that Severus, who depended so much on the support of his army, did not hold a triumph.

A further indication of the importance attached to a triumph by emperors is that after the triumph of Cornelius Balbus in 19 BC, only members of the imperial family were granted this honour. Senators had to be satisfied with grants of the triumphal ornaments.[91] Augustus would not have exluded senators from one of their traditional military honours, had he not thought that the triumph was so

[86] Tac., *A* 12.20.

[87] In the *Penguin Classics* translation (p. 52) Grant takes the passage as expressing a contrast between whole nations or kingdoms and individuals. Only against the former could triumphs be won. But the contrast is between 'supplices' and 'integrae', i.e. the poor suppliant who has tested Roman might, and the proud unconquered nations who rejected Roman power.

[88] Valerius Flaccus (2.8.4.) claimed that a triumph should bring new territory to the empire.

[89] *H* 4.4.

[90] *Vit. Sev.* 9.10.11.

[91] See below, pp. 358ff.

prestigious that no one outside the imperial family should be allowed to share it.

A well-earned triumph could increase an emperor's standing with the army and the rest of the people, and so be important politically. It is also worth asking if an emperor who hoped to secure his position by developing his military reputation would be tempted to provoke campaigns in order to obtain a triumph, since this honour was associated with real military achievement.[92]

Augustus triumphed three times, for Dalmatia and Pannonia, Actium, and Egypt. His propaganda represented these campaigns not as part of a civil war, but the destruction of a foreign foe. The three triumphs held on three consecutive days provided a massive demonstration of military excellence that was not without political purpose. Augustus held more triumphs than any other emperor in the period up to the death of Severus Alexander, and they all took place early in his reign (29 BC). They served to emphasize the overwhelming military prestige of the man who had fought his way to power as one military leader among several, and doubtless bolstered up his political position as he attempted to establish himself securely. Afterwards he felt able to decline further triumphs.[93] Along with other military honours Augustus employed the triumph to enhance the position of those who featured in his dynastic plans. In 7 BC Tiberius received the consulate, a triumph and a second *imperator* acclamation. In the same way, in the reign of Tiberius Germanicus was granted a triumph in AD 17 and further honours in the following year. Both Germanicus and Drusus needed to be distinguished as the emperor's obvious successors. Indeed when Tiberius wrote to Germanicus in AD 16 urging him to desist from the German war, he gave as one of his reasons that some scope for acquiring glory, in particular the honour of a triumph, should be left to Drusus.[94] After Germanicus' death Tiberius brought Drusus to the fore and defended his advancement on the grounds that he had been well tried, suppressing mutinies, completing

---

[92] See further below, pp. 387ff.

[93] *RG* 4.

[94] Tac., *A* 2.26.

wars, and holding a triumph, and the consulship on two occasions. All this meant that he knew the work he was going to share with the emperor.[95] The triumph is here seen as part of the justification for a man's suitability for imperial duties. The same purpose may be seen in the joint triumph of Vespasian and Titus in 71 and the association of Commodus with Marcus Aurelius in his triumph of 176.[96]

Claudius also needed to show that he was capable of fulfilling his imperial duties. The manner of his accession, his uninspiring career, and the strong opposition of some of the upper classes meant that Claudius had to justify his rule and build up his prestige, especially with the soldiers on whom he relied so much. The motive for the invasion of Britain was perhaps largely political. Although it is true that after the invasion of Britain by Caesar the Romans believed that the area was in the orbit of their *imperium* and expected the British to act as their clients, nevertheless a new military initiative still required an immediate motive. Suetonius says that Claudius deliberately chose Britain because he wanted a *iustus triumphus* and thought that Britain was the only suitable place.[97] According to Suetonius, Claudius' compelling motive was the desire for a triumph. This implies that the emperor had already decided to go himself to Britain since the tradition was that to earn a triumph the commander had to be present in person. This is not contradicted by Dio's statement that a British deserter persuaded Claudius to send a force there. The deserter will have provided the pretext and information Claudius needed. Although Claudius merely instructed Plautius to send for him if any major difficulty arose, extensive equipment had already been prepared for an imperial expedition.[98] This, and the fact that Plautius, despite the success of the invasion, very speedily sent for Claudius at the first real sign of trouble, suggest that he had received more explicit instructions from the emperor than

---

[95] *A* 3.56 — 'triumphalem et bis consulem noti laboris participem sumi'.

[96] Jos., *BJ* 7.151f; *Vit. M. Ant. Phil.* 16.1 — 'cito nomen Caesaris et mox sacerdotium statimque nomen imperatoris ac triumphi participationem et consulatum'.

[97] *Cl.* 17.1; for another explanation of Claudius' expansionist policy, see A. Momigliano, *Claudius: The Emperor and his Achievement* (1934), 54.

[98] 60.19.–21.

Dio intimates. Claudius was in Britain for only sixteen days and it is unlikely that his presence had any effect on the course of the campaign. Still, he managed to arrive at the climax of the invasion, the capture of Camulodunum, and it looks as if he was summoned for the denoument of the campaign to claim the maximum glory. The triumph was important for Claudius: it will have increased his authority and majesty with the multitude, made his command of the army more secure, and so made it more difficult to believe in the possibility of his overthrow. Claudius exploited his military success, as we can see from his grandiloquent address to the Senate on the admission of Gallic citizens to Roman offices: '. . . I am afraid that I may seem somewhat arrogant and to have looked for an excuse for boasting of my own extension of the boundaries of the empire beyond the ocean'.[99]

The Jewish triumph of Vespasian and Titus deserves comment in that the suppression of the revolt of an inconsiderable people was now the occasion for a triumph which Augustus would perhaps have despised. Josephus says that the festival celebrated not only victory in foreign wars, but also the end of civil conflict and the start of hopes for happiness in the future.[100] He may well be repeating official propaganda. The triumph was the symbol of the stability of Roman power; both politically and militarily the empire was established on the firmest foundations. All this was emphasized by the building of the new temple of peace.

Domitian was present in person at least in 83 to deal with the Chatti, over whom he triumphed at the end of the year. The emperor's personal success could justify the triumph, which may however be seen as premature if it is true that the war dragged on to 85. His triumph in 89 over the Germans and the Dacians looks suspicious. It is doubtful if anything he did to the Chatti at this time merited their inclusion in a triumph; and his settlement with Decebalus was built on the foundations of the victory won in 88 at Tapae by Tettius Julianus. But after the revolt of Saturninus the emperor badly needed to re-establish his prestige, not

[99] *FIRA*[2] I, p. 282 f. Cf the appearance of Caratacus in Rome, p. 135.
[100] *BJ* 7.157–8.

only with the armies but also in Rome. A triumph was the easy solution, and the emperor could justify it by his personal presence in both Germany and Dacia in 89. Furthermore, Domitian, who had been excluded from the military glory of the house during the reign of his father, was eager to establish his own reputation in the military arts.[101]

It remains curious that Septimius Severus did not celebrate any triumphs at all. His refusal of a triumph in 195 can be explained on the argument that he did not want to appear to be triumphing for a civil war.[102] But it is more difficult to see why he refused a triumph in 202 after his real successes in the Parthian war. The *Historia Augusta* suggests that an attack of gout prevented the emperor from standing in the triumphal chariot.[103] This may be plausible since it would be embarrassing for the emperor to participate in this dignified ceremony in a sitting position. The victories were celebrated with distributions of money and seven days of sumptuous games and spectacles.[104] It was important for Severus to prove himself to his troops as the great warrior and to show the upper classes that he was something more than the victor in a civil war.

(d) Coins and Sculpture

In the arrangement and design of coin types, war memorials, triumphal arches, and statues, emperors had a wide range of material on which to have their achievements and policies expressed. Many coins were minted originally to pay the troops and so types with a military connotation may have had an immediate relevance, but is very difficult to judge the effect pictures on coins had on the people who used them. To answer this we need to know how many people could read the legends or understand the significance of the pictures, what the circulation of the coins was, and how the types were chosen. But little is known about the imperial

[101] For the problem of the first war against the Chatti, see B. Jones, 'The Dating of Domitian's War against the Chatti', *Hist* 22 (1973), 79; J.K. Evans, 'The Dating of Domitian's War against the Chatti again', *Hist* 24 (1975), 121. For the campaigns of 89, see Syme, *CAH* XI, 175 ff.

[102] See above, p. 138.

[103] *Vit. Sev.* 9.10 and 16.6; cf. Birley, *Septimius Severus*, 182-3.

[104] Dio, 76.1.1 f.

mints and the mechanism of coin production. It is impossible that emperors were responsible for every coin type and there must have been much mechanical repetition of already existing and approved types, unless the emperor made a specific intervention, as Claudius clearly did for his series of coins celebrating the Praetorian Guard.[105] Presumably emperors approved a certain general range of types to which they might recommend additions in particular circumstances during a reign. For the historian the impression the coins made on the soldiers and the rest of the population is in a way less important than the intention behind them. For the coins express ideas clearly approved of by the emperor, and sometimes perhaps reflect a direct imperial initiative. Therefore they can provide some indication of the impression an emperor wished to give of his reign.

There was a natural desire to celebrate military victories in grandiloquent terms suggesting Roman power and domination. These types follow a regular pattern: a personification of the defeated country sits in mourning, surrounded by weapons; sometimes a trophy is also represented.[106] A variation of this type shows a trophy with bound enemy captives sitting at its base.[107] The boastful legends identify the victory: for example, 'The Capture of Armenia'; 'The Total Defeat of Iudaea'; 'The Conquest of Germany'.[108] The emperor was directly associated with these victories, of course, since his portrait and titles appeared on the obverse of the coin.[109] Some coins make the guiding role of the

---

[105] *BMC* I, p. 165, nos. 5 and 8. In general the intelligibility of coin types has been much overrated. Cf. the judicious comments by A.H.M. Jones, *Essays in Roman Coinage presented to Harold Mattingly* (1956), 13, and the attempt at refutation by C.H.V. Sutherland, *JRS* 49 (1959), 46.

[106] The following section is not an exhaustive survey of coin evidence. For illustration I have selected coins from: *BMC* I, Augustus, nos. 10, 40, 56, 671 ff.; II, Vespasian, nos. 31 ff.; Titus, nos. 161 ff.; Domitian, nos. 294, 310, 325; III, Trajan, nos. 145 ff.; 785 ff.; IV, Marcus and Verus, nos. 233 ff.; 271 ff.; Marcus, nos. 1413, 1427, 1476.

[107] *BMC* I, Claudius, no. 157; II, Vespasian, nos. 608, 862; Domitian, no. 299; III, Trajan, nos. 250, 826, 905; IV, Marcus and Verus, nos. 578 ff.; 642, 758, 1664; V, Severus, nos. 86, 118, 296, 405 ff.; Caracalla, nos. 520, 718, 803.

[108] e.g. *BMC* I, Augustus, nos. 10, 18, 671; II, Vespasian, nos. 44, 388; Domitian, no. 29; III, Trajan, nos. 381, 474, 1033; IV, Marcus, no. 1413.

[109] On Augustus' Parthian coins the legend is associated closely with his titles — 'Caesar div. f. Armen. Capta Imp. VIIII'.

emperor in the campaign even more explicit. On Vespasian's coins celebrating his victory in Judaea, the emperor, in military dress and holding a spear, towers over the mourning province.[110] The same picture is found on the coins of Trajan.[111] But the coins also make clear that imperial campaigns were on behalf of the Senate and people and directed to achieving the glory and security of the empire. On Augustus' coins celebrating the return of the standards from Parthia, the letters *SPQR* ('Senate and people of Rome') appear.[112] Vespasian's coins referring to the defeat of the Jewish rebels show *Victoria* inscribing *SPQR* on the shield of victory.[113] Even more explicit are coins of Trajan showing the emperor presenting a Dacian prisoner to the Senate, or supporting the globe of the world with a togate senator.[114] These were intended to associate the Senate and entire Roman state with the emperor's victory.[115]

Under Augustus several coins were minted referring to the capture of Armenia and the return of the captured standards from Parthia. The operations concerned here had not been conducted by Augustus and indeed the legends on the coins exceed the strict truth of what had happened. Domitian's coins with 'The Capture of Germany' after the defeat of the Chatti seem optimistic, though 'Germania' was no doubt more comprehensible than the name of a single tribe.[116] Nevertheless, although coins are part of imperial propaganda, with exaggeration and flattery of the might of Roman arms, in general they seem to celebrate significant victories in which the emperor himself had participated. Furthermore, no coin makes direct mention of a success won by a

[110] *BMC* II, Vespasian, nos. 543, 796.

[111] *BMC* III, Trajan, nos. 1033 ff. Trajan also appears standing with his foot on the head of a Dacian, receiving a shield from a Dacian prisoner, and riding down a Dacian soldier (nos. 242, 822, 137, 245, 833, 400).

[112] See n. 108.

[113] *BMC* II, p. 184.

[114] *BMC* III, pp. 38; no. 244.

[115] Note also the coin celebrating the new province of Dacia — 'Dacia Provincia Augusta' (no. 960). There is also an interesting coin of Marcus Aurelius showing the emperor in military dress, holding a spear, and extending his hand to raise the kneeling *Italia* (*BMC* IV, no. 1449). The legend 'Restitutor Italiae' suggests Marcus' labours to save the empire.

[116] For Augustus *BMC* I, nos. 10, 40, 56, 671; Domitian — *BMC* II, nos. 294, 325.

senatorial commander. Coins commemorating a particular victory were probably intended not so much to make an immediate impact and persuade people to support an emperor's policies, as to provide a grand expression of the climax of imperial military excellence.

This theme is continued in the celebration of the emperor's dominant relationship with foreign kings, which appears on coins issued by Trajan and Lucius Verus. The emperor, in military dress, sits on a high platform surrounded by his officers, and he dwarfs the foreign king who crouches humbly to receive his crown. The legend emphasizes Roman power: 'The Bestowal of a King on the Parthians'.[117] These coins were not confined to those emperors who campaigned in person. On two coins issued in the reign of Antoninus Pius, the emperor appears in a toga and performs the same type of ceremony with foreign kings who seem to have virtually equal status with him. The legends proclaim: 'The Bestowal of a King on the Armenians' and 'The Bestowal of a King on the Quadi'.[118] The first apparently derives from a diplomatic success against the Parthians,[119] the second is completely obscure. The nature of the coins suggests that Pius was not claiming any great glory for a minor success that had not been due to his own military efforts.

It is indeed clear that to some extent every emperor propagated a general image of military success even if he had little interest in military affairs and his reign had seen no great activity. The continuity and success of the empire were summed up in the person of the emperor and expressed by abstract conceptions like *Victoria* ('Victory'), *Pax* ('Peace'), *Virtus* ('Vigour' or 'Courage'). *Victoria* emphasized the military vigour of the empire and was a common type under most emperors.[120] It was readily intelligible and needed little elaboration; it could be associated more closely with the person of the emperor — *Victoria Augusti* ('The Victory of the Emperor') — or made even more emphatic, as in the

[117] *BMC* III, Trajan, nos. 588, 1045; IV, Marcus and Verus, nos. 300, 1099.

[118] *BMC* IV, Pius, nos. 1272, 1274.

[119] *Vit. Pii* 9.6.

[120] See in general J. Gagé, 'Victoria Augusti', *Revue Archéologique* 96-7 (1930), 1; T. Holschere, *Victoria Romana* (1969).

Severan type — *Victoria Aeterna* (Everlasting Victory').[121] Victory brought with it peace, which in Roman eyes was the peace of total victory and Roman domination. *Pax* was therefore an honourable and inspiring concept and proclaimed that the empire was inviolate and that all nations stood at peace out of deference to Roman armed might.[122] The *virtus* of the emperor ensured this felicitous state of affairs, and he worked with his loyal troops to establish *disciplina* and efficiency.[123] Even Antoninus Pius is portrayed marching at the head of a file of soldiers, with the legend *Disciplina*.[124]

The military success of the empire and the personal survival of the emperor depended on the loyalty of the army. From the reign of Vitellius types proclaiming 'Loyalty' (*Fides*) or 'Concord of the Armies' (*Concordia Exercituum*) appear regularly.[125] For the historian there is a difficulty. Do these coins mean that armies were loyal and devoted? Or was the emperor attempting to conceal revolt and dissension among his troops? There is no way of telling without external evidence. Nevertheless, such coins perhaps served to remind the soldiers of their oath of loyalty and express the perennial ideal of the relationship between emperor and army.

Sculptured columns, triumphal arches, and statues of the emperor as a warrior provided a less widespread but more dramatic and impressive illustration of the emperor's military prowess. Among such monuments the triumphal columns of Trajan and Marcus Aurelius are outstanding, not only by their size, but also in the idea of recording in detail the progress of an imperial campaign.[126] There is some reason to

---

[121] *BMC* V, p. 178.

[122] Several coin types of Trajan show *Pax* standing with her foot on the head of a Dacian or setting fire to a pile of Dacian arms (*BMC* III, p. 189, nos. 891-2).

[123] Several coin types depict the emperor engaged on the traditional activities and duties of the *imperator: decursio, profectio, adventus* (see R. Brilliant, *Gesture and Rank in Roman Art* (1963); G. Koeppel, *BJ* 169 (1969), 130; S. MacCormack, *Hist.* 21 (1972), 721.), *adlocutio, disciplina.*

[124] *BMC* IV, p. 270, no. 1675.

[125] *BMC* index of legends, s.v. *fides, concordia, consensus.* The type has several variations — clasped hands, soldiers clasping hands, personified *concordia* holding legionary standards; an elaborate version issued under Domitian and Trajan shows the emperor shaking hands with a soldier across a lighted altar; other soldiers are grouped around (*BMC* II, p. 364 no. 301, III, p. 154, no. 742a).

[126] See in general C. Becatti, *La Colonna Coclide Istoriata* (1960); F.B. Florescu, *Die Siegesdenkmal von Adamklissi: Tropaeum Traiani* (1965);

think that these columns contain the quintessence of imperial military propaganda, illustrating how emperors wished to present to the Senate and people their role with the army. The sculptors of the columns have dwelt upon several striking themes. Throughout the story of the campaigns the emperor has a dominant position, not only in artistic portrayal,[127] but also in the sheer frequency of his appearance.[128] It seems that both Trajan and Marcus Aurelius directed virtually every move in the wars. They supervise the start and end of the campaign and sustain it by their personal presence, their involvement in the day-to-day wartime duties of the army, and their encouragement of the soldiers in speeches.[129] The emperors were also responsible for negotiations with foreign envoys and for receiving the surrender of the beaten enemy.[130] In all these duties both Trajan and Marcus appear in full military dress, or in the *paludamentum* and short tunic. And they are usually accompanied by groups of men also in military dress. These are presumably the imperial *comites* and senior officers.[131] This was no doubt a popular idea. Senators too had a share in the military life of the empire and could contribute to the glory of Rome.

Trajanssäule; Caprino, *La Colonna;* W. Zwikker, *Studien zur Marcussäule* (1966); L. Rossi, *Trajan's Column and the Dacian Wars* (1971); G.C. Picard, *Les Trophées Romains* (1957); R. Brilliant, *Arch of Septimius Severus in the Roman Forum MAAR* 29 (1967); *RE VIIA,* col. 373 s.v. 'Triumphbogen'; K. Hopkins, *Conquerors and Slaves,* 221–6. The most detailed representation of the scenes on the column of Trajan is found in C. Cichorius, *Die Reliefs der Trajanssäule* (1896). For a detailed attempt to use the column of Trajan as a historical source, see G.A.T. Davies *JRS* 10 (1920), 1; against, K. Lehmann-Hartleben, *Die Trajanssäule* (1926). The most judicious survey of the art of the column is still that of I.A. Richmond, 'Trajan's Army on Trajan's Column', *PBSR* 13 (1935), 1.

[127] See R. Brilliant, *Gesture and Rank in Roman Art,* 107 ff.

[128] Florescu, *Trajanssäule;* between taf. 4 and 123, Trajan appears in 5–15; 18–21; 22–4; 26–7; 30; 32; 34–41; 43; 45; 49; 52; 55; 58; 60; 62; 65; 68–71; 73–4; 76–7; 84–90; 92; 96; 100; 104–5; 107; 111; 113; 118.
Caprino, *La Colonna;* between figs. 8 and 138, Trajan appears in 10–11; 15–16; 18–19; 21; 25; 28; 30–2; 35; 37; 41–5; 47–9; 51; 53; 57; 59; 61; 65; 69; 71; 75; 77; 83; 91–3; 98; 101; 103; 106; 109; 112; 115; 117; 119; 120–1; 125–6; 128; 131.

[129] For imperial speeches and the emperor's role as 'fellow-soldier', see above, pp. 69ff. and 32ff.

[130] Florescu – 21, 30, 36, 39, 45, 52, 62–4, 100, 104–5, 107, 113; Caprino – 25, 32, 42, 51, 53, 61, 65, 71, 75. For the emperor receiving prisoners, see Florescu – 13, 22, 32, 55, 58; Caprino – 15, 31, 35, 83, 120.

[131] See below, pp. 355ff.

Finally, the sculptured scenes on the columns show that on campaign, besides military organization, an emperor had other duties, including religious sacrifices and receptions by local communities in the empire.[132] The general theme of propaganda on the columns is that the emperor laboured with his brave soldiers to protect, preserve, and enhance the civilized life of the empire. Such monuments, statues of emperors in military dress, and other pictorial records of imperial achievements, served to keep the ruler in the public eye and confirm that he had successfully fulfilled his role as defender of the empire.[133] Similarly the triumphal arches erected throughout the empire (there were over fifty in Rome) were ceremonial rather than functional, and proclaimed the majesty and military success not only of the Roman State, but particularly of the individual emperor to whom each one was dedicated.

(e) Despatches to the Senate; Autobiography; Other Literary Works

In the Republic a military commander normally kept the Senate informed about his operations by means of despatches.[134] It is clear that most emperors who went on campaign continued this practice. Dio's description of a despatch sent by Hadrian shows that the traditional opening words used by Cicero were maintained: 'If you are in good health, it is well, I and my army are in good health'.[135] The sending of despatches in the traditional form kept up the appearance that the Senate had a real share in the military policy of the emperor and that he was not using the army merely at his own whim. An informal process probably carried on by Augustus soon became something expected by the Senate, and even in the third century Dio thought it

---

[132] Florescu, 8, 40, 85, 88; Caprino, 92.

[133] Cf. the picture erected by Severus — Herodian. 3.9.12; and by Maximinus — 7.2.8. For statues of the emperor, see above, pp. 97-9 and K. Hopkins (n. 126).

[134] Cicero, Fam. 5.2.1; 5.7.1; 10.35.1; 15.1.1; 15.2.1.

[135] 69.14.3. Other emperors: Gaius (Suet., Cal. 44.2; 45.3); Domitian (Dio, 67.7.3); Trajan (68.29.1 f.); L. Verus (Fronto, Haines (Loeb), II, pp. 133; 145); Marcus (Dio 71.10.5); Caracalla (77.18.2; 20.1 f.; Herodian. 4.11.8); Macrinus (Dio, 78.27.3; 36.1 f.); Maximinus (Herodian. 7.2.8).

worth mentioning that Macrinus did not send a full despatch to the Senate after his peace settlement with the Parthians.[136] A despatch could also provide an excellent opportunity to broadcast an emperor's achievements. Gaius organized the delivery of his despatches from Germany to create a dramatic impression. The messenger was instructed to ride in a carriage at full speed into the forum and present the despatches to the consuls in person in the temple of Mars Ultor, before a full meeting of the Senate.[137] Doubtless the tone of imperial despatches was often grandiloquent. Trajan wrote frequently to the Senate recounting the names of conquered peoples and claiming that he had marched further than Alexander.[138] Hadrian however adopted a more subdued approach in his despatches about the Jewish war, as was proper for someone who was dealing with a difficult and costly revolt from Roman rule.[139] According to Fronto, Lucius Verus reached a high degree of eloquence and dignity in his despatches about the Parthian war. He apparently mentioned his negotiations with the Parthian king, the storming of towns, and invited Marcus to adopt the title *Armeniacus*.[140] Caracalla wrote alleging that he had subjugated the entire East.[141] Maximinus described in detail a battle against the Germans and dwelt upon his personal bravery.[142]

The more widely the emperor's view of what was happening on military campaigns was disseminated, the better. Announcements of victories were of course made outside the Senate. The Arval Brethren were charged with the performance of certain sacrifices on behalf of the imperial family. As the Arvals were composed of distinguished senators, this provided an excellent way of spreading information favourable to the emperor among the upper classes.[143] This

---

[136] 78.27.3.

[137] *Cal.* 44.2. It was forbidden to ride in a *vehiculum* in the *forum* during the day.

[138] Dio, 68.29.1 f.

[139] 69.14.3.

[140] Haines (*Loeb*), II, pp. 144; 132.

[141] Herodian. 4.11.8.

[142] 7.2.8.

[143] See J. Scheid, *Les Frères Arvales: Recrutement et Origine Sociale sous les Empereurs Julio-Claudiens* (1975); R. Syme, *Some Arval Brethren* (1980).

information often concerned political or military matters. For example, in the *acta* of the year 213 the Arvals sacrificed 'because our lord Antoninus is about to pass through Raetia in order to destroy the enemy forces of the barbarians, so that the enterprise may turn out well and luckily for him'. Later they sacrificed for the German victory of Caracalla.[144]

Many inscriptions in honour of emperors were set up by the Senate and the people and local communities throughout Italy and the provinces. Some were probably directly influenced by the emperor. In a letter to Nicopolis on Ister, Septimius Severus commends the people for their enthusiastic celebration of the emperor's message that peace had been attained throughout the world 'because of the defeat of those savages who are causing disturbance to the empire'. Severus also wrote to the Aezani congratulating them on their celebration of Caracalla's proclamation as Caesar, and added that his victory had occurred after their decrees and that he had written the letter to inform them.[145] Although there is little evidence, we may conjecture that information was regularly sent to the communities in Italy and the provinces. The details of military success may not always have been completely accurate. A dedication from Cyrenaica in 107 records how Trajan captured Decebalus. In fact Decebalus committed suicide and this point may have been obscured later by enthusiastic exaggeration.[146]

In these celebrations of the emperor's military success one theme is prevalent; his army laboured only for the safety and glory of the empire. For some people this was not merely a topic for polite congratulation in a public inscription. Their lives depended on the emperor's military intervention. The province of Further Spain celebrated Augustus 'because through his help and constant concern the province had been pacified'.[147] The town of Sarmizegethusa records how it was rescued by Marcus Aurelius — 'saved by a display of courage from two threatening dangers'.[148] The *Civitas Treverorum*

[144] *ILS* 451.
[145] *IGBR* 659 (Nicopolis); *IGR* IV. 566 (Aezani).
[146] *SEG* IX.101; M. Speidel, *JRS* 60 (1970), 142.
[147] *ILS* 103.
[148] *ILS* 371.

honoured Septimius Severus and the legion *XX Primigenia* 'for uprightness and courage since the state was defended by it [the legion] during a siege'.[149] The important point here is that, although the state was defended by the legion, the honour went in the first place to the emperor, who inspired the victory. This indicates the responsibility of the emperor for the direction of all military activities, and the same idea appears in the inscription from the triumphal arch of Titus in Rome celebrating his glorious victory over the Jews, 'through the instructions, advice, and auspices of his father'.[150] The Roman emperor, whoever he was and whatever his personal inclinations, had to display his *virtus* to preserve stability and internal peace, retain the loyalty of the army, and maintain and perhaps expand the power of the Roman people in war.[151] It is notable that perhaps the most grandiloquent inscription on the theme of martial glory was set up by the Senate and the people to Marcus Aurelius, whose personal interests were more philosophical and scholarly than military.[152]

Most emperors belonged to the upper classes, among whom a high value was placed on literature and learning and many of whom turned their hand to writing in a dilettante fashion. It is not surprising that several emperors recorded their achievements, military or otherwise, in autobiographical works, some of which seem to have been widely published. In these they could defend their actions, expound the drudgery and glory of war, and hope that this would most directly influence the upper classes. Augustus had set the trend with his autobiography written about 25 BC, and in a brief memoir (*Res Gestae*) of his entire career to be inscribed outside his mausoleum. In military affairs he emphasized four main themes: firstly, the vast glory and personal success of the emperor, with a list of titles and triumphs.[153] Secondly, his wars; he stresses that he extended Roman power over new territory, that all the wars were just

---

[149] *ILS* 419.
[150] *ILS* 264.
[151] For celebration of the emperor's role in civil and military affairs, see *ILS* 292; 425.
[152] See above, n. 59.
[153] *RG* 4.

and necessary, and that he restored Roman prestige and the standards lost by other commanders.[154] Thirdly, the establishment of total Roman domination; embassies from far-off places sought Roman friendship, and Augustus was the first to receive envoys from India; foreign kings came as suppliants and offered their children as hostages; Augustus had the power to make kings at will.[155] Fourthly, Augustus established peace through military victory ('parta victoriis pax').[156]

Throughout the *Res Gestae* Augustus uses the first person or the phrase 'meo auspicio' ('under my direction'), showing the personal leadership and achievement of the emperor. But he also insists throughout that his efforts were on behalf of the honour and glory of the Roman people. The words 'Populus Romanus' appear frequently.[157] Naturally, there is no hint in the *Res Gestae* of the military adventurer or the fact that the army was a personal mercenary force. The summary of his achievements expresses what Augustus thought would win popularity and support among those who could read and respond. The writer of the prologue to the *Res Gestae* in the Ancyra inscription understood in the way that Augustus must have hoped, when he summarized the emperor's actions as follows: 'by which he brought the whole world under the power of the Roman people'.

Vespasian and Titus wrote memoirs about the Jewish war. Presumably these were published since Josephus considered that they were valuable sources for the war and failure to use them could be held against a historian. Little can be deduced about style or approach,[158] though it may be assumed that the memoirs described the routine duties, exploits, and decisions of the commanders.[159] Trajan wrote a commentary

[154] 26, 27, 29, 30.

[155] 31.1; 32; 33.

[156] 34.1; cf. 13; 26.2. See in general, S. Weinstock, *JRS* 50 (1960), 44.

[157] In relation to 'amicitia' (26.4; 29.2); 'imperium' (27.1; 30.1); 'exercitus' (30.1); 'imperia' (30.2); 'fides' (32.3).

[158] Josephus, *Vita* 358 and 242; cf. *Ap.* 1.56. There may be a hint of the approach at *BJ* 4.658 ff., where Josephus is describing the march of Titus from Alexandria to Caesarea. In contrast to Josephus' usual style, this passage is very terse and reads like campaign notes. It *may* be taken from the memoirs of Vespasian and Titus.

[159] For the content of the memoirs, see *Vita* 342-3; *BJ* 3.29.

in several books on his Dacian wars. From this work only one, unilluminating sentence survives.[160] It does show however that Trajan wrote in the first person and did not follow the practice of Caesar in using his own name or an impersonal construction. Vegetius, in his *De Re Militari*, mentions *Institutiones* of Hadrian, but there is no sign of the nature of these.[161] Septimius Severus wrote an autobiography which at least covered the civil war against Albinus.[162] It is not clear how much of this Dio used, and there may be some hints of it in his extant history, for example the story of Severus' personal involvement in the battle of Lugdunum, the explanation of his wars in the East and the failure to take Hatra, and the story of the desert well.[163]

Emperors did not always need to rely on their own efforts to broadcast their achievements. The wars waged by the Roman army brought inspiration to many historians and poets. What is more, an emperor often had friends among the artists and writers of the age; patronage and encouragement were extended and an author might feel obliged to celebrate in his work the emperor whom he respected. In the reign of Augustus, although poets like Virgil, Horace, Propertius and Ovid were not mere ciphers, they were influenced by the achievements, views and suggestions of Augustus, and no doubt in their own way expressed much of what he wanted to hear.[164] This will have been particularly true of Ovid after his exile to Tomi, since he needed to regain Augustus' favour. All these poets were much respected and read among the upper classes, and therefore provided an excellent avenue for the expression of Augustus' role as military leader. Several themes are prevalent: the emperor has sole responsibility for the exhaustive military duties of the empire;[165] he has won total victory against Rome's traditional enemies, defeated

---

[160] Priscianus, 6.13 – 'Traianus in I Dacicorum'. The sentence is: 'Inde Bezobim, deinde Aizi processimus'.

[161] 1.8.

[162] Dio, 75.7.3.

[163] See Millar, *Cassius Dio*, 122; 141.

[164] R. Syme, *The Roman Revolution*, 459 ff.; P.A. Brunt, *JRS* 53 (1963), 170 ff.; C.M. Wells, *The German Policy of Augustus* (1971).

[165] Virg., *Georg.* 1.25 ff.; Ovid, *Trist.* 2.1.221 ff.; *Ex Pont.* 2.9.33; 3.3.61; Horace, *Carm.* 4.5.25 ff.

peoples who have never been conquered before, and exacted vengeance from Parthia;[166] he has brought peace based on Roman domination;[167] his management of the empire is supported by the gods' help.[168] In general the emperor appears as the dutiful leader who uses the army in legitimate conquest to strengthen the empire, expand Roman power if necessary, and avenge Roman defeats. The result is an honourable peace which all enjoy. Similarly, the poems of Statius and Martial abound with references to Domitian's wars against the Germans and Dacians. The same type of theme appears: the emperor's personal responsibility; total victory and the bringing of peace; the imperial triumph.[169]

Some writers needed no encouragement from the emperor himself. In a letter to a prospective bard of Comum who intended to write a poem 'The Dacian Wars', Pliny warmly approves and suggests themes — the achievements of Roman military engineering, new bridges and camps, the defeat and death of a foreign king. The poet will invoke Trajan himself and sing of his achievements, deeds, and counsel.[170] Indeed literary works of this kind sometimes got out of hand. In his satire *How to Write History*, Lucian criticizes the laudatory histories that greeted the campaigns of Lucius Verus in Parthia: these works were mostly panegyric, grossly exaggerated the emperor's military prowess, and expended vast space on his actions.[171] In Fronto's *Principia Historiae* we can see one laudatory history in the making. Fronto emphasizes the strength of the enemy and notes how Verus, as a good *imperator*, restored discipline by personal example

---

[166] Virg., *Georg.* 2.167 ff.; 3.25 ff.; 4.562; *Aen.* 1.286 ff.; 8.727; Horace, *Carm.* 1.2.51 ff.; 50 ff.; 1.18.55 ff.; 2.9.18 ff.; 3.3.43 ff.; 3.5.1 ff.; 4.14.4 ff.; Ovid, *Trist.* 3.12.45 ff.; 4.2.1 ff., especially 44 ff.; *Fast.* 5.585 ff.; *Ars Amat.* 1.177-228; Propertius, 2.1.25 ff.; 2.10.13 ff.; 3.4.1-9; 3.5.48; 4.3.7 ff.; 4.6.83-4.

[167] Horace, *Carm.* 4.14.41 ff.; 4.15.5 ff.; Virg., *Aen.* 6.851-3; 1.289; Ovid, *Ex Ponto* 2.6.18 ff.; *Fast.* 1.280 ff.

[168] Virg., *Aen.* 1.278-9; Horace, *Carm.* 1.12.49 ff.; 3.5.1 ff.; Propertius, 4.6.

[169] Statius, *Silvae* 1.1.25 ff.; 78 ff.; 1.2.179 ff.; 4.1.13 ff.; 4.2.66; *Theb.* 1.16 ff. Martial 2.2; 5.1.7; 7.5; 7.80; 8.11.

[170] *Ep.* 8.4.

[171] *How to Write History* 7; 14 (one historian compared Verus to Achilles and the Parthian king to Thersites); 19 (apparently one author spent hundreds of lines in describing the emperor's shield); 20.

and leadership.[172] The emperor's general strategy is praised and possible criticisms are explained away.[173] As Verus had prompted Fronto to write the history, it presumably reflects exactly what he wanted. In a letter to the orator the emperor suggests that his policy and actions should be explained and above all the greatness of his achievements must be made manifest by mention of the lack of success before his arrival.[174] Verus intended the history to be taken seriously, since he arranged for the consular commanders in the war to send their campaign notes to Fronto. It is a good illustration of the importance which an emperor, who was not primarily an enthusiastic soldier, attached to his military role and the creation of a suitable military image.

The emperor was personally responsible for the army's organization and readiness to deal with any military operation. His ability to preserve the empire's territories and the benefits they brought to the people of Rome contributed to the strength of his government. The upper classes, where there was a long tradition of serving the State by commanding armies, could use military ineptitude on the part of an emperor as a means of criticizing his capacity to rule.[175] If the stability of his regime were thus endangered, revolt might appear more likely to succeed. Furthermore, there was special pressure on an emperor since he was so closely associated with the army and had to back up his claim both to be a 'fellow-soldier' and an *imperator* in line with the military traditions of the Roman state.

The presentation of the emperor's role as army commander, his military honours, and the visible monuments of his success were therefore an important part of his relationship with the army, upper classes, and people. To some extent all emperors, even those who had little interest in the military arts, maintained the image of a successful commander. This type of propaganda did not become debased

[172] Haines (*Loeb*), II, pp. 198 ff.
[173] pp. 212–4. Verus negotiated peace terms because he did not wish to purchase glory with the lives of his men.
[174] pp. 194–6.
[175] See below, pp. 398ff.

because usually celebrations of military success were associated with genuine achievement. Finally, in the main emperors propagated only the respectable elements of their association with the army. It was put forward as the background against which were set forth the emperor's military duties and achievements and his conduct of campaigns. The fiction that the army was the 'exercitus populi Romani' was sedulously maintained. The propaganda about emperor and army reflects the idea of a ruler who, like the senators and *equites*, served the State in many capacities and was not committed merely to the image of a soldier, or a civil leader with no military interests or pretensions.

III

THE REWARDS OF MILITARY SERVICE

1. INTRODUCTION

In the last decade of the Roman Republic almost 200,000 Italians were under arms, and probably the large majority of these were conscripts.[1] The military dynasts who hoped to control these men had to make service under their command as lucrative and attractive as possible. The cost was high — in regular pay, cash handouts or donatives, and discharge payments in money or land. Crassus had said that no man could call himself rich if he could not support an army out of his income.[2] It was a commonplace of later historiography that the dependence of leaders on their troops, and large scale financial inducements, inevitably led to the break down of order and discipline, since commanders controlled their men not through any legal right or obligation, but by donatives. 'And so everything was split into factions, and the troops became insubordinate to the leaders of the factions.'[3] In effect, commanders had put their country up for sale.[4]

When Augustus had established himself as master of the Roman world, he needed to fix conditions of military service that would keep the army satisfied, but also well disciplined. He had shared in the dubious practices of his rival dynasts — 'he seduced the army with gifts'.[5] But now, if peace and order were to prevail, the soldiery had to be kept in check.

---

[1] P.A. Brunt, *Italian Manpower* (1971), 410 ff.; 473 ff.
[2] Plut., *Crass*. 2.
[3] Appian, *BC* 5.17-18.
[4] Plutarch, *Sulla* 12. Cf. *Mar*. 7.4; and see above, pp. 32-3.
[5] Tac., *A* 1.2 'militem donis . . . pellexit'.

Augustus accepted the responsibility and himself took charge of the organization of the pay and conditions of the army. Only he knew the numbers of the armed forces and the fleets and the expenditure needed. The precious document containing the information was written in his own hand and was passed on to his successor.[6] In the *Res Gestae* the emperor carefully enumerated his financial disbursements for his veteran soldiers.[7] And in AD 6 Augustus masterminded the creation of the military treasury (*aerarium militare*) to help pay the soldiers' discharge benefits.[8] The treasury was eventually financed by state taxes, but despite this and Augustus' approach to the Senate about the matter, which seems to have been mainly intended to get the senators to associate themselves with an unpopular measure, the emperor remained firmly in control of the army's benefits. He launched the treasury with a gift of 170 million sesterces from his own funds, promised to contribute annually, and controlled the organization of the new treasury and the appointment of its three prefects.

Tacitus was in no doubt that right from the start of the imperial period the emperor personally controlled military pay and benefits. Clearly a ruler who depended on military support could not afford to let another gain credit and favour as financial benefactor of the troops. Tiberius was worried by Agrippina's distribution of gifts and clothes to the legions returning from her husband Germanicus' campaigns in Germany. It looked like an attempt to win the favour of the troops. 'Commanders are superfluous if a woman is to visit the units, approach the military standards, and attempt to distribute money.'[9] It is unlikely that Tacitus had access to these thoughts of Tiberius; he is probably using the occasion to express his analysis of the dilemma perpetuated by the system of Augustus. Tiberius continued to be sensitive to interference by any individual with this idea. In AD 32 he wrote to the Senate violently criticizing Junius Gallio because he had suggested that Praetorian veterans should have the

---

[6] 1.11.
[7] *RG* 15, 16.
[8] Dio, 55.24.9; *RG* 17.
[9] Tac., *A* 1.69.

right to sit among the *equites* at the theatre. What had he to do with the soldiers? They must receive their orders and rewards from the emperor alone. Was he seeking to corrupt military discipline and stir up sedition?[10] The specific charge against Gallio was that he was trying to persuade the Guards to be loyal to the State rather than the person of the emperor.[11] The State, it seemed, counted for nothing; the army was the emperor's personal possession. No doubt Tiberius' suspicions had been aroused after the fall of Sejanus; he actually accused Gallio of being the agent of the prefect. The letter may be the result of increasing disillusionment with his position and his relationship with the Senate. Nevertheless, it shows how anxious Tiberius became if anyone took the initiative in matters affecting the army.

Yet from time to time Tiberius had sought to involve the Senate in business relating to the army. 'There was no matter of public or private business so insignificant or so important that he did not bring it before the Senate . . . even questions of levying or discharging soldiers, and the disposition of the legions and the *auxilia*.'[12] In AD 14 Tiberius wrote to the mutinous soldiers of the Pannonian legions stating that he would put their demands before the Senate. Drusus would make any possible concessions immediately. 'The remaining questions must be reserved for the Senate, which, they should remember, was capable of displaying indulgence as well as severity.'[13] However the mutinies were in fact settled by the emperor's sons by whatever methods the situation demanded, and the results merely communicated to the Senate.[14] But again, as late as AD 32 he commended the Senate when it voted that the pay of the Praetorians should be taken from the public treasury.[15] Tiberius clearly wanted the Senate to play its part in the government of the State, but not all aspects of imperial policy could be equally open

---

[10] *A* 6.3.
[11] Dio, 58.18.4.
[12] Suet., *Tib.* 30.
[13] Tac., *A* 1.25.
[14] 1.52.
[15] Dio, 58.18.3. It is not necessary to place this incident in 32; Dio introduces the story with a vague phrase of time and he may not have known the precise date, but inserted it in his narrative where he thought most appropriate.

to senatorial discussion, and perhaps Tiberius was guilty of inconsistency himself. When the Senate was invited to discuss military affairs, this was a concession not a right. Consequently the senators did not know how long or how far the concession would be extended; the resulting confusion and uncertainty help to explain the fate of Gallio, who had indeed hoped that his suggestion would win the emperor's favour. The management of the army, particularly its pay and benefits, and its connection with the imperial family were from the start one of what Tacitus calls 'the secrets of ruling'. About such matters Sallustius Crispus, Tiberius' confidant, shrewdly advised, 'The emperor must not weaken his autocratic control by referring everything to the Senate; the secret of ruling is that the accounts do not add up, unless the emperor is the sole auditor.'[16]

As for the soldiers, they wanted to be certain that they received all their emoluments. They were far more likely to be able to identify with and trust one man, who needed their support in turn, than any group of people, or the Senate. In a subtle evocation of the feelings of the troops on this matter, Tacitus invents a speech for the centurion Clemens, who is attempting to dissuade the Pannonian legions from supporting the leaders of the mutiny in AD 14, Percennius and Vibulenus. He asks what will happen to their pay and bonuses if the emperor is removed. 'Will Percennius and Vibulenus provide pay for the soldiers and land for the veterans?'[17] Tacitus here illustrates his view that the provision of pay and benefits for the army was an essential function of the emperor, dependent upon his massive resources and fortune, and emphasizes the importance of the emperor's personal association with this obligation.

That the emperor was the sole paymaster and benefactor of the army was obviously politically beneficial in the sense that the soldier, knowing precisely on whom his well being rested, was likely to support the man who guaranteed it. However, the possibility remained that if the emperor failed to ensure the payment of the troops' emoluments regularly and generously enough, the army would hold him responsible

[16] Tac., *A* 1.6.
[17] 1.28.

and support someone who promised to pay more. The loyalty of a mercenary army to an individual was exactly the problem that had plagued the Republic. But the rule of the emperors produced a long period of comparative political and military stability in contrast with the late Republic. With one man in control perhaps the central government was stronger and more able to deal with any threats; or perhaps the soldiers became generally content with their lot.

In this context the cost to the empire of paying the army, the provision of funds for this purpose and for the increasingly expensive donatives, and the relative financial prosperity of the troops are matters which, although difficult to assess, illuminate the interrelation between the army and the social, economic, and political history of the empire. It is striking that although Plutarch recognized the prevalence and importance of lavish gifts of money by the military dynasts, he still believed that the personal conduct of the commander who shared his men's toils was in the end a more effective influence on the troops.[18] In relation to these other factors, how important was money in securing the political loyalty of the Roman army?

2. THE FINANCIAL EMOLUMENTS OF THE ROMAN ARMY: THE COST TO THE EMPIRE

Augustus adapted and developed the republican practice of retaining permanent standing armies in those provinces which needed military defence continuously. He met all the military needs of the empire with a regular professional army of twenty-eight legions, supported by auxiliary troops. This obviated the need for specially levied expeditionary forces to deal with particular crises.[1] Such forces could have a disruptive effect on Augustus' ordered relationship with the army and its commanders. The pay for a legionary soldier was 900 sesterces a year, increased to 1,200 sesterces by Domitian. This sum rose to perhaps 2,000 sesterces a year

[18] Plut., *Mar.* 7.4-5.

[1] See R.E. Smith, *Service in the Post-Marcian Roman Army* (1958), 70 ff. Cf. Dio, 52.27.1 ff.

under Septimius Severus and to 3,000 sesterces under Caracalla.[2] Although there is some doubt about the precise figures, it is clear that there was a substantial improvement in the soldiers' material benefits.[3] Recent studies have convincingly suggested that the *auxilia* were paid at five-sixths of the legionary pay rate. In that case an ordinary soldier will have received 1,000 sesterces a year under Domitian.[4]

Under Augustus the monetary *praemia* paid to discharged soldiers ammounted to 12,000 sesterces for legionaries and 20,000 sesterces for Praetorians. Caracalla fixed the sum of 20,000 sesterces for legionaries and an uncertain amount for the Praetorian Guard. It is not known if he was the first to raise the *praemia* since Augustus.[5]

The recurrent cost of paying the army must have been the single most important financial problem that faced every emperor. Failure to pay promptly might mean political catastrophe. Augustus' twenty-five legions (after AD 9) will have absorbed about 150 million sesterces of State revenue each year, and the various urban troops another 40 million.[6] By the end of his reign there may already have been as many

---

[2] Brunt, 'Pay and Superannuation', 50 ff.; see too G.R. Watson, *Hist.* 5 (1956), 332; *The Roman Soldier*, 104 ff.; D. Breeze, 'Pay Grades and Ranks below the Centurionate', *JRS* 61 (1971), 130; R. Develin, *Latomus* 30 (1971), 687; B. Dobson, 'The Significance of the Centurion and Primipilaris', *ANRW* II.1, 407 ff. Although Develin is right to emphasize the inconclusive nature of the arguments for the amount of the Severan pay rise, his own suggestion that the legionary received 1600 sesterces after Severus' increase is based on the very insecure premise that Dio has correctly preserved the exact total amount of Caracalla's pay rise. In my calculations I have accepted the arguments of Domaszweski and Brunt for legionary pay under Septimius Severus and Caracalla. I find Develin's arguments that Severus introduced the full *annona militaris* (part payment of the troops in kind) inconclusive. The excellent comments of Millar, *Cassius Dio*, 152, n. 3, still seem valid: 'All that can be proved is that this period saw the irregular beginning of what became the system in the fourth century.'

[3] See below, pp. 177-9.

[4] M. Speidel, 'The Pay of the *Auxilia*', *JRS* 63 (1973), 141.

[5] Brunt, (n. 1), 61 ff.

[6] This calculation assumes 25 legions and a paper strength of 5,500 in each legion (Watson, *Roman Soldier*, 13). Legions were perhaps very rarely at full strength, but this variable factor should be balanced by the fact that I have not allowed for the increased pay of the *principales*. To the cost of the legion must be added the salary of 54 centurions (810,000 sesterces) and the *primi ordines* including the *primuspilus* and *primuspilus bis* (240,000 sesterces?) — Dobson, *ANRW*, II.1, 408. The total cost of one legion will have been in the region of

as 150,000 auxiliary troops in the army. If the *auxilia* received five-sixths of legionary pay, this section of the army will have cost about 112 million sesterces a year.[7] On top of all this the emperor had to find money or land for the discharge bonus of veteran troops. These *praemia* perhaps cost Augustus around 48 million sesterces for legionaries and the Praetorians. It is not clear if *auxilia* received *praemia*, but since it was in the emperor's interests to make them an integral and efficient part of the army and cement their loyalty, they must surely have been treated like the rest of the soldiers in this respect. If the auxiliaries did receive *praemia* after twenty-five years service, and this was at five-sixths of the rate for legionaries, about 30 million sesterces will have been added to the bill.[8] This takes no account of increased bonuses for centurions and other officers. On the other hand, land was often given to veterans as their discharge bounty, and this was probably cheaper than a cash handout. All these figures can give no more than an order of magnitude and are certainly an underestimate since they take no account of the cost of the imperial fleets or the salary of senior officers. With these reservations, it may be suggested that annually Augustus needed to find a sum in the area of 350 to 380 million sesterces to finance the army on which the integrity of the empire, and the maintenance of his power within it, depended.

6 million sesterces. If the cohorts of the Praetorian Guard numbered 1,000 men in each (convincingly argued by Passerini, *Le Coorti Pretorie* (1939), 58 ff.; against M. Durry, *Les Cohortes Prétoriennes* (1938), 81 ff.;), the cost will have been 9,000 × 3,000 = 27 million sesterces. To this must be added about 2.25 million sesterces for the 150 centurions who served in Rome (Dobson, op. cit., 427). The soldiers of the Urban Cohorts will have cost about 4.5 million sesterces (3,000 × 1,500), the *Vigiles* about 6.3 million (7,000 × 900).

[7] 150,000 × 750 HS. This calculation takes no account of the increased rates of the officers or cavalrymen. For the number of *auxilia*, see Cheesman, *Auxilia*, 53–6; Kraft, Rekrutierung 140 ff.; *RE* Supp. IX (1962), cols 617–24.

[8] K. Hopkins, *JRS* 70 (1980), 124, has some new ideas for calculating the number of soldiers discharged every year. His figures seem to me too high and to underestimate wastage through war and other causes. In my calculation I assumed that half the soldiers survived until discharge. With an army of about 140,000 and 20 years service, this means that 3,500 men would be discharged every year; 3,500 × 12,000 = 42 million sesterces. About 280 Praetorians were discharged annually; 280 × 20,000 = 5.6 million sesterces. *Auxilia*: with 150,000 auxiliaries and 25 years service, about 3,000 men would be discharged annually; 3000 × 10,000 ($\frac{5}{6}$ of legionary *praemium*) = 30 million sesterces.

A pay rise for such a large force could have widespread financial implications for the empire and must have been a major worry to an emperor, who had to balance the presumed greater affection of the army after such a rise against the possible damage to the economy of Italy and the provinces. After the pay rise granted by Domitian, the annual cost of the army will have been in the region of 600 million sesterces.[9] In Caracalla's reign the cost of the pay of the legions and urban troops alone will have been over 800 million sesterces a year.[10]

These rough calculations allow the conjecture that in the first century AD yearly expenditure on the army consumed at least 40 per cent, and perhaps even up to one half, of the State's available revenue, which has been plausibly estimated at a sum in excess of 800 million sesterces.[11] Dio may not

[9] The cost of one legion will have been c. 8 million sesterces (legionaries — 5,500 × 1,200 = 6,600,000 sesterces; centurions — 54 × 20,000 = 1,080,000 sesterces; *primi ordines* and *primipili* — 360,000 sesterces). Thirty legions in service would cost c. 240 million sesterces. Praetorians — 10,000 × 4,000 = 40 million sesterces; Urban Cohorts — 4,000 × 2,000 = 8 million sesterces; *Vigiles* — 7,000 × 1,200 = 8.4 million sesterces. To these sums should be added 3 million sesterces for the cost of the 150 centurions in Rome; and so the total cost for the urban troops was around 60 million sesterces. The *auxilia* may have numbered about 190,000, of which c.48,000 were *alares* (Cheesman, *Auxilia*, appendix I; *RE*. Supp. IX.), although these figures are probably an underestimate. On a very rough calculation, the auxilia may have cost about 215 million sesterces a year by the second century.

It is not known if Domitian increased the amount of praemia; if he did not, and if soldiers served for 25 years or more, it is possible that the cost of this item remained relatively stable, even though the size of the army had increased: 165,000 legionaries — about 3,300 discharged annually × 12,000 = 40 million sesterces; on the same calculation the urban troops will have cost about 8 million sesterces in *praemia*; 190,000 *auxilia* — 3,800 discharged annually × 10,000 = 38 million sesterces.

[10] *Legionaries* — 181,500 × 3,000 = c.545 million sesterces. *Centurions, primi ordines, primipili* — c.115 million sesterces. And so the cost of the legions will have been c.660 million sesterces. *Praetorians* — 10,000 × 10,000 = 100 million sesterces. *Urban Cohorts* — 4,000 × 5,000 = 20 million sesterces. *Vigiles* — 7,000 × 3,000 = 21 million sesterces. To these figures can be added about 7.5 million sesterces as the cost of the centurions in Rome.

[11] See K. Hopkins, 'Taxes and Trade in the Roman Empire, 200 BC–AD 400', *JRS* 70 (1980), 101, especially 116–20. Professor Hopkins' suggestion of 824 million sesterces as a plausible figure for the budget in the first century of the imperial period, means that the estimates of T. Frank, *An Economic Survey of Ancient Rome*, V, 4 ff. are too high. See too P.A. Brunt, 'The Revenues of Rome', *JRS* 71 (1981), 161, a review of L. Neesen, *Untersuchungen zu den direkten Staatsabgaben der römischen Kaiserzeit* (1980).

have been far wide of the mark when he made Agrippa say in 29 BC: 'You must obtain a large amount of money from all sources; for current revenues will certainly not suffice for the upkeep of the army and everything else.'[12] The cost of the army dominated the financial life of the empire.

The *Res Gestae* give a hint of the relative importance of the army in Augustus' monetary disbursements. He lists several irregular payments to the people, a grant to the public treasury, the cost of gifts to the Capitol, and various public works undertaken at his personal expense. The total is about 800 million sesterces between 31 BC and AD 6. Much of his expenditure, however, is not itemised in detail, for example, the cost of games; in reality, the emperor may have spent as much again. Nevertheless, in the same period 1,550 million sesterces were paid out in *praemia* and other rewards for the troops, and in a grant to help the military treasury.[13] It is significant that in this personal record of Augustus' achievements, these military costs alone (excluding regular pay) seem at least to equal the various other financial demands his position made inevitable. The sheer magnitude of the sums expended on the army may be further illustrated by the recent calculation that in the Roman world at the end of the Republic 4.8 million sesterces would have been sufficient to feed about 10,000 families at subsistence level for one year.[14]

The financial burden imposed by the army was increased by irregular distributions of cash (donatives), usually to celebrate particular events.[15] The amount of these payments was not directly connected with regular pay and owed much to the political circumstances of the time and the character of the emperor. It is necessary, therefore, to examine the evidence reign by reign, though the literary sources give a very incomplete picture. It was not until the second century that donatives regularly matched the extravagance of the late

[12] 52.6.

[13] *RG* 15, 17, 18, 19-21. For the games, see 22, and Brunt and Moore, *Res Gestae Divi Augusti, ad loc.* Payments to soldiers: RG 15-16; cf. 3.3.

[14] K. Hopkins, *Conquerors and Slaves*, pp. 41 and 39, n. 52.

[15] For donatives in general see, *RE* V (1905), 1542 ff.; Passerini, *Le Coorti Pretorie*, 114 ff.; Forni, *Il Reclutamento*, 35 ff. For the occasions on which donatives were distributed, see below, pp. 186ff.

Republic. The soldiers of Lucullus received 20,000 sesterces for his campaigns in the East.[16] At Pompey's triumph the smallest award was 6,000 sesterces.[17] Octavian promised his soldiers 20,000 sesterces after the second capture of Rome.[18] This was about twenty times a full year's pay. The 'Liberators' too were very generous: in the campaign of Philippi a donative of 6,000 sesterces was paid and Brutus apparently offered 8,000 sesterces to the defeated troops of Cassius.[19]

Augustus granted few donatives during his reign. In 29 BC he gave 1,000 sesterces to 120,000 of his veterans, a grant that was bigger than any single gift to the plebs at Rome.[20] In his will he left 1,000 sesterces per man to the Praetorians, 500 to the Urban Cohorts, and 300 to the legions.[21] It seems that Augustus succeeded in ending the tradition of exorbitant donatives established in the late Republic. Tiberius followed his example, although doubled the legacies of Augustus in his own name,[22] and left the same amount in his will.[23] However the grant of 4,000 sesterces to the Guard after the fall of Sejanus shows a dramatic increase in imperial benevolence, even though it was restricted to the Praetorians.[24] Gaius followed the practice of doubling his predecessor's legacies, at least for the Praetorian Guard.[25] In addition he paid 400 sesterces per man to the soldiers assembled for the invasion of Britain.[26] This is important as the first record of the amount of a donative paid to the soldiers in the provinces while on campaign.[27]

The unique political circumstances of the accession of Claudius dictated special measures, and the huge donative of 15,000 sesterces paid to the Praetorians[28] had its

[16] Horace, *Ep.* 2.32.33; Plut., *Lucullus* 37.4.
[17] Plut., *Pomp.* 45.3.
[18] Appian, *BC* 3.94. See R. Syme, *The Roman Revolution*, 177; 187.
[19] Appian, *BC* 4.100; cf. 118; Plut., *Brutus* 44.
[20] *RG* 15.3.
[21] Suet., *Aug.* 101.2; Tac., *A* 1.8.
[22] Suet., *Tib.* 48.2.
[23] ibid. 76; Dio, 59.2.
[24] Suet., *Tib.* 48.2.
[25] Dio, 59.2.3.
[26] Suet., *Cal.* 46.
[27] See below, pp. 188–9.
[28] Suet., *Cl.* 10.4.

precedent in the violent upheavals of the Republic rather than the relative stability of the early empire. The donative was five times the normal year's pay of a Praetorian. Coins celebrating the Guard were perhaps minted to be distributed as part of this donative.[29] On the anniversary of the accession each Praetorian received 100 sesterces, presumably as a token payment.[30]

Suetonius mentions only the promise of money to the Guard, but this cannot be pressed to mean that no other troops got money. Josephus notes specifically that Claudius 'promised a similar grant to the armies wherever they were stationed'.[31] Josephus probably means not that every soldier received 15,000 sesterces, but that they were all promised a donative of some kind. The bequests left by Augustus and Tiberius were paid on a proportional basis in that the urban troops got 50 per cent and the legionaries 30 per cent of the sum given to the Praetorians. It is clear that the *auxilia* were not included in these grants (except perhaps Roman citizens in the *cohortes civium Romanorum*), and Dio confirms that in AD 37 only citizen troops received Gaius' donative.[32] It may be conjectured that Claudius paid a donative to the legionaries consisting of 30 per cent of the sum paid to the Praetorian Guard, namely 4,500 sesterces.[33] In which case, the total cost of Claudius' donative to his troops will have been approximately 833 million sesterces; of this the Urban Cohorts and the Praetorian Guard will have received about 165 million sesterces[34], and the legions

---

[29] *BMC* I, pp. 165–6.

[30] Dio, 60.12.4.

[31] *AJ* 19.247. Josephus, however, thought that the donative was 20,000 sesterces per man.

[32] 59.2.3.

[33] It could be argued that Gaius, by doubling Tiberius' bequest to the Praetorian Guard, but not those to the Urban Cohorts and legionaries (Dio, 59.2.1 ff.), established a new proportional payment, i.e., the legionaries received 15 per cent of the sum enjoyed by the Praetorian Guard. Claudius could hardly be more parsimonious than Gaius, but would he wish to follow the example of his murdered predecessor?

[34] *Praetorians* — 9,000 × 15,000 = 135 million sesterces. *Urban Cohorts* — 4,000 × 7,500 = 30 million sesterces. These calculations are based on the assumption that the Urban Cohorts received 50 per cent of the grant to the Praetorians, and take no account of increased rates for officers.

668 million.[35] This huge expenditure on one donative was more than twice the cost of paying the army for one year.

It is reasonable to assume that all accession donatives after Claudius were paid to the legions in proportion, even when the sources do not mention this specifically. Plutarch records how in 68 Nymphidius promised a donative to the Guard and in proportion to those serving outside Italy.[36] The *Historia Augusta* describes the accession of Marcus Aurelius and Lucius Verus as follows: '. . . castra praetoria petierunt et . . . ob participatum imperium militibus promiserunt et ceteris pro rata'.[37] The phrase 'ceteris pro rata' should most naturally be taken as referring to the rest of the troops in the army: 'They went to the Praetorian camp and promised a donative to the Guardsmen in honour of their joint succession, and in proportion to the other troops'.[38] It is indeed very difficult to believe that emperors could avoid paying a donative at least to all the legionaries at their accession, especially after the civil wars of 68-9 when provincial legions had proved decisive. Furthermore, Trajan, Hadrian, and Commodus assumed the purple while with the legions. It also seems plausible that the auxiliary troops, who formed an increasingly large part of the army and took a great share in the fighting, could not indefinitely be excluded from these donatives. There is some support for this suggestion in the fact that Hadrian, during his inspection of the troops in Africa in 128, granted a donative to the auxiliary cavalry cohort (*Ala I Pannoniorum*) because of the successful performance of their exercises (p.79).

Claudius' donative to some extent acted as a precedent. Dio says that Nero promised the Guard all that Claudius had given them.[39] In addition, after the conspiracy of Piso he bestowed a monthly grain dole on the Praetorians and paid

---

[35] 5,500 × 27 × 4,500 = about 668 million sesterces. If, however, the legionaries received only 15 per cent of the amount paid to the Guardsmen, the cost will have been about 334 million sesterces. These calculations take no account of increased payments to officers.

[36] *Galba* 2.2.

[37] *Vit. Marc. Ant. Phil.* 7.9-10.

[38] Contrast Magie, *Loeb* vol. I, p. 150, n. 4; A.R. Birley, *Lives of the Later Caesars* (Penguin, 1976), p. 115; they believe that the phrase refers to the officers.

[39] 61.3.1.

a donative of 2,000 sesterces per man.[40] Unfortunately, little definite evidence exists for the size of donatives in 68-9. A 'bigger than usual' donative was promised in Galba's name but not paid. Plutarch says that it was 30,000 sesterces for the Praetorians and 5,000 for the soldiers in the provinces.[41] These figures may be hostile exaggeration, but perhaps such amounts would not have been out of place in an attempt to overthrow such a well-established dynasty. Few other definite figures are mentioned. Otho promised 5,000 sesterces to his Praetorians after a serious outbreak of indiscipline; Vitellius' troops were dissuaded from sacking Vienne by a gift of 300 sesterces per man.[42]

Vespasian's initial promises to the Syrian legions were restrained and we are told he did not give more to the soldiers in civil war than others had in peace.[43] This is no help in finding a precise sum, although the mention of what others had given in time of peace probably refers to the donative paid at the accession of Claudius and Nero. But it is not clear if Tacitus means that the total cost of Vespasian's largess to the troops did not exceed 15,000 sesterces per man, or that this was the amount of the donative promised at his proclamation alone. When Mucianus and Domitian arrived in Rome after the defeat of Vitellius, only 100 sesterces were distributed to the troops.[44] But this may have been a gesture of good will until the emperor amassed enough cash to pay the full amount of the donative.

There is no evidence for the cost of donatives paid by Nerva and Trajan. According to the *Historia Augusta* Hadrian granted 'a double largess in honour of his assumption of the imperial power'.[45] This may imply that there was a recognized amount for the donative paid at the accession of an emperor. Perhaps the 15,000 sesterces paid by Claudius and Nero had become the standard sum. Yet it seems unlikely that Hadrian can have doubled this figure in view of his

---

[40] Suet., *Ner.* 10.1; Tac., *A* 15.72.
[41] Suet., *Galba* 16.1; Plut., *Galba* 2.2.
[42] Tac., *H* 1.82.
[43] *H* 2.82.
[44] Dio, 64.22.2.
[45] *Vit. Had.* 5.7. Cf 23. 14.

reputation for good discipline and strict control of the army. We know that Marcus Aurelius paid at his accession a donative of 20,000 sesterces to the Praetorians. It is possible that this figure had been paid by Hadrian and left unchanged by Antoninus Pius, about whom there is no evidence, and Marcus. In that case, since Hadrian doubled the donative, the normal amount before his reign will have been 10,000 sesterces. This figure may have been established by Vespasian, whose offers could be described as 'restrained', perhaps in relation to the promises of Nymphidius and the actual payments of Claudius.

The donative of 20,000 sesterces paid out by Marcus Aurelius and Lucius Verus is the first attested largess comparable in amount to payments made in the civil wars of the late Republic. In 192 Pertinax thought that a promise of 12,000 sesterces was sufficient to win over the Praetorians. However in a speech to the Senate he subsequently pretended that he had offered 20,000.[46] This was apparently now the recognized figure and suggests that Commodus had matched his father's donative. In the so called 'auction of the empire', Didius Julianus offered the Praetorians 25,000 sesterces, only 5,000 more than the respected Marcus had paid.[47] Nevertheless, this grant is the largest attested donative paid by any emperor.

Septimius Severus is alleged to have offered a bigger than usual donative to the Pannonian legions before the march on Rome.[48] In fact he paid only 1,000 sesterces per man, although the troops had demanded 10,000.[49] Even if the sum of 1,000 sesterces was only a down payment, the amount sought by the soldiers was moderate by the standards of the time. On the tenth anniversary of his assumption of power Severus bestowed 1,000 sesterces per man on the Praetorian Guard.[50] Although the extravagance of Caracalla incurred the censure of senators, only one donative is known from his reign — 10,000 sesterces after the murder of Geta and his

---

[46] For Marcus Aurelius, see n. 37; for Pertinax, see Dio, 74.1.2; 8.3.
[47] 74.11.3 ff.
[48] Vit. Sev. 5.2.
[49] Dio, 46.46.7; Vit. Sev. 7.6.
[50] Dio, 76.1.1.

seizure of sole power.[51] Perhaps the pay rises awarded by Severus and Caracalla allowed them to moderate the number and amount of donatives paid. Macrinus gave the soldiers 3,000 sesterces when he took the name 'Antoninus'.[52] Later, faced with the disintegrating loyalty of his army, he offered 20,000, but actually paid 4,000.[53] Elagabal celebrated his marriage to Cornelia Paula with a dinner for the troops costing 1,000 sesterces per man.[54] Beyond this there is no evidence for the amounts paid in donatives in the Severan era.

The amount granted to the soldiers in largess had no obvious or consistent connection with the regular rates of pay. It is true that the donatives of Claudius and Marcus Aurelius are five times the year's pay of a Praetorian. But this may have been merely a convenient round sum. The extent of imperial largess was based on the political circumstances, available resources, the judgement and character of an individual emperor, and what his predecessor had granted.[55] Since donatives were irregular in amount and timing, this may have lessened the drain on imperial finances. But in practice donatives were always paid on certain occasions, notably the accession, and so at the start of every emperor's reign the monetary requirements of the army will have been thrust upon his attention. What is more, since some donatives were needed unexpectedly, this element of unpredictability must have caused difficulty, since the treasury might be empty at the crucial moment. In the context of the financial problems faced by Marcus Aurelius, it is significant that the donative paid at his accession cost 240 million sesterces for the troops in Rome alone, and if it was extended to the legionaries on a proportional basis of 30 per cent, it will have cost in the region of a further 1,000 million sesterces.

It is impossible to produce a detailed and coherent survey of the economic and financial consequences of the pay and emoluments of the Roman army for the emperor and the

---

[51] Herodian, 4.4.7.
[52] Dio, 78.19.2.
[53] 78.34.2; 36.1 f.
[54] 80.9.
[55] See below, pp. 191ff.

territories he ruled. There are only a few scattered indications of the endless problem of filling the imperial coffers to help keep the army contented and loyal. This reflects both the interests of the sources, who rarely seem concerned with economic measures except in an anecdotal fashion, and the fact that the rewards of military service and indeed imperial resources were among the 'secrets of ruling'.

Augustus clearly found difficulty in paying the discharge *praemia* for his veterans. He introduced a proposal in the Senate in AD 6 for the establishment of the military treasury to pay these bonuses.[56] Eventually he persuaded the Senate to agree to his idea of a 5 per cent death duty on the estates of Roman citizens; the treasury was also supported by a one per cent tax on auction sales. Furthermore the emperor accepted gifts from communities, foreign kings, and Roman citizens, and paid in 170 million sesterces of his own money (this would provide discharge payments for 14,000 men), promising a contribution every year. The payment of this sum may indicate that Augustus was not so much worried about cash in hand as the budgeting of this fund for the future. Subsequently, senators objected so much to the new tax that in AD 13 Augustus suggested a land tax instead; but this was even more obnoxious to the Senate, and so the death duties were retained and Augustus got his own way as he had always intended.[57] Obviously the emperor still thought that these funds were essential to the successful operation of the treasury. Indeed they were probably insufficient since one of the complaints of the mutineers in AD 14 was that 'old men disfigured by wounds, are serving in their thirtieth or fortieth year'.[58] If soldiers were being kept beyond the regular twenty years plus five as a reserve, this presumably indicates an inability to pay the discharge bonuses.[59] Tiberius was worried by the cost of the money grants and accelerated discharges (after sixteen years service) conceded to the troops

---

[56] Dio, 55.25.1 ff. (Dio, however, is in error when he says that the treasury was also designed to pay soldiers' salaries; cf. *RG* 17.2.)

[57] Dio, 56.28.4 ff.

[58] Tac., *A* 1.16; 31.

[59] See the interesting note by K. Hopkins, *JRS* 70 (1980), 124; the longer the period of military service, the fewer soldiers survive to discharge age.

by Germanicus in the mutiny of AD 14.[60] The problem of finding cash for the *praemia* persisted, and in 15, amid appeals for the abolition of the one per cent auction tax, Tiberius insisted that the military treasury needed the funds. He added that the state's resources were indeed incapable of meeting the financial burden unless the soldiers were not discharged until after twenty years service. So the concessions hastily made to the mutineers in the previous year were cancelled.[61] If in AD 23 Tiberius really did intend a trip to the provinces because of the large number of veterans to be discharged, it may be that the problem was still so serious that the commanders on the spot were reluctant to act themselves.[62]

Despite these difficulties there was no further trouble with the army in Tiberius' reign and he managed to leave a surplus of at least 2,700 million sesterces to Gaius.[63] However such reserves could easily and quickly be dissipated by extravagant and improvident emperors, and by the end of Nero's reign it was said that he had allowed the army's pay to fall into arrears while the provinces were oppressed by his exactions.[64] He was also unable to pay veterans' discharge *praemia*. If this was widespread and prolonged it doubtless will have seriously damaged his popularity with the army; but it is possible that Suetonius' generalization was based on one or two well known incidents.

Vespasian was bent on creating a reserve of 4,000 million sesterces, and his practice of increasing and sometimes doubling taxes may well have enabled him to go some way towards realizing this aim. This will have made it easier for Domitian to raise the soldiers' pay without a further increase in taxes. Nevertheless, the pay rise, coupled with other heavy expenditure in his reign, seems to have placed him in a difficult position. In a letter to his procurator he says that the provinces were barely equal to the most essential demands, and this suggests that in his view they were now taxed up to

[60] Tac., *A* 1.52.
[61] 1.78. The soldiers were now to serve for twenty years, plus five as a reserve.
[62] *A* 4.4.
[63] Suet., *Cal.* 37.3.
[64] Dio, 62.11 ff.; Suet., *Ner.* 32.1.

the hilt.[65] According to Suetonius, Domitian became 'rapacious because of lack of funds'.[66] The financial difficulties under Nerva and early in Trajan's reign were perhaps due in part to the abandonment of Domitian's rapacious devices. It is worth noting that the treasury had to meet the special calls for donatives to the plebs and soldiers incidental to the accession of new emperors in rapid succession in 79-81 and 96-8. So military costs had some share in creating financial difficulties, and it is possible that the increase in pay under Domitian absorbed more revenue than was prudent unless the emperors practised economies in building and court expenditure, at any rate until Trajan's conquests produced more funds.

Emergencies, particularly military activity, always created financial problems because the empire seemed to lack systematic budgeting. Despite the reserves Antoninus Pius left, Marcus Aurelius was short of money, no doubt because of the cost of the wars and the decline in revenue following enemy devastation and the great plague. His huge accession donative will have contributed to the exhaustion of the treasury. Dio says that the emperor was most economical and did not place extra levies on the people even though he was forced to pay out far more than the usual expenditure.[67] At one stage of the war at least, the shortage of cash was critical. The treasuries were exhausted and Marcus was unwilling to impose fresh exactions. He held an auction of imperial furniture and artefacts in the forum and the proceeds went on military pay.[68] Marcus by this action presumably wished to highlight the state's exceptional financial difficulties and his own willingness to make sacrifices. Another story in Dio illustrates the dilemma that confronted Marcus. After a successful battle against the Germans, the victorious soldiers requested a donative. But the emperor refused, declaring that anything they got more than usual (i.e. normal pay) would

[65] McCrum and Woodhead, *Select Documents of the Flavian Emperors* (1961), no. 466.
[66] *Dom*. 3.2. Suetonius also suggests that military expenses weighed heavily on the emperor — 12.1. I cannot agree with the view of R. Syme (*JRS* 20 (1930), 55 = *Roman Papers* I, 1) about finances under Domitian.
[67] 72.32.3.
[68] Zonaras, 12.1 (see *Loeb* edition of Dio, vol IX, p. 70).

be squeezed from the blood of their relatives and families. He meant that excessive military expenditure could only be recouped by exactions on the provinces. The emperor concluded, 'Only god can decide about the fate of the sovereignty'.[69] Marcus was aware that to oppose the soldiers' wishes and refuse a donative might even place his own rule in some jeopardy.

Septimius Severus, who granted the first pay rise after Domitian, was criticized by Dio 'because he weighed the State down with excessive financial expenditure'.[70] Caracalla effusively promised the soldiers, 'all the treasuries are yours'.[71] He was determined to lavish money on them and apparently was unconcerned about those who had to suffer in the process. 'No one in the world should have any money except me, so that I may bestow it on my soldiers.' When his mother rebuked the emperor for the money spent on the army and the dissipation of the sources of revenue, he pointed to his sword and replied, 'Do not worry, mother, the money will not run out as long as we have this.'[72] Caracalla seems to have lived up to his promises. Dio comments that he was fond of spending money on his soldiers, and to pay for this he crushed and robbed all the rest of mankind, and the senators most of all.[73] This hostile account is likely to be exaggerated, but there is no doubt that senators bitterly resented his huge expenditures on the army and believed that this had a deleterious effect on the financial structure of the empire and the people who had to pay to support it. In this respect Dio is undoubtedly right. Indeed the problems created by Caracalla are illustrated by the fate of his successor Macrinus. He wrote in desperation to the Prefect of the City, pointing out that he found it impossible to give the soldiers their full pay and the donatives they were receiving, and yet impossible not to give it. He pointed specifically to the vast cost of Caracalla's pay rise.[74] Macrinus had intended to leave intact the pay and privileges of serving

[69] 71.3.3–4.
[70] 75.2.3.
[71] 77.3.2.
[72] 77.10.4.
[73] 77.9.1 ff.
[74] 78.36.2.

soldiers but reduce the pay of those newly enlisted to the level established by Septimius Severus. But collusion between the new recruits and the old soldiers prevented this, and an unstable regime proceeded to its ruin.

All this evidence produces a kaleidoscopic and unsatisfactory picture of the interaction of the cost of the army and the social and economic history of the imperial period. We can often only guess at the precise difficulties caused by military expenditure in any one reign, the misery of the people in the provinces, who ultimately bore the burden of cost and suffered the depredations of soldiers whom perhaps the government was unwilling to check, the difficulties of the officials carrying out the exactions, and the anxiety experienced by every emperor as he ensured that there was sufficient ready cash for pay and donatives. For in the end it was not god but the soldiers who 'decided about the sovereignty'. On top of the cost of the army, money had to be found for distributions to the people of Rome (*congiaria*), games, building projects, the imperial court, salaries of officials, and the special burden imposed by military campaigns. Indeed the extra cost of large scale military activity may often have restricted imperial policy except in emergency or unless great booty could be expected.[75] Even the vast personal wealth of emperors[76] could not itself support 400,000 men scattered round the Roman world.

3. FELIX MILITIA?

Juvenal begins his bitter satire on the privileges and advantages of life in the army by asking, 'Who can count up the rewards of prosperous military service?'[1] Elsewhere he paints a picture of a father, greedy for money, who determines to get his son into the army as a centurion.[2] But was the ordinary soldier comparatively well off?

The mutineers of AD 14 complained about the inferior

---

[75] See below, pp. 397ff.
[76] See Millar, *ERW*, 133 ff.

[1] 16.1–2: 'quis numerare queat felicis praemia, Galli,/militiae?'
[2] 14.193–9.

land distributed as discharge *praemia* and the low *stipendium* out of which they had to pay for clothes, weapons, tents, and bribes to the centurions in order to avoid chores. To them military service seemed harsh and unfruitful ('gravis et infructuosa'), and they demanded a wage of 4 sesterces per day (instead of 2½).[3] There is no reason to doubt that these grievances were sincerely felt. After 31 BC, with little prospect of lucrative wars and few donatives in Augustus' reign, life in the army perhaps did not seem very attractive in relation to the physical risk involved.

Domitian's pay rise increased legionary pay from 2½ sesterces to about 3.2 sesterces per day. Auxiliary troopers got about 2.7 sesterces and Praetorians 11 sesterces daily. By the time of Caracalla legionary pay had risen to approximately 8 sesterces daily, Praetorian pay to about 27.3 sesterces. In the first century military pay was certainly not generous. A labourer in Rome could earn 3-4 sesterces per day, and a farm labourer half this.[4] And in Syria a workman could earn one Syrian *drachma* a day (3 sesterces).[5] In addition a soldier's pay was further reduced by the compulsory stoppages for food, clothing, arms, and other payments.[6] Clearly the Roman soldier did not live at subsistence level, since an average family could probably survive on about 450 sesterces a year for wheat.[7] But it is optimistic to think that the soldier was able to spend 80-90 per cent of his salary on items other than food.[8] This does not allow for the stoppages from his pay and the fact that although he was not allowed to marry, the soldier often took a permanent concubine, and presumably he would want to support his woman and the bastard children of such a liaison.[9]

[3] Tac., *A* 1.17.
[4] T. Frank. *ESAR*, I, 188 ff.; 384 ff.; R.P. Duncan-Jones, *The Economy of the Roman Empire* (1974), 11-12; 54.
[5] T. Frank, *ESAR*, IV, 178 ff. This sum probably included the workman's keep.
[6] Brunt, 'Pay and Superannuation', 52 f.; 60; Watson, *The Roman Soldier*, 102 ff. Cf Tac., *H* 1.46: Otho ended the practice by which soldiers were expected to pay the centurions to gain exemption from duties. In future the cost of this was met by the emperor himself.
[7] Hopkins, *Conquerors and Slaves*, 39, n. 52.
[8] As suggested by Duncan-Jones (n. 4), 12.
[9] See below, pp. 301-2.

What made the soldier better off than any civilian labourer was the certainty of regular employment year by year; a labourer who earned 3-4 sesterces daily could not always find work on a day to day basis. If he worked for half the year he would earn only about 700 sesterces. Furthermore, the soldier enjoyed a superior status. There was always the chance of a cash donative and the certainty of a discharge bonus; even if the plots of land were not always satisfactory, they went part of the way towards freeing the soldier from anxiety about old age. In addition, he was not subject to taxes and requisitions and enjoyed certain other privileges.[10] To many people in the empire who lived at subsistence level, the well-fed soldier with his ordered existence in well-built and hygenic barracks must have seemed comfortably off.

Pay rises for the army were few because it was simply too expensive, given the overall cost of the military establishment. By the time of Caracalla, however, the legionary's pay had increased by nearly three and a half times its face value. It is another question whether military pay kept pace with the debasement of the silver coinage and possible price rises. Certainly in the second century there was a marked decrease in the silver content of the *denarius*, which, by the time of Septimius Severus, contained only 43-56 per cent of pure silver.[11] At the same time papyri provide some evidence for a rise in prices. But the debasement of the coinage may well have passed unnoticed until the time of Commodus. Furthermore, most of the evidence for big price rises concerns Egyptian wheat, the price of which fluctuated greatly because of local and seasonal difficulties.[12] Therefore its price is not good evidence for the effects of inflation in general terms and the debasement of the silver coinage. A recent study has concluded that the worst period of price increases was in the last part of the third century, and that

[10] See pp. 207ff. and Appendix 3.

[11] T. Frank, *ESAR*, V, 92-3; T. Pekáry, 'Studien zur römischen Wahrungs und Finanzgeschicte', *Hist.* 8 (1959), 443; M. Crawford, 'Finance, Coinage and Money from the Severans to Constantine', *ANRW* II. 2, 560; see also K. Hopkins, *JRS* 1980, 115 ff.

[12] Frank, *ESAR*, II, 303.

rates of inflation were slow during the first two centuries of the principate, with relatively stable prices.[13]

Even if this is so, the financial position of the soldiers improved only slowly, until the time of the Severi, particularly Caracalla. It should be emphasized, however, that donatives, which increased in frequency and amount in the first two centuries, helped to make soldiers better off. Some, indeed, are found owning slaves, land, and other property, and contracting financial deals.[14] And they were able to save money. Saturninus financed his revolt against Domitian from the savings of the camp bank of the legions of Upper Germany. The emperor subsequently prohibited the deposit of more than 1,000 sesterces by any one soldier in the camp bank.[15] A papyrus from Alexandria, apparently relating to the pay accounts of two legionaries, shows that in the course of one year Q. Julius Proculus, after all deductions, was able to save about 28 per cent of his pay, and with previous savings had 343 *drachmae* on deposit. C. Valerius Germanus was not so lucky, and saved only 22 per cent of his pay and had 188 *drachmae* on deposit.[16] There is still no general agreement on the question why the two men do not receive the full amount of each pay installment, at this time 300 *drachmae*. Nevertheless, the point is that both these soldiers, despite the compulsory deductions, were able to save a comfortable proportion of their salary.

Not all the money acquired by soldiers can be explained on the hypothesis of legacies or peculation and extortion. It seems that in the first two centuries of the imperial period the overall financial and social position of the troops was superior to that of most common people. By the time of the Severan dynasty the material position of the ordinary soldier had improved well beyond anything a civilian of the lower orders could expect. Furthermore, apart from the possibility

[13] Duncan-Jones (n. 4), 12. It is, however, not safe to use military pay rates as a guide to levels of inflation in the first two centuries (p. 10). Increases in military pay had more to do with politics than economics (see below, pp. 181ff). Cf. M. Crawford (n. 11), especially, 568; Hopkins (n. 11), 115, and n. 40.

[14] See below, pp. 280–1.

[15] Suet., *Dom.* 7.3.

[16] R.O. Fink, *Roman Military Documents on Papyrus* (1971), 243 ff. and the bibliography there quoted.

of enrichment by war or donatives, there was the chance of promotion to the ranks of the *principales* or junior officers, the highest class of whom received three times as much as a legionary. A soldier who managed to gain promotion to the centurionate could look forward to a very lucrative career. It can be surmised that this was the attraction of military service. Soldiers were hardly well off in absolute terms and no doubt often grumbled; but although there were risks inherent in the profession, the regularity of payment, the discharge bonus, the various additional privileges and opportunities, and perhaps the conviviality of camp life could make men of low degree reasonably content in relation to the opportunities otherwise open to them. Of course much depended on luck and what the individual made of it. One young soldier wrote home to his parents thus:

Dear mother, I hope that you are in good health. When you get this letter please send me some money. I have absolutely nothing left since I bought a donkey-cart and used up all my money on it. Please send me a riding coat, oil, and especially my monthly allowance. The last time I was home you promised not to leave me without any money, but now you are treating me like a dog. My father came to visit me yesterday, but he gave me nothing. Everyone is making fun of me now and saying that although my father is a soldier, he gives me nothing. Valerius' mother sent him a pair of pants, some oil, a food parcel, and some money. Please send me some money and don't leave me in this state. Love to everybody at home. Your loving son.[17]

It is interesting that this family with two members in the army was apparently quite well off; the young soldier could expect a regular allowance and gifts, and was rich enough to buy a cart and donkey. His own improvidence had caused his plight. For this recruit at least, life in general seems to have been quite pleasant. Indeed many soldiers may well have agreed with the sentiments of Apollinaris, a recruit to the fleet who had been sent to Misenum, and who wrote to his mother sometime in the second century:

I want you to know, mother, that I arrived in Rome in excellent health on 25 September, and was posted to Misenum, although I do not yet

[17] *BGU* 814.

know the name of my unit. For I had not yet set out to Misenum when I wrote you this letter. I want you, mother, to look after yourself and not to worry about me. For I have come to a fine place.[18]

4. PAY AND POLITICS

A 'money-maker' is how Dio describes Julius Caesar. The money was mainly for military expenditure, and Caesar declared that power was obtained, protected, and developed by two things, soldiers and money, and that they were closely connected with each other. For armies were kept together by proper pay and emoluments and these were obtained by force of arms; and if one of the two were lacking then the other would collapse at the same time.[1] At least from the time of Sulla[2] the Roman legions had frequently been virtually a mercenary force hired by individual commanders to execute their private political plans.[3] Commanders over-indulged their troops; for they might be outbid,[4] unless they could build up loyalty by other means.[5]

In the Republic money was sometimes given to individual soldiers as a reward for valour,[6] and doubtless a great public spectacle was created on these occasions. Even on routine pay distributions the commander himself might take charge. Livy, writing of Scipio in 206 BC, states that the absence of the commander through illness prevented the payment of the troops on time,[7] which implies that it was normal at least for this commander to preside personally while the money was being counted out. Indeed this may have been the usual practice, and when the emperor or a member of the imperial family was present with the troops, he might take personal charge. In AD 70, during the siege of Jerusalem, Titus, who ranked as a prince, staged a formal pay parade at which he presided himself while the troops paraded in full armour

---

[18] *Select Papyri* (*Loeb*) I, no. 111.

[1] Dio, 42.49.4.

[2] Plut., *Sulla* 12.8-9; cf. Nepos, *Eumenes* 8; Appian, *BC* 5.17; Sallust, *Cat.* 11.5 f.

[3] Appian casually refers to Octavian's troops as mercenaries — *BC* 3.197.

[4] Appian *BC* 3.43-4. Octavian circulated pamphlets contrasting the alleged miserliness of Antony with his own generosity.

[5] See above, pp. 32ff.

[6] Caesar, *BC* 5.53.5; cf. *BG* 8.4.1; *TLL* s.v. 'duplex'.

[7] 28.29.2; cf. Caesar, *BC* 3.53.5.

and the officers counted out the money to each man in a ceremony that lasted for four days.

The idenfication of the emperor as the sole source of the army's financial benefits is vividly illustrated by a letter written in the second century by Apion, a new recruit to the fleet, to his father: 'When I arrived in Misenum, I received from Caesar three gold pieces as my travelling expenses. And everything goes well with me.'[8] Of course the emperor did not stand on the quayside to hand over the travelling expenses. But it is important that Apion, who must have received his gold pieces from some officer, assumes that they came directly from the emperor.

There is a little more evidence for the association of emperors with donatives. It is helpful to consider the occasional distribution of money by the emperor to the plebs (*congiarium*). Several coin types bearing the legend 'congiarium' or 'liberalitas' ('generosity') portray this event, and it is possible that the coins were specially minted for the distribution. A coin of Nero with the legend 'The Bestowal of Money on the People' shows the emperor togate sitting on a stool on a high platform approached by a ladder. An official hands out the money to a citizen with a child.[9] However a coin issued under Hadrian shows the emperor seated alone on a platform, distributing money in person.[10] This became the normal way of depicting the distribution scene; other officials disappear or fade into the background and emphasis is placed on the direct contact between emperor and citizen, although sometimes the 'generosity' is personified. In all these scenes the right hand of the emperor is extended, symbolizing his personal participation in the distribution of cash.[11]

[8] Jos., *BJ* 5.349 (Titus); *BGU* 423 = *Select Papyri* I, no 112 (Apion). Money, and officials to organize the payment of the troops, accompanied imperial campaigns — Pflaum, Carrières, 224; *ILS* 1573; Pliny, *NH* 7.129.

[9] *BMC* I, p. 274, no. 136. See in general, P. Hamberg, *Studies in Roman Imperial Art* (1945), 32. The same general type is found for other emperors: Titus (*BMC* II, p. 139, no. 629), Trajan (III, p. 147, no. 712), Hadrian (III, p. 404, no. 1136).

[10] III, p. 275, nos. 291-5.

[11] Other emperors: Pius (IV, p. 201), Marcus and Lucius Verus (IV, p. 589), Commodus (IV, pp. 700; 826), Marcus and Commodus (IV, p. 658), Pertinax (V, p. 8), Caracalla (V, p. 482), Macrinus (V, p. 506), Severus Alexander (VI, nos. 6,8, 206, 564). For the personification of Liberalitas, see Hamberg, op. cit. For the significance of the gesture, see Brilliant, *Gesture and Rank*, 132-3.

To have had any point at all these coin types must have given a reasonably accurate picture of what went on at these well-known events. Perhaps, then, the emperor usually presided and occasionally handed out the money himself. Pliny gives a vivid account of the expectancy with which the appearance of Trajan at a *congiarium* was awaited. The people lined the route and held their children on their shoulders to get a better view of the emperor.[12] On this occasion Trajan apparently did distribute some money himself — 'you ordered all the children to be received and inscribed on the register before they saw you and approached you'. According to Dio, at a *congiarium* in 45 Claudius did not distribute all the money himself; but this was because he wished to hold court, and his sons-in-law took over the ceremony.[13] Claudius obviously wanted a member of the imperial family to preside.

Since emperors took this kind of trouble over the *congiarium*, it is a plausible suggestion that they normally distributed personally all donatives to the Praetorian Guard in Rome. When the emperor was on campaign and awarded a donative, he presumably took the opportunity to distribute the money to a larger body of troops. Gaius' distribution of money to the Guard in AD 37[14] is portrayed on a coin which shows the emperor, togate, addressing the Praetorians.[15] One of the few coins that show a distribution of a largess to soldiers was issued under Septimius Severus and Caracalla, and shows the emperors seated on a platform before which stands a soldier; the legend celebrates the 'Generosity of the Emperors'.[16] The literary sources in general suggest that it was normal for the emperor to go in person to the Praetorian camp to promise or distribute the donative.[17]

The donative ceremony conducted on campaign is illustrated by a relief from Trajan's column.[18] Trajan, in full military dress and surrounded by his officers, sits on a *sella*

[12] *Pan.* 26.1 ff.   [14] 59.2.1.
[13] 60.25.7.   [15] *BMC* I, p. 151, no. 33.
[16] Cohen, vol. IV, p. 157, no. 126.
[17] Claudius — Suet., *Cl.* 10.4; Nero — Tac., *A* 12.69; Domitian — Dio, 66.26.3; Antoninus Pius — *Vit. Pii* 10.2; Marcus Aurelius *Vit. Marc. Ant. Phil.* 7.9; Caracalla — Herodian, 4.4.7.
[18] Florescu, taf. 35.

castrensis on a raised piece of ground. The soldiers grouped round cheer and embrace one another as one soldier kneels to kiss the emperor's hand. Since one soldier is seen leaving the emperor apparently carrying a small sack over his shoulder, it is likely that he is carrying money and that the scene depicted is indeed the award of a donative, and perhaps military decorations.[19] The scene conveys what impressed the artist about ceremonies where the emperor distributed benefits to the troops — the benevolent majesty of Trajan, the personal contact between emperor and soldier, the enthusiasm of the troops on a grand and splendid occasion, which was doubtless designed to emphasize the role of the emperor as generous commander-in-chief and comrade.

When he was addressing the *III Augusta* in Lambaesis, Hadrian bestowed a donative on the troops as a reward for their excellent performance in their exercises. 'It is apparent that your prefect trains you diligently. Take this donative . . .'.[20] This speech was probably addressed to the *Ala I Pannoniorum* and it is clear that the money was given out while Hadrian presided; again we see the emperor's personal responsibility for the donative.

This practice persisted into the fourth century. The sixth-century writer Cassiodorus describes in his *Historia Tripartita* how the emperor Iulian (360–3) ordered his soldiers to burn incense before they received the donative from his own hand.[21] Later, when Christian soldiers realised what they had done, they hurled the money back at the emperor's feet. The occasions on which donatives were distributed, while being solemn and impressive and emphasizing the emperor's authority and generosity, were also festive. Tertullian describes how soldiers usually wore laurel wreaths as they went forward to collect the money: 'When the generosity of the most mighty emperors was being displayed in the camp,

[19] The scene obviously portrays a special occasion and not just the routine distribution of pay. It might be argued that the soldier carrying the sack belongs to the preceding scene. But that scene appears to be complete, and the soldier is contained within the sweeping gesture of one of Trajan's officers. Cf. C. Cichorius, *Die Reliefs der Trajanssäule* vol. II (1896), 214 f.

[20] *ILS* 2487.

[21] 6.30.6.

the soldiers decked in laurel-leaves approached.'[22] Even when
the emperor was not present, his name and the reason for the
donative were no doubt emphasized.[23]

A pay rise or cash handouts naturally earned good will and
popularity among the troops. Significantly, Julius Caesar
doubled his soldiers' pay before the civil war in 49.[24] After
this Domitian was the first emperor for over a hundred years
to raise the military *stipendium*.[25] This cannot be securely
dated, but it is plausible to associate the concession with the
aftermath of the revolt of Saturninus in 89.[26] Domitian
found that he had to fight several campaigns in his reign, and
in addition he encountered increasing difficulty in his
relationship with the Senate. The defection of the governor
of Upper Germany must have added a sinister new dimension
to the emperor's problems. His concern can be seen in his
decision that in future two legions should not be stationed in
one camp and that the amount of money deposited by
soldiers with their commander should be limited.[27] In the
circumstances a military pay rise in the order of 33 per cent
was no doubt intended to boost Domitian's prestige with the
army and cement the loyalty of the troops to his house.

Herodian places the pay rise of Septimius Severus among
the list of rewards and benefits conferred on his troops after
the victory over Clodius Albinus in the civil wars. It was
intended as an incentive for continuing loyalty in his attempt
to make himself politically supreme. The reaction of some
soldiers to the emperor's largess may be seen in the inscrip-

[22] *De Corona* 1.1.
[23] Cf. T.C. Skeat, *Two Papyri from Panopolis* (1964), 56 ff. This papyrus of
AD 300 contains orders for the payment of donatives to the troops stationed in
Egypt. When the procurator of the Lower Thebaid issued the requisite order, he
always stated very carefully the name of the emperor and the reason for the
donative; e.g., col. vi 161 f.; vii 186 f.; x 260 f. This was probably also read out to
the troops.
[24] Suet., *Div Iul.* 26.3.
[25] Suet., *Dom.* 7.3.; Dio, 67.3.5.
[26] Dio thought that the pay rise was to celebrate a victory in Germany, but
he did not really know since he says 'perhaps because of this victory'. I do not
believe that the coin with the legend *Stip Imp Aug Domitian*, apparently dated
to 84 (C. Kraay, *ANS Mus N* 9 (1960), 114-16), necessarily refers to his pay rise
since we do not know to whom such coins were distributed, nor in what context.
[27] Suet., *Dom.* 7.3. Saturninus financed his revolt against Domitian from the
savings in the camp bank.

tion set up by the *optiones* of the *III Augusta* in Africa: 'For the safety of the emperors, the *optiones* have established a shrine with statues and images of the divine house and also their protecting deities, out of the very generous pay and benefactions which they confer on them.' Here, this military *collegium* had acted as a channel for expression of good will from the army to the emperor.[28] Caracalla distributed a donative and promised a large pay rise immediately after the murder of his brother Geta.[29] His extravagant largess was designed to win the crucial support of the soldiers for his assumption of sole power, and the breaking of his father's dynastic plans.

A pay rise for the entire army cost a huge amount and could not often be contemplated, even though it would make an emperor popular. Donatives might provide an easier way of buying loyalty. Augustus' regime had a strong bulwark in the 120,000 veterans settled in colonies in Italy; all received 1,000 sesterces in 29 BC on the occasion of his triumphs [*RG* 15.3]. Those occasions when an emperor regularly bestowed largess on the army confirm how this was used for political purposes.

The most sensitive and difficult time for any dynasty is the transition from one ruler to another. Augustus aimed to ensure not only that Tiberius was pre-eminent in power and prestige, but also that the army should be bound in loyalty to him and in expectation of benefits. In his will he left money to the urban troops and the legions, as well as the plebs in Rome.[30] As it happened he failed to ensure a trouble-free time for Tiberius, since there were disturbances among the troops in Pannonia and Germany, partly because of pay and conditions and indeed the failure to pay Augustus' bequests.[31] Tiberius, however, was strong enough to overcome this discontent and he emphasized his concern for the army by doubling Augustus' bequests in his own name.

[28] 3.8.4 f. *CIL* VII. 2554; cf. 18070. For Military *Collegia*, see *Dizionario Epigrafico* s.v. 'collegia'. cf. also G.T. Murphy, *The Reign of the Emperor Septimius Severus from the Evidence of Inscriptions* (1945), 76.

[29] Herodian, 4.4.7; Dio, 78.3.

[30] See above, p. 166.

[31] Tac., *A* 1.35.

Gaius followed his example,[32] but it was Claudius who brought a dramatic development. The donative he offered was significant in two ways; firstly, its extravagant amount was in contrast to the comparative moderation of previous awards;[33] secondly, previous donatives had been in the form of a voluntary grant, mainly testamentary bequests. Claudius' payment established the idea that an emperor should pay a donative on his accession in his own right, not connected with the bequests of his predecessor. The payment to the troops at the start of the reign became now virtually an obligation, not a gift, and tied the emperor more closely to the support of the army. Suetonius was essentially right in his analysis of the importance of Claudius' accession: 'He was the first of the emperors who indeed used bribery to secure the loyalty of the troops.'[34] After Claudius the distribution of money to Praetorian Guard and to the other troops became a regular feature of imperial accessions, designed to bind the army to the emperor in good will and mutual benefit.[35] It was arranged to suit the political circumstances of the time.[36]

It was particularly important that the intended heir be brought before the troops and identified with their benefits as soon as possible. In 8 BC Augustus distributed a donative because Gaius Caesar had accompanied the army on military exercises for the first time.[37] This largess, probably in the prince's name, would bind the troops to him as an important member of the imperial family and possible successor of Augustus. In 51, when Nero adopted the toga of manhood, Claudius distributed a largess to the soldiers and the people in the young prince's name.[38] In the same way a donative accompanied the adoption of L.Ceionius Commodus by

[32] Dio, 59.2.1 ff.
[33] See above, p. 166.
[34] Suet., *Cl.* 10.4.
[35] e.g., Trajan — Pliny, *Pan.* 25.1 f.; Hadrian — *Vit. Had.* 5.7; Antoninus Pius — *Vit. Pii* 4.9; Marcus Aurelius and Lucius Verus — *Vit. Marc. Ant. Phil.* 7.9; Commodus — Herodian. 1.5.1.
[36] Cf. Hadrian's double donative in 117 — *Vit. Had* 5.7. Perhaps he was worried by the execution of four consulars, or the morale of the army after the set backs in the East.
[37] Dio, 55.6.4.
[38] Tac., *A* 12.41.

Hadrian, and later the adoption of Antoninus Pius.[39] Pius himself celebrated the marriage of Marcus Aurelius and Faustina with a donative to the troops.[40] It was expedient to associate the army with these public ceremonies designed to promote the future security of the dynasty and the advance of the emperor's chosen successor. The dynastic pretensions of such occasions are well illustrated by the *tirocinium* of Lucius Verus, at which Pius sat between Marcus and Lucius while the quaestor counted out the largess to the people.[41]

The army was even more clearly linked with the fate of a dynasty when a donative was awarded after a conspiracy. After the fall of Sejanus, Tiberius gave 4,000 sesterces to the Praetorians and gifts to the Syrian legions, who alone had not placed statues of the prefect in the camp shrine.[42] Tiberius was not as lucky as Augustus, who had avoided this kind of donative which placed imperial largess back in the context of political strife as a reward for loyalty in time of personal danger for the commander. Gaius also distributed money to the soldiers after he had executed Aemilius Lepidus, who may have been involved in a serious conspiracy.[43] This use of the donative reached a particularly disreputable level in the distributions of money by Nero after the murder of his mother.[44] Dio comments sarcastically that the purpose of such a largess was presumably to persuade the Praetorian Guard that many crimes like this would be committed.

The regular association of the donative with imperial accessions and the introduction of intended heirs, and its use in times of political crisis to cement the loyalty of the army, inevitably focused attention on this aspect of bribing the soldiers for political support. It is impossible to say how many donatives were given to the soldiers in each reign and

---

[39] *Vit. Had.* 23.14; *Vit. Pii* 4.9.
[40] Ibid. 10.2.
[41] *Vit. Veri* 3.1.
[42] Suet., *Tib.* 48.2.
[43] Dio, 59, 22.7. And see Balsdon, *The Emperor Gaius*, 74.
[44] 62.14.3. Note also the donatives distributed after the conspiracy of Piso: 62.27.3; Tac., *A* 15.72.

how many of these were associated with political events.[45]
Certainly most of the donatives regularly mentioned in the
sources seem to be 'political' largess of the type described
above. There were others, especially after military campaigns[46] or visits to the troops.[47] The demand for a donative
by Marcus Aurelius' troops after a victory over the Germans
may indicate that a largess was expected in such circumstances.[48].

Emperors could not avoid paying donatives, but the matter
was perhaps rather embarrassing in their relationship with the
senatorial class. In his *Panegyric* Pliny discusses Trajan's
generosity. He devotes most of his account to the *congiarium*
paid to the people, and the soldiers are only briefly
mentioned.[49] Pliny knew better than to dilate upon one of
the 'secrets of ruling'. But he was perhaps relieved to be able
to pass over it quickly. He praises the equality of the whole
distribution – the plebs get the whole *congiarium*, the
soldiers receive only half their donative, but before the
plebs – 'in this way the soldiers were made equal with the
people'.[50] The argument seems forced and artificial, almost
as if Pliny is trying to put the military donative in the best
light. The soldiers received more money than the plebs in
hand-outs, and they received their largess first because their
support was essential. It is true that *congiaria* were used to
obtain the support of the plebs, which was not to be

---

[45] We cannot assume that a donative was bestowed on the troops on each
occasion that a *congiarium* was given to the people, though it is difficult to
imagine that money was given to the people and not at least to the Praetorian
Guard.

[46] Suet., *Cal.* 46. Suetonius is critical, implying that Gaius thought that the
donative was generous when it was not. Balsdon follows this view and thinks that
the emperor intended the donative to be an insult to the legions *The Emperor
Gaius*, 92). But it is unlikely that even Gaius would have attempted such a
dangerous exercise. Suetonius' comment may be anachronistic. This was probably
the first donative since early in Augustus' reign made to the legions in the
provinces because of a campaign. It was an important extension of the use of the
donative, and since the usual bequest to a legionary was 300 sesterces, this grant
of 400 was relatively generous.

[47] See n. 20.

[48] See above, pp. 174-5.

[49] 25.2.

[50] 'Aequati sunt enim populo milites eo quod partem sed priores, populus
militibus quod posterior sed totum statim accepit.'

despised.[51] But, while the *congiarium* to the people stood as an additional security for good order in Rome, the military donative could be vital to the survival of an emperor's regime. Pliny's treatment of the subject has some significance for upper-class attitudes. Extravagance and ill-discipline were hated and feared. When senators approved of an emperor they sought to rationalize the donative as part of his dual responsibility for the civil and military duties of the State.[52]

But if, in reality, the army was a private mercenary force subject to the whims of one man,[53] then he might find it difficult to avoid extravagant payments and the consequent threat to the army's discipline. The success of emperors in dealing with this problem depended on the character of the individual and the pressures he came under. It is important that donatives got bigger and appear to have been distributed more frequently. The amount of money given to the soldiers was governed more by political needs than rational consideration of the economic requirements of the troops, or the resources of the empire. Once an emperor had paid out a large donative it will have been difficult for his successor to avoid following his example.

It presumably did not escape the notice of the army commanders in 41 that Claudius, at first an unlikely aspirant to the purple, had encouraged the military basis of his support with a huge largess. Although Claudius succeeded in keeping discipline during his reign,[54] it was possible that someone who so openly and extravagantly bought the loyalty of the troops could be outbid. Tacitus' succinct observation on the events of 68-9 — 'one of the secrets of ruling had been revealed, it was possible for an emperor to be made outside Rome' — sums up the consequences of the break-down of the

---

[51] Z. Yavetz, *Plebs and Princeps* (1967), 131 ff.; Brunt and Moore, *Res Gestae Divi Augusti* (1967), 58.

[52] Emperors perhaps sought to encourage this idea. It may be significant that, whereas *congiaria* are frequently celebrated on coins, donatives to soldiers are rarely portrayed.

[53] See n. 3.

[54] There was one military revolt, which petered out after a few days — Suet., *Cl.* 13.2; and one mutiny among the troops who were preparing to embark for the invasion of Britain — Dio, 60.19.2 f. This may reflect the natural reluctance of the troops to go to fight in an unknown part of the world.

mystique and aura of the Julio-Claudian dynasty.[55] Men of
energy and ambition outside the ruling family could move in;
military power and money were inextricably linked;
discipline and parsimony could be fatal. Galba's attitude was
severe, but ruinous to his chances. 'I pick my soldiers,' he
said, 'I do not buy them.'[56] But he was inconsistent and his
rigorous approach did positive harm; it was said that his
troops could have been won over by even a small donative.
But the emperor was too niggardly, and the standards of the
time demanded a different approach.[57] It opened the way for
Otho to outbid him in a race to win the loyalty of the
troops.[58] But no one could monopolize the award of
donatives, as Tacitus illustrates in a speech put into the
mouth of Galba's heir. Piso hopefully promises a largess to
secure the loyalty of the Guard, but there is a gloomy fore-
boding that the donative may in fact be paid by Otho to
secure the murder of Galba.[59]

Naturally, in this period grand promises and donatives
became very important as the most direct way of persuading
a large number of troops quickly. But the soldiers *were*
influenced by other factors.[60] Emperors sought to bind the
soldiery to their house in affection and sentiment; personal
devotion to a respected commander, and the local loyalty
and rivalry of the legions in the various provinces also played
a part. Galba's mistaken parsimony was possibly based on the
belief that he could play down the support of the army
because he had won without any real fighting; and he may
have found it difficult to change his natural tendency as a
disciplinarian. Otho, so far as is known, offered no donative
before the battle of Bedriacum, presumably because he had
no ready cash; but in the main, his troops fought well during
the battle.[61] The known donatives of Vitellius and Vespasian

[55] *H* 1.4. Tacitus was critical of the decline in discipline partly brought about
by Nero's neglect and extravagance — 1.5; *Ag.* 16.3-4 for the state of the legions
in Britain.
[56] *H* 1.5.
[57] 1.18.
[58] 1.37.
[59] 1.30.
[60] See above, p. 17.
[61] Tac., *H* 2.42 f.

seem ridiculously small.[62] Vespasian indeed earned the praise
of Tacitus. He was the only emperor up to then who had
changed for the better. 'He took a splendidly strict line
against indulging the troops, and for that reason had a better
army.'[63] Vespasian succeeded with his tough discipline
because the sheer exhaustion of the leading men and the
armies helped to stabilize the situation. No one wanted more
war. And he had sons, so the soldiers could see that they
were fighting not for one adventurer, but for a dynasty that
could offer them security. Finally, the fighting in Rome and
Italy probably produced enormous booty, at least for some
of the troops. And so formal donatives may have been less
necessary, though the soldiers received at least one, on
Vespasian's return to Rome.[64]

Stability and discipline prevailed throughout the Flavian
dynasty. However, because of unrest among the soldiers at
the murder of Domitian, it is likely that Nerva was forced to
pay or promise a large donative, and in general his relationship with the army may have been uneasy.[65] The long campaigns of Trajan and the rigorous inspections of Hadrian indicate a strict maintenance of discipline and efficiency, without
which indeed the army could not have resisted the onslaught
of the northern tribes in the reign of Marcus. But there are
in this period some indications in the legal codes of relaxation of discipline, and desertion was a serious problem in
the last years of Marcus. The long wars and the plague may
have undermined the morale of the army. If so, Commodus
did nothing to repair it, and his reign witnessed a serious
decline in discipline. Although the claim that he wished to
distribute the property of the rich among the soldiers may be
exaggerated, the Praetorians were allowed to do virtually
whatever they wanted. His successor Pertinax won favour
because he recalled the Guard to orderliness and discipline
and forbade them to attack passers-by or seize property.[66]

[62] See above, p. 169.
[63] *H* 2.82; cf. Suetonius, *Vesp.* 8.2.
[64] Dio, 65.10.19.
[65] See R. Syme, *JRS* 20 (1930), 55 ff. = Roman Papers I, 1; D.M. Robathan,
'Domitian's "Midas-Touch"', *TAPA* (1942), 130.
[66] Herodian, 1.17.2; 2.4.1–4; Dio, 74.8.1.

There was trouble too in at least one provincial army.[67]

Pertinax's attempt to restore discipline was doomed to failure. He tried to do too much too quickly,[68] and could not escape the repercussions of the manner of his accession, which was brought about by the violent death of an emperor whose extravagance and licence had made him popular with the troops. The new emperor was obliged to offer a large donative, although the treasury was empty and he had to sell Commodus' personal effects to raise cash.[69] Pertinax was obviously aware that his donative of 8,000 sesterces was less than the immediate precedents. In a speech to the Senate he lied that he had given the soldiers as much as Marcus. According to Dio, this infuriated the soldiers present in the Senate,[70] and it would be wrong to reject the word of a probable eyewitness that this incident was a factor in turning the troops against Pertinax.[71] The murder of Pertinax marks a decisive development. For the first time an emperor fell largely because of his inability to pay the Praetorians as much as they wanted. What is more, Pertinax was the first emperor to die at the hands of his own troops acting largely on their own initiative.[72]

The sequel to his downfall produced the 'sale' of the empire in the Praetorian Camp to the highest bidder.[73] This episode, sordid as it seemed to contemporaries, was the inevitable conclusion of the persistent use of the donative to bolster the emperor's political control and security. Nevertheless, the disgraceful scene not only dramatically illustrated again the value of bribing the soldiers, it also marked a further decline in the mystique and prestige of the imperial position. It was impossible for Didius Julianus to have any authority or control over the troops since his tenure of power depended merely on the bribery of men who had already

[67] P.A. Brunt, 'The Fall of Perennis: Dio-Xiphilinus 72.9.2', *CQ* 23 (1973), 172.

[68] 74.10.3.

[69] 74.5.4.

[70] 74.8.3 ff.

[71] Dio was present in Rome during these years — Millar, *Cassius Dio*, 16–17; 134.

[72] There is no certain evidence for any plot on this occasion. See A.R. Birley, 'The Coups d'Etat of the Year 193', *BJ* 169 (1969), 272–3.

[73] Dio, 74.11.2; Herodian, 2.6.5; 6.12; 6.14.

murdered one emperor and gone unpunished.[74] The discipline of the Guard collapsed and it is likely that events in Rome and the prevailing instability influenced the decision of Septimius Severus and Pescennius Niger to seek the purple by force of arms.[75]

When Severus captured Rome in 193, it was the first time in one hundred and twenty-four years that the legions, bribed by a military usurper, had marched on Rome. Severus could not escape the consequences of his action. During his first meeting with the Senate, some soldiers burst in and shocked him with a demand for what Octavian had given his troops in 43 BC.[76] If this detail is correct (and Dio was a horrified eye witness of the scene), it is a remarkable indication of how an emperor was expected to live up to a predecessor's generosity. The soldiers were in fact satisfied with only 1,000 sesterces each, and this sum must have been paid on account because Severus had little ready cash.

The traditional view is that Severus completely corrupted the discipline of the army.[77] Herodian states that he was the first to corrupt discipline and the tradition of obedience.[78] This contradicts his earlier discussion of Didius Julianus,[79] and the evidence he adduces does not support his contention. According to Herodian, Severus was the first to increase military pay. This of course is not true, and the distribution of donatives to win political support had been employed since the late Republic. It is inaccurate for Herodian to say that 'Severus taught the soldiers to love money and introduced them to a soft life'. The pay rise and the booty gained from the sack of Ctesiphon in the second Parthian war and from the destruction of Lugdunum perhaps enabled the emperor to avoid extravagant donatives, while keeping the soldiers content.[80]

---

[74] Herodian. 2.6.14.

[75] In the same way as the events in Rome in 68 influenced the leading army commanders.

[76] Dio, 46.46.7; *Vit. Sev.* 7.6.

[77] Rostovtzeff, *SEHRE*[2] (1957), 353 ff.; H.M.D. Parker, *A History of the Roman World AD 138-337* (1935), 86 f.; for a more judicious, though basically hostile estimate, see S.N. Miller, *CAH* XII, 32 ff. Against — E.B. Birley, *Epig. Stud.* 8 (1969), 63; A.R. Birley, *Septimius Severus* (1971), 283 ff.

[78] 3.8.5.   [79] 2.6.14.   [80] See below, pp. 309-10.

And so, although the soldiers were reasonably well off under Severus,[81] the indications are that he attempted to maintain strict discipline. Drastic measures were necessary in 193 to reassert imperial authority and instill the concept of obedience. When Severus entered Rome he boldly disbanded the Praetorian Guard and replaced it with men from his own armies. The soldiers who had murdered Pertinax were executed.[82] In a speech he bitterly criticised the troops 'because of the lawlessness of their action against their emperor'.[83] Severus was no doubt aware of the value of his posing as the avenger of lawlessness, and he will have wished to reward his own troops with service in the Guard. But he probably also realised the need to take decisive action against the treacherous Guard which had betrayed two emperors. This is a good indication of his determination to preserve discipline in his own army. Despite two civil wars and long campaigns in Parthia and Britain, there was surprisingly little trouble. We hear of a mutiny at Saxa Rubra on the way to fight Niger;[84] and at the siege of Hatra some European troops refused an order to advance.[85] But both these disturbances originated in particular circumstances and do not imply general indiscipline. The armies remained loyal to the dynasty at the accession of Geta and Caracalla and even after the murder of Geta. It seems that by his personality, judgement, and luck Severus did restore the habit of obedience to the army and made a firm distinction between the commander and the commanded.

Nevertheless, Severus recognized the importance of seducing the army with money, and on his death bed he is supposed to have said, 'enrich the soldiers and ignore the rest'.[86] Caracalla took his father's advice and carried his methods to their logical conclusion. His reign reached a peak of extravagance,[87] but despite this he apparently kept the army under control. Dio and Herodian, although very hostile

---

[81] See above, pp. 177–9.
[82] Dio, 75.1.1; Herodian. 2.12.2 ff.
[83] ὑπερ τῆς ἐς τὸν αὐτοκράτορα σφῶν παρανομίας.
[84] *Vit. Sev.* 8.10. The mutiny was over the choice of a camp site.
[85] 75.12.3–5.
[86] 76.15.2.
[87] See above, pp. 175–6.

to the emperor, did not traduce him by alleging indiscipline and disturbance among the soldiery. However Dio does say that the troops in the Parthian campaign became corrupted by a winter spent in houses.[88] This may be hostile gossip, like the story that Caracalla was eventually deserted by his soldiers.[89] But underneath the calm surface, the frequent cash hand-outs and Caracalla's extravagant talk and reduction of the imperial dignity by excessive comradeship were producing a dangerous legacy for the future.

Macrinus had to deal with the consequences of this. He could not afford to alienate the troops, who were resentful at the murder of Caracalla, but he found it impossible to keep giving them their full pay and donatives.[90] Dio approved in principle of Macrinus' attempt to impose some restraint, but questioned the political timing of the move. Macrinus should have waited until the soldiers had been dispersed to their various units for the winter.[91] In fact Macrinus was forced to restore full pay and grant a large donative. This was another blow to imperial dignity. Macrinus failed to deal with the linked problems of military discipline and the increasing expectations of the troops for financial rewards. The nemesis of Caracalla's policy was that his successors were in a much weaker position to deal with the soldiers on whose support they depended.

For the unstable times after the death of Macrinus it is difficult to get a clear picture of the discipline and efficiency òf the armies or what factors most influenced the troops. Herodian at least believed that money continued to be the greatest attraction for the men.[92] This may be merely a personal opinion, but it seems plausible. The emperor Elagabalus himself lamented, 'I find no acceptance among the Praetorians, to whom I am giving so much'.[93] Dio gives an alarming account of the breakdown of military discipline in the reign of Severus Alexander. The Praetorian Guard murdered Ulpian, their prefect, and for a long time the

[88] 78.3.4.
[89] 78.6.4.
[90] 78.36.2.
[91] 78.12.7; 28.1 ff.; 29.1–2.
[92] 5.8.3; cf. 5.3.11; 5.4.2.
[93] 80.18.4.

instigator of the crime went unpunished;[94] the soldiers engaged in a three-day battle with the populace of Rome and this ended only when parts of the city were set on fire.[95] There were complaints from the Praetorians about Dio in his capacity as consular governor in Pannonia because he attempted to enforce discipline. Indeed they even demanded his surrender and this hostility became common knowledge, since Alexander had to advise Dio to spend his second consulship outside Rome in case the troops tried to murder him in his robes of office.[96] Dio naturally had a poor opinion of military discipline and efficiency in this reign and he believed that the luxury, licence, and indiscipline of the troops in the East were such that they refused to fight and preferred to surrender to the enemy.[97] All this shows an extensive breakdown in the capacity of the emperor to control the army, for which there were doubtless many reasons, most importantly the decline in the prestige of the Severan dynasty, the feeble nature of Alexander himself, who appeared to be no soldier and to be completely dominated by his mother's advice, and the lack of real military success at a time during which the empire was coming under increasing pressure. Nevertheless, Herodian was convinced that the emperor's miserliness (partly the result of his mother's greed) and slowness to bestow donatives were important factors in the soldiers' dislike of Alexander.[98] Since Herodian is generally favourable to Alexander in his history, this particular criticism acquires a certain credibility. The emperor was the victim of a long, but inconsistent process of bribing the troops which eventually helped to destroy the army's discipline and morale. By 235 restraint was virtually impossible, and it was increasingly difficult to satisfy the soldiers' expectations.

The army's financial emoluments, for which emperors

[94] 80.2.2 f. For the fate of Epagathus, see R. Syme, *Emperors and Biography* (1971), 153. Chapter IX in general provides an excellent account of the realities of the reign of Severus Alexander, in contrast to the idyllic picture presented by the *Historia Augusta.*

[95] Dio, 80.2.3.

[96] 80.4.2–5.1.

[97] 80.4.1.

[98] 6.9.4; cf. 6.1.8; 8.4; 9.8. There is however no reason to think that Alexander reduced military pay, as argued by Domaszweski, *Rh.M* 58 (1903), 383. Refuted by Passerini, *Athenaeum* 24 (1946), 158.

took responsibility and with which they identified themselves, always had the most direct influence on the troops.
An emperor could not have survived long if he failed to
provide the troops with their pay and benefits, even if he
was well liked for other reasons. Hence the provision of such
benefits was a most urgent priority. A military usurper
naturally would have little time to develop his personal
relationship with the troops and so was bound to use money
as the quickest way to win over a large number of soldiers.
Nothing could disguise that the Roman army was a
mercenary force, perhaps up for sale to the highest bidder.
During much of the imperial period no bidder was to be
found, or at least none who could hope to appeal to a
sufficiently wide audience and convince enough troops and
their officers that he had the backing and resources to make
it worth their while to risk everything in rebellion against the
reigning emperor. But the events of 68-9 made it clear that
soldiers could be successfully bribed even against a well-
established dynasty, and this was an important precedent.

By the end of the Severan dynasty much of the mystique
and awe surrounding the emperor had been eroded and
discipline had seriously deteriorated. The excessive indulgence of the army with monetary and other privileges played
a major part in this. The soldiers, repeatedly courted, bribed
and pampered, expected to profit greatly from military
service, and rebellion had a high price. Furthermore,
emperors now identified themselves so closely with the
troops that it was difficult to control their demands
effectively. The army was more mercenary than ever and
more people were prepared to bid for its support.

5. MILITARY DECORATIONS

As commander-in-chief the emperor could take personal
control of any aspect of the army's administration, including
the promotion and decoration of individual soldiers. It is
unlikely that emperors often had the leisure to deal personally with the award of decorations; but imperial campaigns
could provide just such an opportunity. Moreover, it is a
plausible assumption that any soldier who particularly dis-

tinguished himself in combat was brought to the ruler's attention. Doubtless an obvious display of interest from the commander-in-chief was useful, even in a small way, for building up a rapport between leader and troops.

Augustus took great care over the distribution of military honours, and himself decided on the type and value of each award. He granted the highest honours with great circumspection and without bias, and even bestowed them on ordinary soldiers.[1] This may suggest that he actually handed out some of the decorations himself at special ceremonies.

Apronius, proconsul of Africa in AD 20/21, awarded military decorations to an ordinary soldier who had saved a comrade's life in battle. Tiberius added the *civica corona* and complained that Apronius could have awarded this himself 'through his right as proconsul'.[2] Apparently Apronius had the right to grant military decorations because, as proconsul, he was in a sense acting under his own auspices. In addition Augustus had established that senators who had been awarded triumphal ornaments could also bestow decorations.[3] This practice was perhaps peculiar to his reign, and in any event the implication of this evidence is that imperial *legati*, since they were acting under the emperor's auspices, had no right to award military decorations and that the decision for such awards lay with the emperor himself. This means that when proconsuls ceased to have troops under their command, the initiative for all decorations would emanate from the emperor.

It is not necessary to believe that since the emperor alone possessed *auspicia* and had the right to grant military decorations, these could be bestowed only in campaigns where the emperor was present.[4] It would have been foolish to discriminate against soldiers who distinguished themselves in campaigns not personally directed by an emperor. No one could doubt that his overall responsibility for the army and

---

[1] Suet., *Aug.* 25.3. 'Has quam parcissime et sine ambitione ac saepe etiam caligatis tribuit.' For military decorations in general, see now V.A. Maxfield, *The Military Decorations of the Roman Army* (1981).

[2] Tac., *A* 3.21.

[3] 'triumphales . . . quod ipsi quoque ius habuissent tribuendi ea quibus vellent' (Suet., *Aug.* 25.3).

[4] P. Steiner, 'Die Dona Militaria', *BJ* 114 (1906), 89.

his total control over military affairs allowed him to confer decorations on whomever he wished. We see this in the inscription of an equestrian military tribune who received decorations 'from the emperor Nerva Caesar Augustus Germanicus in the war against the Suebi'.[5] Nerva himself did not conduct this campaign. When an emperor was present on campaign, he presumably received reports from his officers about the distinguished conduct of soldiers, authorized awards on their advice, and if possible bestowed them himself. When he was not present, then either he, or whomever he delegated for the job, will have received reports and recommendations from his commanders, and authorized them to make the appropriate award.[6]

The important point is that, in the mind of the soldiers, military decorations were associated with the emperor. The large majority of inscriptions set up by soldiers to celebrate the award of military decorations specifically mention that the award was made by the emperor, and his name and titles are usually given in full.[7] This need not mean that all the soldiers received their decorations from the hand of the emperor. But clearly they had been impressed by the idea that their decorations depended on his personal initiative. This appears even more obviously in an inscription which records how a soldier of *III Gallica* was 'decorated with gold collars and armlets on the vote of the legion in accordance with the wishes of Hadrian Augustus'.[8]

The importance of the emperor's involvement is highlighted by the ceremonies at which the decorations were distributed. Josephus gives an excellent description of one such ceremony when a member of the imperial family was present.[9] After the fall of Jerusalem Titus congratulated the army in a formal speech, and afterwards bestowed decorations on those who had distinguished themeselves. The prince stood on a high platform surrounded by his senior officers and in the presence of the entire army. Officers read out the names of the men to be honoured; then Titus called

---

[5] *ILS* 2720. And see Maxfield, 115 ff.; 255 ff.
[6] As Tiberius did in the case of Apronius (n.2).
[7] Maxfield, 116-17, 265 ff.
[8] *ILS* 2313.
[9] *BJ* 7.5-17.

each man forward by name and applauded as he approached. He placed a crown of gold on the soldier's head and handed over the appropriate decoration. It is clear that Titus himself decided on the proper award for each man;[10] in addition, all the soldiers who were decorated received promotion and a reward from the booty. The ceremony was followed by a sacrifice and a banquet. The event was designed to make a grand impression on the troops and it perhaps helped to tie them emotionally to the imperial family when they saw Titus exhibiting such interest in their comrades.

Equites and other junior officers made the most out of personal interest by an emperor. The long career inscription of the *eques* Valerius Maximianus, who began as prefect of *Cohors I Thracum* and was eventually adlected into the Senate,[11] shows that when he was prefect of *Ala I Aravacorum* he was honoured by Marcus Aurelius: 'In the German war Maximianus was congratulated in public by Imperator Antoninus Augustus, and a horse, trappings, and weapons were bestowed upon him because he killed with his own hand Valaon, the leader of the Naristae.' This is interesting because it shows that Marcus made a speech of praise before the army, and the use of the subjunctive mood may indicate that this is part of the original citation which the emperor read out.[12] Apparently, as an additional reward, Maximianus received immediate promotion. Some soldiers were lucky enough to attract imperial attention on several occasions. Maximus, the captor of Decebalus, was first decorated by Domitian in his Dacian campaigns; then he was 'promoted to the rank of *duplicarius* by the deified Trajan, by whom he was also appointed scout in the Dacian War'. After this, he was twice decorated by Trajan in the Dacian and Parthian wars.[13]

The association of military decorations and promotion by the emperor is also seen in the career of Octavius Secundus, a centurion of the *X Fretensis*.[14] In addition to his military decorations from the Jewish war, he was 'promoted by the

---

[10] 7.16: πάντων δὲ τετιμημένων ὅπως αὐτός ἕκαστον ἠξίωσε.

[11] *AE* 1956.124. Pflaum, *Carrières*, 476 ff.; no. 181.

[12] Cf. M. Speidel, *JRS* 60 (1970), 142.

[13] Ibid.; note especially 149 ff. See above, p. 105.

[14] See *ILS* 2080.

same emperor [Hadrian] through transfer to *I Italica*, where he became *primuspilus*'. In at least one case Caracalla, in place of a military decoration, bestowed a sum of money on one of his senior centurions as well as immediate promotion.[15] The gift of money seems to have been on the initiative of the emperor, and may well have been taken from the booty of a successful campaign in the same way as Titus had done at the siege of Jerusalem.[16]

Any reward received by the soldiers had to be seen to come from the emperor, and could not be left entirely in the hands of army commanders, who might seek to win favour by generous bestowal of rewards and decorations and so build up a rapport with the troops. The soldiers indeed believed that military decorations were decided on by the emperor and came directly from him even when he was not present in person. This reflects the efforts made by emperors to convey their concern and personal initiative. When the commander-in-chief appeared with his army, a great display was organized through which his interest in and care for his brave troops could be emphasized. Of course only a few men in any reign received their military decorations from the emperor's own hand, but stories and gossip in the army could perhaps spread the rumours of such ceremonies, in the same way as it got around that Trajan tore up his own clothes to make bandages for his wounded soldiers.[17] As patron, benefactor, commander-in-chief, and 'fellow-soldier', each emperor sought to dominate his relationship with his army and present himself as the only conceivable focus of loyalty and affection.

It is the custom for rulers and sovereigns in many societies to accumulate military honours to enhance their dignity and prestige. It would be interesting to know if Roman emperors themselves accepted military decorations in order to identify with the army. In 27 BC Augustus was granted by the Senate the right to hang on his door the crown of oak leaves (*civica corona*) normally awarded to a soldier for saving a comrade's life in battle. Augustus' crown symbolized that he was always

---

[15] *ILS* 7178. See p. 106.
[16] Josephus, *BJ* 7.15.
[17] See above, p. 46.

victorious over his enemies, and was the saviour of his fellow-citizens.[18] This presumably refers to his ending of the civil wars. The oak wreath was portrayed on his coinage with the legend 'ob cives servatos' ('to celebrate the preservation of the citizens').[19] This theme does not appear subsequently, except possibly in the coinage of Vespasian.[20] That may be significant. He too had to restore order and stability after prolonged war and military upheaval. The *civica corona* could be seen as a sign of his determination to preserve peace, and it had strong military connotations appropriate to a man who had notable martial achievements to his credit. Apart from these examples, there is no sign that emperors regularly took military decorations for campaigns waged under their direction, and it is possible that the traditional and dignified honour of the Roman military commander, the acclamation as *imperator*, was considered more suitable.

---

[18] Dio, 53.16.4.
[19] *BMC* I, pp. 2, 7, 26, 57, 66, 118.
[20] See *BMC* II, p. 7.

PART TWO

THE SOLDIER AND THE LAW

IV

THE LEGAL PRIVILEGES OF THE ARMY

1. INTRODUCTION

Roman legal procedure was affected, at least from the reign of Hadrian, by discrimination in various ways in favour of a particular class, known as the *honestiores*, who consisted largely of senators, *equites*, decurions, and magistrates.[1] Emperors wished to support that class from which they themselves came and which had an inherited dominance in society, and those people who contributed to the administration of the empire and the smooth functioning of its component parts.

The Roman soldier, who generally came from the lower classes, did not possess any of the usual criteria for legal privilege in Roman society. It is therefore significant for the role they played and the attitude of the emperor that they possessed privileges in certain aspects of the law. There are two possible explanations, which may indeed be connected. The exceptionally exacting nature of the professional soldier's career and the special problems created by long absence from home in the service of the State demanded a relaxation in some areas of the law. Obviously the need to keep the army relatively contented with its lot was of great importance to an efficient military establishment. This leads to the second explanation of the army's legal privileges. The soldiers comprised the largest group of people who were

---

[1] P. Garnsey, *Social Status and Legal Privilege in the Roman Empire* (1970), 234 ff.; especially, 245 ff.

performing a vital service for the State and whose loyalty was essential to the emperor. He must therefore ensure that his soldiers were satisfied with service under him, since that was one way to retain their personal loyalty. Therefore, although some of the legal privileges of the army may have been intended originally to sort out anomalies in the law, few emperors will have been unmindful of the good will and affection to be gained by an indulgent attitude to the troops.

Yet at the same time the emperor also had to keep in mind the interests and feelings of the upper classes and the needs of the empire as a whole. Soldiers might have certain privileges, but they could not be allowed to aspire to the dignity and social prestige that were the prerogative of men of rank.[2] A conscientious emperor who desired to perpetuate the rule of law and a stable government had an obligation to protect the interests of all his subjects and to ensure that as far as possible their rights were not infringed.

Nevertheless, the soldier was entitled to legal privileges not enjoyed by any other sector of the community, no matter how rich and well connected. Ulpian speaks of 'the most extensive indulgence displayed towards soldiers' ('plenissima indulgentia in milites') in relation to the military will.[3] This privilege was authorized by law, yet it was still considered to be 'against the strict rule of law' ('contra iuris regulam'). The paradox illustrates the problems faced by jurists, who by their training and inclinations sought an equitable operation of the law for the parties involved, and who had to interpret soldiers' legal privileges. In addition, a jurist doubtless found it difficult not to be influenced by the attitudes and decisions of the emperors themselves who, by extending their indulgence generously and perhaps in rather effusive language, helped to create a general attitude towards the legal position of soldiers. And so, although the legal privileges extended to the army were in certain ways limited, it can be suggested that the benevolent attitude of officials gave soldiers advantages exceeding any formal rights.

---

[2] Cf. Dio's view of the common soldier – 52.25.6–7.
[3] *Tit. Ulp.* 23.10; *D* 29.1.1.

In fact the privileged position of the army and the indulgent attitude of the authorities may have contributed in some way to the aggressive behaviour of the troops to the civilian population and the consequent distress and injustice for which there is much evidence in the imperial period. In particular, the treatment of soldiers in court repays investigation. For the ordinary citizen an appearance in court was a difficult and anxious time. Juvenal pointed out some of the usual hazards faced by litigants — endless delays, assignment to crowded court sessions, frequent adjournments — and boldly declared that soldiers, by contrast with the unfortunate civilians, received special treatment when they appeared in court. Can this be dismissed as merely the venomous exaggeration of a clever satirist? In this context it is also relevant to consider the possible effect on the legal process of the increasing employment of centurions to judge certain cases.

Behind the law and the jurists, the emperor was the guarantor of the legal privileges of the army. The desire of successive emperors to benefit the soldiers, and their willingness to make themselves available to hear complaints and requests from ordinary soldiers and provide replies, perhaps gave the troops a greater opportunity than the civilian population to gain access to the emperor, and contributed to the privileged position of the army before the law.

Civilians might suffer as a result of the legal privileges conferred on the army, or at the hands of the arrogant soldiery, confident of its immunity from investigation and serious punishment, or through the carelessness and indifference of officials. This, while no doubt undesirable to many emperors, could be tolerated. On the other hand the soldier's conduct as a soldier was governed by Roman military law, and to modify this or treat soldiers leniently in matters of military discipline and organization could have a direct and deleterious effect on the efficiency and good order of the army itself. An examination of the ways in which the regulations governing the soldiers' military obligations developed may provide a further test of the determination of various emperors to maintain discipline, and not succumb to the temptation to court the affection and loyalty of the army at all costs.

2. THE SOLDIER'S WILL

A special concession permitted soldiers to make a will that was considered to be formally valid even if it did not conform to the strict legal requirements normally enforced in the case of civilians. Ulpian traces the history of this concession.

Julius Caesar was the first to extend to the soldiers the right to make a will free from formal legal requirements [*libera testamenti factio*]. However this concession was for a limited period only. Titus was the next to grant it; and after him Domitian. Then, after this, Nerva displayed the most extensive indulgence to the troops. Trajan followed this practice and then the following heading began to be included in the instructions to governors.[1]

Caesar's privilege may have been extended to all Roman soldiers by an enactment during his dictatorship. But it is more likely that it was granted during his time in Gaul, by virtue of his power as proconsul, and was confined to the troops who served with him at that time. During the period of their active service he will have ensured that the wishes of any soldier who was killed in battle were carried out. As justification Caesar could invoke the tradition of the 'testamentum in procinctu', a will lacking the usual formalities ('sine libra et tabulis') made by a soldier on his way to war.[2] This was apparently obsolete,[3] and it is possible that Caesar either revived or extended it to suit his own purposes. He needed to build up a good reputation with his men, and this concession would be an excellent mark of his concern for them.

After this the privilege of 'libera testamenti factio' was not formally revived until the reign of Titus. A story in Josephus, however, suggests that soldiers had received some kind of similar concession before this. During the siege of Jerusalem in 70 one of a group of Roman soldiers cut off by the Jews persuaded a comrade to come to his aid by offering to make him heir: 'I leave you heir to my possessions if you come and

---

[1] *D* 29.1.1.

[2] Cicero, *De Orat.* 1.228; Aulus Gellius, 15.27.3; Gaius, *Instit.* 2.101.

[3] Cicero, *De Nat. Deor.* 2.9.

catch me.'[4] This verbal contract without formal witnesses or the necessary legal observances ressembles the 'testamentum in procinctu', and the soldiers seem to have believed that this agreement would be valid. In this case the validity was not tested since the soldier who came to the rescue was killed. It may be suggested that Vespasian granted special privileges to the troops who first supported him, and Titus and Domitian later extended this to especially favoured soldiers. Nerva then may have granted to all soldiers in the army the formal privilege of making a will that was held to be valid despite non-conformity with strict legal form. This would explain Ulpian's reference to 'the most extensive indulgence'. Nerva needed to placate the troops enraged at Domitian's assassination, for which thcy might havc hcld him responsible as he was the principal beneficiary. It was natural then for Trajan to confirm this measure along with the other *beneficia* conferred by his 'father'. Emperors are often commended for confirming the benefactions of their predecessors *en bloc*. If Nerva introduced the privilege of 'libera testamenti factio' late in his reign, it is reasonable that the necessary action to publicize it and make it effective was taken by Trajan. He ordered a definition of the privilege to be set out in the *mandata* of provincial governors. The governors were presumably asked to publish those parts of the *mandata* which were of general concern and needed to be known. Gaius records that the *mandata* on military wills went into the edicts of proconsuls, and legates will probably have acted in the same way.[5]

It seems odd that Augustus, who gained power by military force, did not follow his adoptive father's policy on military wills. Augustus indeed was concerned to preserve the façade of good discipline and forceful control of the troops.[6] Nevertheless he did conccrn himself in another way with the problems of soldiers and the inheritance of property. In his *Sententiae* the jurist Paul wrote: 'A soldier who is a *filius familias* [a son whose father is alive and in whose power legally he still is] must, just like a civilian, either be expressly

---

[4] *BJ* 6.188 ff.
[5] *D* 29.1.2.
[6] See above, p. 33.

written as heir or formally disinherited; for the edict of *divus* Augustus has now been rescinded, in which it was forbidden for a father to disinherit his son, if a soldier.'[7] It is strange that Augustus interfered with the traditional right of the *testator* to dispose of his property as he wished, but the edict must have been designed to protect the son from the injustice of being disinherited while he was away on active service and not in a position to find out what was happening or to petition for a 'complaint against an undutiful will'.[8] However, it may be that Augustus' usual practice was to make concessions to certain favoured individuals and intercede his own *auctoritas* with the consuls, provincial governors, and other officials who had to deal with the cases of soldiers. Augustus perhaps gave no orders, but only recommendations to officials, who would subsequently enforce them by their *imperium*, so that eventually the emperor's suggestions acquired the force of law.

The development of *fideicommissa*[9] seems to offer a parallel to the development of legislation in military wills. Until the time of Augustus *fideicommissa* had no legal force.

But on frequent occasions the emperor, because he was inclined to support certain individuals, or because the person who was designated to carry out the trust had been appealed to 'in the name of the emperor's own safety', or because of some outrageous perfidy, ordered the consuls to interpose their authority. Since this seemed to be just and was also popular, gradually the practice was turned into regular jurisdiction.[10]

Here new law is created out of an informal process by the magistrates acting with the approval of the emperor and the full support of popular opinion. The privilege of the military will may have developed in much the same way in this period, rather than by formal enactment.

[7] *D* 28.2.26.

[8] See, Buckland, *Text-Book*, 327 ff.

[9] Buckland, *Text-Book*, 353. *Fideicommissa* were bequests for the benefit of a third party, in the form of requests and not of command; they were not subject to all the restrictive rules surrounding a will.

[10] Justinian, *Inst.* 2.23.1. 'Gratia personarum motus, vel quia per ipsius salutem rogatus quis diceretur, aut ob insignem perfidiam iussit consulibus auctoritatem suam interponere.'

In this context it is worth noting that under Augustus a *fideicommissum hereditatis* (a trust involving all or part of the inheritance) to a non-citizen was held to be valid. Vespasian, however, withdrew this validity.[11] This may have had something to do with the problems encountered by soldiers in the disposition of their property under the Julio-Claudians and Flavians. The soldier could profit from the *fideicommissum* by leaving his estate to a non-citizen, in particular his concubine and bastard children, who normally would not be Roman citizens. It is unlikely, however, that many soldiers could benefit from this without aid from legal advisers who would prepare written documents (*tabelliones*).

The privileges associated with the military will were extended to all soldiers in the army who were Roman citizens, not merely those who were engaged on active service. In his *mandata* Trajan spoke in effusive general terms about his 'most excellent and loyal fellow-soldiers', and it is clear that he meant all soldiers. That is certainly how Ulpian interpreted it.[12] Imperial rescripts concerning the military will convey the same impression of an act of benevolence generously conferred on all soldiers. 'The emperor Caracalla to Vindicianus: "The wills of soldiers are not subject to the regulations of the law, since on account of the troops' simple mindedness they are permitted to make them in whatever way they wish and in whatever way they can." '[13]

However in one rescript in 212 Caracalla concluded, 'for the wishes of a soldier engaged on an expedition are held to be legally binding'.[14] In the light of the other evidence, this cannot mean that *only* those soldiers on active service were entitled to the privileges of the *testamentum militare*.

---

[11] *Gnomon* of the *idios logos*, 18 (Riccobono, *FIRA*[2] I, 469 ff.); see also, *Il Gnomon dell' Idios Logos* (1950).

[12] *Tit. Ulp.* 23. 10: 'Milites quomodocumque fecerint testamenta, valent, id est etiam sine legitima observatione. Nam principalibus constitutionibus permissum est illis quomodocumque vellent, quomodocumque possent, testari. Idque testamentum, quod miles contra iuris regulam fecit, ita demun valet, si vel in castris mortuus sit vel post missionem intra annum.'

[13] *CJ* 6.21.3 (213); cf. 21.5 (224); 21.6.1 (225); 21.7 (229); 21.8 (238).

[14] 6.21.1 (212).

Presumably the author of the rescript included a reference to the 'expeditio' because the petitioner had specifically mentioned this in his description of the circumstances surrounding the case. It may also be true that soldiers actually involved on campaign received specially favourable consideration in respect of their last wishes, though in fact the rescript gives no hint of this.

Few soldiers seem to have been specifically excluded from the right of 'libera testamenti factio'. Hadrian granted in a rescript that even a soldier who had been condemned to death for an offence against military law could make a will about property he had acquired in military service. Ulpian was of the opinion that such a will was valid 'iure militari'.

It is preferable that they should make their testament according to the rules governing military wills; since the right of making a will is conceded to them in their capacity as soldiers, it is a reasonable conclusion that they should act in accordance with the *ius militare*. But this interpretation depends on the condition that the military oath was not broken.[15]

Hadrian allowed that the will of those who had committed suicide with good reason should be valid in accordance with the rules governing military testaments;[16] this right was also granted to men discharged from the service for medical reasons (*causarii*).[17] But troops who had been dishonourably discharged, and those who were the captives of enemy forces were denied any testamentary privileges. Tribunes and equestrian officers were permitted to make a military will, but they did not enjoy the year's grace after service in which to convert it into a normal one.[18]

The *testamentum militare* had to be completed during military service (and that was considered to commence when the soldier was included in the ranks);[19] furthermore, 'the will which a soldier makes contrary to the strict rule of law is valid if the soldier dies in his military service or after his

[15] *D* 29.1.11; cf. 28.3.6.
[16] 28.3.6.7.
[17] Lenel, *Palingenesia* (1898), vol. I, p. 574.66 (Macer).
[18] 'ignominiosi' — 29.1.26 (Macer); captives — 29.1.10 (Ulpian); officers — 29.1.21 (Africanus).
[19] 29.1.42.

discharge, up to the period of one year'.[20] These regulations, first attested in the jurist Africanus (c.180),[21] were presumably first defined by Nerva or Trajan, when the privilege of *testamentum militare* was established for all troops. It may seem like a display of cynical indifference on the part of the emperor, in that he was less concerned with the welfare of the soldier once he had been discharged, when his contentment and loyalty to the reigning emperor would be of less pressing importance. But in general veterans continued to be well looked after by the government, which could justifiably argue that the year's grace was sufficient for the veteran to find competent legal advice and make a will that conformed with the strict rule of law. If he did not do so, he could be held to be negligent.

Furthermore, depending on the circumstances this rule concerning the time limit could be rather vaguely interpreted. The jurist Paul raised the case of a soldier who had been honourably discharged and then joined up with another military unit within the year. But during this year, when his will was still valid 'iure militari', he failed to renew it under the same regulations. The question was therefore whether the will would be valid in the event of the soldier's death after the year of grace following the first period of service had expired, but while he was still in the second period of military service. Paul was doubtful because the soldier had failed to declare his intention that the will made in the first period of service should be renewed 'iure militari' when he joined the army for the second time. And so, technically the will's time limit of one year had expired and it was no longer valid. Paul was however inclined to give the soldier the benefit of the doubt. 'But it is more compassionate to say that the will is valid on the grounds that the two periods of military service count as one, so to speak.'[22] The language

[20] *Tit. Ulp.* 23.10; *D* 29.1.38 (Paul); 1. 21 (Africanus); 1.15.6 (Ulpian); 1.34.1 (Papinian). For an example of a soldier's will made after discharge, see *FIRA*[2] III, pp. 196 ff.

[21] See W. Kunkel, *Herkunft und soziale Stellung der römischen Juristen, Forschungen zum römische Recht* 4 (1952).

[22] 29.1.38.1. Krüger impugned this passage, without giving a reason. Presumably he thought that Paul's decision was different or expressed in different terms. But there is no good reason to suspect interpolation here.

reflects the jurist's difficulty in deciding between what he knows to be correct in strict law, and his desire to be benevolent to the troops.

It may have been difficult to enforce the rule that the military will retained its validity for only one year after service. The *gnomon* of the *idios logos* in Egypt, which sets out the regulations governing the duties of that office, is rather imprecise on the question of soldiers and their wills. 'Soldiers in service and also those who have left the service are permitted to dispose of their property by both Roman and Greek wills and to use whatever form of words they choose.'[23] The author is clearly referring to the *testamentum militare*, and it seems that in Egypt at least, no definite time limit was imposed upon veteran soldiers.

The troops' privilege of making a will unimpeded by the normal legal regulations was conferred and confirmed by emperors in effusive language with sweeping generalizations. Trajan's *mandata* provide the best example:

It has been brought to my attention that wills made by my fellow-soldiers are being produced which would be the subject of dispute if the full rigour of the law were strictly applied to them. Therefore in response to the justness of my feelings for my excellent and most loyal fellow-soldiers, I have decided that due consideration must be made for their simple-minded innocence. Consequently, regardless of the way in which their wills have been drawn up, their wishes are to be considered valid. And so, they may draw up their wills in whatever way they wish and in whatever way they can, and the mere wish of the maker of the will is to be sufficient for the division of his property.[24]

The language is striking for the flattering reference to the emperor's fellow-soldiers,[25] and also for its vague benevolence. Trajan's obvious concern for his troops and the

---

[23] Riccobono, *FIRA*[2] I, p. 476; *Gnomon*, 34.

[24] 29.1.1: 'Cum in notitiam meam prolatum sit subinde testamenta a commilitonibus relicta proferri, quae possint in controversiam deduci, si ad diligentiam legum revocentur et observantiam: secutus animi mei integritudinem erga optimos fidelissimosque commilitones simplicitati eorum consulendum existimavi, ut quoquomodo testati fuissent, rata esset eorum voluntas. Faciant igitur testamenta quo modo volent, faciant quo modo poterint sufficiatque ad bonorum suorum divisionem faciendam nuda voluntas testatoris.'

[25] See above, pp. 37-8.

impression created by his words doubtless ensured that governors and other officials interpreted this concession as liberally as possible. But the soldiers may have been encouraged to exploit their privilege too enthusiastically, and Trajan later had to modify his decision.

He had received an enquiry from one of his governors, Statilius Severus, who had to adjudicate in a case involving the will of a soldier. The emperor replied:

The privilege conferred on soldiers that their wills are to be considered valid regardless of how they have been executed, should be interpreted as follows. The first point to be ascertained is that the will was completed, and that can be done without putting the will in writing and also applies to people who are not soldiers. Therefore if the soldier, about whose property the case before you is concerned, called his colleagues together for the purpose of making his will and specifically declared whom he wished to be his heir and on which slave he wished to confer liberty, then you may conclude that he did make his will in this way without putting it in writing and that his wishes should be honoured. But if, as often happens in casual conversation, the soldier said to someone: 'I make you my heir', or 'I leave my property to you', then this should not be regarded as a valid will. It benefits no one more than the soldiers to whom this privilege was given that this kind of disposition should not count as a valid will. For otherwise it would be easy for witnesses to appear after the death of a soldier and declare that they had heard him say that he was leaving his property to someone whom they wanted to benefit, and in this way the true wishes of the soldier would be frustrated.[26]

The language of this rescript is more businesslike and straightforward than that of the original *mandata*, since

---

[26] 29.1.24: 'Divus Traianus Statilio Severo ita rescripsit: Id privilegium, quod militantibus datum est, ut quoquo modo facta ab his testamenta rata sint, sic intellegi debet, ut utique prius constare debeat testamentum factum esse, quod et sine scriptura et a non militantibus fieri potest. Si ergo miles, de cuius bonis apud te quaeritur, convocatis ad hoc hominibus, ut voluntatem suam testaretur, ita locutus est, ut declararet, quem vellet sibi esse heredem et cui libertatem tribuere: potest videri sine scripto hoc modo esse testatus et voluntas eius rata habenda est. Ceterum si, ut plerumque sermonibus fieri solet, dixit alicui: "Ego te heredem facio", aut, "tibi bona mea relinquo", non oportet hoc pro testamento observari. Nec ullorum magis interest, quam ipsorum, quibus id privilegium datum est, eiusmodi exemplum non admitti: alioquin non difficulter post mortem alicuius militis testes existerent, qui adfirmarent se audisse dicentem aliquem relinquere se bona cui visum sit, et per hoc iudicia vera subvertuntur.'

Trajan is attempting to sort out the uncertainty created by his instructions and the change in the accepted process of the law. Indeed there is an implied rebuke for the greed and dishonesty of some soldiers, although the emperor is still concerned that they should get the full benefit of the privilege. The difficulty encountered by Statilius Severus was the result of the vagueness of the *mandata* and the grandiose and generous language which suggested a sweeping privilege, with few if any restrictions. Even if the amendment suggested in the rescript had been systematically enforced, it gave governors little scope seriously to limit the extensive privileges of the military will, especially in view of Trajan's benevolence towards the troops, of which Pliny was well aware during his governorship of Bithynia: 'I thought it hard to refuse [to forward a petition from a centurion], since I know how willingly and sympathetically you respond to appeals from the soldiers.'[27]

Subsequent emperors reaffirmed the privilege of the *testamentum militare* in the same benevolent terms as Trajan. Caracalla also spoke of the simple-mindedness of the troops and their right to make wills 'in whatever way they wish and in whatever way they can'.[28] Severus Alexander spoke of the 'soldiers' own special privilege' ('proprium privilegium'),[29] of their 'free decision to leave their property to whomever they want',[30] and of the 'prerogative of the military privilege' ('praerogativa militaris privilegii').[31] The concern of emperors that soldiers should receive the full benefit of the concession can also be seen in the specific instructions issued to imperial legates in the *mandata*.[32] According to Gaius, a proconsul issued a separate edict on the wills of soldiers, 'because he knew very well that in accordance with the constitutions of the emperors, unique and extraordinary regulations were applied to their wills'.[33]

[27] *Ep.* 10.106.
[28] *CJ* 6.21.3.
[29] 21.6.
[30] 21.5.
[31] 21.7.
[32] *D* 29.1.1. For the sending of *mandata* to proconsuls, see G.P. Burton, 'The Issuing of Mandata to Proconsuls and a New Inscription from Cos', *ZPE* 21 (1976), 63.
[33] 29.1.2: 'propria atque singularia iura in testamenta eorum observari'.

The generalizations used by emperors create an impression of goodwill and generosity, but to what extent were soldiers better off than civilians, who did not enjoy any privileges in the making of a will? There are three main areas in which the soldier was substantially assisted by his privileged position — the technical problems encountered in formally drawing up a will, the people to whom he was permitted to leave property, and the process of altering an already completed testament.

Normally in Roman law, failure to adhere to the strict and extensive regulations governing the formal presentation of a will meant that it became invalid.[34] But a soldier did not have to bother with the required number of witnesses or the formal announcement of the will (*nuncupatio*).[35] He could even make a will in Greek, though normally all wills had to be in Latin.[36] Unfinished wills were generally regarded as valid, because the wishes of a soldier were held to be paramount, no matter how they were expressed.[37] Paul was called upon to decide in a peculiar case.

Lucius Titus, a soldier, dictated his will to his scribe to be written up from notes, and before it could be formally written out, the soldier died. I consider if the dictation counts as a valid will. I replied that soldiers are permitted to execute a will in whatever way they want and in whatever way they can, as long as this is done in a way which can be proved by proper evidence.[38]

Here it is interesting to note the influence of the generous wording of Trajan's *mandata*, but also a concern that injustice and misrepresentation should not take place, as the emperor had made clear in his reply to Statilius Severus.

Because of ignorance, carelessness, or for convenience, soldiers were often in breach of many of the usual regulations concerning wills. The writings of the jursits show some of the

---

[34] Buckland, *Text-Book*, 282 ff.
[35] Gaius, *Inst.* 2.109–10. For a general description of the legal privileges of soldiers, see E. Sander, *RhM* 101 (1958), 152.
[36] *Gnomon* of the *idios logos*, 34; cf. 8.
[37] *D* 29.1.35 (Papinian).
[38] 29.1.40.

unusual actions they were obliged to tolerate. A soldier could institute heirs in two or more wills, and they remained valid if he expressed this wish specifically; indeed, as Papinian puts it, 'a soldier who makes several wills on different days is held to make his will frequently'.[39] Furthermore, a soldier was permitted to institute several heirs for his property acquired in military service and his other property;[40] he could institute an heir by *codicilli* and by testament;[41] he could even make a will for part of his property and remain intestate for the rest;[42] he could institute an heir for a limited amount of time, or on a condition.[43] This contravened the principle of law otherwise applicable, that once someone had been invested as *heres*, he could not remove himself from this position.[44] In addition, the *testamentum militare* was protected from 'bonorum possessio' (i.e., control of property, though not in the formal capacity as heir) in respect of property acquired by a soldier in military service, and this was confirmed by Antoninus Pius in a rescript.[45] Sometime in the second century soldiers were exempted from the *Lex Falcidia*, which laid down that the legacies in a will should not exceed three-quarters of its total value.[46] There could be no 'querella inofficiosi testamenti' (a complaint that a will was undutiful) against the will of a soldier;[47] and a change in his status, for example by adoption, did not invalidate the will.[48] The usual regulations governing gifts made in the expectation of death (*donationes mortis causa*) were relaxed in the case of soldiers.[49] Finally, a soldier who was afflicted by deafness and dumbness was permitted to make a military will while he was still in the ranks awaiting his discharge on medical grounds. Normally this was for-

[39] 1. 35; cf. 1.19 (Ulpian).
[40] 1.17.1 (Iulianus apud Gaium); cf. Buckland, *Text-Book,* 294–5.
[41] 1.36. pref; 1.35 (Papinian); and see O. Seecke, *RE* IV col. 174 f.; Marcus Aurelius established that if for some reason the will was invalidated, the *codicilli* would also be invalidated (1.3).
[42] 1.6 (Ulpian); *CJ* 6.21.3 (213); for civilians see Just. *Inst.* 2.14.5.
[43] *D* 29.1.15.4 (Ulpian); 1.41 (Tryphonius).
[44] Buckland, *Text-Book,* 282.
[45] 29.1.30; 1.29.3 (Marcellus).
[46] 1.17.4 (Gaius); 1.18 (Tryphonius).
[47] 5.2.8.3 (Ulpian); cf. 5.2.1.
[48] 29.1.23 (Tertullian).
[49] 39.6.15; cf. Buckland, *Text-Book*, 256 ff.

bidden on a legal technicality even for those who had been deaf mutes from birth.[50]

The privileges outlined above appear to have developed in an unsystematic way from Trajan's general grant of 'libera testamenti factio'. The vague nature of his *mandata* meant that when particular problems arose in respect of soldiers' wills, emperors or jurists produced a ruling according to the circumstances. And so eventually there was a relatively coherent body of examples or precedents for the extent of the concessions soldiers could expect. Although the first mention of some of these privileges occurs in the Severan jurists, it is clear that most of them had been discussed and confirmed by Trajan and his immediate successors from the early second century onwards, and were not introduced by Septimius Severus.[51]

In a will made by a civilian there were strict regulations governing the people who could become heirs or receive a legacy. 'Only those people can be instituted as heirs who have, along with the testator, the right of making a will themselves.'[52] The military will largely absolved soldiers from these restrictions: 'Those who have been deported, and nearly everyone who does not have the right of making a will, can be instituted as heir by a soldier.'[53] This is confirmed by a rescript of Severus Alexander:

In the will of a soldier, whether he was still in service or had died within a year of an honourable discharge, the inheritance and the legacies must be conferred on all to whom they were left, since among the other concessions granted to soldiers they also have the right to leave, without restriction, their property to whomever they wish, unless the law specifically prohibits them.[54]

In fact there were few specific restrictions on this right. A soldier could not name a slave as heir, without first granting him his freedom. And if he thought that a slave was

---

[50] 29.1.4; cf. *Tit. Ulp.* 20.13.
[51] 29.1.1; 1.2; 1.24; *Gnomon* of the *idios logos*, 34; Gaius, *Inst.* 2.110–11; D 29.1.9; 1.17.1-2; 1.20.1; 1.21; 1.30; 28.3.6.7; 40.5. 42.
[52] *Tit. Ulp.* 22.1.
[53] D 29.1.13.2.
[54] *CJ* 6.21.5 (224).

free and made him his heir, then the institution was not valid.[55] Hadrian laid down in a rescript that 'a woman who can be suspected of being licentious cannot receive anything from the will of a soldier'.[56] This presumably refers to prostitutes. Soldiers will frequently have been in contact with such ladies and Hadrian may have been anxious to ensure that prostitutes did not profit by falsely alleging that the soldiers had left property to them.[57]

Gaius tells us that the soldiers' right of instituting as heirs or legatees whomever they wished included peregrines, Latins, and childless and unmarried persons.[58] This was perhaps introduced by Trajan and may have had its origin in an attempt to ameliorate the legal consequences of the ban on military marriages, or the difficulties of soldiers who had just acquired citizen rights.[59] In this case it seems that a special concession in the making of a will was being extended to soldiers to help deal with another problem they faced through military service. The *testamentum militare* had here been developed beyond the idea of the minimum necessary change in the law to assist the simple-minded troops distribute their property. The military will produced an open-ended privilege for soldiers, and it is easy to see how further rights could be usurped, be confirmed in individual cases, and then become a general rule.

Soldiers were also treated as special cases in the matter of leaving property to children. A civilian testator could not disinherit children who were in his control, unless he specifically excluded them by name in his will. For this purpose he had to disinherit all who might be born after his will was completed or after his death (*postumi*).[60] But if a soldier passed over an existing child without mentioning him in his will, this constituted an act of disinheritance.[61] It is true

[55] *D* 29.1.13.2-3. See below, p. 224.
[56] 1.41.1.
[57] Cf. pp. 290-1.
[58] *Inst.* 2.110-11.
[59] See Campbell, *JRS* 1978, 158.
[60] Gaius, *Inst.* 2.127-30.
[61] *CJ* 6.21.9 (238), 6.21.10 (246). Before Septimius Severus removed the ban on marriage, these regulations will have referred to children born before or after military service.

that the birth of a *postumus* could also break a military will if the child were under the legal control of the *testator*. But if the soldier were still in the army when the *postumus* was born, and merely expressed a wish that his will should remain valid, 'it will be valid, just as if another will has been made'.[62] On the other hand, if the soldier had left the army before the birth of the *postumus*, the broken will could not regain its validity and a completely new testament was needed.[63] Jurists were sympathetic towards the problems faced by soldiers as a result of these privileges. So it was established that a child passed over in silence in a soldier's will by mistake, did have a claim on the estate.[64] In this the jurists were undoubtedly influenced by the considerate attitude of emperors.[65]

The principle of 'libera testamenti factio' centred on the idea that the wishes (*voluntas*) of the soldiers should be paramount. This concern is also apparent in the wide latitude granted to soldiers to alter their will with the minimum of formality. Papinian states the general rule: 'For in whatever way a soldier makes a will, it will become void if he makes a new one, since for a soldier a mere expression of wish is a will.'[66] The lack of formality can be seen in another statement by Ulpian: 'Just as a soldier can confer an inheritance by a simple expression of his wishes, so he can also take it away. Therefore, if he cancelled a will and then wanted it to be valid again, it will be valid in accordance with his last expression of his wishes.'[67]

Even if a soldier made a second will in which he instructed the heir by *fideicommissum* that the first will was to be valid, his wishes were respected and he was held to have two

---

[62] *D* 29.1.33.pref.—33.1 (Tertullian). Cf. 1.7; 1.36.2.

[63] 1.33.2–3.

[64] Ibid; cf. 1.36.2 (Papinian). Note that a soldier could execute a will on behalf of his child — *D* 29.1.15.5.

[65] Cf. *CJ* 6.21.9 (Gordian); 10 (Philip).

[66] *D* 29.1.34.2; 1.27.

[67] 1.15.1; he goes on to advise the judge to consider the soldier's motives; if it is proved that the soldier repented of his change of mind, then the will should be held as renewed. But if his intention was that what was written in the will should not be read, the decision will be that he acted in this way in order to cancel his will.

wills.[68] Indeed Gaius was apparently prepared to allow a military will in which the soldier had changed his mind about the heir. 'If in the same will a soldier institutes a certain person as heir and then disinherits him, the heir will be considered to have been deprived of the estate, whereas in the will of a civilian the estate cannot be removed by mere disheritance of this kind.'[69] Presumably the will of a civilian was rendered invalid by such a mistake.

Most of the discussion about the expression of a soldier's wishes and the changing of his will occurs in the works of the Severan jurists. But the passage of Gaius quoted above shows that even in the second century the concept of allowing a soldier to change his will by a mere expression of his wishes was well established. In fact Antoninus Pius showed a similar concern for the *voluntas* of a soldier in a rescript. He ruled that a will made under the usual rules of law before military service should be valid 'iure militari' merely by the expression of the soldier's intentions ('voluntas').[70]

The rescripts and pronouncements of emperors were decisive in determining the attitude of the other officials who had to interpret the privileges associated with the *testamentum militare*. It is notable that Statilius Severus, when confronted with the case involving the disposal by will of the estate of a soldier, had not the confidence to decide for himself, but instead referred a relatively unimportant matter to Trajan. A benevolent rescript would be influential, especially since military privileges were open to wide interpretation. For example, Severus Alexander, when dealing with the problem of a will which referred to a slave as if he were a free man, replied:

The phrase 'I grant and bequeath to my freedman Fortunatus' does not entitle you to obtain your freedom, if you are referring to the will of a civilian. But since you claim that the *testator* was a soldier, if he genuinely intended to give you your freedom and did not in error believe you to be his freedman, then you are entitled to your freedom,

[68] 1.19 (Ulpian).
[69] 1.17.2.
[70] 1.9; Julianus wanted a clearer indication of the soldier's wishes — 1.20.1.

and indeed directly, and the prerogative of the military privilege entitles you to claim the legacy.[71]

Normally the will of a soldier was subject to the provisions of the *Lex Aelia Sentia,* which governed manumissions.[72]

Once again it should be emphasized that the generous attitude of emperors was not a phenomenon of the Severan age. A rescript of Antoninus Pius considered the case of a soldier whose wishes had been disrupted by the death of his heir and his substitute.

Our emperor Antoninus Pius, in order that the final wishes of his soldiers should be valid in all respects, instructed that in a case where an heir and his substitute had died suddenly before assuming the inheritance, those to whom freedom and the estate had been left under a trust by the soldier through the heir and his substitute should become free and heirs to the estate, just as if they had received these directly. However, in the case of those who had received their freedom and inheritance from a civilian *testator* through a trust, when the heir and his substitute died suddenly, the emperor thought it sufficient in this case to confirm only their freedom.[73]

Jurists like Javolenus Priscus, Salvius Julianus, Ulpian and Papinian were not mere imperial ciphers, but responsible and learned men who had a sincere respect for the principle of the law. But they also took a favourable attitude towards the troops and their privileges, and repeated the expansive pronouncements of the emperors.[74] They recognized explicitly

[71] *CJ* 6.21.7: 'Ex his verbis: "Fortunato liberto meo do lego", vindicare tibi libertatem non potes, si pagani testamentum proponatur. At enim cum testatorem militem fuisse proponas, si non errore ductus libertum te credidit, sed dandae libertatis animum habuit, libertatem et quidem directam, competere tibi, sed et legati vindicationem habere praerogativa militaris privilegii praestat.' Cf. *D* 29.1.40.2 (Paul).

[72] *D* 29.1.29.1. Cf *CJ* 6.21.4: 'Si Rufinus vir clarissimus tribunus laticlavius maior annis lege definitis faciens testamentum te manumisit, iustam tibi libertatem competisse scire debes. Quod si minor annis ex lege constitutis fuerit, cum faceret testamentum, lege impediente nullam libertatem adeptus es, quae in hac parte nec militibus remissa est. Quod si idem testator causam manumittendi te habuit, quae probabilis vivo manumittente consilio futura esset, quia per fideicommissum data libertas a quolibet minore annis ei, cuius causa probari potuit, praestari debet, et ex testamento militis eiusmodi servis iustam libertatem competere consequens est.' And see Buckland, *Text-book,* 79.

[73] *D* 40.5.42, cf. the rescript of Severus and Caracalla: 29.1. 13.4; 1.14.

[74] 29.1.40 (Paul); *Tit. Ulp.* 23.10.

the distinction between soldiers and civilians, in that the former were entitled to a variety of privileges not enjoyed by the latter. These privileges could easily be extended through the indulgent attitude of the men who administered the law.[75]

The jurists seem to have accepted Trajan's explanation for the privilege of the *testamentum militare*, that the simple-mindedness and inexperience of the troops made it necessary.[76] Gaius observed that in the constitutions of the emperors the strict enforcement of the law in the wills of soldiers was relaxed 'because of their extreme ignorance' ('imperitia').[77] A second reason, namely that soldiers laboured on behalf of the State and deserved reward, is reflected in Ulpian's extraordinary etymology for the word *miles*. Among a number of suggestions he said that it was derived from 'the rigours ['malitia'], that is the austerity which they endure on our account', or from 'the evil ['malum'] which soldiers usually protect us from'.[78]

It must be doubted if either the *simplicitas* or *imperitia* of the troops, or the onerous and dangerous nature of their duties on behalf of the State, provided sufficient justification for the privileges they received. The first explanation has some plausibility since the rescripts of the *Codex Justinianus* show that soldiers were often incapable of understanding their rights.[79] What is more, many soldiers will have been new citizens or from families who had recently acquired the citizenship. No doubt they were unfamiliar with the traditions of Roman law and the making of wills. But the rest of the lower orders in the empire were just as likely to suffer from lack of knowledge of the law. As Roman citizenship spread, many even of the higher classes will have had the difficulty of making a will in an unfamiliar legal system. When the law did take more care of soldiers than of others,

---

[75] Distinction between *milites* and *pagani* — 29.1.14 (Maecianus); 1.33.2 (Tertullian); 1.34.2 (Papinian). Benevolent attitude — 28.3.6.6; 29.1.11; 1.38.1; 39.6.15.

[76] *D* 29.1.1.

[77] Gaius, *Inst.* 2.109.

[78] *D* 29.1.1.1. The true etymology of *miles* is unclear; cf. *Thes. Ling. Lat.* vol. 8, col. 939.

[79] See below, pp. 273ff.

it surely suggests that the troops were considered more important to the emperor than civilians, whose *imperitia* could be ignored.

However, the privilege of the military will can perhaps partly be explained by the fact that the soldier might be engaged on campaign in remote areas where it would be difficult to get advice, and that in the camp itself there was an absence of legal advisors (*tabelliones*)[80] because of the small scale of business. This may help to explain why some of the officers also received the privilege of 'libera testamenti factio'. But the soldier could at least look to his immediate commander for advice. One of the duties of the military tribune was to listen to the complaints of his fellow-soldiers. In many areas poor Roman citizens no doubt also found it hard to obtain legal advice, yet the government made no special provision for their interests.

The likelihood of sudden death could also serve to justify the principle of *suprema voluntas* in a soldier's will, and the right of making a will free from legal nicities. But the evidence shows that up to the time of Constantine the privileges were allowed to all soldiers during military service. There is little reason why a soldier engaged in routine camp duties far from the dangers of war should receive any special freedom to make a will, or why the privileges associated with the *testamentum militare* should be so extensive.

Originally additional motives probably lay behind the development of the military will. If a soldier failed to make his will in due form, then, before the Flavians at least, it was invalid and his property went to the intestate heirs. The effect would often have been to disappoint the expectations of his own comrades, or perhaps of his concubine and children (who, being non-citizens could not inherit).[81] Moreover, there might be no intestate heirs (for example, a new citizen whose kinsmen remained non-citizens), or none aware of their position and effectively able to claim. In that case the *bona vacantia* (property without an owner) would fall to the *fiscus*. The case would come before the legate,

[80] See F. Schulz, *History of Roman Legal Science* (1946), 109 ff.
[81] See below, pp. 301-2.

or perhaps the procurator, and the emperor's officials would be forced to sequester the property for the emperor. It is possible to imagine a case in which a soldier's comrade or natural son were disinherited on a technicality and the emperor was forced to sequester the estate. Cases of this kind would cause great resentment and discontent, and it is easy to imagine that long before soldiers were permitted to make a military will, emperors chose to neglect any claims to *bona vacantia*.[82] But if the *fiscus* were not to profit by strict observance of the laws, why should third parties, as interested heirs? But it was quite another matter if the soldier had been discharged. Once he had been settled as a veteran, the upsetting of his will on a technicality would be much less likely to bring the emperor into bad repute, for it would not have the same publicity among the serving troops. Furthermore, the discharged soldier would find it easier to obtain legal advice.

The privilege of the military will may have originated as a means by which emperors attempted to avoid discontent in the army, provide some protection from the rigours of military life, and perhaps assist recruitment. But in itself it had a wider significance, for most emperors will surely have realized that the *testamentum militare* would help to convince the soldiers of their concern and interest, increase the rewards of serving in the army, and so help to develop personal loyalty and affection for the emperor who guaranteed these privileges.[83] There is much truth in the opinion of

---

[82] Cf. *D* 38.12.2: 'Bona militis intestati defuncti castrensia fisco non vindicantur, cum heres legitimus ad finem quinti gradus exstitit aut proximus cognatus eiusdem gradus intra tempus possessionem acceperit.' I wish to thank the Council of the Society for Roman Studies for permission to quote in this paragraph a passage from my article in *JRS* 1978, 157.

[83] Naturally the privilege of 'libera testamenti factio' described in this chapter could apply only to Roman citizens, i.e. legionaries. The auxiliaries, who consisted largely of *peregrini*, will not have been making Roman wills. But I find it hard to accept that the auxiliaries were completely ignored, especially since by the end of the first century they made up half the numbers of the army and took an increasingly large part in the fighting. It is possible that the consular legate in the provinces where auxiliaries were stationed informally ensured that the provisions of a will made by a peregrine soldier that did not accord with any legal requirements of the practice in his country of origin, were nevertheless carried out. A will made after discharge, when the auxiliary had acquired citizenship, would have to conform with Roman legal requirements.

the jurist Macer, who, in discussing the soldier's right to dispose of his property acquired in military service, describes it as a 'privilege extended to deserving soldiers as a kind of reward'.[84] In the eyes of the soldiers at least, their legal privileges were part of their emoluments, like pay and discharge *praemia*.

For each emperor there was a delicate balance. He needed to indulge the army to preserve its contentment and loyalty, but he must also maintain the law and the rights of others. This concern is discernible in the restrictions on the military will, which were designed as far as possible to prevent the infringment of the rights of others.[85] Since most emperors claimed to rule by sanction of the law, they must at least pay lip-service to its principles.[86] And many were probably sincerely concerned, in particular because by upbringing, education, and sentiment emperors identified themselves with the upper classes, for whose privileged position the law was a considerable bulwark.

3. THE SOLDIER'S PROPERTY

The Roman *filius familias* (i.e., a man whose father was still alive and in whose control legally he was) owned no property of his own and could therefore not make a will, since he had no estate to dispose of.[1] Everything was in the power (*potestas*) of his father and was owned by him. The soldier's *castrense peculium* consisted of property acquired in or because of military service, over which he had complete control. The significance of this privilege depends

---

[84] *D* 29.1.26.

[85] A soldier could not dispose of his wife's dowry (29.1.16 — Paul); he could not order a slave's punishment in a will (1.13.2 — Ulpian); he could not appoint tutors for his son who was still not of age and who was still in the control of his grandfather (1.28 — Marcus Aurelius and Lucius Verus).

[86] Cf. Severus Alexander — *CJ* 6.21.5. The soldiers can leave property to whomever they like, 'nisi lex specialiter eos prohibuerit'. It is possible that this final phrase is a later interpolation. On the other hand, it is consistent with Alexander's desire to live by the rule of law: 'nihil tamen tam proprium imperii est, ut legibus vivere' (*CJ* 6.23.3).

[1] *Tit. Ulp.* 20.10: 'Filius familiae testamentum facere non potest, quoniam nihil suum habet, ut testari de eo possit.'

on the legal importance in the imperial period of the 'father's power' (*patria potestas*).

It has been suggested that for the bulk of the citizen population the rules of *patria potestas* did not apply, and that it was relevant to only the upper class élite.[2] But this idea runs counter to the available evidence. Firstly, Juvenal, writing in Hadrian's reign, says that soldiers alone have the right of making a will while their father is still alive — 'for it has been decided that emoluments acquired by military service should not be included in the bulk of the property over which the father has total control'.[3] Juvenal must have believed that the concept of *patria potestas* was relevant to men of the lower classes. Secondly, imperial rescripts affirm that Roman citizens of whatever social class were under their father's legal control. For many rescripts on this point are addressed to soldiers and they emphasize the principle of the father's power: 'for, none the less soldiers remain in the power of their parents';[4] 'If your son was in your control at the time when you acquired certain items in his name, there is no doubt that these belong to you.'[5] These and many other similar examples show that the question of *patria potestas* and the ramifications caused by the privilege of *castrense peculium* continued to be important and contentious issues for ordinary people.

Finally, it seems that *patria potestas* applied to Roman citizens in the provinces. A papyrus of AD 267 records the sale of a slave by a father and son, both mailed cavalrymen stationed in Egypt.[6] Both have semitic names. It is clear that the father acts on behalf of his son 'according to the laws of the Romans'; the son, therefore, is not in control of his own affairs. This confirms the contention that *patria potestas* was generally accepted by citizens in the provinces, though it was frequently misunderstood and weakened into a kind of 'Vulgarrecht'.[7]

---

[2] D. Daube, *Roman Law: Linguistic, Social and Philosophical Aspects* (1969), 81.

[3] 16.51 ff.   [4] *CJ* 12.36.3.   [5] 36.1.   [6] *P.Ox.* 2951.

[7] L. Mitteis, *Reichsrecht und Volksrecht* (1891), 151 ff.; 209 ff. He also believed that the idea of *patria potestas* was a practicable concept among Greeks of the second century; cf. especially Dio of Prusa, 15.20; Philostratos, *VS* 521.

If Roman citizens were still under the control of their father, legally owned no property, and could not make a testament, the privilege of *castrense peculium* was a significant addition to the special rights accorded to soldiers. It was first introduced by Augustus, who allowed the soldiers to have control over the property they had acquired through military service, and to dispose of it by will.[8] These rights were confirmed again by Nerva and by Trajan, and up to this time applied only to those soldiers still serving in the army. We may compare the development of the military will, where Nerva's benevolence was confirmed and publicized by Trajan. However, whereas Augustus may have intervened informally in the case of the military will, his support for the privilege of *castrense peculium* clearly consisted of a formal authorization. It is interesting that Hadrian extended the privilege of *castrense peculium* to veteran soldiers, a principle apparently maintained by subsequent emperors.

The *castrense peculium* is defined as whatever was given by his parents or relatives to a man embarking on military service, or whatever the *filius familias* himself acquired during military service, and which he would not have obtained had he not been a soldier. For anything which he would have acquired anyway without being a soldier is not defined as part of the *castrense peculium*.[9]

This definition was not sufficiently exact to prevent several areas of doubt about what the soldier was permitted to consider as property associated with his military service. The jurists were concerned to ensure that the privilege was not exploited unfairly at the expense of others. So the dowry of a soldier's wife, whom he had married before joining up, was held to be outside the *castrense peculium*, especially since the dowry was heavily involved with the rights of the

[8] Justinian, *Inst.* 2.12. pref; *Tit. Ulp.* 20.10: 'Sed divus Augustus constituit ut filius familias miles de eo peculio quod in castris adquisivit testamentum facere possit.'

[9] *D* 49.17.11 (Macer); 17.4 (Tertullian); 17.6 (Ulpian); 17.16 (Papinian); *CJ* 12.36.1 (223): 'Peculio autem castrensi cedunt res mobiles, quae eunti a patre vel a matre aliisve propinquis vel amicis donatae sunt, item quae in castris per occasionem militiae quaeruntur. In quibus sunt etiam hereditates eorum, qui non alias noti esse potuerunt nisi per militiae occasionem, etiamsi res immobiles in his erunt.'

other family, and could not be set aside in the soldier's private property over which he had sole control.[10] Papinian ruled that anything left to a soldier by his cousin, who had served as a soldier in another province, should not be in the *castrense peculium*, since the reason for the bequest was not military service but their blood relationship.[11] But as Scaevola pointed out, the difficulty was in deciding whether in a case where the two men were related and also fellow-soldiers, that is presumably serving in the same province, their joint military service had increased the affection already existing between them. In that sense it could be argued that the inheritance had been acquired through military service and should be defined as part of the *castrense peculium*.[12] As a solution another jurist proposed that if the will concerning the inheritance had been made before the period of joint military service, then the inheritance could not be in the *castrense peculium* of the soldier who received it; but if the will had been made after their *commilitium*, then the inheritance could be classed as part of the *castrense peculium*.[13] Ulpian took a strict view of bequests made to soldiers by relatives.

If his wife, or a relative, or anyone else not known to him from military service, donates or bequeaths anything to a soldier who is a *filius familias*, and expresses a specific wish that he should have it in the *castrense peculium*, can it really be included in the *castrense peculium*? My view is that it should not. For I consider the truth of the matter, and whether the acquaintance and affection were derived from military service, not what someone imagined was the case.[14]

Significantly, some emperors took a much more liberal view. Hadrian ruled that, in a case where a soldier who was a *filius familias* was instituted as heir by his wife, he became heir and that when he manumitted those slaves who were

[10] *D* 49.17.16: 'nam hereditas adventicio iure quaeritur, dos autem matrimonio cohaerens oneribus eius ac liberis communibus qui sunt in avi familia, confertur.'
[11] 49.17.16.1.
[12] 17.19. pref.
[13] Ibid.
[14] 17.8.

part of the inheritance, they became his own freedmen. This means that the inheritance had been included in the soldier's *castrense peculium*.[15] Since at this time soldiers were not permitted to marry, it follows that the soldier had married this woman before military service and therefore the inheritance had nothing to do with his military career, and in accordance with the strict definition should not have been included in the *castrense peculium*.

When Gordian III was petitioned about a case concerning an inheritance bequeathed to a soldier by a relation who was also a soldier, he displayed none of the doubts and anxieties that had affected Papinian and the other jurists.

The emperor Gordianus Augustus to Gallus the soldier. Since you claim that you have been instituted as heir by your brother who is a fellow-soldier serving in the same camp, your request that this inheritance should pass to your *castrense peculium*, rather than to the father in whose control you still are, seems entirely reasonable. For I am compelled to believe that your toils away from home and the company of your joint military service, and the fellowship in the carrying out of your duties, must certainly have added considerably to your brotherly love, and rendered you both more affectionate to one another.[16]

The emperor has generously given the soldier the benefit of the doubt and has not troubled to enquire when the will was made, as Tryphonius suggested. The effusive language employed in this rescript doubtless made clear to officials how they should interpret similar cases in the future.

Once it had been decided what was in the *castrense peculium*, the *filius familias* who was a soldier had complete control over it, and could employ or dispose of it in whatever way he pleased, even against the wishes of his father.[17]

---

[15] 17.13; cf. 17.16.

[16] *CJ* 12.36.4: 'Cum adlegas te a fratre tuo eodemque commilitone in isdem castris institutum heredem, successionem eius potius ex castrensi peculio tuo quam patri cuius in potestate es per te quaesitam videri rationis est. Etenim peregrinationis labor sociatus commilitii eius et obeundorum munerum consortium adfectioni fraternae nonnihilum addidisse, quin immo vice mutua cariores invicem sibi reddidisse credendum est.'

[17] *D* 49.17.7 (Ulpian); 17.4.1 (Menander) — 'actionem persecutionemque castrensium rerum semper filius etiam invito patre habet'; 29.1.30.

Both emperors and jurists strove to protect the *peculium* against encroachment by fathers who resented the intrusion upon their traditional rights. Maecianus stated the principle firmly: 'Any actions of the father which for the time lead to the alienation of any right belonging to the *castrense peculium*, are prohibited.'[18] Hadrian confirmed that a soldier could manumit a slave belonging to the *castrense peculium*.[19] On the other hand, if a father tried to manumit a slave in the *castrense peculium* while his son was still alive, the grant of freedom was prohibited.[20] Moreover, the father could not take possession of the *castrense peculium* if he gave his son in adoption or emancipated him.[21]

However, a conscientious emperor would be anxious to preserve the delicate balance between the traditional rights of the *pater familias* and the privileges of the soldiery. Two rescripts of Severus Alexander illustrate some of the problems:

The emperor Alexander Augustus to Felix. A *filius familias* cannot take any property for himself without the permission of his father, unless he has it as the *castrense peculium*.[22]

The emperor Alexander Augustus to Felicianus the soldier. The man who told you that you were freed from the ties of your father's control by your position as a soldier, is in error. Like everyone else soldiers remain in the control of their fathers, but they have the *castrense peculium* as their own property and the father has no rights over this.[23]

The rights of the father with regard to the *castrense peculium* when his son died intestate, also give a good indication of the balance between a military privilege and the principle of the law otherwise applicable. For if the *filius familias* who was a soldier died without making a will, his father received the *castrense peculium* as if it were the freely

[18] 49.17.18.1.
[19] 17.19.3.
[20] 17.9 (Ulpian).
[21] 17.14.2 (Tertullian); 17.12 (Papinian).
[22] *CJ* 12.36.2: 'Filius familias alienationem nullius rei sine voluntate patris habet, nisi si castrensi (?) peculium habet.'
[23] 36.3: 'Errat, qui tibi persuasit, quod nexu paternae potestatis iure sacramenti solutus es. Manent enim nihilo minus milites in potestate parentium, sed peculium castrense proprium habent nec in eo ius ullum patris est.'

revocable *peculium* that a father could bestow on his son. Indeed it was held that the *castrense peculium* had never left the father's control.[24] Again, if the son instituted heirs for the *castrense peculium* and they refused to accept the inheritance, it then passed to the father.[25] All this perhaps shows a latent respect for the father's rights and a desire to upset as little as possible the normal process of the law.

It is plausible to suggest that the privilege of *castrense peculium* was necessary to keep the troops in good heart. On a reasonable estimation of the expectation of life in the Roman empire, many soldiers who were legitimate sons of citizens would have lost their fathers, and many, whether sons of non-citizens or of citizens born from non-citizen mothers, were not subject to *patria potestas*. All these soldiers had full rights over their property and earnings. By contrast, if the law had not been modified, *filii familiarum* would have had no title even to keep and spend their army pay and donatives, except in so far as their fathers gave them a freely revocable administration of *peculium*. It would presumably have been the duty of the imperial legate to enforce the right of a father to take what his soldier son had earned. This would have been all the more intolerable in that so many of the men's comrades were not in the same position. One conceivable device was to exempt soldiers from *patria potestas*. But the privilege of *castrense peculium* involved less disturbance of the law and the traditional rights of fathers.[26] Augustus in fact established a right that could satisfy soldiers and yet also showed restraint and avoided reckless indulgence of the army.

[24] *CJ* 12.36.5 (Diocletian); *D* 49.17.14 (Papinian); 17.17 (Papinian); 19.3 (Tryphonius). Tryphonius could describe this process only by comparing it to the right of *postliminium*, by which one who returned from captivity abroad might be restored to his old position.

[25] 49.17.17. Note that if the father was instituted as *heres* of the *castrense peculium*, he could refuse the inheritance and obtain the property as *peculium* in which he would be regarded as resuming his original rights. As *heres* he was liable up to the hilt for debts on the *peculium*, whereas if he simply resumed his rights on the *peculium* he was liable only to the extent the *peculium* permitted.

[26] I wish to thank the Council of the Society for Roman Studies for permission to quote in this paragraph a passage from my article in *JRS* 1978, 157.

Clearly a man should not feel that he was being penalized by military service, and it was essential to develop a content and efficient fighting force. But, as in the case of military wills, emperors naturally sought the good will, affection, and personal loyalty of their troops, and were willing to foster the idea that the army was a highly privileged group with a special place in the ruler's attentions. Hadrian's extension of *castrense peculium* to veterans is significant. It is unlikely that many soldiers who survived military service will have had fathers still alive, and so there can hardly have been much discontent among veterans over *patria potestas*. The reason for the extension of the privilege in this way was perhaps the desire to create a good impression of the emperor's benevolence and concern for his troops right through their lives.

Juvenal was right to emphasize the uniqueness of the soldiers' position in Roman society: 'To the soldiers alone is given the right of making a will while their father is still alive.'[27] Once again it seems that the soldier, who had none of the usual criteria for legal privilege, enjoyed a substantial advantage, which in this case was possessed not even by a consular legate who was still a *filius familias*.

4. THE SOLDIER AND THE DEFENCE OF HIS INTERESTS

Soldiers were held to be in a special position because of the service they performed for the State. 'All soldiers, who cannot leave the military standards without risk to themselves, are considered to be absent in the service of the State ['rei publicae causa absens'].[1] This status also applied when the soldier was on leave and travelling either to or from home, but not, on one interpretation, when he was actually at home.[2] Others too besides soldiers were classified as absent in the service of the State — tribunes of the soldiers, equestrian officers, imperial legates and their official *comites*,

---

[27] 16.51 ff. — 'solis praeterea testandi militibus ius/vivo patre datur. Nam quae sunt parta labore/militiae, placuit non esse in corpore census/omme tenet cuius regimen pater.

[1] *D* 4.6.45 (Scaevola).
[2] 6.35.9 (Paul); cf. 6.34.

proconsuls, the prefect of Egypt, procurators, army doctors, recruiting officers, anyone sent out to suppress 'evil men', those on embassies, and those who left Rome on public errands.[3]

A man could be classified as absent in the public service only if he was away not for his own convenience but from necessity,[4] and this status lasted only for the time during which he fulfilled a particular office.[5] It is hard to think of anyone who more obviously came into the category of those *rei publicae causa absentes* than the troops. The other groups of men who qualified for this status were small in number and most were absent only temporarily. The army, by contrast, comprised by far the largest group on public service and each soldier was on average absent for twenty-five years. Therefore the rights associated with this status will have been more important to soldiers than to anyone else, the more so in that soldiers perhaps did not have the resources or legal knowledge to appoint someone to look after their interests in their absence.

The basic right associated with absence in the State's service was *in integrum restitutio*. 'By this *in integrum restitutio* the praetor promises to order all necessary steps to be taken to set aside the legal consequences that had started with a certain event, as if that event had not occurred, whether the event was a legal act or merely the passage of an appointed time.'[6] This process could be invoked by someone who had suffered loss because he had been unable to defend his legal interests and property since he had been detained away from home. The right of *in integrum restitutio* was enshrined in the praetor's edict, which, although not codified or stereotyped until Hadrian's reign, had for the most part been fully developed by the end of the Republic. The surviving parts of the edict provide that *in integrum restitutio* will be given to make good loss in property sustained by anyone 'who was absent without trick or deceit on public service'.[7] It should be noted that the Table of Heraclea

---

[3] 6.32; 33.2; 35.1 ff.
[4] 6.36 (Ulpian).
[5] 6.38.1 (Ulpian).
[6] M. Kaser, *Römische Zivilprozessrecht* (1966), 330.
[7] *D* 4.6; Lenel, *Ed. Perp.* 109 f.

disqualifies from municipal office anyone whose property had been sold up by order of a court, unless he was a ward or absent without trick or deceit in the public service.[8] It therefore seems reasonable to suppose that the relevant terms of the edict go back to the late Republic.

If soldiers and others legitimately absent in the service of the State failed to sue or were not defended, this might result in the other party acquiring ownership by *usucapio* (the acquisition or control by possession for a certain period of time), or by *praescriptio longi temporis* in the case of provincial lands.[9] Usufructs, that is the right to enjoy the property of another and take its profits, but not to destroy it or dispose of it, would be lost by non-use for one year in the case of movables and for two years in the case of immovables.[10] It was against losses such as these that the right of *restitutio* was intended to protect soldiers and others absent on state business. Again, those *rei publicae causa absentes* could not have their property taken over if they failed to defend a suit for *damnum infectum* (when the ruinous state of private property affected the security of that of a neighbour).[11] Furthermore, the man on state business had the right to *restitutio* even after the four years had elapsed during which actions had to be brought against the *fiscus* for anything it had sold off.[12] Particular provision was made for anyone engaged in state service who had suffered injustice or loss of property while they were under age (twenty-five). Normally minors could claim restitution within a year of coming of age.[13] But if a man joined up while under twenty-five or before the end of the year's grace, he was entitled to restitution for up to one year after discharge even with regard to transactions of his minority.[14] If it were correct to give all men who had just passed the age of twenty-five a year's grace in which to review the transactions that could justify a claim for restitution, and bring an action, it is clear that

---

[8] *FIRA*[2] 1.13.
[9] See Buckland, *Text-Book*, 241–51.
[10] *D* 4.6.23.3 (Ulpian); Buckland, *Text-Book*, 269 ff.
[11] *D* 4.6.15.2. (Ulpian).
[12] *CJ* 2.50.5 (240).
[13] See in general *D* 4.4.
[14] *CJ* 2.52.1–4.

recruitment into the army would deprive a man of this opportunity. And so the soldier was regarded as coming of age on the day of his discharge, and the year's grace in which he could claim restitution was calculated from that date.[15]

In the matter of a law suit by creditors, the property of a man absent on public service could be taken over, but not sold up;[16] the sale was to be deferred until he had ceased to be absent in the service of the State.[17] Severus Alexander was able to bring reassurance to a soldier on such a matter:

> The emperor Alexander Augustus to Aristodemus the soldier. If part of anyone's property is taken over by another while he is on military service, the usual provision for acquisition through possession for a length of time is rescinded, and he is allowed to reclaim his owner-ship after he has ceased to be absent on the State's service, rightfully within one year. It is not correct, however, for the legal rights of the man in possession to be infringed any further than this, contrary to that provision.[18]

The one year time limit, during which an action for *restitutio* had to be brought, was presumably to guard against deceit and an improper exploitation of the privilege.[19]

It is worth noting that soldiers were most prominent in making use of the right of *restitutio*. Out of seven rescripts in the *Codex* on this subject down to 294, six are concerned in some way with the problems of soldiers.[20] Probably many soldiers did own property; imperial rescripts show them in possession of vines, houses, land, slaves, movables, and receiving inheritances.[21] Much of this property was doubtless in the area of their origin, but some will have been acquired in the province where they served, despite the fact that in theory soldiers were forbidden to acquire such property.[22] For if a soldier were instituted as heir he was allowed to

---

[15] Ibid.
[16] *D* 42.4.6.1 (Paul).
[17] *CJ* 2.50.4 (239).
[18] 2.50.3 (223); cf. 2.50.2 (222).
[19] For the 'annus utilis', see Buckland, *Text-Book*, 719 f.
[20] *CJ* 2.50.1, 2, 3, 5, 6, 7. The heading of this *caput* is: 'DE RESTITUTIONE MILITUM ET EORUM QUI REI PUBLICAE CAUSA AFUERUNT'.
[21] See below, pp. 280–1.
[22] *D* 49.16.9.pref (Maecianus); 16.13 (Macer).

accept an estate where he served; and there was nothing to prevent his acquring land in another province.[23] What is more, in practice the rule about the acquisition of land where a soldier served was not strictly enforced. For if he actually purchased land contrary to the rule and no one complained or discovered it until after his discharge, he could not be disturbed.[24]

Many soldiers then may have had interests in property and movable possessions both in the area of their home and where they served, and will often have found it difficult to protect these interests at law because of the length of military service, the infrequent periods of leave,[25] and the demands of active military duties which could prevent them from defending a suit even close to the military camp. A soldier could indeed be expected to appear in court to defend his interests, presumably if this was compatible with his military duties.[26]

The entitlement of the soldiers to restitution was subject to the same restrictions as were imposed upon anyone who was held to be absent on public service. It was subject to the decision of the praetor, or, in the provinces, the decision of the provincial governor when he administered the law.[27] The right could not be extended to those who were not legitimately absent in the State's service,[28] or to those who had been negligent and failed to defend a case when it was possible for them to do so or appoint a procurator to act for them,[29] or to those who sought to profit through the punishment or loss incurred by a third party.[30]

It clearly was possible to exploit the privilege of *restitutio* improperly. For example, the appropriation of property

---

[23] 16.9.1; 16.13.

[24] 16.9 pref; 16.13.1.

[25] If the soldier was not held to be *rei publicae causa absens* when home on leave (see n. 2), it could be argued that he should defend his interests then; but his leave might not afford him the time to complete a protracted legal case.

[26] This is implied by Ulpian, *D* 4.6.15.2. See further below, pp. 254ff.

[27] Many provincials had the citizenship and it was natural for them to sue and be sued where they had their property. Therefore the provincial governor would also have to administer *in integrum restitutio*.

[28] *D* 4.6.4 (Callistratus).

[29] 6.16 (Paul).

[30] 6.18 (Paul).

or assets (*possessio*) was not necessarily the inevitable result of an action brought against those absent in the service of the State. Perhaps the potential plaintiffs would see little advantage in prosecuting their full rights, until the time came when the privilege ceased to be available. However, in the meantime the privileged person could have obtained himself full title to the disputed property by *usucapio* or *praescriptio longi temporis*. But in such an eventuality the praetor's edict provided restitution for the plaintiff. For a clause of the edict granted *restitutio* for all parties against those who tried to acquire property when they were absent on public business.[31] The praetor was concerned to ensure that while men *rei publicae causa absentes* should suffer no harm, they should not be allowed to gain an improper advantage.[32]

There is indeed little sign that soldiers were treated any differently than others absent on State business.[33] However, there is an interesting rescript from Severus Alexander to a lady called Secundina, who was apparently the wife of a soldier. 'In the case of women who have been abroad with their husbands who are absent in the service of the State, if these women are excluded from 'actiones temporariae' [i.e., a legal process that could take place only inside a certain time limit], it is not unknown to come to their assistance, on the precedent of the treatment of the soldiers themselves.'[34] This is a notable extension of the privilege of restitution for the benefit of the wives of men absent on public service. The phrase 'ad exemplum militum' suggests that the emperor naturally thought of the soldiers as the principal beneficiaries of *restitutio*, and may indicate that

[31] 6.21 (Ulpian).

[32] 6.22.1 (Paul). 'Sicut igitur damno eos adfici non vult, ita lucrum facere non patitur.' cf. 6.28.6 (Ulpian).

[33] It is worth noting a case described by Paul (4.6.30). If a soldier's *usucapio* was invalid and he died before completing the time required but this was completed by his heir, the heir had to make good the loss to the plaintiff. This was true even though the soldier acted 'sine dolo'. This process was exactly parallel to the way in which a soldier's heir could enjoy his claims under *in integrum restitutio*, as indeed could the heirs of all who were entitled to this privilege (4.1.6; *CJ* 2.50.1 (197)). In all this there is no indication of any special treatment of the troops.

[34] *CJ* 2.51.1 (226). 'Temporalibus actionibus exclusis mulieribus, quae cum maritis rei publicae causa absentibus peregrinatae sunt, ad exemplum militum subveniri solere non est ignotum.'

this privilege had been extended first to the wives of soldiers, and subsequently to others absent on state business.

The status of soldiers serving in Rome itself in the Praetorian Guard and the Urban Cohorts produced another problem. Ulpian thought that 'all who serve the State in Rome are not absent on public business'.[35] However, elsewhere he pointed out that soldiers were an exception: 'But soldiers who serve in Rome are certainly considered to be absent in the service of the State.'[36] It was Antoninus Pius who established or confirmed this right for the troops.[37] It seems that Pius was attempting to sort out the problem of definition; could soldiers who were Italians and served in Rome really be classed as *rei publicae causa absentes?* Normally a man was held to be on public business from the time he left Rome until he returned.[38] Clearly the urban troops would have been in an anomalous position had Pius not made his ruling, which displayed the usual concern to satisfy the army's needs.

No doubt soldiers, who particularly required the help of *restitutio* because they were absent for long periods and lacked expert advice, saw this right as another benefaction from the emperor.[39] It is likely, however, that others were seriously inconvenienced by the soldier's ability to be absent for a long time, not defend himself, and get restitution of property. But once again emperors and jurists attempted to hold the balance, and the discretionary aspect of *restitutio* allowed officials to ensure that the principle of the law was disturbed as little as possible, and that the privilege was not exploited to the detriment of others.

---

[35] *D* 4.6.5.1.

[36] 6.5.7.

[37] 6.35.5: 'Praefectus quoque Aegypti rei publicae causa abest, quive aliam ob causam rei publicae gratia extra urbem aberit. Sed et in urbanicianis militibus idem divus Pius constituit.' This does not mean that Pius was the first to introduce this measure. Paul may have come across a rescript of the kind so common in the *Codex*, in which an emperor reaffirms the law.

[38] *D* 4.6.38.1; cf. 35.7. Someone who lived outside Rome and had to travel to the city was held to be on state business.

[39] The right may well have originated in the Republic (see n.8) when soldiers started to serve for long periods of time in the army.

V

THE SOLDIER AND THE COURTS

1. INTRODUCTION

When Encolpius, the hero of Petronius' *Satyricon*, rushed into the streets of Puteoli armed with a sword to find his slave and lover Giton, he unfortunately met a soldier.

> A soldier spotted me; he was probably a deserter or a nocturnal cutthroat. 'Hey there comrade,' he said, 'what legion and century do you belong to?' I boldly lied about my century and legion. But he said, 'Well then, in your army do the soldiers walk about wearing white shoes?' Since, by my expression and trembling, I showed that I had been telling a lie, he told me to hand over my sword and to watch out that I did not get a beating. So I was robbed . . . .[1]

In his novel the *Golden Ass*, Apuleius describes a similar incident.[2] Lucius, the hero of the book, had been changed into an ass and was in the service of a vegetable grower. His master encountered a soldier on the road. The subsequent incident provides a glimpse of what Apuleius thought it was like for poor provincials when they met a soldier face to face. The vegetable grower was defenceless, the soldier tall, well-armed, and aggressive. His proud and arrogant demand for the ass was spoken in Latin, and the vegetable grower, not understanding, rode past. At once the soldier struck him and

---

[1] *Satyricon*, 82. The consensus of scholarly opinion is that the work was composed in the first century; see R. Browning, *CR* 63 (1949), 12; H.T. Rowell, *TAPA* 89 (1958), 14; H.C. Schnur, *Latomus* 18 (1959), 790; K. Rose, *Latomus* 20 (1961), 821.

[2] 9.39 ff. Apuleius was born at Madaura in Africa c.125. A man of wide learning, he became an *advocatus* and travelled extensively in the empire. See especially F. Millar, 'The World of the *Golden Ass*', *JRS* 71 (1981), 63.

in Greek demanded the ass, on the excuse that it was needed
to carry the baggage of the provincial governor. In fact, as
the rest of the story shows, the soldier wanted the ass for
himself. There was no protection against, or escape from,
this kind of assault and extortion, except to fight physically.
But even then the odds were heavily in favour of the military.

The vegetable grower in the story managed to get the
better of the soldier, beat him up, and sought sanctuary in
a friend's house. The soldier, however, got the help of his
comrades and, acting on a tip-off, approached the magistrates
of the town, complaining that the vegetable grower and the
ass were hiding in a certain house and that some of the
governor's property had been stolen. Immediately, although
there was no evidence, the magistrates accepted the soldier's
word, went to the house, and had it searched while holding
the inhabitants under threat of death. Eventually the culprit
was found, and dragged off to prison and summary execution
while the soldier got possession of the ass.[3]

The story shows a local population[4] fearful of meeting
Roman troops and helpless against brutality and aggression.
For the local magistrates were intimidated by armed might,
the use of the governor's name, and frequent references to
the emperor.[5] In this society the civilian had little hope of
even bringing a soldier to court. The army which supposedly
protected the provinces could be seen as a destructive
parasite upon them.

These ideas in Apuleius are echoed by Juvenal in his incomplete sixteenth satire, which is so bitterly devoted to
exposing the privileged position of the army that it has been
suggested that it was censored by Hadrian, who resented any
criticism of his beloved army.[6] No civilian would dare to
attack a soldier, and if he gets beaten up himself 'he will
conceal the fact and will not dare to show the magistrate his

---

[3] 9.42.

[4] The story is set in Achaea and Macedonia.

[5] 'Contra commilitones ibi nec uspiam illum delitescere adiurantes genium
principis contendebant ... Tum gliscit violentior utrimque secus contentio:
militum pro comperto de nobis asseverantium fidemque Caesaris identidem
implorantium ...

[6] See G. Highet, *Juvenal the Satirist* (1954), 156 ff., who rejects this theory.

knocked out teeth, the black lumps and swelling weals all over his face, or the remaining eye which the doctor offers little hope of saving.' A wise man will not prosecute a soldier, since the redress will be worse than the original offence and will require the assistance of a doctor.[7]

These three authors, Petronius, Apuleius, and Juvenal, are virtually the only literary sources that may help us to see what life was like for the ordinary man in the Roman empire in his relations with the army. How reliable is the picture they paint? One of the strengths of Apuleius' novel is that in it he sets his fantastic plot in the plausible context of incidents from real life. It is hard to believe that Apuleius or Petronius did not seek to make their work more entertaining and comprehensible to their audience by creating a background of recognizable social and economic details from contemporary life.[8] Again, a satirist is likely to be most effective if his attacks are plausibly directed at activities and injustices, past or present, known to the readers.[9]

Yet this picture of soldier and civilian in the Roman empire is in stark contrast to the conventional encomion of Aelius Aristides, who praised the wondrous efficiency of the army spread round the frontiers guarding the grateful peoples,[10] or Dio of Prusa who said that the soldiers were like shepherds who, with the emperor, guarded the flock of the empire.[11] These Greeks, protected by their eminence and influential contacts, may not have troubled to understand the effect the army had on the ordinary people of the empire. An examination of the evidence for the conduct of the troops in the provinces, the opportunities for a civilian to gain redress, and the position of the soldier in court, will help to show how successful emperors were in protecting the welfare of their 'flock'.

[7] 16.9-12; 21-22.
[8] For Apuleius, see Millar (n. 2), 63.
[9] See Highet, op. cit., 161 ff.
[10] J.H. Oliver, 'The Ruling Power: A Study of the Roman Empire in Second Century after Christ through the Roman Oration of Aelius Aristides', *TAPhA* 43.4 (1953), sects. 67; 72 f.
[11] 1. 28 f.

2. MILITARY OPPRESSION OF CIVILIANS

The poor man probably sought to avoid the soldiery as much as possible. But from time to time large numbers of troops passed through provinces on military expeditions.[1] More frequently small groups of soldiers travelled through in detachments (*vexillationes*) and on recruiting missions, or on their way to the various outposts scattered round the empire.[2] Individual soldiers often journeyed through a province on official business or as couriers on the public post, or on their way to and from leave. The army was not entirely shut away in permanent camps, and doubtless soldiers had the opportunity to exploit their superior power and status against civilians. Although we may distinguish between soldiers who acted on the orders of others, for example, in the matter of requisitions, and soldiers who acted entirely in their own interests, it is unlikely that this distinction made much difference to the suffering provincials.[3]

The Romans themselves recognized the danger of oppression, corrupt officials, and the alienation of the civilian population. Under the *caput* 'Concerning the duties of a provincial governor', Ulpian declares that the governor must see that men of humble means are not deprived of their single light or meagre furniture for the use of others, under the pretext of the arrival of officials or soldiers. He must take care that 'nothing is done by individual soldiers exploiting their position and claiming unjust advantages for themselves, which does not pertain to the communal benefit of the army'.[4] In an edict published in 133-7 Mamertinus, the prefect of Egypt, admitted that illegal and violent requisitions by troops had turned the local population against the

---

[1] See in general, Rostovtzeff, *SEHRE*² (1957), 358 ff.; 424 ff.

[2] Cf. Arrian, *Periplous* 3, 6, 9, 10; Ritterling, *JRS* 17 (1927), 20; Sherk, *AJP* 76 (1955), 400; MacMullen, *Soldier and Civilian*, 49 ff.; *RE* s.v. *frumentarii*.

[3] For the oppressive nature of Roman provincial administration, see P.A. Brunt, 'Charges of Provincial Maladministration under the Early Principate', *Hist.* 10 (1961), 189; MacMullen (n.2), chapters III and IV; S. Mitchell, 'Requisitioned Transport in the Roman Empire: A New Inscription from Pisidia', *JRS* 66 (1976), 106.

[4] *D* 1.18.6.5-7. 'Ne quid sub nomine militum, quod ad utilitates eorum in commune non pertinet, a quibusdam propria sibi commoda inique vindicantibus committatur, praeses provinciae provideat.'

Roman army: 'And so it has come about that private citizens are insulted and abused and the army is criticised for greed and injustice.'[5] Augustus himself seems to have been worried about possible misuse of soldiers if they were taken from their military duties. 'Although I am aware that it is not inappropriate for soldiers to work in building activities, I am nevertheless worried that, if I give my permission for anything of this sort, which might be in my or your interests, a sufficient degree of restraint, which would be acceptable to me, would not be applied.'[6] Augustus must have feared the kind of misuse of troops for personal ends that came to light in the case of Lucilius Capito, the procurator of Asia in the reign of Tiberius. This official had used groups of soldiers to which he was not entitled, and had oppressed the province.[7] These signs of anxiety on the part of emperors and their officials suggest that the complaints levelled against Roman provincial government in general and the conduct of soldiers in particular, by historians like Tacitus and Cassius Dio, who themselves had experience as governors, are not mere rhetoric and imagination.[8]

Other observers make similar criticisms. Epictetus advises that it is better to let your mule go if a soldier attempts to commandeer him during a requisition. For if you argue or resist, you will get a beating and lose the mule anyway.[9] Elsewhere Epictetus classes the Guardsman with the 'tyrant' and others who cause grief and fear to those who are not prepared against them by philosophy.[10] Epictetus taught in Rome for some time before AD 89 and he may be referring to the conduct of the Praetorian Guard towards the people in Rome. It is interesting that he does not recommend any attempt to obtain redress against injustices perpetrated by soldiers.

[5] *PSI* 446 = *Select Papyri* II, no. 221.
[6] *D* 49.16.12.1.
[7] Tac., *A* 4.15; Dio, 57.23.4. In a letter to Pliny, Trajan set out his rule on the matter: 'sed et illud haereat nobis, quam paucissimos a signis avocandos esse' (*Ep*. 10.20.2.).
[8] e.g. Tac., *Ag*. 15; 19.2, 30 ff. (speech of Calgacus), *A* 14.35; Dio, 62.3 ff.
[9] 4.1.79.
[10] 3.24.117. See in general, F. Millar, 'Epictetus and the Imperial Court', *JRS* 55 (1965), 141.

In the New Testament it is made clear that the soldiers in the East had an appalling reputation, and this cannot entirely have been the result of hostility between the Jews and the gentile auxiliary troops in Judaea. To soldiers asking what they should do, John the Baptist replied: 'Do not extort money from anyone, do not act as an informer, and be satisfied with your own pay.'[11] This may refer to the soldiers of king Herod, but the behaviour of Roman troops is not likely to have been any better. Already it is assumed as a matter of course that soldiers will supplement their pay with illegal exactions and act as informers, presumably for profit. The development of the verb διασείω, which literally means 'I shake violently', to refer to the process of extortion seems sinister. Indeed the troops are classed with tax-gatherers, the most hated of all groups.

Two other stories in the New Testament concern Roman centurions. In Acts we hear about Cornelius, a Roman centurion who saw a vision from the Lord.[12] The point of the story is that the kindness and justice displayed by the soldier are exceptional. He was 'pious and god-fearing', helped the people, and was known as a 'just man'. The argument is that *even* a centurion by his conduct can win the favour of god. In St. Matthew's gospel there occurs the story of a centurion who asked Christ to heal his sick servant.[13] Here the object is to contrast the faith of the Gentiles with the Jews' lack of faith. It is a reasonable suggestion that a Roman centurion was deliberately chosen as the subject of the story in order to emphasize this contrast, precisely because people had a low opinion of soldiers in general.[14] Furthermore, the supposedly brutal behaviour of the troops at the crucifixion was an integral part of the tradition surrounding Christ's death.[15] Perhaps the well-known reputation of the troops was exploited by Christ's supporters to stir up feeling in his favour.

The noun διασεισμός ('shake-down' or 'extortion') occurs in two personal financial accounts found in Egypt, dating

[11] St. Luke, 3.14.
[12] Acts. 10.2, 7; 22.
[13] 8.5 ff.
[14] Cf. 8.8: οὐκ εἰμι ἱκανὸς ἵνα μοῦ ὑπὸ τὴν στέγην |εἰσέλθῃς.
[15] St. Matt., 27.27 ff.; St. Mark, 16.16 ff.; St. John, 19.23 ff.

from the mid-second century AD.[16] They are in fact half-yearly accounts, and on the first are registered payments to the 'stationarius', to two police agents, and 'for extortion' (ὑπὲρ διασεισμοῦ). The payment for extortion is 2,200 *drachmae*, the second largest on the entire account. It seems likely that the other payments to officials were also for extortion or blackmail. In the account for the second half of the year, on two occasions substantial sums were paid out 'to the soldier at his demand'.[17] On the same document is a payment to the local chief of police, and in the context this too seems suspicious. It is extraordinary that these sums for extortion should be entered so casually; the owner has clearly accepted the financial loss as irretrievable. It is perhaps an indication of the attitudes prevailing at the time that soldiers had the confidence simply to demand large sums of money. Another papyrus shows a system of extortion in operation in Egypt as early as AD 37.[18] A village scribe swears that he does not know any of those who have suffered extortion by a soldier and those with him. It seems that the soldier was working a kind of extortion ring.

Requisitions of animals and provisions, usually carried out by soldiers, were a major source of grievance to the civilian population.[19] But when soldiers exceeded their authority and added violent aggression to illegality, the burden became intolerable. We have already seen the evidence of Epictetus, Petronius, and Apuleius. The theme is further illustrated by a series of edicts, the earliest issued by Germanicus during his visit to Egypt in AD 19, forbidding the forcible occupation of lodgings and the taking of property without payment.[20] The other edicts were issued by prefects of Egypt — Aemilius Rectus in 42,[21] Vergilius Capito in 49,[22]

---

[16] L. Robert, *Revue de Philologie*, 3 series 17 (1943), 111.

[17] Lines 8-9; 11-12. The restoration ⟨στρα⟩τιώτῃ ἀπαιτοῦντι is almost certainly correct.

[18] *P. Ox.* 240.

[19] See especially Mitchell, (n. 3), and the bibliography quoted there.

[20] Ehrenberg and Jones, *Documents Illustrating the Reigns of Augustus and Tiberius*[2] (1955), no. 320 = (*Select Papyri* II, 211).

[21] Abbott and Johnson, no. 162.

[22] Ibid., no. 163; cf. H.G.E. White and J.H. Oliver, *The Temple of Hibis in El Khargeh Oasis*, Part II (1938), no. 1.

Tiberius Alexander in 68,[23] and Mamertinus in 133-7,[24] and all deal with the same problem. It is notable that in all these edicts except that of Tiberius Alexander, soldiers are specifically mentioned as culprits. In fact the soldiers are mentioned first and seem to cause most of the trouble as the edict of Mamertinus makes clear. They seized property without authorization, and even those who did have the requisite *diplomata* violently took more than was necessary and did not pay.

So, when Christ taught, 'If someone forces you to go with him for one mile, go with him for two',[25] he was preaching a doctrine of common sense. If a soldier forced you to act as guide or perform another duty, it was better to go willingly with him. It is significant that a word (ἀγγαρεύω) developed especially to describe the practice of forcing people into providing certain services. This was the fate of Simon, arbitrarily compelled to carry the cross to the crucifixion.[26]

It cannot be argued that since most of this evidence comes from Egypt and Judaea, these provinces were untypical. It is true that the soldiers who misbehaved in Egypt and Judaea were generally on service detached from their units, but this practice was widespread in the provinces of the empire. We hear more of military misconduct in Egypt precisely because there is more evidence from Egypt for life under Roman rule, and also evidence which relates to the common people. Moreover, other scattered evidence shows that the same problems existed in other provinces. We now have the edict of the governor of Galatia early in Tiberius' reign dealing with abuses of the system of requisitioning transport and mentioning soldiers in particular as culprits.[27] Domitian's letter to his procurator in Syria, while not singling out the troops, deals with the kind of illegality soldiers had been involved in elsewhere.[28] The town of Juliopolis in Bithynia

[23] Abbott and Johnson, 165; cf. White and Oliver, op. cit., 23 ff.
[24] See n. 5.
[25] St. Matt. 5.41.
[26] 27.32.
[27] Mitchell, (n.3).
[28] McCrum and Woodhead, no. 466; cf. the edict of Claudius found at Tegea (*CIL* III. 7251 = Smallwood, *Documents*, no. 285).

suffered because it was on the frontier and a lot of traffic passed through. Pliny wrote to Trajan asking him to grant it relief from some of its burdens. In his reply the emperor assumed that part of the injustice suffered by the local population was caused by soldiers.[29] A letter from Julius Saturninus, legate of Syria c.185/6, to the people of the village of Phaenae promises action against soldiers who forcibly acquired accommodation and entertainment which they were not required to provide.[30]

In addition, a group of petitions from the villages of Mendechora in Lydia (c.200-250),[31] Scaptopara in Thrace (238),[32] and Arague in Phrygia (244-7),[33] all beg the emperor for relief from the brutal conduct of officials. Soldiers had been leaving their approved routes to seek hospitality and take peasants and oxen from the fields. These abuses had been going on for a long time and previous decisions to punish the wrong-doers had been disregarded. In particular, Scaptopara possessed attractive hot springs and had the misfortune to be situated between two military camps. The troops had persistently ignored the instructions of the legate of Thrace that the villagers were not to be disturbed.[34]

Finally, even the population of Rome itself did not escape from the exactions and violence of the soldiery. In Juvenal's sixteenth satire, the unfortunate civilian who is soundly thrashed by a soldier and contemplates the pleasures of pleading his case in the military camp, has obviously been assaulted by a Praetorian Guardsman.[35] Perhaps this happened fairly regularly. Pertinax (193) was congratulated

---

[29] Ep.10.77-8.
[30] IGR 3.1119 = Abbott and Johnson, 113.
[31] Abbott and Johnson, 143-4.
[32] IGRB 2236 = Abbott and Johnson, 139.
[33] CIL III. 14191 = Abbott and Johnson, 141.
[34] Cf. the plight of Aga Bey in late second, early third century — Abbott and Johnson, 142. Note also the similar tale from the village of Euhippe — L. Robert, 'La Ville d'Euhippe in Carie', CRAI 1952, 589; Abbott and Johnson, 144; I. Stoian, 'Sur la plainte des Paysans du Territorie d'Histria', Dacia (1959), 369; L. Robert, REG 1958, 283; 1961, 202. Daremberg-Saglio, s.v. hospitium. For the behaviour of stationarii and frumentarii, see G. Lopuszanski, 'La Police Romaine et les Chrétiens', Antiquité Classique 1951, 5.
[35] See above, p. 244.

because he curbed the Praetorian Guard and did not allow the troops to go on the rampage, insult or strike passers-by, or carry axes.[36] Something of the hatred existing between the Guardsmen and the population of Rome can be seen in the furious outbreak of fighting in the reign of Severus Alexander; the battle went on for three days with many deaths on both sides and ended only when the Praetorians set fire to parts of the city.[37]

Although the ordinary people will have seen the soldiers as their main oppressors, on many occasions the troops were carrying out the orders of other officials, who were, it seems, often themselves corrupt[38] and quite willing to employ the army against their accusers or against the civilian population in general. We have already seen that Augustus, Tiberius, and Trajan were concerned to prevent the use of soldiers ouside their strictly military duties, or their exploitation by unauthorized people.[39] Some offenders were fairly innocuous, like the *legatus legionis* dismissed by Tiberius because he gave his freedmen some soldiers for a hunting expedition.[40] We also hear from Lucian how, in the reign of Marcus Aurelius, he received two soldiers from his friend the governor of Cappadocia as a personal escort on his way to the Black Sea.[41] Far more sinister was the behaviour of the procurator of the imperial estates at Sûk-el-Khmis who used soldiers to arrest and torture the imperial tenants and even to beat Roman citizens.[42]

It is true that emperors frequently had good intentions in dealing with corruption and abuse, and were willing to respond to appeals from the oppressed.[43] Domitian in his

---

[36] Dio, 74.8.1; Herodian, 2.4.1.

[37] Dio, 80.2.3.

[38] For example, at Socnopaei Nesos in Egypt it seems that not only the superintendent of the customs house, but also the overseers of the nome were involved in concealing a tax fraud (*P. Amh.* 77, lines 1–33 = *Select Papyri* II, 282). On the imperial estates at Sûk-el-Khmis in Africa, the procurator was in league with the chief lessee (*FIRA*² 1, p. 496 ff; = *ILS* 6870).

[39] See above, p. 247.

[40] Suet., *Tib.* 19.

[41] *Alexander the False Prophet* 55.

[42] See n. 38, lines 10 ff.

[43] e.g., the edict of Libuscidianus, *JRS* 1976, p. 107, lines 1–4; Commodus — *FIRA*², 1, p. 498, lines 1 ff.; Philip — Abbott and Johnson, 141.

letter reminds his procurator in Syria of his responsibility to observe the rules himself.[44] Furthermore, the series of edicts from the prefects of Egypt illustrates the efforts of imperial officials to deal with abuses. Means were provided for making complaints known: Germanicus appointed his secretary Baebius to look after petitions of this kind;[45] the legate of Syria asked the people of Phaenae to write to him if they suffered any injustice and told them to place his letter in a conspicuous place so that no one could plead ignorance.[46] Severe punishments were frequently threatened,[47] and sometimes exacted. Cumanus, procurator of Judaea, summarily executed a soldier who had torn up a copy of the Holy Law in a Jewish village.[48]

Nevertheless, the accumulation of evidence leaves little doubt about the behaviour of the army in the Roman empire. It bears small relation to Dio of Prusa's concept of stout shepherds guarding their flock. Many of the poorer inhabitants would have much more easily recognized Apuleius' vegetable grower, the victim of a brutal soldiery. In view of the need often to repeat edicts forbidding certain abuses, and the fact that even imperial rescripts seem to have brought little respite to the provincials, and that the petitioners rarely asked for the guilty to be punished,[49] it is difficult to take very seriously the protestations of determination by emperors and their officials to deal with injustice and illegality from whatever source.

To some extent the abuses committed by soldiers were part of the wider malady of provincial misgovernment and inefficiency that involved many more imperial officials. Was the widespread oppression of civilians by soldiers a symptom of the general inability of emperors to control any of their servants (a problem encountered in most empires),

---

[44] See n. 28.

[45] See n. 20, lines 22 ff.

[46] See n. 30.

[47] Aemilius Rectus said: 'I shall employ the most severe punishment' (n. 21); Vergilius Capito laid down a tenfold fine for those found guilty (n. 22); Mamertinus promised to chastise wrong doers strictly — ὡς ἐμοῦ κολάσοντος ἐρρωμένως (n. 5).

[48] Jos., AJ. 20.115 f.

[49] It is notable that Commodus did not even reprimand the rascally procurator at Sûk-el-Khmis, and apparently has no thought of punishing him (n. 38).

or did it at least in part result from the difficulty of prosecuting soldiers in court and a deliberate reluctance by
officials and governors, who took their guidance from the
emperors, to proceed against soldiers on behalf of civilians,
who were not as important to the welfare of the empire and
its ruler?

3. THE SOLDIER IN COURT

Serving soldiers had the right of bringing an accusation pertaining to criminal law. 'If it is in the power of a soldier to
bring forward criminal proceedings during the time when he
is serving the interests of the State, he is not forbidden to do
so.'[1] However a soldier could institute proceedings only
when the action involved his own interests or those of his
family. This was confirmed by a rescript of Gordian III in
238. 'The emperor Gordianus Augustus to Gaius the soldier.
Soldiers are not forbidden to undertake legal proceedings
which pertain to trial by a permanent jury court, as long as
they are seeking to avenge an injustice done to them or a
member of their family. Therefore we grant that you may
institute proceedings to avenge the death of your cousin.'[2]
The implication is that a soldier was not permitted to begin
criminal proceedings on behalf of anyone outside his immediate family; and this explains why Macer placed soldiers
among those who could not bring accusations.[3]

The soldier's right to bring criminal charges was also
restricted by the demands of his military duties. Another
rescript from Gordian III illustrates the unfortunate predica-
ment of one soldier in 242 concerning his adulterous wife.

The emperor Gordianus Augustus to Hilarianus the soldier. If your wife
left the province before she could be brought to trial for adultery, an
accusation cannot be brought in her absence and the request that she
should be brought back to the province where you are serving as a
soldier is not just. But you will be able to bring a formal accusation

---

[1] *D* 4.6.40 (Ulpian).
[2] *CJ* 9.1.8; cf. 10.
[3] *D* 48.2.8; cf. 11. pref. In the first reference Macer is presumably referring
to an accusation made by a soldier on behalf of another.

against her when your military duties permit. For the time which you
have given to your military obligations should not deprive you of the
retribution which, with the grief of a betrayed husband, you demand.[4]

In one area of criminal law, treason against the emperor
(*Lex Iulia de Maiestate*), soldiers were positively encouraged
to bring proceedings, apparently without any restriction. The
language used reflects the close relationship between emperor
and soldier. 'Soldiers too, who normally may not bring an
accusation on behalf of another, are to be allowed to
institute proceedings in this case. For those who are vigilant
in guarding the peace are much more than any one else to be
permitted to bring this accusation.'[5]

It is evident that soldiers could sue in their own interests
in cases pertaining to civil law, and many imperial rescripts
show that they did so.[6] Presumably the restrictions that
applied to criminal prosecutions undertaken by soldiers also
applied to civil suits.

Of all the advantages of army life Juvenal chose to treat
legal privileges first, and he believed that when the soldier
appeared in court he was greatly advantaged over and above
civilian plaintiffs and defendants.[7] A civilian who began proceedings soon became entangled in the lengthy process of the
law with its crowded sessions and frequent adjournments.[8]
By contrast, the soldier had his case heard when it suited
him, and it would be settled quickly so that his property was
not worn away by endless wrangling in court.[9] Juvenal
also contrives to leave the impression that the outcome of the
case would usually be favourable to the soldier. It is sufficient to recall briefly the dramatic impact made by the name

---

[4] *CJ* 9.9.15; cf. 2.12.9.

[5] *D* 48.4.7.1 'nam qui pro pace excubant, magis magisque ad hanc accus-
ationem admittendi sunt'.

[6] Juvenal, 16.36 ff.; *D* 49.1.24.1 (Scaevola); *CJ* 3.32.4; 33.4, 7; 4.34.3, 4;
35.7; 51.1; 54.2; 64.1.

[7] For a survey of Satire 16, see M. Durry, 'Juvénal et les Prétoriens', *REL*
13 (1935), 95; O. Behends, *Die römische Geschworenenverfassung* (1970), 211;
in general on soldiers' rights, E. Sander, 'Das römische Militarstrafrecht', *RhM*
103 (1961), 289.

[8] 16.42 ff.

[9] 48–50: 'ast illis quos arma tegunt et balteus ambit,/ quod placitum est ipsis
praestatur tempus agendi,/ nec res atteritur longo sufflamine litis.'

and appearance of a military *accusator* in the story in Apuleius.[10]

The prospects of a civilian were no brighter when a soldier was the defendant. The unlucky man who had been beaten up by a soldier would perhaps be reluctant to seek redress for the assault.[11] But if he did, then, Juvenal alleges, he was wasting his time and likely to suffer even greater injury.[12] The praetor was approached and granted a judge (*iudex*) in the usual procedure; but the judge was a centurion and he heard the case in the military camp before the soldier's hefty colleagues; the plaintiff was intimidated and unable to persuade witnesses to appear:—

The man who wants redress for this receives a hobnailed centurion as judge, and a beefy crowd of jurors cramming the benches. For the ancient military rule and the long standing tradition from the time of Camillus are preserved, that a soldier should not be involved in a court case outside the camp and far from the standards. Of course the centurions will follow an impeccably just procedure and I am bound to obtain redress if my complaint is justified. But the whole unit is hostile, and all the company agrees to make your redress require a doctor, an outrage more serious than the original offence. It would be extremely stupid to plead your case and, since you have two legs, provoke all those heavy military boots, all those hobnails. What is more, who would come so far from the city to act as a witness? What friend could be so loyal as to venture inside the rampart of the military camp?

Juvenal concludes: 'It would be easier to find a witness to perjure himself against a civilian, than someone to tell the truth against the interests and honour of a soldier.'[13]

The satirist imagines a case in Rome conducted in the Praetorian camp where the centurion *iudex* used the soldiers as his *consilium*,[14] but he obviously believed that all soldiers

[10] See above, pp. 243-4.
[11] 16.7 ff.
[12] 13 ff.
[13] 32-4.
[14] He may have in mind a *cognitio extra ordinem*, where the praetor could appoint whomever he wished as judge and issue instructions to him in any form. In the formulary process the choice of judge was restricted and the instructions to him had to be in a particular form.

were advantaged whenever and wherever they appeared in court as defendants. He mentions long-standing military regulations that required a soldier who was at law to have his case heard within the confines of the camp. The reference to Camillus is presumably to emphasize the antiquity of these regulations. This seems plausible and we should not expect to find corroborating evidence in the writings of the jurists unless magistrates were compelled to give military *iudices*, and that is unlikely. In origin the intention was probably innocent enough, to prevent the removal of soldiers from their military duties to pursue their own interests. If the soldier had to make this sacrifice, there was no reason why he should be released from his military obligations to answer the charge of a civilian plaintiff. Furthermore, this was in line with the general principle of Roman law that a suit should be brought in the *forum* of the defendant, that is, where he actually lived.[15] It could be argued that in the case of a professional soldier, his *forum* was the military camp.

Hadrian confirmed the general reluctance to release soldiers from the camp in order to appear in court to give testimony. 'Witnesses are not to be summoned rashly from a long distance away; much less should soldiers be called away from the standards or their duties in order to give evidence; this was stated by the defied Hadrian in a rescript.'[16] The phrase 'multo minus avocandi sunt' emphasizes the emperor's unwillingness to let this happen, and it must have made it very difficult for the civilian plaintiff to get a soldier into court. Furthermore, if a defendant could not appear in court because he was sick or was absent on state business, any action to enforce a judgement against him was, in the opinion of Paul, to be denied, or the praetor should not carry through the legal consequences.[17] In these circumstances it would be difficult for the plaintiff to obtain redress unless he was prepared to confront the soldier in the military camp.

The problem will have been specially difficult for a civilian who suffered an injury at the hands of a man who then became a soldier and moved away from the area. In fact

[15] *D* 5.1.19.2; Crook, *Law and Life*, 75.
[16] *D* 22.5.3.6.
[17] 5.1.75.

provision was made against this. 'If anyone, after he has been summoned to appear in court, becomes a soldier or moves into another jurisdiction, he does not have the right to have his case transferred to that jurisdiction, on the grounds that he has already been brought to court.'[18] However, this rule did not necessarily make it any easier for the plaintiff to get the soldier back to stand trial. Furthermore, the implication of the rule is that a man who was already a soldier at the time when he was summoned to appear in court could insist that the suit was heard in his own *forum* by another court, possibly in the military camp. In this way, a soldier who was, for example, on leave and who committed an offence against a civilian, could make it impossible for the injured party to pursue him. The award of this right may have been at the discretion of the praetor or the provincial governor.

There are several other rather vague indications in the legal sources that soldiers in some way were advantaged in a court of law.

When a soldier petitioned to sue in his own name for goods which he claimed had been given to him as a gift, the reply was made that if the gift had been given to change the conditions of a suit, the previous owner should be responsible for the case in order that it may be clear that he transferred to the soldier property and not a law suit.[19]

---

[18] 5.1.7: 'Si quis, posteaquam in ius vocatus est, miles vel alterius fori esse coeperit, in ea causa ius revocandi forum non habebit quasi praeventus.' And see further below, p. 261. For capital charges, Trajan established or confirmed the following rule (49.16.4.5): 'Reus capitalis criminis voluntarius miles ... capite puniendus est, nec remittendus est eo, ubi reus postulatus est, sed, ut accendente causa militiae, audiendus: si dicta causa sit vel requirendus adnotatus, ignominia missus ad iudicem suum remittendus est nec recipiendus postea volens militare, licet fuerit absolutus.' I interpret this to mean that if a defendant on a capital charge joined up before the case began and had not been detained or registered as missing with an accusation pending, then he was to be tried on the spot, presumably by his own commander, since his entry into military service had added a new factor to his position. But if the case had begun, then he was to be dishonourably discharged and sent back for trial. The tone of the rescript is stern throughout and there was clearly a desire to stop the exploitation of military service by those outside. But what happened if the 'reus capitalis criminis' was already in the army before the crime was committed? Was he to be tried by his immediate commander?

[19] *D* 4.7.11.

Here a civilian had made a gift to the soldier of property under dispute at law, in the hope that he would have a better chance of winning the case. The implication is that a soldier would be a more powerful adversary in the legal sense (*potentior adversarius*). Dishonest exchanges of property in this way were forbidden.[20] Now a *potentior adversarius* was normally someone who acquired an advantageous legal position by circumstances, for example if he lived in another province and therefore might prove difficult to sue.[21] Yet it seems that the soldiers were by virtue of their military status in an advantageous position at law.

In the same way, if a man joined the army while involved in litigation, his purpose might be to gain an advantage over his opponent. 'Not everyone who joined the army while involved in a legal case should be dismissed from the service, but only the man who joined up with the intention of giving himself, under the protection of military service, a more weighty influence than his opponent.'[22] The phrases 'pretiosior' and 'optentus militiae' are vague, but suggest that by virtue of being a soldier a man would make himself superior to his adversary in court. Menander is not disputing the soldier's right to this superiority, only the self-interested exploitation of it by those outside the army. This is further illustrated by a rescript of Septimius Severus and Caracalla. 'If you wish to volunteer for military service, present yourselves to the men who have the right of checking recruits. However you are not unaware that those who seek to become soldiers because they are involved in litigation, are normally dismissed from the service on the demand of their opponents.'[23]

It is likely that these hints of military privilege in court

---

[20] In the praetor's edict – 4.7.1. pref.-1.

[21] Ibid. 'Itaque si alterius provinciae hominem aut potentiorem nobis opposuerit adversarium, tenebitur.' See in general, A. Wacke, *ANRW*, II.13, 562 ff.

[22] *D* 49.16.4.8: 'Non omnis, qui litem habuit et ideo militaverit, exauctorari iubetur, sed qui eo animo militiae se dedit, ut sub optentu militiae pretiosiorem se adversario faceret.' Menander thought that if a man were engaged in his legal case before he joined up, he should be dismissed; but if he gave the case up, he should be allowed to stay in the army.

[23] *CJ* 12.33.1.

refer firstly to the ability of the soldier to avoid the impartial process of law and be tried in the military camp in front of his own comrades; and secondly to the fact that civilians were reluctant to face up to soldiers, who seemed to have a superior status and to have the support of the emperor and his officials, because they knew that a specially favourable attitude would be taken to them.

In this context the prohibition on a soldier's acting as procurator on behalf of the interests of a third party, even a member of his family, perhaps acquires a sinister significance.

It is not correct for a soldier to act on behalf of his father or mother or wife or, in accordance with the sacred rescript, in the name of a procurator, since in the public interest ['utilitas publica] a soldier is not permitted to undertake a case on behalf of a third party or to undertake business matters or to present himself in the capacity of supporter of another.[24]

The question is exactly how the appearance of a soldier in court on behalf of a third party would be detrimental to the public interest. One explanation is that the State could not afford to spare a soldier from his military duties in order to conduct the affairs of another person in court. It is interesting that soldiers were also forbidden to act as 'tutor' or 'curator'.[25] This provision must sometimes have been to the detriment of a soldier's interests, and so the motive was presumably that soldiers, who could be called away on military duties, were not considered competent to fulfil the task. Moreover veterans were permitted to act as procurators, which suggests that after a soldier was freed from the demands of his military duties, there was no objection to his acting in this capacity.[26] But the eagerness of

[24] *CJ* 2.12.7 (223). For the term *procurator*, see Crook, *Law and Life*, 236 f. Soldiers were not permitted to undertake criminal accusations on behalf of third parties outside their family; see above, p. 254.
[25] *CJ* 5.34.4 (244). Soldiers, along with others 'rei publicae causa absentes', women, the chronically sick, and those entering magistracies, were also prohibited from acting as *defensor* (*D* 3.3.54, Paul).
[26] *D* 3.3.8.2. Ulpian's statement that a soldier could not act as *procurator* even if his legal opponent was agreeable to this, may suggest that the object of the rule was not so much to protect civilians as to ensure that soldiers did not take on an obligation that their military duties would not allow them to fulfil properly.

some to have their interests defended by a soldier, and the suggestion that he was a *potentior adversarius*, seem to offer a further explanation. By his position and status a soldier would be able to exercise an unfair advantage in court, and the public interest can be interpreted as the need to protect the weaker citizen against the privileged soldier. It was acceptable that the soldier should be allowed to protect his own interests, but not to exercise his special influence for the benefit of others.[27]

This was not so important in the case of veterans, whose absence at law would not damage the efficiency and good organization of the army, and whose influence in court was probably less than that of a serving soldier.[28] It can also be suggested that the prohibition on the acquisition by a soldier of land in the province where he was serving was dictated not only by the ostensible desire to prevent troops from being distracted from their military duties, but also by a fear that they could use their power and influence to acquire and retain property dishonestly.[29]

Finally, soldiers were exempt from certain types of penalty — torture and consignment to work in the mines.[30] Veterans were even better off in this respect. They could not be tortured, beaten, given to the beasts, or sent to the mines or to public labour. Indeed they ranked in this respect with the *decuriones,* who were classed among the *honestiores.*[31] These exemptions confirm the privileged legal position of soldiers, although of course in the question of punishments they remained subject to military discipline.[32]

Even if a civilian obtained a judgement against a soldier,

[27] The rule concerning the role of soldiers as procurators was not strictly enforced. If the fact that a soldier was ineligible to act as *procurator* was overlooked when the case began, he was permitted to continue to act in that capacity; *CJ* 2.12.13 (239) — 'Ita demum super lite persequenda, quam tibi mater mandavit, actionem intendere potes, si, cum primo litem contestareris, non est tibi eo nomine opposita praescriptio militiae: quod nec, cum appellatio agitur, tibi obici poterit. Nam si integra res est, ratio perpetui edicti acceptam tibi non permittit alieno nomine actionem intendere.'

[28] The veteran's *forum* was not the military camp and he may not have found it as easy as the serving soldier to obtain a trial there.

[29] See above, pp. 239-40.

[30] *D* 49.16.3.1 (Modestinus); cf. *CJ* 9.41.8 (Diocletian).

[31] *D* 49.18.1; 18.3; Garnsey, *Social Status and Legal Privilege*, 245 ff.

[32] See below, pp. 303 ff; Garnsey, op. cit., 247.

the execution of this judgement was perhaps quite another matter. In Roman law it was the responsibility of the successful plaintiff to follow up the decision of the judge.[33] For example, in the case of a debt the plaintiff could seize the debtor, retain him in private custody, and enter his property to sell it off. If the debtor were a soldier, this procedure might be inadvisable or impossible; and the soldier could no doubt call upon his comrades for any physical assistance needed. It may be significant that Ulpian thought it necessary to mention specifically that a soldier had to pay up if he lost a suit. 'When a decision is given against a soldier who has served his time in the ranks, he is compelled to pay up, so far as he is able.'[34]

There are considerable grounds, therefore, for accepting Juvenal's account of the privileged position of the soldiers in court. Juvenal does not mislead on what *could* happen to a civilian plaintiff against a soldier; he may exaggerate in suggesting that it happened invariably. In practice in Rome in matters of civil law, the praetor, though competent to receive suits brought against soldiers by civilians or by soldiers against others, and to appoint whomever he wished as *iudex*, may, for convenience and in keeping with military regulations and the wishes of the emperors, have appointed a military *iudex*. In time this convention became an unwritten rule. This idea can help to explain the expedition of soldiers' cases alleged by Juvenal.[35] If a soldier were the plaintiff or defendant in a case pertaining to criminal law, then in Rome the matter would be decided by the appropriate public jury court, and it is less easy to see how he might be advantaged in this way. It is possible, however, that the Praetorian prefect at some stage acquired a capital jurisdiction in cases involving his own soldiers and tried them himself.[36]

---

[33] Crook, *Law and Life*, 82–3.

[34] *D* 42.1.6, pref.; I take Ulpian'a argument to be that even a soldier has to pay up so far as he is able, if the decision goes against him. For 'condemnatus eatenus qua facere potest', see Buckland, *Text-Book*, 693–4.

[35] See above, p. 255.

[36] There is no evidence for this guess. For a survey of the development of the jurisdiction of the Praetorian prefect, see Howe, *The Praetorian Prefect from Commodus to Diocletian*, 32 ff. See too Millar, *ERW*, 122 ff. It was always possible for the emperor himself to take any case involving a soldier; cf. Pliny, *Ep.* 6.31.

In the provinces the provincial governor will have decided the appropriate course of action in both civil and criminal cases;[37] and he was also the commander of the troops in his province. It is easy to see how, in order to cause the minimum disruption to the administration of the army, he would appoint a judge from among the troops and order the trial to be held in the miltary camp. The centurion would be an obvious choice as *iudex*.[38] In criminal cases the governor himself officiated; but when a soldier was involved he may well have heard the case in the military camp.[39] It should be emphasized that civil suits and criminal trials need not invariably end up in this way. It was up to the magistrate or governor to decide what to do, and in a situation where a soldier could be released from his duties and was in his own *forum* he could be expected to defend his interests in the normal way.

Nevertheless, in general the civilian plaintiff will have found it difficult to bring a soldier before a civil court; and a civilian defendant was no better off, in that he was likely to be tried in the soldier's *forum*. A trial in the military camp was technically not a court martial, but it is unlikely that the civilian would have had an opportunity of gaining justice, especially if a campaign threatened and the soldiers were urgently needed. The whole ambiance of the trial would be military, and as Tacitus observed, 'legal jurisdiction in the camp is direct, knows no appeal, and has many summary decisions'.[40] The civilian, perhaps already thoroughly intimidated by the tough and often dishonest soldiery, could have little confidence about braving the rigours of such a trial. It is possible that the difficulty of bringing soldiers to justice, and the bewilderment and despair of the poorer citizens, contributed to the abuse and corruption in the provinces and the inability of those in authority to remedy the situation.

---

[37] For an example of a criminal case, see *CJ* 9.1.10 (239): 'Si crimen ad tuam tuorumque iniuriam pertinens exsequeris, sollemnibus te inscriptionibus adstringe, ut praesidem provinciae habere iudicem possis.'

[38] See below, Appendix 1.

[39] For a possible example see below, pp. 294f. In these circumstances the governor might use army officers as his advisers.

[40] *Ag.* 9.4.

VI

IMPERIAL RESCRIPTS TO SOLDIERS

1. INTRODUCTION

Through rescripts emperors dealt with all kinds of legal queries raised in written petitions by ordinary people. The rescript was not intended to promulgate law or make a judgement; usually it stated what the law was, without any kind of modification. 'They are rather authoritative opinions which a petitioner can use in any way he pleases, for example as an argument in court.'[1] Many of the questions raised were within the competence of the appropriate officials to decide, and the petitioners approached the emperor evidently because they feared that they would not receive justice in the ordinary run of things.

It is clear from the *Codex* that soldiers are often among the recipients of rescripts, and in many cases they addressed the emperor on just the same kind of points as civilians. Soldiers had the same rights in going straight to the head of state (who in their case was also commander-in-chief) as civilians had. However, some petitions from soldiers arose specifically from the circumstances of their military service or military privileges, and here it is notable that in this way the troops could have recourse directly to their commander-in-chief on military business. Soldiers enjoyed privileges in various aspects of the law and when they appeared in court; they were also the 'fellow-soldiers' of the emperor, who desired the army to identify closely with him. The response of emperors to petitions from the troops is therefore import-

---

[1] Honoré, *JRS* 1979, 52; *Emperors and Lawyers* (1981); see also, Williams, *JRS* 1974, 86; *JRS* 1976, 67; Millar, *ERW*, 240–52.

ant as a guide to their attitudes to the soldiers and the law, and the extent to which they were prepared to indulge the army.

But do rescripts and other imperial documents embody decisions taken personally by emperors and their advisers, and do they contain the actual words in which an emperor expressed his decision, or a summary of them? This subject has provoked long-standing controversy among scholars. Honoré has argued from the style and content of the rescripts that they were composed by the *a libellis* (the secretary in charge of petitions) and that the tenures of the various holders of this office can be traced.[2] On the other hand W. Williams, while accepting the role of the imperial secretary in rescripts relating to private law, believes that in general the emperor was all-important, and attempts to trace in the public pronouncements of emperors the individuality of imperial authorship.[3]

However the arguments seem inconclusive. Honoré makes a strong case for the role of the *a libellis* in composing some rescripts, but it is plausible to suppose that the secretary could express in his own words and style a decision effectively made by the emperor, perhaps with his advice. In the same way we may explain signs of individuality in imperial documents on the hypothesis that the efficient secretary adopted the *persona* and tone of his master. It may be surmised that when an emperor received a petition, he might answer it at once in the context of his own experience and immediate wishes; or he might seek advice and then reply himself; or he might seek advice, expecting and receiving a draft reply, which he would then send off unchanged, amend or re-write. Or he might delegate the matter entirely to a subordinate official. 'Purely as a hypothesis, we may surmise again that emperors now [after 193] tended to decide the main tenor of a *subscriptio*, perhaps after consultation, and to leave its precise wording to be composed by the *a libellis*.'[4]

From the point of view of this study, two considerations

---

[2] See n. 1; also *Studia et Documenta Historiae et Iuris* 28 (1962), 162.
[3] *JRS* 1976, 69.
[4] Millar, *ERW*, 251.

should be emphasized. Firstly, whoever composed the rescripts would not draft a reply which he knew would be rejected by his master. He must write in accordance with the known principles, slogans, and attitudes of the emperor, who could intervene himself at any time, and who could reply personally if he wished. In any event, it is likely that the final version of a rescript was submitted for imperial inspection and approval. For it is easy to forget that the Roman emperor was an autocrat who could do what he liked and who had in practice the power of life and death over his subjects and officials, many of whom perhaps were unwilling to use their initiative or proceed far on their own responsibility. Therefore, rescripts and other public documents ought to be valid evidence for the known attitudes of emperors towards the army and its privileges.

Secondly, if there was one area of the law where officials and jurists would be unwilling to use their own initiative, it was surely the privileged position of the army. The extensive military privileges created an unusual and delicate situation where the interests of one group to which emperors showed special favour had to be balanced against the rights of others and the principle of the law. It is difficult to believe that the emperor was not consulted in questions concerning military law and the rights and emoluments of his troops. Indeed it was probably advisable for others not to get involved, as Junius Gallio discovered in the reign of Tiberius.[5] Pliny's letter to Trajan from Bithynia asking about the punishment of two slaves who had enlisted in the army is instructive: 'I postponed punishing them until I could consult you, as the founder and bulwark of military discipline, about the type of punishment'; he also pointed out that the decision would be a precedent.[6] Pliny believed that only the emperor could decide on questions of military discipline.[7] Moreover,

---

[5] Tac., *A* 6.3.

[6] *Ep.* 10.29.

[7] The phrase 'te conditorem disciplinae militaris firmatoremque' may have been inserted by Pliny to attract the emperor's attention. He obviously expected Trajan to read his letters, or if someone else read them first, that they would be referred to the emperor. It is difficult to believe that a conscientious emperor would not want to know what his governors were doing. See A.N. Sherwin-White, *The Letters of Pliny: A Historical and Social Commentary* (1966), 536 ff.

Pliny forwarded a centurion's petition to Trajan because he knew that the emperor was personally ready to respond to such pleas.[8] We may suggest that it was precisely in the case of soldiers' petitions that emperors were most likely to take a personal interest and communicate their ideas directly to the person who drafted the reply.[9]

2. INDIVIDUAL ACCESS TO THE EMPEROR

Petitions from private individuals had to be delivered in person to the emperor, wherever he was, by the petitioner himself or by a close relation. It was not the responsibility of the provincial governor to forward petitions addressed to the emperor through the public post or by any other means, unless in exceptional circumstances.[1] Therefore civilians who lived outside Italy could find it very difficult to communicate their problems to the emperor. But soldiers had a much better opportunity, in the first place because they were treated exceptionally in the forwarding of petitions. Pliny's letter to Trajan about the centurion Aquila is once again relevant.[2] It shows that Pliny had read the petition or had been apprised of its contents; he had been asked formally by the centurion to send the document to Trajan; it was possible for Pliny to think of not forwarding the plea. The phrase 'durum putavi negare' must refer to the fact that it was not usual for a governor to send on a petition to Rome, but that in the case of a soldier Pliny was prepared to make an exception because he knew that Trajan took a generally favourable attitude towards the troops. If this was the usual procedure, then soldiers were significantly advantaged in their access to the emperor.

[8] 10. 106.

[9] In the following chapters dealing with rescripts and other documents, I write throughout as if the emperor made the decision himself. This conveniently avoids long periphrases, but in my view is also accurate enough since I believe that the emperor was likely to be consulted on most matters involving soldiers, even if the form of a reply or statement was worked out by a secretary.

[1] Williams, *JRS* 1974, 86 ff.

[2] *Ep.* 10.106 — Rogatus, domine, a P. Accio Aquila, centurione cohortis sextae equestris, ut mitterem tibi libellum per quem indulgentiam pro statu filiae implorat, durum putavi negare, cum scirem quantam soleres militum precibus patientiam humanitatemque praestare.

Furthermore, the provincial governor was also the commander of the troops in his province and was responsible for the organization, administration, and well-being of the army with which he was entrusted. It was reasonable that he should make himself accessible to his men, and ensure that their problems were settled. One of the duties of the *tribunus militum* was to 'listen to the complaints of his fellow-soldiers'.[3] And the troops had the power of their numbers; several rescripts are addressed to units or groups of soldiers who had banded together to make a joint petition, no doubt in the hope that they would have greater impact. Caracalla replied to the 'soldiers of the first cohort' about the military duties they were required to undertake;[4] Gordian III provided a rescript for 'Valentinus and the other soldiers' concerning the position of Valentinus' brother-in-law, who had been reinstated after deserting.[5]

Even if a soldier was unsuccessful in bringing a formal petition to the emperor's attention, other methods were possible which certainly were not available to civilians. The circumstances of the mutiny in Pannonia in AD 14 were of course exceptional, but the riotous soldiers prevailed upon Blaesus, the governor of the province, to send his son, a military tribune, as a delegate to convey the complaints of the men to Tiberius.[6] It was said that under Claudius the German soldiery 'wrote secretly to the emperor in the name of all the armies', complaining about the hard work to which they were subjected by commanders hoping to obtain triumphal ornaments in this way.[7] It is not clear how these letters were conveyed to Claudius. Possibly the soldiers sent a messanger or a deputation, or they may have approached the procurator, who also had a direct channel of communication with the emperor.[8] Josephus records how several

---

[3] 'Officium tribunorum est . . . querellas commilitonum audire', *D* 49.16.12.2. Cf. the petition by twenty-two veterans of the *X Fretensis* to their legionary legate: *Italian Society Papyrus* no. 1026 (AD 150).

[4] *CJ* 12.35.2.

[5] 35.5; cf. 9.16.1.

[6] Tac., *A* 1.19.

[7] *A* 11.20.

[8] Classicianus, Nero's procurator in Britain, reported to the emperor about the behaviour of Suetonius Paulinus — *A* 14.38.

auxiliary units in Judaea, who objected to being transferred to Pontus, sent a deputation to Claudius and won their case.[9] Commodus received courteously a large group of legionaries who had travelled from Britain to Rome to complain to the emperor about the conduct of Perennis, the Praetorian prefect[10]

Again, as emperors increasingly visited the armies and went on campaign, the troops had greater opportunity to present their problems in person. When Caracalla was on campaign in the East, he was approached by two soldiers who asked him to judge a dispute over a skin of wine. Dio was surprised: 'They displayed so little respect for their emperor that they bothered him with such a trivial matter.' But it is notable that Caracalla gave judgement in the case and ordered the soldiers to divide the wine equally. Whereupon they cut the skin in half with a sword and lost it all.[11]

Civilians also took the opportunity of the presence of an emperor in the provinces to present petitions.[12] But it seems that for a variety of reasons soldiers had a significantly better chance of gaining the attention of an emperor, wherever in the empire he was. This may be reflected in another fact. Williams has argued that, since petitions usually had to be delivered in person, the great majority of petitioners must have come from areas with easy access to the emperor's usual residence in Rome. Therefore most of the petitioners would be Latin speaking, and this can help to explain why most of the rescripts in the *Codex* are in Latin.[13] Private persons who wished to consult an emperor, but who lived in the provinces and particularly in the East, had less chance of making their problems known.

In the *Codex* between 211 and 244 there are 934 rescripts probably addressed to private individuals.[14] In the same

---

[9] *AJ*. 19.365-6.   [10] Dio, 72.9.2.   [11] 78.1.3.
[12] Cf. Williams, *JRS* 1974; Millar, *ERW*, 28-40. When Trajan arrived in Antioch in 115, a huge crowd of people came to the city with law suits and petitions — Dio, 68.24.1.
[13] *JRS* 1974, 96.
[14] Honoré, *Emperors and Lawyers*, tables 1 and 2. Not all private rescripts to civilians can be definitely identified. Between 193 and 282, 495 rescripts of uncertain status are noted (pp. 35-6). In Honoré's view, most of these are to private individuals, though the criteria for this judgement seem imprecise.

period 81 rescripts in the *Codex* are addressed to soldiers (excluding veterans). This means that between 211 and 244, soldiers received about 8.5 per cent of all private rescripts. On the basis of individual reigns, under Caracalla *c*.7.5 per cent of private rescripts were issued to soldiers, under Severus Alexander *c*.6 per cent, and under Gordian *c*.13 per cent. There are in addition in the *Codex* between 211 and 244 9 rescripts about soldiers, but not necessarily addressed to them.[15] Since the compilers of the *Codex* will normally have chosen most of the rescripts to illustrate points of law and not according to recipient, the *Codex* should provide a good random sample of the type of people who received rescripts. The proportion of rescripts concerning soldiers may be significant. The army in the imperial period hardly numbered more than 400,000–500,000 men. Beloch calculated that the total population of the empire at the death of Augustus was between 50 and 60 millions.[16] Some of his computations have been recently confirmed by P.A. Brunt and seem now to be accepted by scholars.[17] If Beloch's figure is roughly accurate, the army comprised less than 0.75 per cent of the empire's population, yet soldiers received more than 8 per cent of all rescripts addressed to private individuals. Even if this calculation seems tenuous and subject to a considerable margin of error, it is still important that soldiers received so many rescripts, in view of the fact that, as Williams suggested, people with easy physical access to Rome had a better chance of getting their petitions through. Since most soldiers served far from Rome, how did so many get petitions to the emperor? The petitions preserved in the *Codex* cannot merely be from Praetorian Guardsmen. It seems that as individuals, or a group performing a particular function in the empire, soldiers were likely to receive from an emperor more attention than civilians could expect.

[15] Evidence in Appendix 2; see also Honoré, table 2. Reign by reign, Caracalla has 18 rescripts to soldiers out of 236, Alexander 27 out of 427 Gordian 36 out of 268. If we include in the overall figures the rescripts issued by Severus and Caracalla, the soldiers still receive about 7.5 per cent of the total.

[16] *Die Bevolkerung der Griechisch-Römanischen Welt* (1886), 375 ff.; especially 507.

[17] P.A. Brunt, *Italian Manpower* (1971), 121 ff.; R.P. Duncan-Jones, *The Economy of the Roman Empire* (1974), 2; the conventional figure is apparently accepted by K. Hopkins, *Conquerors and Slaves* (1978), 1.

Most of the rescripts in the *Codex* which concern soldiers specifically mention the status of the petitioner — for example, 'Imp. Antoninus A. Maximo militi'.[18] A few are addressed to 'evocatus' or 'veteranus'. No other group or profession in the empire have their occupation designated in this way in rescripts. Rescripts to civilians take no cognizance of the petitioner's occupation; usually only his name appears and there is no sign that he had even mentioned his profession except when it was specifically relevant. But it is clear that soldiers, when writing to the emperor, mentioned that they were or had been in the army. Now, although several petitions concerned the military duties of soldiers, many others dealt with purely personal problems. Here too the soldier made known his military status.[19] This suggests that soldiers were proud of their status as *milites* and expected it to have influence with the emperor.

Why should the status of a petitioner who was a soldier be recognized in the designation of a rescript? The procedure is so common that whoever composed the rescripts must have been following some kind of general rule, which, in my view, is likely to have originated with the emperors themselves. Possibly if the petitioner had made it clear that he was a soldier, an emperor would want to show that he had noted the status of its author. But the use of *miles* in rescripts also suggests that, even in the context of civil law, emperors conceived of their relationship with the petitioner in terms of commander-in-chief and soldier, rather than emperor and citizen.

This leads to another consideration. When a petition from a soldier reached an emperor it is plausible to suggest that there was less chance of it being ignored, rejected, or deferred. Emperors may have been more disposed to accept and respond to queries from soldiers than from civilians. Pliny had spoken of Trajan's 'patientia' and 'humanitas' towards his troops. The emperor lived up to this reputation:

[18] *CJ* 1.18.1. A few rescripts to soldiers do not include 'miles' in the designation, e.g., 2.18.8; 3.36.4. It might be argued that if a rescript to a soldier gave only his name but not status, and did not reveal this by its content, we would not know that it was addressed to a soldier. But there are so many rescripts addressed specifically to soldiers that it is a plausible conjecture that this was the normal practice.   [19] e.g. 4.34.2.

'I have read the petition that you sent me from P.Accius Aquila, a centurion of the sixth cohort of auxiliary cavalry. I have been moved by his plea and have bestowed Roman citizenship on his daughter. I have sent a copy of my reply which you may give to him.'[20] Trajan also professed to cherish the justice and fairness of his reign,[21] and it is likely that other emperors were at least equally concerned to look after the interests of their troops.

It is interesting that the peasants of Scaptopara presented their complaint to the emperor Godian 'through Aurelius Purrus, a soldier of the tenth loyal, faithful, Godian Praetorian cohort, who lived in the same village and owned land along with them'.[22] Similarly, a petition from the community of Arague was presented to Philip by a soldier.[23] Did the petitioners hope not only that their soldier friends could get the complaint to the emperor's attention more effectively, but also that the emperor would be more willing to respond favourably in the interests of one of his soldiers?

That these notions are not merely fanciful is shown by an inscription from Tufici in Umbria honouring one of its citizens, Aetrius Ferox, a centurion of *II Traiana Fortis* who had been specially honoured with promotion to the centurionate by Antoninus Pius because of his energetic conduct of his military duties.[24] Ferox had used the emperor's good will to the benefit of his fellow-citizens:

Through all the promotions in his military service he gave great assistance to our state on every single occasion, as often as it was necessary; and most recently he followed up our petition so eagerly that he gained from the best and greatest emperor Antoninus Pius the right of paying late the tax for the paved road, and through his generosity relieved the community of civic expenses.

Here it seems that the local town benefited not just because Ferox had access to the emperor and could present the

---

[20] *Ep.* 10.107.

[21] e.g. *Ep.* 10.55; 97.2.

[22] *IGB* 2236 = *IGR* 1.674 = *FIRA*² 1. 106 = Abbott and Johnson, 139.

[23] *CIL* 3.14191 = *IGR* 4. 598 = *FIRA*² 1. 107. The usual reading is 'per Didymum mili<t>e<m f>rum<entarium>'. But Williams, *JRS* 1974, p. 97, n. 87, has suggested 'per mili<tem>generum'.

[24] *ILS* 2666; see above, p. 106.

petition, but also because he was especially well thought of by Pius and used his influence to gain a personal concession.

Such influence will of course have been less marked in the case of ordinary soldiers, but it is interesting that some petitions were presented by common soldiers on behalf of members of their family:

The emperor Alexander Augustus to Aurelius Maro the soldier. If your father sold his house under the compulsion of force, the sale will not be considered valid since it was not carried out in good faith; the purchase of the property is invalidated because it was completed dishonestly. Therefore if you approach the governor of the province in your name, he will use his authority to intervene, especially since you claim that you are ready to refund the buyer the sum paid over as the cost of the property.[25]

It is worth noting that the soldier is advised to take up his father's case in his own name with the governor, which perhaps suggests that he could gain an advantage in so doing.

Of course civilians too petitioned on behalf of members of their family;[26] but it may well have seemed to the poor civilian that the powerful soldier with his privileges in law and in court, and his apparent ability to influence officials, had a much superior opportunity of effectively taking action about a complaint. In the resolution of their anxieties and problems, the soldiers enjoyed opportunities not open to the majority of the population of the empire; this was another advantage of military service and part of the bond between emperor and army.

3. THE SUBJECT MATTER OF THE RESCRIPTS TO SOLDIERS

The subject matter of the rescripts shows the range of material that came before the emperor and his officials concerning the problems of the soldiers and the administration of the army. The rescripts fall into three main categories: those dealing with questions that originated in the privileges

---

[25] *CJ* 4.44.1 (222); cf. 2.19.5 (239); 22.1 (238); 9.16.1 (215); 12.35.5.
[26] There are three examples in the *Codex* listed by Honoré (*Emperors and Lawyers*, 27) of civilians petitioning on behalf of members of their family.

granted to soldiers; those concerned with matters or army discipline and organization; and those answering petitions from soldiers concerning purely private matters in civil law.

The rights associated with the military will seem to have created the greatest amount of work for emperors and their advisers.[1] Petitions were submitted concerning the details of what rights soldiers possessed and the validity of the *testamentum militare*,[2] the question of substitution;[3] the undutiful will;[4] and the problem of those who had inherited under a military will and were in doubt over their rights.[5] Difficulty arose from the right of soldiers effectively to disinherit a child by not mentioning it in a will[6] The right of a soldier to leave the property acquired in military service to one heir and be intestate for the rest of his property also caused confusion. Caracalla had to explain the point to a baffled soldier:

If a soldier instituted his comrade as heir of only his camp property, then it is legally right for his mother to take possession of the rest of his property on the grounds that he died without a will. But if he made an outsider his heir and that person has accepted the inheritance, then your wish to have his property transferred to you is not legally justifiable.[7]

No doubt it was difficult to convince the dead man's comrade, who hoped to acquire all his property, that he was not entitled to this.

In general, the number of petitions submitted on the question of military wills shows the importance of this privilege and its relevance to the needs and desires of the troops. This is important since, as it happens, the only two extant wills made by soldiers are both 'iure civili'.[8] The emperor

---

[1] *CJ* 6.21.
[2] 21.8 (238); 50.7 (226); 9.23.5 (225); *D* 29.1.9; 1.24.
[3] *CJ* 6.21.6 (225).
[4] 3.28.9 (223).
[5] 21.4 (222); 7 (229); *D* 40.4.52; 29.1.41.1; *CJ* 6.21.5 (224); 30.3 (241).
[6] 6.21.9 (238).
[7] 21.2 (213); cf. 21.1 (212).
[8] *Etudes de Papyrologie* 6 (1940), 1 = *FIRA*² 3, no. 47 (AD 146); *Select Papyri* I, no. 85 = *FIRA*² 3, no. 50 (AD 191).

and his officials were regularly called upon to interpret, explain, and if necessary modify the privileges enjoyed by the troops. Sometimes this involved questions of extraordinary triviality, which however in themselves help to illustrate life in the empire. Severus Alexander and his advisers replied to Cassius the soldier:—

The wishes of a soldier expressed in his will about the construction of his funeral monument should not be neglected by his mother and father and heirs. For although the right of bringing an accusation on these grounds has been rescinded in previous decisions, nevertheless they cannot avoid the ill will and the guilty knowledge that surrounds the failure to carry out a last duty of this nature and their contempt for the last wishes of the deceased.[9]

We may surmise that Cassius, shocked by the neglect of his slain comrade's last wishes in the failure of his relatives and heirs to erect a headstone, had appealed to his emperor for retribution. It is interesting that although the emperor insists that no formal accusation can be brought, he adopts a high moral tone in favour of the correctness of the soldier's sentiments.

The rescripts on the privilege of the *castrense peculium* reveal an eager acceptance of the right by soldiers who were still in the control of their fathers, and a determination by the fathers to hold on to their traditional prerogatives. Rescripts deal with what was legally in the *peculium*, and the criteria governing this decision, and attempt to prevent encroachment by either side.[10] Severus Alexander is found sorting out the complications of a family wrangle over *castrense peculium:*

The emperor Alexander Augustus to Antonius. If you were a *filius familias* and movable property of various kinds, which was permitted to be in the *castrense peculium*, was given to you by your father, you retain it in the rest of your *castrense peculium* and do not hold it in common with your brothers. But estates cannot be in the *castrense peculium* even if your father gave you them as you went off on your

---

[9] *CJ* 3.44.5 (224).
[10] *CJ* 3.36.4 (Severus Alexander); 12.36.1-4 (Severus Alexander and Gordian); *D* 29.1.30.

military service. However a different rule applies to those estates that came to a *filius familias* as a result of his military service; for such estates do belong to the *castrense peculium*.[11]

A series of rescripts deals with the rights of soldiers for *restitutio* since they were 'absent in the service of the State', and the problems of those who had been prevented by military service from rectifying an injustice suffered when they were minors.[12] The troops sought reassurance about their ability to protect and recover their property:

'The emperor Gordianus Augustus to Secundinus the soldier. Once *restitutio in integrum* has been requested, it is certainly legally correct that everything has to remain in its own position until the business is completed; and whoever has responsibility for the matter will see to this.'[13]

Obviously it was incumbent upon emperors to explain the privileges they had granted to the army and sort out the complications arising from them. These problems extended to the families and heirs of soldiers; therefore an emperor's responsibility for the army had fairly wide social and legal implications. More importantly, precisely because there was some doubt over the exact extent of military privileges, much was left to the interpretation of the emperor and those who administered the law. Their attitude could directly influence the development of the army's privileged position.[14]

'Someone who has been born with one testicle, or who has lost one, can legally serve in the army, according to the rescript of the deified Trajan; for both the commanders Sulla and Cotta are said to have been in this condition.'[15] It is remarkable that Trajan was consulted on such a trivial matter, and even more surprising that a list of precedents of famous commanders with this embarrassing affliction had

[11] *CJ* 3.36.4.

[12] 2.18.8 (Caracalla); 2.50.1-6 (AD 197-254); 2.52.1-3 (Gordian).

[13] 2.49.1 (239).

[14] For the development of the importance of imperial rescripts as precedents, see W. Kunkel, *An Introduction to Roman Legal and Constitutional History* (1973), 128 ff.; H.F. Jolowicz, *Historical Introduction to the Study of Roman Law* (ed. Nicholas, 1972), 368 ff.

[15] *D* 49.16.4. pref.

been kept. But the emperor, as an active commander-in-chief, had to assume responsibility for the discipline and organization of the army and make himself available to answer queries on military law, pay, and conditions of service, which perhaps a jurist or secretary would not be willing or competent to deal with. Trajan may have been exceptional in the amount of interest he devoted to the army, though even he realized that there was a limit to what he could do personally. In a case referred to him by a provincial governor, concerning adultery by a centurion with the wife of a military tribune, Trajan announced the name of the guilty centurion and added a general statement about military discipline, lest it seemed that he wanted all cases of that type referred to him. However the emperor was also petitioned about various other military activities – the treatment of slaves who had volunteered as soldiers,[16] the use of soldiers outside strictly military duties,[17] the punishment of those who volunteered for military service while facing a capital charge,[18] and the treatment of fathers who mutilated their sons to make them unfit for military service.[19]

The range of Hadrian's contact with army matters was very wide. In general his attitude was benevolent and helpful, even in matters of discipline. He issued several rescripts setting out the treatment of soldiers who returned after a period of captivity, depending on how they had behaved during their absence; replied to a legate and a governor of Aquitania on the case of a soldier who allowed a prisoner to escape; and gave detailed instructions about soldiers who tried to commit suicide:

If a soldier stabbed himself or attempted to commit suicide in some other way, the emperor Hadrian replied that the circumstances of the case should be established, so that, if he wished to die because he could no longer endure pain, or because of weariness of life, or illness, or insanity, or shame, he should not be executed, but dishonourably discharged; but if none of these reasons was applicable, then the soldier should be executed.

[16] Pliny, *Ep.* 6.31.4 ff. (centurion); 10. 29–30 (slaves).
[17] 10.19–20; 21–2; 27–8.
[18] *D* 49.16.4.5.
[19] 16.4.11.

Hadrian also considered the wills of suicides:

In a letter to Pompeius Falco, the divine Hadrian stated that if a soldier committed suicide because of some military offence, his will was to be invalid, but if he killed himself because of weariness of life or pain, the will was to be valid; if he died intestate his property was to go to his relatives, or if there were none, it was to be appropriated to his legion.[20]

The emperor extended the privilege of *castrense peculium* to veterans, and was generous in his interpretation of what might be included in this *peculium*. Even prostitutes and their designs against the property of soldiers caught his attention. Moreover, it was Hadrian who forbade soldiers from being summoned from the military camp to give testimony;[21] he also found the time to help the illegitimate children of soldiers who had ignored the ban on military marriages (p. 285). This collection of rescripts and letters allows us to see what Dio meant when he said, 'Hadrian personally investigated absolutely everything . . . the private affairs of everyone, including ordinary soldiers and their officers, their lives, quarters, and conduct.'[22]

Antoninus Pius is found deciding on the appropriate punishment for a deserter who had been given up by his father, for it must not seem that the father had surrendered his son to execution.[23] Septimius Severus and Caracalla were consulted on several minor points concerning the crime of desertion; what happened when a deserter gave himself up after five years? What was to be done if a deserter committed a more serious offence in the province where he was found?[24] These emperors also received an enquiry from a group of potential recruits who were worried about the legal problems involved.[25] Other rescripts deal with the situation of those dismissed from military service on the grounds of ill health,[26] the problems of those seeking reinstatement to

[20] 49.16.5.6 and 8; 48.3.12; 49.16.6.7; 29.1.34; 28.3.6.7.
[21] *Inst.* 2.12. pref.; 49.17.13; 17.19.13; 29.1.41; 22.5.3.6.
[22] 69.9.
[23] 49.16.13.6.
[24] Ibid; 16.3. pref.
[25] *CJ* 12.33.1.
[26] 5.65.1 (239); 12.35.8 (Philip).

the army,[27] the rights of army doctors,[28] the position of soldiers who had committed an offence and were anxious about their pay and *praemia*,[29] the property of deserters and soldiers who had been deported, and the pay of troops captured by the enemy.[30] One soldier had apparently asked for his usual discharge benefits although his dismissal had been dishonourable.[31] The question of pay and *praemia* was obviously very important to the soldiers, but that they should petition the emperor on such matters rather than their immediate commander may suggest how closely the former was associated in the minds of the troops with the discharge privileges and material benefits of the army.

The sum of the matters dealt with in these rescripts amounts virtually to the administration of the army. It seems that the immediate commanders were unwilling or unable to deal with these questions, and that emperors like Trajan and Hadrian and Caracalla, all of whom had an attested interest in military affairs, or like Septimius Severus who was forced by the circumstances of his reign to cultivate the army and an appearance of military excellence, were willing to extend imperial responsibility to nearly every aspect of army life and to the veterans.[32] Other emperors, either from disinclination, indifference, or carelessness may have been more prepared to delegate responsibility for such matters to subordinates. In any event, the rescripts provide a unique vignette of the life and organization of the Roman army, the fears and hopes of the soldiers, the dishonesty of some, the loyalty of others to their comrades, the expectation of help from their emperor, and indeed the enthusiasm of some to get into or stay in the army:

The emperor Gordianus Augustus to Brutus the soldier. Once a soldier has been discharged for medical reasons, he cannot usually be reinstated on the grounds that he has recovered a better state of health. For

[27] 12.35.6 (Gordian); 9.51.7 (Philip).
[28] 10.53.1 (Caracalla).
[29] 7.53.4 (216); 2.35.5; 7 (Gordian).
[30] 9.49.3 (Severus Alexander); 12.35.4 (Alexander); 35.1 (Caracalla).
[31] 12.35.3 (Caracalla).
[32] 7.35.1 (224); 9.47.5 (Caracalla); 10.44.1 (Severus Alexander); 12.35.7 (Gordian); *D* 49.18.5 (Severus and Caracalla).

soldiers are not discharged lightly and only after doctors have declared that they have contracted a defect and this has been rigorously investigated by a suitable judge.[33]

Many of the rescripts in the *Codex* deal with the private affairs of soldiers in civil law. Soldiers owned slaves, houses, vines, and estates.[34] They are found buying and selling, contracting debts,[35] speculating with interest, lending money,[36] acting as surety, and as guarantor for a tax-gatherer, which implies considerable wealth and status, and depositing their property in charge of others.[38] They faced problems of inheritance in civil wills and sometimes failed to master the intricacies of legal procedure.[39]

Clearly some soldiers enjoyed a comfortable life. For example, Severus Alexander dealt with the problem of one apparently wealthy soldier, concerning his farmland:

The emperor Alexander Augustus to Aurelius Fuscus the soldier. It is not necessary for the buyer of a farm to allow a tenant farmer established by the previous owner to remain unless he bought the farm with such an agreement. But if it is proved that the buyer did give his consent in an agreement of some kind that he should remain in the same position on the farm, even though it was not in writing, then he must carry out what was decided according to a contract based on good faith.[40]

Others of course were not so lucky. Antigonus, a soldier in the reign of Caracalla, had got himself in debt with a lady usurer:

If in the presence of witnesses you gave the money you owed along with the interest to the creditor who holds property belonging to you by way of a pledge, and if when she did not accept it you placed a seal

[33] 12.35.6.
[34] 3.33.7 (243); 4.51.1 (224); 3.32.4 (238); 37.2 (222); 42.1 (222); 4.31.8 (Gordian); 54.2 (222); 3 (Alexander).
[35] 4.32.6 (212); 10 (Caracalla); 48.4 (239); 65.9 (234).
[36] 4.35.7 (Gordian); 54.5 (Gordian).
[37] 4.35.6 (238); 65.7 (227).
[38] 4.34.1–4 (Severus Alexander and Gordian).
[39] 4.39.6 (230); 52.1, 2 (Gordian); 5.72.1 (205); 6.22.1 (243); 30.2 (Alexander); 30.3 (241); intricacies of legal procedure — 1.18.1 (212); 2.9.2 (238); 4.21.5 (240); and see further below, pp. 291ff.
[40] 4.65.9 (234).

on the money and deposited it, then you cannot be compelled to pay any interest from the time when you made this deposit. In the absence of the creditor you ought to approach the governor of the province about this.[41]

In this type of legal evidence we have a further illustration of the range of contact between the soldiers and the ordinary inhabitants of the empire. The injustice was not always perpetrated by the troops. But at least when the soldier was wronged or had a complaint, just or unjust, he had a direct channel of communication to his emperor and commander-in-chief, and could expect a reply. The question is what kind of response emperors made to petitions from soldiers and how firmly the rule of law was upheld.

4. EMPEROR AND ARMY: 'EDICTA', 'EPISTULAE', 'MANDATA', RESPONSE TO PETITIONS FROM SOLDIERS

Most of the evidence for communication between emperor and troops from the time of Septimius Severus and his successors is in the form of rescripts addressed to individual soldiers.[1] For the earlier period, although there are few rescripts, we have a range of more public documents that can shed some light on how emperors addressed or spoke about their troops in written communications, and their attitude towards the army and the law. It is likely that emperors adopted a different tone when initiating a communication about the army in general, than when replying to the private enquiry of an ordinary soldier. Formality and dignity would be required in letter or edict, or indeed in the more private *mandata* to a governor, as befitted the utterance of an emperor and commander-in-chief, but his words should also have a wide general impact and secure his wishes for the army. It is plausible to suppose that an emperor would supervise the composition of such documents fairly closely. On the other hand, a rescript to one soldier did not matter so much, since its impact was so much less. But that is not to say that an emperor did not care about queries raised by

[41] 4.32.6 (212).

[1] See below, Appendix 2.

individual soldiers. Every favourable rescript from emperor to soldier would have some effect, if the man told his comrades in his unit or detachment.

In 31 BC Octavian issued an edict setting out privileges for his veterans. It was designed to bind leader and troops more closely together at a crucial time.[2]

Imperator Caesar, son of a god, *triumvir* a second time for organizing the state, declares: I have decided to decree that all veterans should be exempt from tribute . . . to grant to them, their parents, children, and the wives they have or will have, exemption from all taxes; and also that they should be Roman citizens with every possible legal right, exempt from all taxes, free from military service, and exempt from compulsory public service . . . In the same way, just as I desired the veterans to be privileged in the matters mentioned above, I extend my permission for them to keep, use, and enjoy whatever priesthoods, offices, emoluments, benefits, and rewards they have possessed. It is my wish that no other magistrate, nor governor, nor procurator, nor tax collector shall be in their homes against their wishes for the purpose of getting lodging or spending the winter . . .

The language, suggesting the universality and extent of the grant of privileges, which indeed included the wives, children, and even parents of veterans, emphasizes Octavian's generosity to his men.[3] As usual in edicts, the first person is employed; this indicates that the grant of citizenship and other rights mentioned in the document could be bestowed only by Octavian, but also served to underline his personal concern for his army. The text of the edict survives in an Egyptian papyrus because a veteran was sufficiently interested in the privileges conferred to take a copy, which he

[2] *FIRA*[2] 1, no. 56: 'Ipsis parentibus liberisque eorum et uxoribus qui secumque erunt immunitatem omnium rerum dare, utique optimo iure optimaque lege cives Romani sint, immunes sunto, liberi sunto militiae, muneribus publicis fungendi vocatio. Item . . . quemmotum veterani immunes esint eorum esse volui quaecumque sacerdotia quosque honores quaeque praemia beneficia commoda habuerunt, item ut habeant, utantur, fruanturque permitti do. Invitis eis neque magistratus ceteros neque legatum neque procuratorem neque emptorem tributorum esse placet neque in domo eorum divertendi iemandique causa . . .'

[3] Note the phrase 'veteranis omnibus . . . immunitatem omnium rerum', the extensive use of indefinite pronouns in lines 11 f., and the collection of synonyms in line 18 'habeant, utantur, fruanturque'.

then proceeded to read out in court.[4] Once secure in power, Augustus avoided in edicts and speeches terms of endearment and comradeship.[5] Nevertheless it was he who established the idea of the army as a specially privileged group, requiring particular attention from the emperor.

Tiberius professed to be 'master of the slaves, *imperator* of the soldiers, and pre-eminent among the rest'.[6] When he wrote to the mutinous Pannonian legions in AD 14 he adopted a different tone; the emperor expressed his outstanding concern for those heroic legions with whom he had endured countless wars, and promised his good will. This recalls the rapport he had enjoyed eight years before with the German legionaries; some of them rushed up to touch his hand and remind him of the campaigns they had shared.[7]

In 46 Claudius wrote to the Anauni and other tribes attributed to Tridentum, formally granting Roman citizenship, which they had unofficially usurped some time previously. The emperor mentions the disruption that would be caused to the community by revocation of the rights they believed were theirs, and then continues:—

I permit them by my favour to remain in that legal status which they thought they had, and I do so all the more willingly because several of that group of men are reported to be actually serving in my Praetorian Guard, and indeed some of them have become centurions; furthermore some have been enrolled in the jury panels and are judging cases in Rome.[8]

It is notable that Claudius was apparently especially concerned by the plight of some of his Guardsmen, who would have been in an awkward legal position if their citizenship were held to be invalid, and that he mentioned it so emphatically in his edict where it was not really necessary to do so. Had he perhaps been influenced by petitions from some of the soldiers?

---

[4] 'cum Manius Valens veteranus ex<..>ter recitasserit partem edicti hoc quod infra scriptum est'.

[5] See above, pp. 33–4.

[6] Dio, 57.8.2.

[7] Tac., *A* 1.25. See above, p. 35; Velleius, 2.104.4.

[8] *CIL* V, 5050 = *FIRA*[2] 1, no. 71.

Domitian's edict of 88/9 on veterans' privileges closely follows the pattern of Octavian's similar measure. There is the same impression of the emperor's personal indulgence to the soldiers, the breadth of his concern, and the extent of his benevolence:

I have decided to declare by edict that the veteran soldiers among all of you should be freed and exempt from all the taxes of the state and customs dues; furthermore their parents, children, and women whom they take in marriage may be Roman citizens with every possible legal right and are to be excused and freed with every possible exemption; and the parents and children mentioned above by the same condition and right have total exemption . . .[9]

The date of the edict makes it probable that it was published just after the revolt of Saturninus when Domitian, like Octavian, was anxious to secure the good will of his army as quickly as possible. This measure, linked to the pay rise for serving troops, was no doubt effective in this respect.[10]

Trajan's *mandata* to provincial governors concerning military wills are remarkable for a number of reasons.[11] Here it is enough to stress the use of the phrase 'fellow-soldiers', especially in the notable address 'my excellent and most loyal fellow-soldiers', the emphasis on the emperor's personal initiative and benevolence towards the troops, and the effusive repetition of the army's privilege.[12] The language may reflect that fact that Trajan is asking for something the troops should not get, a modification of the *ius commune*; the association of emperor and soldier is indeed very strongly

[9] *FIRA*[2] 1, no. 76: 'Imp. Caesar divi Vespasiani f. Domitianus Aug. Germanicus pontifex maximus trib. potest. VIII imp. XVI censor perpetuus p. p. dicit: Visum est mihi edicto significare universorum vestrorumve veterani milites omnibus vectigalibus portitoribus publicis liberati immunes esse debent ipsi coniuges liberique eorum parentes qui conubia eorum sument omni optimo iure cives Romani esse possint et omni immunitate liberati apsolutique sint, et omnem immunitatem qui supra scripti sunt parentes liberique eorum idem iuris idem condicionis sint. . . . .'.

[10] For the privileges of veterans, see below Appendix 3.

[11] *D* 29.1.1.

[12] '. . . ut quoquomodo testati fuissent, rata esset eorum voluntas. faciant igitur testamenta quo modo volent, faciant quo modo poterint sufficiatque ad bonorum suorum divisionem faciendam nuda voluntas testatoris.'

expressed since the *mandata* would be used and read by senators who were provincial governors.[13]

In 119 Hadrian wrote to Rammius Martialis, prefect of Egypt, conferring certain rights on the illegitimate children of soldiers.[14] The subject matter, relevant to the complicated legal position of a soldier's children and the discipline of the army, and the distinctive language suggest strongly that Hadrian himself dictated this letter:[15]

I know, my dear Rammius, that children born to soldiers during their military service are not permitted to be heirs to their father's property. This did not seem to be harsh since they had acted against military regulations. But I am delighted to seize every opportunity to interpret more benevolently the rather tough decisions of my predecessors. Therefore, since children born in military service are not the legitimate heirs of their fathers, I have decided that even they be admitted to a claim on the property in accordance with that part of the edict that allows a claim to *cognati*. You should make this benefaction of mine known to my soldiers and veterans, not so that I may take the credit for it in their eyes, but in order that they may make use of it if they do not know about it.

Hadrian emphasizes strongly his own responsibility for the new concession, and the pleasure he took in bestowing this personal gift, which indeed served to contrast his benevolence with the rather more strict attitude of earlier emperors. Like Trajan, Hadrian brings out his personal association with the troops, and it is significant that he expresses openly and without explanation that his measure involves a breach of military regulations, and that the soldiers are in the wrong; there is no motive for the privilege except his benevolence. A Greek translation of the letter was displayed in the winter quarters of the *III Cyrenaica* and *XXII Deiotariana* in Egypt and it may have been read out to the troops first.[16] There can be little doubt that Hadrian intended his letter to make a favour-

---

[13] Cf. the subsequent rescript to Statilius Severus – *D* 29.1.24.

[14] Mitteis, *Chrestomathie* II.2, no. 373 = *Select Papyri* II, 213; see Campbell, *JRS* 1978, 158-9.

[15] See now, Williams, *JRS* 1976, 72.

[16] The privilege was presumably extended to the other troops by imperial letters or *mandata*.

able impact on the troops and impress them with the concept
of the emperor's generosity and good will towards his men.

Antoninus Pius made a ruling on the treatment of the will
of a soldier if the heir and his substitute died.[17] The general
tone of the emperor's decision, as it is recorded in the summary of Maecianus, suggests that it was intended to have a
wider relevance than the settlement of the case of one
soldier. It may have been a section from the emperor's
mandata to all governors. If Maecianus provides an accurate
summary of how the original pronouncement began, the use
of the word 'suus' in the phrase 'quo militum suorum per
omnia rata esset voluntas suprema' ('in order that the last
wishes of his own soldiers should be satisfied in every
respect'), seems redundant and therefore significant. Is the
jurist attempting to convey the emperor's emphasis on his
personal association with his troops? Moreover, Pius affirmed
generous support for the last wishes of his troops in everything, and openly distinguished between what was appropriate for soldiers and for the less favoured civilians.

In January 168 Marcus Aurelius delivered in the Praetorian
camp a speech in which he announced a new privilege to
assist veterans of the Guard.[18] The content of this speech
was presumably accepted as law in the way in which the
oratio principis in the Senate is cited as authority.[19] Marcus
expressed his association with the troops ('veterani nostri');
and his personal concern to benefit them and ensure that
they found wives after discharge is emphasized in the word
'sollicitabimus', with its suggestion of winning support with
the seductive offer of another privilege, that is, in addition
to those the soldiers themselves already had.[20] It is of some
interest that Marcus Aurelius, renowned among contemporaries for his moderation and equity, and unlikely recklessly
to indulge the army, should benevolently identify himself
in this way with the interests of the troops in a pronouncement that was to have the force of law.

---

[17] *D* 40.5.42; see p. 225.

[18] *Frag. Vat.* 195 = *FIRA*[2] 2, p. 503. See above p. 84.

[19] H. F. Jolowicz, *A Historical Introduction to the Study of Roman Law*[3] (ed.
Nicholas, 1972), 374.

[20] The object of 'sollicitabimus' seems to be the prospective fathers-in-law.

Finally, the language of the discharge *diplomata* awarded to auxiliaries, sailors of the fleets, and Praetorians,[21] confirms that the terminology used in addressing the soldiers was held to be important. The *diplomata* of the auxiliaries and sailors begin with the emperor's name and full titles, followed by the identification of the soldiers who receive the award of citizenship and then the verb 'dedit':

The Emperor Caesar Vespasianus Augustus, Chief Priest, holding the tribunician power for the second year, Victor for the sixth time, Father of the Fatherland, Consul for the third time and designated for a fourth, has granted citizenship to the veteran soldiers who served in the fleet at Ravenna under Lucilius Bassus, have completed twenty-six or more years service, have been settled in Pannonia, and whose names have been written below; he has also granted citizenship to their children and their posterity . . .[22]

The emperor is therefore the source of their benefits and their immediate commander is relegated to a subordinate clause. But the *diplomata* of Praetorians are significantly different. In them the emperor uses the first person, expressing a closer association with the men of his body-guard, and an honorary phrase is inserted:

I, the Emperor Caesar Vespasianus Augustus, Chief Priest, holding the tribunician power for the eighth year, Victor for the eighteenth time, Father of the Fatherland, Censor, Consul for the seventh time and designated for an eigth, have appended the names of the special troops who served in my bodyguard, and also the names of the soldiers who served in the nine Praetorian Cohorts and the four Urban Cohorts. Since they have bravely and loyally completed their service, I grant them the right of marriage . . .[23]

The personal award of privileges by the emperor, the reference to the brave and loyal service of the Praetorians, and the omission of all mention of the Praetorian prefects, suggest that it was thought worthwhile to alter the language of the *diplomata* to express the emperor's especially close

[21] The legionaries did not receive *diplomata*. See below, Appendix 3.
[22] *FIRA²* 1, no. 27.
[23] *ILS* 1993. See further, Appendix 3.

relationship with the Praetorian Guard; this confirms that the manner in which an emperor addressed his troops in written documents was important.

In these documents concerning the army, almost all of which will have been brought to the attention of large numbers of soldiers, several general characteristics should be emphasized. The nature of the material, and the language sometimes employed to express it, are such that we may plausibly suggest that the emperor himself was responsible, or at least communicated his ideas directly to whatever official did the drafting. The use of the first person (and not only in edicts) will have expressed to the soldier his emperor's personal responsibility and his close association with the troops. Moreover, an emperor sought to affirm a benevolent and special attitude to his 'comrades', through which the privileged soldiers and veterans were distinguished from the civilian population. Yet in these public documents emperors still maintained restraint and dignity and avoided any open statement of their dependence on the soldiery. It is indeed the *mandata* of Trajan, the 'Optimus Princeps', which make the most notably enthusiastic assertion of the association of emperor and army.

In structure and presentation the rescripts to soldiers are similar to those given to civilian petitioners.[24] However in those rescripts confirming established privileges of the soldiery, the emperor could insert a general declaration of the privileged position of the army, to serve as an explanation for the decision taken in the rescript. Severus Alexander ended a rescript thus. '. . . for among the other privileges granted to soldiers they are permitted a free choice to leave their property to whomever they please, unless the law specifically prohibits them'.[25] Caracalla began one rescript with a sweeping statement of imperial benevolence towards soldiers: 'Although the wills of soldiers are not subject to the rules of

[24] See Honoré, *JRS* 1979, 53; *Emperors and Lawyers*, 50 ff. He thought that variations in rescript structure were relevant to the differing approach of various secretaries. The common pattern is: existing situation described — answer to query — explanation of answer.

[25] *CJ* 6.21.5; cf. 5.16.2; 6.21.1; 21.4.2; 6.1.

law, since on account of the simple-minded inexperience
associated with the troops they are permitted to make their
wills in whatever way they wish and in whatever way they
can ...[26] In the interpretation of the extent and consequences of military privileges, declarations like this were
perhaps intended to remind the magistrate or governor of the
special position of the army, and to protect the soldier's
interests.

The rescript of Caracalla also adduced the 'simplicitas
militaris' as a reason for special consideration. In this he
followed Trajan's *mandata*, where the emperor spoke of the
simple-mindedness of the troops.[27] It could be widely propagated that the army performed great labours on behalf of the
empire; the phrase 'munera armatae militiae' no doubt
sounded impressive.[28] In conventional eloquence this idea
was accepted. Dio of Prusa, in a speech delivered to Trajan,
compared to a bad shepherd a ruler who suspected his
army 'and never or rarely met those who endured dangers
and toil on behalf of the empire'.[29] In his Roman oration
Aelius Aristides favourably compared the Roman army to
that of other nations where 'the soldiers were worse off than
those who remained inactive since they alone toiled throughout their lives'.[30] When Seneca said, 'It is the duty of all the
good men, if I may put it like this, to be a soldier and
perform their labours on behalf of all', he probably had in
mind a direct metaphor from the accepted role of the
soldier.[31] Furthermore, Pliny, referring to Trajan's soldiers,
spoke of their 'wounds on behalf of the State';[32] the idea
that the army existed only for the benefit of the empire, and
deserved reward for its labours, was probably encouraged by
emperors.[33] The expectations of the soldiers themselves may
be seen in the petition of a veteran in Egypt about compul-

---

[26] 6.21.3.
[27] *D* 29.1.1; cf. *CJ* 1.18.1. Gaius, *Inst.* 2.109, states that the 'diligens
observatio' was not carried out in the will of a soldier – 'propter nimiam
imperitiam constitutionibus principum remissa est'.
[28] *CJ* 5.34.4; cf. 2.50.6; 9.9.15; 1.18.1; 2.18.8.
[29] 1.28.
[30] J.H. Oliver, 'The Ruling Power', sects. 73; 78.
[31] *De Provid.* 5.1.
[32] *Pan.* 15.5.
[33] Note Ulpian's etymology for *miles*, above p. 226.

sory offices; it was probably addressed to the *Epistrategus:* 'As such a prolonged burden is universally forbidden in the case of natives, much more ought the rule to be observed in my case since I have served such a long time in the army'.[34]

Furthermore, several of the rescripts in the *Codex* are phrased in language that directly contrasts the soldier in his privileged position with the mass of the *pagani.* Severus Alexander explained to a slave who hoped to obtain his liberty through the will of a soldier: 'You cannot claim your liberty if the will of a civilian is being described, but since you claim that the *testator* was a soldier . . . you are entitled to your freedom, and directly . . .'[35] Significantly, it became necessary to point out that not even soldiers had certain privileges. Severus Alexander had to inform a soldier who believed that being a soldier automatically freed him from *patria potestas*, 'for none the less soldiers remain in the power of their parents'.[36] And the same emperor, referring to the manumission of slaves by a *testator* under the legal age, stated that in this respect there could be no concession, not even to soldiers.[37] Most interesting is the case of a lady named Sulpicia, who petitioned Gordian seeking permission to marry again within the fixed period of mourning for her first husband. The emperor however threatened both woman and prospective husband with the provisions of the edict, 'even if he is a soldier'.[38] The last phrase suggests that in certain cases special consideration could be extended to a soldier. It is possible that Sulpicia mentioned that her intended husband was a soldier deliberately, in the hope of winning sympathy for her plight.

But very few rescripts in the *Codex* grant a privilege, as distinct from the usual military privileges, to an individual soldier merely because he is a soldier.

The emperor Antoninus Augustus to Marcus the soldier. If you prove to the provincial governor that the slave girl was bought with your money, and for the purpose of making a gift the receipt of purchase was written in the name of your concubine, he will order that she be

---

[34] *BGU* 180 = *Select Papyri* II, 285.
[35] *CJ* 6.21.7; cf. 21.6.   [36] 12.36.3.   [37] 6.21.4.2.   [38] 2.11.15.

returned to you. For although the consequences of a formal marriage do not apply in this case and therefore a gift could be completed, nevertheless I forbid my soldiers to be robbed in this way by their concubines through deceitful displays of affection.[39]

Here the case against Marcus was very strong. He was not formally married but had a concubine, and so the *donatio*, invalid between man and wife, was valid in this instance. And there was proof of it in the formal written receipt for the purchase of the slave girl in the name of the *focaria*. Caracalla admits all this, but dismisses it with a statement of benevolent concern for his troops, in which he imagines the wily mistress playing upon the honest affections of the simple soldier in order to get gifts from him. The tone and attitude, the effusive language (unusually for rescripts, the first person singular is employed in the emphatic 'nolo'; there is also the emotive word 'spoliari'; the phrase 'fictis adulationibus' is striking and provides a personal note), and the personal association in 'milites mei', all suggest that Caracalla himself made the decision and ensured that his own ideas and expressions were directly conveyed to the person who drafted the rescript. In fact the rescript is thoroughly typical of Caracalla's comradely attitude towards his soldiers, and fits in well with some of his expansive pronouncements quoted by Dio.[40]

The emperor Antoninus Augustus to Maximus the soldier. Although when you were conducting your case, through ignorance of the law on account of the simple-minded inexperience of those in military service, you neglected to submit the relevant proofs, nevertheless if you have not yet made reparation, I grant that you may use the evidence for your defence, if an action is now being brought against you in accordance with the decision.[41]

[39] 5.16.2: 'Imp. Antoninus A. Marco militi. Si ancillam nummis tuis comparatam esse praesidi provinciae probaveris donationisque causa focariae tuae nomine instrumentum emptionis esse conscriptum, eam tibi restitui iubebit. Nam licet cessante iure matrimonii donatio perfici potuerit, milites tamen meos a focariis suis hac ratione fictisque adulationibus spoliari nolo'.

[40] e.g. 78.3.2; 4.1a; 13.6.

[41] *CJ* 1.18.1: 'Imp. Antoninus A. Maximo militi. Quamvis cum causam tuam ageres, ignorantia iuris propter simplicitatem armatae militiae adlegationes competentes omiseris, tamen si nondum satisfecisti, permitto tibi, si coeperis ex sententia conveniri, defensionibus tuis uti'.

This seems to be a personal concession by Caracalla, emphasized by the use of the first person — 'permitto tibi' — and
the excuse of the habitual inexperience of the troops.
Apparently steps were being taken against the soldier to
execute the decision reached in the case. It is remarkable that
he was allowed to continue his defence at this stage.
Ignorance of the law itself was not normally held to excuse
failure to comply with legal procedure, as Gordian pointed
out in a rescript to a civilian in 243.⁴² If soldiers were often
permitted to adduce ignorance of the⋅ law as a reason for
reopening a completed case, it will have made life very difficult for their legal adversaries.

The emperors Severus and Antoninus Augusti to Ingenuus the soldier.
We have ensured on behalf of all our soldiers that they should not
suffer the penalty of confiscation of property if they omit to make a
declaration. And so lay aside your anxiety, and if it seems that you owe
some customs dues, pay them.⁴³

The circumstances described in this rescript are that an article
subject to customs duty and not declared was normally confi-
scated. Severus and Caracalla had provided that no soldier
should be subject to this threat.⁴⁴ The use of the first person,
the verb 'prospicio', and the word 'omnes' indicate a personal
concession by emperors watchful for the interests of all their
army. From this expression of imperial concern, they
proceed to dispel the individual petitioner's anxieties.
Civilians, apparently, had to take their chance with the
customs officials.

Although only in these three rescripts was any kind of
special concession made to a soldier, in a few cases an
emperor generously extended the benefit of the doubt.

The emperor Alexander Augustus to Gallicanus the soldier. Since you
were asked to write out your comrade's will and on his instructions

---

⁴² 1.18.2.
⁴³ 4.61.3: 'Impp. Severus et Antoninus AA. Ingenuo militi. Omnibus militibus
nostris prospeximus, ne ob omissas professiones poena commissi tenerentur.
Proinde deposito hoc metu, si qua portoria debere te apparuerit, exsolve'.
⁴⁴ Domitian had extended exemption from customs dues to veterans, their
parents, wives, and children. This presumably referred only to personal property,
and it is not clear if it was systematically enforced after Domitian's death.

assigned a slave to yourself in the will, it is considered invalid, as if it had never been written, and you cannot take up that legacy. But following my usual tendency to display benevolence, I grant that you should be exempt from the penalty of the Cornelian law, whose precepts you have infringed more through inadvertence, in my opinion, than with fraudulent intent.[45]

The first person ('permitto tibi') is used to convey this interpretation of the law favourable to the soldier. The general statement of imperial benevolence is closely similar to Trajan's *mandata* ('secutus animi mei integritudinem'), and may refer in particular to the soldiers, for whom imperial 'indulgentia' was principally reserved. In a rescript to a civilian concerning an exactly similar case, the same emperor returned a bluntly unhelpful rescript:

According to the decree of the Senate and the edict of the divine Claudius, anyone who is required to write out a will is forbidden to include any advantageous bequest to himself, even if the *testator* dictates it to him, and anyone who does so has the penalty laid down by the Cornelian law invoked against him. Even if he begs for remission because of ignorance of the law and promises not to accept the legacy left to him, the Senate and the divine emperors have rarely extended their forgiveness.[46]

The rescript from Gordian to a soldier concerning the inclusion in the *castrense peculium* of an inheritance from his brother who served in the same camp has been considered in detail above. Gordian allowed the soldier to keep the *hereditas* in the *castrense peculium* although there was great dispute among jurists on this general question. The effusive last sentence with its emotive phraseology and accumulation of reasons to explain why, in the emperor's opinion, military service must have increased fraternal affection, is striking, and perhaps reflects the fact that the emperor and his advisers are so readily granting a right that required more investigation.[47]

[45] 8.23.5.   [46] 23.3.

[47] 12.36.4 "Etenim peregrinationis labor sociatus commilitii eius et obeundorum munerum consortium adfectioni fraternae nonnihil addidisse, quin immo vice mutua cariores invicem sibi reddidisse credendum est.' See above, p. 233.

Severus Alexander confirmed for the benefit of Aufidius, who may have been a provincial governor, that a soldier could act as *procurator* for his own affairs and that this right was not affected by the ban on a soldier acting as *procurator* on behalf of another party. This was not a concession, but the last sentence contains an emphatic statement of the emperor's good will towards the army: 'It is not only ridiculous but also unfair for my soldiers to be barred from this.'[48] If the secretary *a libellis* wrote this, adopting the *persona* of his master, was he possibly influenced by a desire among the emperor's advisers at this time to make a good impression on the troops wherever possible?

In 215 Caracalla was called upon to reply to a petition from a group of his soldiers about the fate of a man apparently on the run from a murder charge:

The emperor Antoninus Augustus to Aurelius Herculianus and the other soldiers. Your brother will be acting more correctly if he presents himself to the governor of the province. If he proves that he struck Iustus with no premeditated intention of killing him, then the governor will withdraw the penalty for murder and bring in a judgement in line with military discipline. For the charge of murder applies only when there was a deliberate intention of injuring someone. But those actions that occur as a result of unexpected incidents rather than criminal intent are held to be accidents rather than crimes.[49]

It is not clear from the context if Iustus was a soldier or civilian when he was killed by Herculianus' brother, who probably was a soldier.[50] Since his brother was reluctant to

---

[48] 2.12.9. Cf. 9.1.8; this rescript concerns the soldier's right to bring an accusation; this was permitted in certain circumstances, but other restrictions on the appearance of soldiers in court may have caused some uncertainty. Perhaps this is why the first person is used, though no privilege is being granted: 'ideoque consobrini tui necem defendere tibi permittimus'.

[49] 9.16.1: 'Frater vester rectius fecerit si se praesidi provinciae obtulerit: qui si probaverit non occidendi animo Iustum a se percussum esse, remissa homicidii poena secundum disciplinam militarem sententiam proferet. Crimen enim contrahitur si et voluntas nocendi intercedat. Ceterum ea, quae ex improviso casu potius quam fraude accidunt, fato plerumque, non noxae imputantur.'

[50] Herculianus' brother is almost certainly a soldier, since otherwise it would be very odd that the other soldiers stood up for him in this way. Since Caracalla speaks of a verdict consistent with military discipline, at least one of the two men involved must have been a soldier, and if it was Iustus then the soldiers would be

footnote continued at foot of next page

surrender himself, Herculianus persuaded some of his comrades to combine in a petition to the emperor, alleging that it had been manslaughter not murder. Caracalla's rescript instructs the governor on what verdict to bring in, provided that Herculianus' brother can prove that there had been no premeditation. The interests of Iustus do not receive much attention, and this would be particularly significant if he were a civilian. The phrase 'secundum disciplinam militarem sententiam proferet' is obscure, but may suggest that the governor would eventually decide the case in the military camp.[51] In any event, this favourable rescript fully justified the confidence of Herculianus and his fellow-soldiers in approaching the emperor directly on behalf of a man who had to some extent prejudiced his own case by not submitting himself immediately to the authorities.

Indeed the patience of emperors must sometimes have been tried by petitions they received in which soldiers confidently sought imperial good will on matters affecting military discipline. Caracalla made no concession in his reply to a soldier who had managed to get back after being captured by the enemy: 'The emperor Antoninus Augustus to Annaeus the soldier. It is not right for you to ask for your pay and donatives to be restored to you for the time when you say you were a prisoner with the enemy, because you have returned and have been restored to your old position by *postliminium*.'[52] The same emperor upheld a petition from long-serving members of the 'first cohort': 'If you have completed twenty years service, the menial duties associated with military service will not be assigned to you.'[53]

Severus Alexander was approached about the position of soldiers dishonourably dismissed from the service. The rescript was helpful, but reinforced the usual rule:

Since soldiers who have been dishonourably discharged are designated with a mark of bad repute, they may not have the benefit of the

---

defending Herculianus' brother against the interests of their comrade. Perhaps both men were soldiers, but in that case it would be superfluous for Caracalla to speak of a verdict 'consistent with military discipline'. And so perhaps the most likely explanation is that Herculianus' brother, who was a soldier, killed Iustus, a civilian. But no certainty is possible.

[51] See further above, pp. 256-63.   [52] *CJ* 12.35.1.   [53] 35.2.

privileges normally given to men of unstained character. They do however have the right of living wherever they wish, provided that it is not
in one of those places from which they are specifically excluded.[54]

The position of the soldier who had not actually been dishonourably discharged was not so gloomy, as Gordian III
pointed out to a veteran:—

Your fears are groundless that a mark of disgrace incurred on account
of an offence committed during military service should be held to have
damaged your good name now that you are a veteran. This is especially
true since it has been decided that if a soldier has been censured in
respect of an offence which could also be committed by a civilian,
he should not after discharge be designated as being of bad repute.[55]

Gordian was also approached by a group of soldiers on the
treatment of a comrade who had been a deserter of long
standing:

'The emperor Gordianus Augustus to Valentinus and the other soldiers.
Since you claim that your sister's husband spent seven years as a
deserter and was reinstated through my benevolence, your wish that it
should be considered as if he had spent this time in the military camp is
not correct. Indeed with the exception of that period of time which
relates to deserters, the man restored by our benevolence will be
obliged to serve out the remainder of his military service. And so he
will not be able to request his pay for the time he spent as a deserter.[56]

As a deserter of seven years standing Valentinius' brother-in-
law was in line for stiff punishment,[57] and it is interesting
that Gordian had already displayed his 'indulgentia' by

---

[54] 35.3.

[55] 35.7.

[56] 35.5: 'Cum adlegas septem annos in desertione egisse maritum sororis
vestrae et indulgentia nostra esse restitutum, non recte desideratis, ut id tempus,
ac si in castris fuerit, habeatur. Proinde excepto eo tempore, quod ad desertores
pertinet, restitutus nostra indulgentia residuo militare debebit: ideoque nec
stipendia temporis, quo in desertione fuerit, exigere poterit.'

[57] D 49.16.13.6.

restoring the soldier, apparently without punishment. Here again the comrades of the delinquent soldier have combined to approach the emperor; and they have displayed great confidence in their commander-in-chief's good will by asking even that the restored deserter should receive his pay for the time spent in absence from the ranks. In view of the impropriety of the request, the rescript is indeed very politely expressed and gives a full explanation.

There was clearly considerable pressure on emperors and their advisers arising from the hopeful petitions of soldiers who had fallen foul of military discipline. If the soldiers were encouraged to think of their emperor as their benefactor and patron, it was natural that they hoped to evoke a favourable response from him towards their problems, not only in military but also in civil life. It may be significant that in the short reign of Gordian III (238-44), out of 268 private rescripts in the *Codex*, 36 are addressed to soldiers (i.e., about 13 per cent).[58] Does this indicate a special determination by the emperor's advisers to respond personally to as many petitions as possible from soldiers? Gordian owed his success largely to the personal choice of the troops; after years of disorder and the murder of emperors, every opportunity had to be taken to establish their absolute loyalty. If Gordian's regime was noted for a generally favourable attitude towards the army, this may help to explain the confidence of the petitioners about the deserter discussed above, and the emperor's *indulgentia*. But this would produce embarrassing requests that presumed too much on the emperor's good will and which could not be allowed.

In conclusion, it seems that it was very rare for an emperor to grant a special privilege in civil law to a soldier merely because of his service in the army. Most rescripts on matters of civil law were in line with existing legal principle and

---

[58] See above, p. 270. It should be noted that most of the rescripts issued by Severus Alexander and Gordian to soldiers do not belong to periods when they were on campaign; on the other hand, 8 out of 18 of Caracalla's rescripts can be dated in or after 213 when the emperor was on campaign. It does not seem to be generally true that emperors issued more rescripts to soldiers because they happened to be present with them on campaign and therefore were more readily available.

showed no particular favour.[59] In dealing with queries from soldiers, emperors seem to have been able to combine their approachability, their personal association with the army, and their benevolent support for its privileged position in certain areas, with a restraint and moderation that aimed to ensure the minimum necessary disruption of the traditional order of things. When an emperor was dealing with the problem of an individual soldier, it was not worth compromising the principle of the law for the gratitude to be gained; and he could hope that an unfavourable reply to one soldier was unlikely to cause widespread dissatisfaction even if the soldier told his comrades.

On the other hand it was always in an emperor's power to grant any privilege to a soldier if he wished. We do not know how often imperial *indulgentia* was extended in this way. The evidence has many limitations. What we can say is that the language and presentation of documents about the army and the way the troops were addressed in such documents were important; furthermore, in rescripts emperors sometimes intervened directly, and it is plausible to suppose that they were consulted by the appropriate officials about petitions from soldiers, at least those involving established

[59] In most rescripts dealing with private matters and civil law there is no demonstrable difference from those addressed to civilians, and it is only the designation *miles* that identifies the recipient. As an example I have selected rescripts concerned with the dealing of soldiers in financial affairs:

debts — *CJ* 3.37.2; cf. *D* 10.3.6.8; 7.12.

   CJ 4.13.1; cf. Buckland, *Text-Book*, 529 f.

   CJ 4.32.6; cf. 32.8; 32.9.

deposita — *CJ* 4.34.1; cf. *D* 16.3.20; 3.10.

   CJ 4.34.2 — 'sicut in ceteris bonae fidei iudiciis'.

   CJ 4.34.3; cf. Gaius *Inst.* 3.196.

   CJ 4.34.4 — here the law is upheld against the claims of a soldier.

mandated actions — *CJ* 4.35.6; cf. *D* 17.1.6.2

   CJ 4.35.7; cf. 8.40.2, 5, 6, 17.

   CJ 4.65.7; the emperor's attitude seems entirely fair.

buying and selling — *CJ* 4.54.3; cf. 4.54.1.

   CJ 4.54.2 and 5; cf. *D* 19.5.

   CJ 4.65.9 — it is stated that soldiers are subject to the 'iudicum bonae fidei'.

   CJ 2.43.2; cf. 2.43.3.

These texts show that in private matters of civil law, soldiers were in general subject to the same provisions as civilians.

military privileges or army discipline, whatever the usual role of the *a libellis* in producing rescripts. In dealing with the army emperors were perhaps prepared to take a general initiative more readily than in other areas of the administration.

But the legal advantages of the ordinary soldier derived from his accepted privileges in certain areas of the law, his ability to gain a special consideration in the hearing of cases, and his superior opportunity for gaining access to and response from the emperor, rather than through immediate concessions by emperors to individual soldiers, which then became established law. Moreover, there is no sign that the civil wars and turmoil of 193–7 significantly enhanced the army's legal privileges. On the contrary there is continuity from the first to the third century in the struggle of emperors to preserve the balance between the support of the troops, the good will of the upper classes who desired the maintenance of their traditional rights and prerogatives, and the defence of law and order.

VII

ROMAN MILITARY LAW

1. INTRODUCTION

Traditionally the Romans took great pride in the strict military discipline through which their forefathers had established Roman supremacy. T. Manlius typified the ferocious determination to put the *res publica* before personal feelings. He executed his own son for attacking the enemy contrary to orders, and Livy makes him say. 'You have undermined military discipline, by which the Roman state has stood to this day'.[1] This kind of 'disciplina maiorum', no doubt much idealized, was inappropriate to the end of the Republic and the imperial period. But there was still a recognition of the value of good discipline and military organization. When Caesar recruited a new legion, the *Alauda*, from the people of Transalpine Gaul, he first trained them in the 'disciplina Romana'.[2] Tacitus spoke of the outstanding qualities of a German tribe, the Chatti, and their rare ability to place more reliance on the general than on the army, 'an achievement usually reserved for Roman discipline'.[3] Outsiders too were impressed by the seemingly invincible discipline of the Roman army. Aelius Aristides in his Roman oration specifically mentions how the soldiers 'lived day by day in good order and never failed to do what had been commanded'.[4]

---

[1] 8.7.16: 'disciplinam militarem, qua stetit ad hanc diem Romana res, solvisti . . .'; cf. 8.32; 34; 35.
[2] Suet., *Caes.* 24.2.
[3] *Germania* 30.2; cf. 25.2.
[4] J.H. Oliver, sect. 87.

In the years of civil war at the end of the Republic discipline had become of secondary importance, to be enforced or relaxed as suited the individual commander's ambitions and the need to win the approval of his troops.[5] It was in Augustus' interests to show that he was not merely another military adventurer, and prove to the upper classes his ability to preserve the *disciplina militaris*, since they too would appreciate a curb on the indisciplined and licentious conduct of the armies which had settled the fate of the Republic. An emperor could not allow his regime to become unstable through the pressures of a turbulent soldiery. Dio has praise for Trajan because he disciplined the soldiers so strongly that they did not become proud and arrogant 'as usually happens in these circumstances', that is, when there had been a successful war.[6]

How far could an individual emperor influence or be responsible for the discipline of a large professional army scattered round the empire? Much depended on the character and abilities of the governors, who had to oversee the training and organization of the legionaries and auxiliaries. An emperor could seek to control military discipline by appointing the right kind of commander in the first place, by travelling round and inspecting the troops in their training, as Hadrian did, or by taking personal charge of a campaign. But many other factors also influenced the appointment of consular legates, not many of whom had extensive military experience before taking up their posts;[7] and Hadrian was unique in his peregrinations round the army camps in time of peace. An emperor might have to rely on specific or general instructions to his governors and hope that they could carry them out, and also give a lead when questions of military discipline and organization were brought to his attention.[8]

The ban on the contracting of marriages by soldiers during service provides a good illustration of the different and often conflicting pressures on emperors and their reaction to them.[9] The ban was presumably thought necessary to preserve the efficiency and good order of the army as a

---

[5] Appian, *BC* 5.17; Plut., *Mar.* 7.4–5.   [6] 68.7.5.   [7] See below, pp. 325ff.
[8] See above, pp. 276ff.   [9] See in detail, Campbell, *JRS* 1978, 153.

fighting machine unencumbered by the presence of wives
and children. It may well have been introduced by Augustus
to tighten up discipline when he reduced and reorganized the
legions that fell into his control after Actium. Perhaps he
intended to discourage as many soldiers as possible from
forming liaisons with women, with the threat of non-
recognition of these in law. However the prohibition ran
counter to the natural desire of some soldiers to cohabit with
local women, whom they regarded as their 'wives'. And to
contemporaries a legal restriction on married life would be
unwelcome.[10] It was important also to keep the army
contented and make military service as attractive as possible,
partly in order to encourage new recruits. Consequently,
the imperial administration found itself in a muddle; no
emperor seemed willing to remove the ban, possibly because
of traditional military thinking on the maintenance of
discipline. Instead individual emperors reacted in different
ways to the various problems created by the denial of the
consequences of a legal marriage to soldiers. Some did
nothing, but others — Claudius, who was particularly anxious
to secure the good will of all the troops, possibly Trajan,
and Hadrian — ameliorated some of the consequences of the
marriage ban, but in a piecemeal fashion.

Although this brought about a gradual improvement in
the army's position, the decisive change was made by
Septimius Severus. In a dramatic act of good will, he swept
away the ban and allowed soldiers to contract a legally valid
marriage. This decision was the emperor's own initiative and
was apparently part of his attempt to confirm the loyalty
of his army after the defeat of Clodius Albinus in 197.
The army was a personal mercenary force and Severus'
decision on military marriages emphasizes how an emperor
could at any time intervene and establish or amend whatever
rules and traditions of discipline he pleased.

The history of the ban on the marriage of soldiers, and its
removal by Severus, raise more general questions about
Roman military law and discipline. Since an emperor could
do what he liked with the army, and since his conduct would
be dictated by his character and the prevailing political situ-

[10] Ibid., 155.

ation, the application of military discipline was a variable factor in the history of the Roman army. But however much emperors needed to flatter the soldiers, they all needed to preserve the army's ability to resist foreign foes, and of course to some extent centurions and junior officers could provide some continuity in the enforcement of discipline. Once again it was a delicate balance for each emperor to get from the troops the correct blend of affection, loyalty, contentment with their lot, and yet efficient fighting prowess.

2. LEGAL PENALTIES AND THE ENFORCEMENT OF MILITARY DISCIPLINE

A soldier needed a good record and an honourable discharge to be eligible for the privileges of a veteran.[1] Desertion from the ranks and insubordination were the most serious military crimes, and here an important distinction was made between times of war and times of peace.[2] In principle desertion in face of the enemy brought death,[3] and a soldier who ran away in battle was executed in full view of his comrades 'to create an example'.[4] Similarly a soldier 'who pretended to be sick because of fear of the enemy' was punished with death;[5] desertion when the army was on the march, and disobedience of the express order of the commander, brought the same penalty.[6] *Transfugae*, that is, soldiers who deserted with the intention of joining the enemy, were held in even greater disapprobation. If they returned they were to be tortured and condemned to the beasts or to be bound on the 'fork'. The severity of this treatment is emphasized by the fact that soldiers did not normally suffer these punishments.[7] And a soldier who was caught in the act of going over to the enemy was executed immediately.[8] Indeed Taruttienus

[1] See further below, pp. 311ff.
[2] D 49.16.5.1 (Menander). For Roman military law in general, see Mommsen, *Römische Strafrechts* (1899), 31 ff.; E. Sander, *Rh. M* 103 (1960), 289.
[3] 49.16.3–4 (Modestinus).
[4] 16.6.3 (Menander).
[5] 16.6.5.
[6] 16.3.15–16.
[7] 16.3.10 (Modestinus).
[8] 16.3.12.

Paternus, who was Praetorian prefect under Marcus Aurelius and wrote on *Res Militaris* confirms that *transfugae* were to be tortured and executed, and classes them as enemies ('hostes'), not soldiers ('milites').[9] In this category of *transfugae* were also placed soldiers who had been captured and yet ignored an opportunity of escaping and returning to the ranks.[10] Moreover, scouts who betrayed secrets to the enemy were held to be traitors ('proditores') and were executed.[11] In general, the loss of weapons was considered to be a serious offence during a campaign and could involve the death penalty, though a more humane interpretation laid down that the soldier could be demoted to another arm of the service.[12] And in peacetime a scale of penalties was employed. If the soldier lost or sold his armour for the legs and shoulders, he was beaten, but the loss of cuirass, shield, helmet, and sword was tantamount to desertion. Nevertheless, exceptions could be made for a new recruit, and in cases where the custodian of the weapons had distributed them at the wrong time.[13]

Obviously in time of war the efficiency and morale of the army demanded that discipline be sternly enforced. Several emperors, princes, and senatorial commanders exercised the rigorous control of the troops provided for in these tough regulations. Suetonius says that Augustus exercised discipline very strictly. He dismissed the tenth legion in disgrace for insubordination and decimated any units that gave way in battle; individual soldiers or centurions who left their posts were executed, and the emperor devised various ignominious penalties of his own for minor offences.[14] Suetonius is apt to generalize from single instances, but it does seem that Augustus made an effort to set an example of tough discipline on campaign. Germanicus too apparently issued an edict tightening up the rules on desertion.[15] During his exploits in Germany, Gaius is said to have exercised a strict if

[9] 16.7.
[10] 16.5.5 (Menander).
[11] 16.6.4.
[12] 16.3.13 (Modestinus); 14.1 (Paul).
[13] Ibid.
[14] *Aug.* 24.1-2. For a general survey of military discipline in relation to increasing financial inducements, see above, pp. 190ff.
[15] *D* 49.16.4.13.

erratic control;[16] it was alleged that he thought of executing the legionaries who had mutinied against his father Germanicus in AD 14.[17] Galba had the reputation of being a strict disciplinarian, though in the end it did him no good.[18] In fact discipline could more easily be enforced on active service. In the difficult siege of Jerusalem Titus displayed great severity to maintain the army's morale and discipline. He ordered the execution of a cavalryman who had lost his horse in a Jewish raid.[19] He dismissed with dishonour a soldier who had been captured and then escaped in full view of his comrades, for in Titus' opinion a Roman soldier should not be taken alive.[20] Few emperors were as strict as Titus, but in their own way both Trajan and Hadrian became renowned for their control over the army. The statement of Marcus' Praetorian prefect Paternus, who held a command in the Marcomannic wars, that 'traitors and those who deserted to the enemy are considered as enemies not as Roman soldiers',[21] certainly reflects the severe enforcement of the rules on desertion. The brutal struggle saw large numbers of desertions from the legions, as is clear from the terms of the peace treaty which included a provision for the return of deserters.[22]

Among consular legates, Corbulo and Ulpius Marcellus were famous for their strict discipline. Indeed Corbulo virtually made his reputation in this way. He trained the lazy and inefficient Syrian army with exemplary severity. Although Tacitus may have exaggerated his toughness, it is clear that Corbulo did not allow first offenders to escape. Deserters were executed; an officer who disobeyed his commander's order not to engage the enemy was made to camp with his troops outside the wall of the camp.[23] Ulpius Marcellus is the subject of a detailed description in Dio: 'He always conducted himself like a soldier in respect of what he ate and in everything else.' He forced his subordinate officers to stay awake by sending them instruction at all hours.[24]

[16] Suet., *Cal.* 43 ff.
[17] *Cal.* 48.
[18] Tac., *H* 1.5.
[19] Josephus, *BJ* 6.155.
[20] 6.362.
[21] *D* 49.16.7.
[22] Dio, 73.2.2.
[23] Tac., *A* 11.17; 35–6.
[24] Dio, 73.8.2 ff.

Similarly, the redoubtable Pontius Laelianus earned a reputation for his tough treatment of the Syrian legions.[25] Although his methods were less dramatic, Agricola during his governorship of Britain, by personal example and courage, resolutely trained and guided his forces through tough campaigns.[26]

But the application of strict rules of discipline in the style described above may have been unusual, and for that reason attracted the particular attention of contemporaries. When writing about Corbulo's strictness, Tacitus implies that most commanders did not punish first offenders, even for desertion.[27] Tacitus had evidence to suggest that the Syrian legionaries were in an appalling condition before the arrival of Corbulo. They had become sluggish because of the long period of inactivity on the eastern frontier. 'It is established fact that some veterans of that army had never been on guard duty or on watch, found a rampart and ditch a strange novelty, and had neither helmets nor armour; they were sleek businessmen who had conducted their military service in towns.'[28] These troops were a poor reflection on the work of the previous legate, Ummidius Quadratus. Yet only a few years previously, Gaius Cassius had kept strict discipline as governor of Syria.[29] This is an indication of the uneven enforcement of discipline, apparently according to the character of individual governors, although the Syrian legions seem to have been particularly prone to disorderly conduct. In the *Principia Historiae* Fronto describes how Lucius Verus reduced to obedience troops who rarely stayed with their units or at the posts to which they had been assigned. They wandered outside the camp, frequently drunk and rarely carrying their weapons.[30] This is doubtless exaggerated in order to magnify the achievements of Verus. Fronto is perhaps stating a well-known theme, but it was a theme that could be applied with justice to the Syrian legions under the administration of some governors. And the army in Syria

[25] Fronto (Haines, *Loeb*), II, p. 148).
[26] Tac., *Ag.* 19–22.
[27] *A* 13.35.
[28] Ibid.
[29] 12.12.
[30] Haines, II, p. 208; cf. p. 148.

may not have been unique. In Britain, Trebellius Maximus (63-9), and his successor Vettius Bolanus (69-71) were, in Tacitus' opinion, completely incapable of maintaining discipline in the legions. Trebellius actually had to go into hiding; 'disgraced and humiliated, he commanded on sufferance'.[31]

The evidence shows that despite the efforts of individual emperors and provincial governors, in time of general peace periods of relatively severe discipline alternated with periods of great slackness, and the enforcement of military regulations was varied and inconsistent. When soldiers were not on active service there was a wide scope in the provisions of military law for a generous interpretation and reduction of the penalty that strictly should have applied.

Even in time of peace desertion was still a serious offence and much occupied the writers on military law. But once the harsh realities of war were removed, a more lenient view was often taken. There was a careful distinction between 'emansor' and 'desertor': 'An *emansor* is a man who, having been absent for a long time, returns to camp voluntarily. A deserter is a man who has been absent for an extended time and is brought back.'[32] The *emansor* presumably exceeded his furlough or was absent without leave for so long that it could not be considered an accident. He was distinguished from the deserter by his voluntary return and the length of his absence. But there is no evidence for the number of years that constituted the criteria for the distinction.[33] The vagueness of the definition may have allowed a liberal interpretation of the law. Indeed, many extenuating circumstances were accepted. The *emansor* was to be pardoned if he were prevented from returning from leave by illness, travel difficulties, or was detained by robbers.[34] Special concessions were made to the inexperience of the new recruit 'who still does not understand the rules of discipline'.[35] When punishment was being assigned, attention should be paid to the rank, pay, and previous record of the

[31] *Ag.* 16.3-4.
[32] *D* 49.16.3.3; 3.7; 14. pref.
[33] Cf. 16.4.14 (Menander).
[34] 16.3.7 (Modestinus); 16.14.1 (Paul).
[35] 16.4.15 (Menander).

culprit.[36] All this seems very reasonable. However some concessions made to the *emansor* seem rather generous.

And so the reasons for a man's absence are always considered, why, and where he was, and what he was doing; forbearance should be displayed if he was sick or if he was held by affection for his parents or relations, or if he pursued a fugitive slave, or if there was any other reason of this nature for his absence.[37]

It is remarkable that such concern was shown for the filial affection of a soldier, and that, if the slave mentioned is his own, he was allowed to leave his military duties to deal with his own property. These considerations applied to the *emansor*, whose punishment must have been at the discretion of the commander depending on the length of his absence and other relevant circumstances. A soldier who left his post was described as 'worse than an *emansor*' and received a beating or lost his rank.[38]

In the case of deserters, their rank, pay, the post they deserted, and their previous record should be taken into account; it was also relevant if the soldier had deserted alone or with a group, if he had committed any other crime during his desertion, and of course the length of his absence. A deserter who eventually surrendered himself, without being compelled to do so, was more leniently treated.[39] A cavalry-man who deserted in time of peace was reduced in rank, an infantryman was transferred to another unit.[40] Deserters found in Rome were executed, those found elsewhere could be reinstated after a first offence, although execution was the punishment if they deserted again.[41] This can be explained on the hypothesis that the man who fled to Rome was likely to be a more determined deserter than a man found wandering in the provinces. A soldier who committed another offence during a period of desertion was more heavily punished. For example, a theft was considered tanta-mount to a second act of desertion.[42]

[36] 16.5. pref.
[37] 16.4.15.
[38] 16.3.5 (Modestinus).
[39] 16.5 (Menander). Although voluntary return remained one of the distinctions between an 'emansor' and a true deserter.
[40] 16.5.1.   [41] 16.5.3.   [42] 16.5.2.

At least in peacetime the deserter could escape with fairly light punishment; and at all times he could be pardoned by the emperor, whatever the circumstances. It appears to have been normal practice in the Severan period for a soldier who had deserted, presumably in time of war, and had given himself up within five years, to be deported to an island. Septimius Severus and Caracalla decided this in a rescript, and Menander believed that the ruling should be used as a precedent.[43] The decision could be described as an act of imperial 'indulgentia',[44] and this generosity was sometimes extensive.[45] Indeed, Papinian found it necessary to confirm that a soldier guilty of desertion, who had been reinstated, did not receive pay for the time of his absence from military service.[46] However, there could be exceptions: 'When after a period of desertion a soldier has been reinstated in the army, he should not receive his pay and donatives for the intervening time, unless the generosity of the emperor has granted this as a special favour.'[47] This kind of 'special favour' from emperors can hardly have been extended very often. But the fact that Paul thought it worth mentioning specifically indicates that it cannot have been entirely unusual.

Nevertheless, there is no certain evidence for a weakening of discipline in the Severan era after the civil wars of 193-7, since we do not know what special circumstances were relevant to the cases discussed above. Moreover, it seems that the same liberal interpretation of existing military regulations sometimes occurred in the second century. Antoninus Pius ordered that a deserter who had been surrendered by his father should be demoted to an inferior unit 'in case it should seem that the father had given his son up to execution'.[48] This may have been designed to encourage parents to surrender their children who had fled home. But it also shows

---

[43] 16.13.6; cf. 5.4 (Menander).

[44] Ibid.: 'Qui in desertione fuit, si se optulerit, ex indulgentia imperatoris nostri in insulam deportatus est.'

[45] CJ 12.35.5, Gordian pardoned and reinstated a man who had been a deserter for seven years.

[46] D 49.16.10; cf. n. 45. Gordian specifically discounted the possibility of pay for the seven years the man had spent as a deserter.

[47] Ibid.

[48] 16.13.6.

a willingness to find yet another extenuating circumstance in the treatment of deserters.

Another concession made by Hadrian allowed even deserters to the enemy (*transfugae*) to escape punishment if they captured bandits and informed on other *transfugae*. But this concession was not made if the deserter merely promised to do these things.[49] Presumably that would look too much like a deal. Hadrian also ruled that soldiers who could prove that they had escaped from captivity and were not *transfugae* could be reinstated. If the soldier had a good record then his story should be believed, but if he had been neglectful of his duties and wandered out of camp, no credence should be placed in it.[50]

Other military regulations governing the relationships between soldiers their comrades, and their officers can be reviewed briefly. There was a simple general principle. 'A military offence is committed whenever a soldier acts contrary to the demands of the general discipline of the army, as for example laziness, insolence, and cowardice are crimes.'[51] The range of punishments included beating, fines, imposition of fatigues, demotion to another part of the army, loss of rank, and, most seriously, dishonourable discharge.[52] Soldiers could not normally be sent to the mines or tortured.[53] Some offences, like disobedience and insubordination, were regarded as especially serious. A soldier who was a 'disturber of the peace' was executed. Presumably this refers to a soldier who encouraged other soldiers to disobey commands. Modestinus remarks that death was the penalty for a soldier who instigated a serious disturbance among the troops; but if the uproar he caused stopped short at 'abuse' and 'minor complaints' then he was merely demoted.[54] A soldier who struck the commander or showed insolent insubordination to him was to be executed.[55] Acts of disobedience to a centurion were punished according to the gravity of the insult: if a soldier grabbed the centurion's baton (*vitis*) he was demoted to another arm of the service; if

---

[49] 16.5.8.
[50] 16.5.6.
[51] 16.16.6. pref.
[52] 16.3.1. (Modestinus).
[53] Ibid.
[54] 16.16.1 (Paul); 3.20 (Modestinus).
[55] 16.16.1.

he broke the stick or struck the centurion he was to be executed.[56] In theory at least, major acts of disobedience by large bodies of troops were punished by dishonourable discharge.[57] These penalties demonstrate the strict framework of Roman military law, necessary to preserve the authority of the officers. However, much depended on the strictness of the individual commander, and it is perhaps unlikely that the maximum penalty was exacted except for the most hardened offenders. We may note that even if a large body of troops deserted together and returned 'inside a specified time', they did not suffer capital punishment and were not even dishonourably discharged; the soldiers were to be reduced in rank and distributed to different units.[58]

Good order and discipline partly depended on a stable relationship between soldiers serving in the same camp. A strict view was therefore taken of assault against a comrade, or theft. A soldier who wounded a fellow-soldier with a stone was to be discharged from the army; it was a capital offence if he used a sword.[59] Dishonourable discharge was the penalty for soldiers caught stealing in the baths,[60] and for those who committed adultery.[61] The rules governing the treatment of attempted suicides in the army again illustrate the existence of detailed military regulations that nevertheless had wide scope for interpretation.[62]

Apart from the death penalty, dishonourable discharge was the most serious punishment a soldier could face, since it excluded him from all the privileges enjoyed by veterans. The *honesta missio* (honourable discharge) was the reward for good discipline and a satisfactory record. The position of those soldiers who failed to complete their period of service because of illness or disability, and who were discharged on medical grounds (*causaria missio*), is a good test of the attitude of the military authorities — and ultimately of the

[56] 16.13.4 (Macer).
[57] 16.3.21 (Modestinus).
[58] 16.3.9. The purpose was presumably to keep them from concerting similar action again.
[59] 16.6.6 (Menander).
[60] 47.17.3 (Paul).
[61] Pliny, *Ep.* 6.31.5; cf. 48.5.12 (Papinian).
[62] 49.16.6.7 (Menander). See above, p. 277.

emperor — towards soldiers who were of no further use to
them.

It has been argued that discharge on medical grounds was
only a temporary classification and that *causarii* could be
upgraded 'after consideration' to the status of honourably
discharged soldiers. Whether or not a soldier who had been
invalided out was upgraded in this way depended on the
nature of his ailment; for example, honourable wounds could
be distinguished from psychological or physical infirmity.
Any *causarii* who were not upgraded to the new classification
were regarded as dishonourably discharged soldiers.[63]

However this theory does not fit in with the impression
given by the jurists and the imperial rescripts. Macer sum-
marizes the status of those discharged from the army:

> The benefit of this ruling [about land acquired in service] certainly
> does not apply to those who have been dishonourably discharged, since
> it is held to be a privilege granted to veterans as a reward; and so it
> can be said that it does apply to the man who has been dismissed on
> medical grounds, since the reward is given to this man also. In general
> there are three kinds of discharge: honourable, medical, and dishonour-
> able. An honourable discharge is granted when the full period of
> military discharge has been completed; a medical discharge when some-
> one is pronounced to be unsuitable for military service through mental
> or physical infirmity; a dishonourable discharge when someone is
> dismissed from the service because of an offence.[64]

The only soldiers classed as dishonourably discharged were
those who had committed a specific offence, and it would be
ridiculous to classify soldiers who were physically ill with
such men. Macer clearly distinguishes between *ignominiosi*,
who received no privileges, and *causarii*, who did. This
appears even more clearly in Macer's description of the
validity of the military will: 'The wills of those who have
been dishonourably discharged immediately cease to be valid
according to military regulations, although a year's validity

---

[63] G.R. Watson, *The Roman Soldier*, 123 ff.; Nesselhauf, *CIL* XVI, no. 10,
n. 2.
[64] *D* 49.16.13.3.

is given to the wills of those who obtain an honourable or medical discharge'.[65]

The evidence suggests that all *causarii* received exactly the same privileges as those with *honesta missio* and were not looked on with any disfavour. In a rescript of 213 Caracalla states that *causarii* of twenty years' service' keep a clear record and are eligible for the general privileges granted to veterans'.[66] The emperor Philip confirmed that a *causarius* 'has no stain on his record'.[67] Diocletian, in reply to a query from a veteran, stated that veteran soldiers received the benefit of exemption from local offices and impositions if they had served for twenty years and it was shown that they had received an honourable or medical discharge.[68]

In principle then, *causarii* were eligible for the privileges of a veteran according to a time scale. Herennius Modestinus in his *De Excusationibus* provides the key to this. In his discussion of the exemption of veterans from *tutela*, he defines the categories who had this privilege: there are those honourably discharged, 'or those who because of illness receive a medical discharge (for this is also honourable)'.[69] Officially the *causarius* was formally distinct from the man with an honourable discharge, but from the point of view of his reputation and privileges the *causarius* was considered to have what approximated to the *honesta missio*. In this sense *honesta* is used non-technically as an expansion of the definition *causarius*. This principle was applied to all those discharged on medical grounds on the basis of the following time scale: a soldier who had served for twenty years received full exemption; five years service brought one year's exemption, eight years brought two years exemption, and so on. Although Modestinus is referring to exemption from *tutela*, the rescripts show that this kind of scale was applied to all veterans' privileges.[70]

This helps to explain a couple of inscriptions, one of which describes a soldier as 'ex causa missus honesta missione'.[71] And in a discharge *diploma* a marine from the *II Adiutrix*

[65] 29.1.26.
[66] *CJ* 5.65.1.
[67] 12.35.8.
[68] 10.55.3; cf. 7.64.9.

[69] *D* 27.1.8.2–5.
[70] nn. 66–8.
[71] *CIL* VI. 3373.

receives 'honesta missio' although he is a *causarius*.[72] It is
easy to see why *causarii* might unofficially usurp the words
'honesta missio'. To all intents and purposes their discharge
was honourable, but officials in the provinces might be suspicious of the title *causarius*, which perhaps they did not
meet very often. The *diploma* of the marine is the only
known official document to speak of 'causarii . . . honesta
missione'.[73] It may be an example of the non-technical use
described above. Was it devised to emphasize the loyal service
of the men who had helped Vespasian in 69?

The treatment of *causarii* seems to have been scrupulously
fair; the authorities, without conceding too much, protected
the rights of ill or crippled ex-soldiers. Men discharged for
reasons of poor health before they had completed their
service were expendable, and since they were no longer in
the limelight, there was not much danger of an outcry among
serving soldiers if they had not been well treated. But the
generally helpful attitude of emperors and their officials
confirmed imperial benevolence towards the army, and had
a chance of consolidating good will among veterans. Recruitment could also benefit if it were clear that the interests of
soldiers who were disabled by or during military service were
properly looked after.

---

[72] *CIL* XVI, no. 10.
[73] The phrase 'exauctorati et dimissi honesta missione' is unparalleled in these
documents. It is tautological and the words 'dimissi honesta missione' look as if
they have been added as an afterthought.

PART THREE
THE ORGANIZATION OF MILITARY COMMANDS

VIII

SENATORS AND *EQUITES* IN COMMAND OF TROOPS; THE SCOPE FOR MILITARY GLORY

1. INTRODUCTION

It is absolutely essential for you to have many people helping you since you rule over such a huge area; and they all should be men of courage and resolution. But if you entrust armies and posts to men of this nature, you will run the risk that both you and your rule will be destroyed. For a man is not worth anything if he has no spirit . . . and the one who has shown a self-confident spirit will inevitably love freedom and hate all tyranny. If you do not entrust affairs to men like this, but only to humble men of low birth, you will incur the anger of the first group since they will feel that they are not trusted, and secondly you will suffer disaster in your most important enterprises. For what success could an inexperienced man of humble birth attain? Could any of our enemies fail to despise him? Which of our allies would obey him? Even the soldiers themselves would surely all despise taking orders from such a man?[1]

In this invented speech in which Agrippa points out some of the dangers of monarchy to Augustus, Dio sums up the dilemma encountered by emperors in the use of their army. The emperor, by his sole control of the army and his usurpation of the senate's old prerogative of appointing ex-magistrates to a province, was an intruder in the usual pattern of upper-class activity. The commanders had to maintain discipline among the troops, keep order in their province, and defend it against outside attack. They had, therefore, to be men of education and status, for they must give commands

[1] 52.8.4 ff.

and inspire respect. In the context of Roman society this meant that the military commanders would be either senators or *equites*. In fact most were senators. This is not surprising since senior senators traditionally commanded the armies of Rome, and originally Augustus desired to satisfy them and whatever military ambitions they had. Indeed the senatorial class, with its long experience of government and military life, was initially the only body capable of providing enough suitable men to govern the major provinces. Other emperors no doubt accepted without question the situation as they found it. The ideal was to find commanders who combined loyalty and ability. No emperor could afford military disasters in terms either of the loss in troops and cost to the provinces, or the damage to his own reputation and prestige. When Varus and his three legions were destroyed in Germany in AD 9, the jolt to Augustus' careful organization of the army and his record for invincibility was considerable. The emperor had good reason to tear his clothes and call upon Varus to return his legions.[2]

Dio of Prusa, in a discourse probably addressed to Trajan, also comments on the problems faced by an autocrat in controlling his armies:

I think that the most important of those essential things, weaponry, walls, armies, cities, are neither useful nor beneficial without friends to control them; indeed they are extremely dangerous.[3]

But how was a king to find such friends?

Kings cannot seek protection against the betrayal of their trust from the law, but from the affection in which they are held. It is natural that those who take their position near the king and assist him in governing the country are the strongest men. The only protection that the king has against these men is their affection for him. Therefore it is certainly not a secure policy for the king to bestow power on anyone at all; his own strength is in proportion to the strength he gives his friends.[4]

---

[2] Dio, 56.23.1; Suet., *Aug.* 23.2.
[3] 3.94.
[4] 3.88-9.

To choose the right man for a military command, an emperor would have to weigh up carefully his character and ambitions. There may be a hint of this painful process in the *Meditations* of Marcus Aurelius.[5] Marcus imagines a match in a gymnasium where one contestant uses his nails or his head unfairly:

We do not make a protest or become offended, and we do not suspect that he will be treacherous in future. Nevertheless we keep a watchful eye on him, not treating him as an enemy or with suspicion, but good-naturedly avoiding him . . . For, as I pointed out before, it is always possible to avoid someone without suspecting or hating him.[6]

He goes on to praise Antoninus Pius' shrewd judgement of men and their actions, and his reluctance to listen to tales.[7] In this context we can understand the anxious hesitation of Tiberius before making appointments to provincial commands, even if Tacitus has exaggerated the actual threat to him from outstanding men: 'He did not give his support to men of outstanding talent, but at the same time he detested incompetence. For he was afraid that the most able men would be a threat to himself, while fools would cause a public disgrace.'[8]

An emperor's chances of achieving an amicable relationship with the upper classes would certainly be affected by his success in dealing with those who aspired to military commands, and his willingness to reward obvious merit. At the same time, if such a relationship could be achieved, it would allow an emperor to be more confident in choosing the best man as his governor.

2. THE ATTITUDE OF THE UPPER CLASSES TO MILITARY COMMANDS

In the Republic the provinces with standing armies and special commands were much sought after, for the prestige and glory to be gained, and increasingly because command of

---

[5] P.A. Brunt, 'Marcus Aurelius in his *Meditations*', *JRS* 64 (1974), 1, suggests that this work was intended for the emperor's eyes only, and so expresses the inmost thoughts of the ruler.

[6] 6.20.   [7] 6.30.3.

[8] *A* 1.80: 'neque enim eminentis virtutes sectabatur, et rursum vitia oderat: ex optimis periculum sibi, a pessimis dedecus publicum metuebat.'

an army seemed to be one route to political success. But quite apart from this, military talent was respected in the Republic for its own sake.[1] Although the civil wars must have reduced men's appetite for conflict and battles, in the principate many senators remembered the military traditions of their ancestors and the obligation upon their class to serve the state in war if required.

Tibullus celebrated the exploits of Marcus Valerius Messalla Corvinus, the consul of 31 BC, patron of letters, and eminent soldier, who won a triumph in 25 BC. By waging war by land and sea and emulating the glory of his forebears in war, we read, he has achieved true *virtus*.[2] The inscription set up by L. Apronius, proconsul of Africa (AD 18-21), and his son, who was serving with him, expresses a bloodthirsty delight in the valorous deeds of the young man, an honour to his father and family tradition: 'What great courage is revealed! The sword is red from killing the enemy and worn away with the slaughter; the spear by which the fierce barbarians were pierced and fell completes the trophy.'[3]

These feelings were perhaps strongest among the heirs of the Republican *nobiles*. Men of famous name, respected and honoured by the new regime, could have avoided military service if they had wished. Instead some chose the arduous and possibly dangerous path to a type of military distinction that was much more circumscribed than it had been in the old days. In the forty-two recorded awards of triumphal honours to senators for military achievement from Augustus to Hadrian, twelve were made to men of old noble families, mostly within the first fifty years of the period.[4]

---

[1] This theme needs no elaboration here; see *Römische Wertbegriffe*, ed. Oppermann, 284 ff.; D.C. Earl, *The Political Thought of Sallust* (1961), 8 ff.; 21 ff.; Cic., *Ad Fam.* 15.2.8; 15.5; 15.6; *Ad Att.* 5.20.1; *De Off.* 1.116; 121; *Pro Murena*, 19-34. See in general D. Stockton, *Cicero, A Political Biography* (1971), 121 ff. Cf. K. Hopkins, *Conquerors and Slaves*, 25-8.

[2] 1.1.53-4; 1.7.1 ff.; 2.1.31 ff.; 2.5.115 ff.; 3.7 (*Panegyricus Messallae*), 83 ff.; 118 ff.; 149 ff.   [3] *ILS* 939.

[4] Evidence in A.E. Gordon, *Quintus Veranius, consul AD 49* (1952), 312 ff. L. Domitius Ahenobarbus, L. Calpurnius Piso, Cn. Cornelius Lentulus, M. Valerius Messalla Messallinus, M. Plautius Silvanus, Cossus Cornelius Lentulus, M. Aemilius

footnote 4 continued at foot of next page

In only a few cases do we hear about the emotions and frustrations of the upper classes in military commands. In the early first century, Africa was the only place where a senatorial proconsul still commanded an army.[5] The war against Tacfarinas provided scope for active service. In 17–18 a proconsul of famous name, M. Furius Camillus, achieved some success. The great family had suffered humiliation while for years the 'general's laurels' lay with others. Camillus wanted a decisive battle, for his peers were interested in the outcome of his command, and gossip had it that he was no soldier.[6] In granting the triumphal honours, Tiberius professed himself delighted that military glory had returned to this famous family. He knew that this would be well received by senators, and it fitted in with his desire to see distinguished men playing an active role in the state.[7] Others, however, did not have the chance of satisfying family honour. C. Cassius, legate of Syria under Claudius, was an eminent jurist. But since his family was famous, and especially in the East, he felt it 'worthy of his ancestors' to establish strict discipline, train the legions, and act as if war was on the way.[8] It is interesting that a man of no military inclination felt inspired by family tradition to put up a credible show in the commander's role, and apparently hope for war.

As the numbers of the old noble families declined in the Senate, the strength of these great traditions may also have waned.[9] But newcomers to the ranks of the Senate probably assimilated many of its traditions, and contests for military honour and renown continued. The abrasive relations between Ummidius Quadratus, legate of Syria, and Corbulo in 55, and later between Corbulo and Caesennius Paetus, are

footnote continued

Lepidus, M. Furius Camillus, M. Licinius Crassus Frugi, Aulus Plautius, Servius Sulpicius Galba, Plautius Silvanus Aelianus. The *triumphalia* of Junius Silanus Torquatus and Cocceius Nerva were purely honorific.

[5] See below, pp. 349–52.

[6] Tac., *A* 2.52.

[7] *Ibid.*: eo pronior Tiberius res gestas apud senatum celebravit.'

[8] *A* 12.12.

[9] It seems that the sons of consuls were often passed over for consular appointments and an ever widening area of recruitment established; cf. R. Syme, *Hist.* 14 (1965), 361.

well known.[10] These disputes were partly caused by rivalry
for military honour, and eventually Nero himself had to
intervene.[11] It was also rumoured that Suetonius Paulinus
was the rival of Corbulo in military affairs; in his British
command he was determined to surpass the latter's success
in Armenia.[12]

Moreover, senators from the provinces may have had
their own military traditions. Julius Quadratus Bassus, the
Pergamene aristocrat, had an outstanding military career
under Trajan; from his consulship (105) until his death in
office in Dacia (117), he was continuously employed in
various military commands. On instructions from Hadrian,
his body was conveyed to Asia by his soldiers and borne
round the city of Pergamum in solemn procession. Finally
a monument was set up, a benefaction of the emperor at
his own expense.[13] Hadrian had, in this case, gone out of his
way to show that senators could win honour for their
military exploits in the service of the empire. Even in the
third century martial *virtus* still had its attractions.
Decrianus, legate of Numidia, celebrated victory over a
marauding tribe, 'the capture of their notorious leader, and
their rout and slaughter'.[14] The sentiments expressed are not
markedly different from those of L. Apronius' son in the
early first century.

The continuing respect for military attainments in Roman
society during the principate may also be seen in Tacitus'
biography of his father-in-law Agricola, which is predominantly an account of his governorship of Britain. As
Tacitus naturally wished to create a favourable picture of
Agricola, he must have expected his audience to approve of
the virtues he recounts. Agricola sought glory 'more energetically than warily'; but that was a noble fault.[15] It was
indeed military glory Agricola wanted,[16] and from the start
he was 'anxious and eager for action', hard working and

[10] Tac., *A* 13.8-9; 15.6.
[11] 13.9.
[12] *A* 14.29; cf. *A* 13.53.
[13] *PIR*² I 508; cf. *AE* 1933.268. For the *beneficium*, see F. Millar, *JRS* 53
(1963), 39.
[14] *ILS* 1194: 'capto famosissimo duce eorum caesis fugatisque'.
[15] *Ag.* 4.3.   [16] 5.3.

vigorous.[17] As a general in the field he displayed judgement
and courage and did not shrink from toil and danger.[18]
Brave and decisive under pressure, he led the troops
personally and chose camp sites himself.[19] Although Agricola
was competent and reliable in his other civil duties, it was
the performance of his military duties that brought him to
the peak of success. 'On a man who had held the consulship
and had received triumphal ornaments, what else could
Fortune bestow?'[20]

The honour accorded to Domitius Corbulo in senatorial
sources is significant. He rapidly became a hero, being the
only senatorial commander of the imperial period to be
mentioned in Frontinus' *Strategemata*,[21] and receiving
effusive praise from historians and others.[22] Muscular of
body, eloquent of speech, and a tough disciplinarian, he
looked the part.[23] Yet Tacitus frankly admits that Corbulo
had certain faults of character; and that his successful
conduct of several commands depended more on diligence
and careful preparations than on startling achievements
in battle.[24] It is curious that Corbulo receives so much praise,
perhaps indeed more than his victories merited.[25] This presumably indicates senatorial enthusiasm at the great military
honour of one of their number and his important command
in a war against Parthia, traditionally one of Rome's greatest
enemies.[26]

Naturally, the concept of military success was not equally
valued by all, and other skills and achievements were held in

[17] 5.1; 6.5; 7.3: 'anxius et intentus agere', 'diligens', 'strenuus'.
[18] 18.4–5: 'ratio', 'constantia', 'labor', 'periculum'.
[19] 20.2; 22.1; 35.
[20] 44.3.
[21] 2.9.5; 4.1.21, 28; 4.2.3; 6.7.2.
[22] Tac., *A* 11.18 f.; 13.8, 35,38,40; 14.24; 15.12; Dio, 62.19.1 ff.; Ammianus,
29.5.4; Statius, *Silvae* 5.2.34–47; Pliny, *NH* 2.180; 5.83; 6.23, 40; Themistius, *Or.*
16.210.
[23] *A* 13.8.
[24] To the discerning reader Corbulo's autobiography showed some failings of
character: 13.9, 34; 15.6. And note the criticisms Tacitus ascribes to 'alii' – 15.6.
[25] R. Syme, *Tacitus*, 493 ff.
[26] Note too the detailed accounts of the war of Poppaeus Sabinus against the
Thracians (*A* 4.46–51), and the campaigns against Tacfarinas conducted by
various proconsuls of Africa – R. Syme, *Studies in Roman Economic and Social
History in Honour of A.C. Johnson* (1951), 113 = *Roman Papers* 218 ff.

high regard — intellectual ability, eloquence, pleading cases
as an *advocatus*, and of course generally good conduct.[27] It
would not do merely to be a dumb soldier. Fronto, while
praising Lucius Verus for his eloquence and military achievements, comments sarcastically on the limitations of some of
the emperor's predecessors, 'who were no more able to
describe their feats of military genius than helmets could'.[28]
Even winners of triumphal ornaments might encounter the
jibe that this distinction was handed out for all kinds of
minor military operations.[29] There were also senators who
had limited ambition for high office and who were satisfied
with local affairs and life on their estates.[30]

Nevertheless, although Tacitus and those like him would
have disputed the primacy of the military arts in the service
of the State, it is clear that there was an underlying respect
in Roman society for proficiency in the skills of military
command, even among those who held provincial governorships merely out of a sense of duty or for their general
advancement, and among those who did not themselves
wish to hold army commands. Some senators indeed were
eager for military responsibility and action, either because
of family tradition and pride, or personal inclination, or
both. Yet not all of these men could be presumed to be
competent; they may not have thought to ask themselves
if they were fit for military duties. And it may have been
impolitic for an emperor to refuse to grant a command to
such men. Then again, there were senators who may have
been able enough, but who preferred the gilded life style of
the capital with easy honours and prestige. For the emperor
there was no easy analysis of the hopes and aspirations of

---

[27] Cicero, *De Off.* 2.44–8.

[28] Haines (*Loeb*), II, p. 136.

[29] *A* 13.53; cf. Pliny, *Ep.* 2.7. Note that in discussing the *triumphalia* of
Pomponius Secundus, Tacitus affirms the superiority of his literary fame (*A*
12.28). Syme says of Pliny's letters, 'he is eager to assert the primacy of literary
fame over military honours' (*Latomus* 23 (1964), 750 = *Danubian Papers* (1971),
245).

[30] Cf. Pliny, *Ep.* 10.12.2; note also Cornutus Tertullus, 'ab omni ambitione
longe remotus' (5.14.2). Pliny believed that a conscientious and diligent man
could hope for a period of retirement and leisure — 1.9; 8.9.1; 9.36. As the letters
were intended to appeal to conventional sentiment, Pliny must have believed that
his readers would find these views acceptable.

the upper classes. Tiberius, despite the difficulty of finding suitable men, tried to cope with these variable factors: 'He distributed offices by considering carefully each man's birth, the distinction of his military record, and his qualities in civil life; and it is generally agreed that no better men could have been chosen.'[31] Tacitus accepted that this was true for only a relatively short part of Tiberius' reign, to AD 23. How often could an emperor achieve these ideals?

3. PROFESSIONAL OFFICERS? FACTORS IN THE APPOINTMENT OF ARMY COMMANDERS

The literary sources suggest that in Roman society, despite the admiration of military skills, all round merit was most appreciated and likely to earn recognition. The tradition of the Republic was that a Roman senator should be prepared to serve the State in whatever capacity it demanded, and be proficient.[1] The Romans probably believed that the man chosen by the competent authority would be capable and efficient. In the Republic that authority would be the *Comitia,* in the imperial period the emperor. The man sent to command an army would have to learn the skills himself, from text books or the harder lesson of personal experience. The qualities of a good general could be summed up as knowledge of military arts, courage, personal status, and good luck.[2] Cicero describes how Lucius Lucullus was not expected to achieve military glory in the war against Mithridates, after spending his early years in legal studies and a quaestorship in which he saw no military action. 'And so he spent the entire voyage partly in inquiring from experienced men, partly in reading the achievements of others, and arrived in Asia a commander, although he had been ignorant of military affairs when he left Rome.'[3]

---

[31] *A* 4.6: 'mandabatque honores, nobilitatem maiorum, claritudinem militiae, inlustris domi artes spectando, ut satis constaret non alios potiores fuisse.'

[1] Cic., *De Off.* 1.71; 116; 2.45–9; *Pro Sest.* 139; Tusc. 3.2.3; Sallust, *Bell. Iug.* 3.1.

[2] *De Imp. Cn. Pomp.* 28

[3] *Acad.* 2.2.

Cicero exaggerates, but the general idea of an amateur approach to military commands remains. Polybius had described the three methods by which men acquired the art of generalship — consultation of handbooks, advice from knowledgeable men, and immediate personal experience.[4] And, in a speech put into the mouth of Marius after his election to the consulship, Sallust makes a telling criticism of the ineptitude of some senators: 'I know some men, citizens, who after their election as consul began to read up history and Greek military handbooks. They got things the wrong way round. You can carry out the duties of an office only after you have been elected to it, but practical experience and action should come first.'[5]

It is interesting that handbooks on military tactics and the art of generalship continued to be written in the imperial period, notably by Onasander (first century AD), Frontinus (late first century), Aelian (in the reign of Trajan?), Arrian (governor of Cappadocia *c*.134), and Polyaenus (*c*.160). All these authors claim to be writing with a practical purpose, namely to elucidate military tactics and stratagems for the benefit of officers and commanders, and even the emperor himself. In Chapter 7 of his treatise Aelian points out his early table of contents, so that the emperor (probably Trajan) can pick out what interests him. In the prologue to the *Strategemata*, Frontinus explains his objectives:

For in this way army commanders will be equipped with examples of good planning and foresight, and this will develop their own ability to think out and carry into effect similar operations. An added benefit will be that the commander will not be worried about the outcome of his own stratagem when he compares it with innovations already tested in practice.[6]

In the light of the other evidence, it seems arbitrary to consider these sentiments merely as a literary *topos*, a conventional statement of the usefulness of the author's subject, rather than a genuine assertion of the expected relevance of military handbooks. Consular legates perhaps did prepare for their posts by reading up what Hannibal did at Cannae.

[4] XI.8.1-2.   [5] *Bell. Iug.* 85.12 ff.   [6] 1.1.

This idea is particularly true in the case of Arrian's work. He was governor of Cappadocia at a difficult time and led the Roman resistance to the invasion of the Alani. It has been convincingly argued that his *Tactica* attempted to adapt Greek phalanx tactics to enable the Roman infantry to deal with the massed, armoured cavalry attacks of the Sarmatians; the work was also intended to raise the skill of the Roman cavalry, and was a genuine response, perhaps encouraged by Hadrian, to the unusual tactics of the enemy.[7]

By using handbooks and by taking advice, a man of average ability could direct an army. So far as we can recover what Romans of the imperial period thought about these matters, it seems that they aimed to serve the State in whatever capacity it required, both civil and military, and that there was no concept of civil or military 'careers', involving a duty to stay in one sphere of activity and acquire specialist skills. Pliny praises his friend Vestricius Spurinna in these general terms: 'As long as it was his duty, he held public offices, accepted magistracies, and governed provinces; he has earned his present peaceful retirement by a great deal of hard work.'[8] Flavius Sabinus, brother of the future emperor Vespasian, received a worthy accolade from Tacitus for the conduct of his duty:

He had served the state for thirty-five years, and had won fame in his civil and military duties; no one could dispute his integrity and justice; he talked too much and that was the one criticism alleged about him in the seven years he spent as governor of Moesia, and the twelve years in the post of prefect of the city.[9]

Moreover, although Tacitus sincerely appreciated his father-in-law Agricola's predilection for military glory, he emphasizes that he was well versed in all the qualities appropriate

---

[7] F. Kiechle 'Die Taktik des Flavius Arrianus', *45 Bericht der röm-ger. Kommission 1964* (1965), 85. A.B. Bosworth, *HSCPh* 81 (1977), 242-7, doubts this hypothesis. I find his arguments unconvincing: (i) Arrian's phalanx in the *Ectaxis* bears little resemblance to that described in the *Tactica*. But Arrian has adapted it for a special situation. (ii) The real value of the Greek Phalanx was the momentum of the charge; but the strength and cohesion of the phalanx were also important and that is what Arrian thought was necessary against massed cavalry. (iii) The detailed description in the *Tactica* of the Hellenistic phalanx is irrelevant; but a commander would have to understand how the Hellenistic phalanx worked before he could adapt it. See too P.A. Stadter, *Arrian of Nicomedia* (1980), 41-9.

[8] *Ep.* 3.1.12   [9] *H* 3.75.

to a Roman senator; his conduct in the civil duties that fell to him, and that in his governorships of Aquitania and Britain, formed a considerable part of his reputation.[10] No ancient source suggests that the specialist military man (*vir militaris*) was a feature of Roman society or government.[11]

Here, I may only reaffirm my belief, argued in detail elsewhere, that the evidence of the career inscriptions of senators does not support any idea that in the imperial period there evolved a bureaucratic system to train future military commanders, and that there was no group of specialist *viri militares* with a distinctive career and special patterns of rapid promotion to the consulship and thence to the great provinces. The careers of consul legates in general show no particularly significant military emphasis and it is very difficult to see any deliberate attempt to prepare them specifically for military duties.[12] Even under an emperor like Trajan, who may perhaps be expected to have favoured military talent and experience, there is little sign of specialized military men.[13] As far as the evidence extends, consular legates did not receive early consulates; in fact it was usually men from noble families who were granted the consulship at an early age, and they tended not to command armies.[14] In the posts that most consular legates held before their consulship, the military responsibilities will often have been limited; even in the case of legionary legates, the administrative and legal duties inherent in this post may have been

[10] *Ag.* 9.2 ff.; 19.

[11] Campbell, *JRS* 1975, 11–12.

[12] *Ibid.* 12–14; 17–24; 27.

[13] *Ibid.* 14–15. For an attempt to find career patterns during the reign of Domitian, see B.W. Jones, *Domitian and the Senatorial Order* (1979), 64 ff.; especially, 74 ff. I find his arguments unconvincing and marred by a too schematic treatment of career inscriptions. The shorter the period examined the easier it is to see patterns of promotions. For example, if there are five certain cases out of twenty-five praetorian proconsuls in Domitian's reign who went on to govern a consular province, it is surely misleading to state, 'one of the important praetorian posts under Domitian was that of praetorian proconsul' (p. 74). It is of course not surprising that *legati legionis* frequently went on to be consuls and consular governors; men given command of troops were obviously trusted. Jones thinks that Vespasian's practice here differed from that of Domitian in that only two-thirds of Vespasian's *legati legionis* went on to be consuls, while all of Domitian's did (p. 77). But his testimonia do not make clear if the careers of the relevant *legati legionis* are completely known.

[14] *JRS* 1975, 16–17.

considerable.[15] And there is no clearly discernible attempt to give future commanders experience in certain areas of the empire in order to create, for example, specialists in the government of Dacia or Pannonia.[16]

The idea that senators were prepared from early in their careers for certain posts by a deliberate pattern of earlier offices, seems a fundamentally anachronistic conception based on modern methods of government and army command. The inscriptions recording senatorial careers are also to blame. It is all too easy when we have a complete career to assume that all the earlier posts were a training for, and channel to, the consular governorships which came towards the end of a senator's career. A career inscription by itself can tell us only what posts a man held; it cannot explain why he held them, how well he performed, or exactly what he did in them, what his thoughts and ambitions were for his 'career', and what the emperor thought about all this. For example, the holding of an important praetorian post need not imply further advancement according to some presumed plan; was not the tenure of such a post merely an indication of imperial favour and trust which might naturally lead to further appointments, if the senator wanted? There is nothing to tell us what a senator thought on what he might

[15] *Ibid.* 20-21.

[16] *Ibid.* 23-4. A.R. Birley's survey of senatorial careers in *The Fasti of Roman Britain* (1981) appeared too late for me to take any systematic note of it here. I observe the correction (p. 21, n. 18) to my no. 72, and possibly no. 49, but am highly doubtful about Statius Priscus (no. 65). In any event my argument is misrepresented. Birley points to my 'artificially restricted category' of those who held a legionary command and a praetorian military province, as if this were the sole justification of my view that 'there are no clearly discernible patterns of promotion'. But at pp. 12-24 I deal with the other combinations of posts and hypotheses about rapid advancement suggested by the proponents of the theory about 'viri militares'. Naturally, it is another reason for doubting patterns of promotion if few men held exactly the same combination of posts, whatever they happened to be.

It also seems strange that at p. 21, n. 18, Birley refers to the small number of one-legion provinces for most of the period AD 69-235, but at p. 33 says: 'It made a particular difference when a number of one-legion provinces were available. This meant that, even if a senator had learned little enough as a military tribune, he could have five or six years, as legionary legate and governor of a province like Numidia, Arabia, Upper Dacia, or Lower Pannonia, during which he commanded troops.' But how many senators could have such a career, given the small number of such provinces? Of the five listed by Birley (p. 33, n. 5), two did not govern a one-legion praetorian province.

do after his praetorship. He might reasonably desire a consulship for the prestige it would bring to his house. What was to
happen next could be decided then, and each senator's
decision will surely have depended on what posts were available, who the emperor was and his continuing good favour,
the circumstances of the reign, what his friends were doing,
what advice he received, and, most importantly, his own
inclinations. He needed time for administering and building
up his own estates, for reading and perhaps writing, for
relaxing, for drinking, for loving. It must be remembered that
we are discussing a prestigious and pampered aristocracy who
turned away from their private pursuits from time to time to
serve the State, not bureaucrats inured to a tedious routine
of service and regular promotion.

Even when a man had gained a consular province, he
rarely enjoyed a tenure of more than six years, and even that
was usually not continuous or spent in the same province.
The most prestigious provinces were Spain and Syria, but
these were not the provinces with the greatest military responsibilities. 'What made a province important in the eyes of
its governor and the man who appointed him, was not necessarily its troops and military duties, but the whole complex
of its administrative demands and obligations, and the
prestige to be obtained there.'[17]

It follows from these general conclusions that there was
no military oligarchy or 'high command', and that it is misleading to speak of 'generals' or 'marshals'. The absence of
professional army officers was not disastrous. The consular
governor could consult the military handbooks and employ
whatever experience he had gained from active service in his
previous posts. For advice, he could look to the legionary
legates, some of whom might at least have been in the
province longer than the governor himself, the junior officers,
and the centurions. The centurions probably played an
important role here because of their experience and closeness
to the troops. Indeed, Julius Caesar had had centurions on
some of his councils of war. In minor campaigns this would
suffice, given that the Roman army was better equipped,

organized, and disciplined than most of its potential adversaries. Arrian's account of his expedition against the Alani gives an excellent picture of the conservative tactics, well-organized preparations, and meticulous planning of an amateur but shrewd senatorial commander who served the empire well.[18] In a major war the governor could expect help from the emperor himself (another amateur), and advice from whatever experienced commanders were available.

Finally, the careers and promotion of *equites*, on a recent investigation, do not admit of patterns or schemes of promotion, and tell against specialization in Roman imperial administration. Other factors must be considered in appointments, especially patronage and the favour of the emperor.[19]

It should be emphasized in respect of the careers of consular legates, that the Roman concept of serving the State was flexible enough for individuals to concentrate on particular activities if they wished.[20] In time of military crisis in one area of the empire, it is natural to suppose that men of experience and proven talent, if they could be found, would be sent to such provinces, or at least that their advice would be sought. In these circumstances a man who seemed particularly able could be advanced rapidly so that he could hold the top posts with the necessary status and prestige. In even the most rudimentary organization of military commands such a procedure is merely common sense. During the serious wars in the reign of Marcus Aurelius, several men who had held praetorian posts in the critical northern provinces were sent back to this area after their consulship and were moved around to deal with various danger points.[21] However these men also tended to hold one or more of the usual consular, civil posts before proceeding to the great commands.[22] What is more, of the *equites* who were adlected into the Senate in this period and gained military commands,

[18] See below, pp. 354-5.
[19] P.A. Brunt, 'The Administrators of Roman Egypt', *JRS* 65 (1975), 124; R.P. Saller, 'Promotion and Patronage in Equestrian Careers', *JRS* 70 (1980), 44; *Personal Patronage under the Early Empire* (1982).
[20] *JRS* 1975, 27.
[21] *Ibid.*, 22.
[22] Cf. especially, Claudius Fronto: *PIR*² C 874; *ILS* 1097-8.

most still held praetorian or consular civil posts.[23] It seems that the government reacted to a military crisis only after it had developed and that there was no planned preparation of commanders to deal with such an eventuality. Practical experience counted for much, but men who had this were still expected to serve the State in a variety of other capacities, and the promotion of talented men outside the senatorial class was not so rapid that it ignored the conventions of the *cursus honorum* and the considerations of status and prestige so important in Roman office holding. We see here not a well-organized bureaucracy and high command, but the Roman upper classes pulling together, making sacrifices, devoting themselves to serving the empire, and defending its integrity and honour.

The emperor had first to decide what senators were available and suitable for appointments in the provinces, and then whom he should pass over, and how the rest were to be apportioned to the various commands. Even if it is right that the emperor did not have his choice dictated by a system of related posts and patterns of promotions to a high command, it is plausible to suppose that he was guided by rational criteria of some kind. In normal times a conscientious emperor would surely aim to reward merit, good character, and energy in the upper classes, with suitably prestigious and responsible posts. This was necessary, both in order to achieve efficiency in the discharge of duties, and also to encourage others to offer their services to the State. It is clear that senators believed that an emperor should properly reward men of ability. Dio of Prusa, speaking before Trajan, noted that whereas most kings favoured flatterers, the good king makes his choice from everyone. The implication is that Trajan would follow such a course.[24] Pliny dwells on this theme in the Panegyric. There is proper scope for *virtus*; now initiative and courage are stimulated, since the emperor does not intimidate his governors.[25] Marcus Aurelius said

---

[23] *JRS* 1975, nos. 12, 33, 65.

[24] 3. 128 ff.; 3.2 ff.; cf. 1.33. See now, Saller, *Personal Patronage under the Early Empire* 94 ff., particularly in relation to *equites*; cf. G. Alföldy, 'Consuls and Consulars under the Antonines; Prosopography and History'. *Anc. Soc.* 7 (1976), 291.

[25] 44.6 ff.; cf. 18–19; cf. Dio, 53.33.8.

of Antoninus Pius: 'He resolutely insisted that offices should be distributed according to the merit of the individual.' And he expressed the ambition to be 'a good pupil of Antoninus'.[26] To appoint men of ability required careful consideration of character and conduct, but that must not involve suspicion.[27] Cassius Dio, in the speech of Maecenas, describes how emperors ought to discuss decisions with prominent men. 'The point of this is that you should get to know well their characters and therefore employ them in the right kind of post; and also that they will go out as governors of the provinces with advance knowledge of your opinions and wishes.'[28]

In the sources, emperors are often praised for the advancement of men according to their reputed merits.[29] Perhaps Velleius was not merely flattering Tiberius when he said that in his reign offices were always open to the worthy.[30] In doing this Tiberius would have been following one of the injunctions left in writing by Augustus — 'to give the administration of affairs to those who had the ability to understand them and to act'.[31] Even Nero created a good impression by his appointment of Corbulo for the Parthian war — 'it seemed that room was being made for men of talent'.[32]

Although the senatorial tradition on Hadrian is ambiguous, Dio praises his careful choice of Julius Severus for the Jewish war.[33] Widespread approval of Marcus' appointments can be inferred from the comments of the sources on various commanders. It is clear that in P. Martius Verus, Marcus found the perfect combination of military and diplomatic proficiency and personal loyalty.[34] Pontius Laelianus, legate of Syria c.153 and comes of Veres c.165, was praised as 'an eminent man who believed in old-style discipline'.[35] Even

---

[26] 1.16.1; 6.30.2.
[27] 6.30.3.
[28] 52.33.3–34.8.
[29] Cf. Tacitus on Tiberius: A 4.6.
[30] 2.126.4 — 'honor dignis paratissimus'.
[31] Dio, 56.33.4.
[32] A 13.8.
[33] 69.13.2.
[34] Dio, 71.3.1.
[35] Fronto (Haines, Loeb) II, p. 148.

Avidius Cassius was recognized by Fronto as a man of energy and alertness.[36] In the reign of Severus Alexander, according to Herodian, military commands were bestowed on men well tested in maintaining discipline, and in the military arts.[37] These stories need not all be true; they nevertheless show that the concept of the reward of merit was widely approved of by senators and recognized by at least some emperors.

In practice it could, of course, be disrupted by mere capriciousness or carelessness on the part of the emperor. But, much more importantly, the holder of the supreme authority naturally thought first of his own safety and security. And merit in the upper classes could most freely be rewarded when an emperor had a good working relationship with senators and *equites* and felt that he could trust them.

It was widely believed that Tiberius in the later part of his reign was suspicious of talented men. Tacitus thought that his reluctance to appoint provincial governors was one possible explanation of the long tenures during this reign.[38] L. Arruntius was hated because he was rich, able in noble activities, and with a reputation to match.[39] C. Silius' friendship with Germanicus was his ruin. Although left in command of an army for seven years, he eventually succumbed to Tiberius' suspicion; his rapid demise had something to do with his rash assertion that Tiberius owed the purple to the loyalty of the troops of Silius.[40] Quiet men were at a premium. Like Poppaeus Sabinus, they need have no special ability, but a modest competence and the art of winning the imperial trust.[41] How much of this is true is another matter. However, it is helpful if Tacitus has preserved the prevailing mood of senators; they hated the emperor and so believed that a bad man could rarely recognize merit and rewarded it only grudgingly. In these circumstances senators were perhaps less eager to accept public service.[42]

---

[36] *Ibid.*, p. 190.   [37] 6.1.4.
[38] *A* 1.80.
[39] *A* 1.13.   [40] *A* 4.18.
[41] *A* 6.39. Not all governors were so quiet. Lentulus Gaetulicus, governor of Upper Germany, allegedly wrote to Tiberius refusing to surrender his province, and promising loyalty if he were not plotted against (*A* 6.30).
[42] See below, pp. 341ff.

At the start of his reign Claudius owed much to the Praetorian Guard, and nothing to the Senate. He was un-certain and suspicious. It was decreed that no soldier should enter the house of a senator even to greet him. He ordered Corbulo back across the Rhine when the commander was preparing to attack the Chauci. Tacitus lets it be inferred that the emperor was cowardly and terrified of Corbulo's power.[43] Dio is even more explicit.[44] Claudius' suspicion caused great anxiety and frustration among senators. If Corbulo provoked the enemy and things went well, the lazy old Claudius might take offence — 'a man of outstanding talent was a threat to peace and quiet'.[45] Here again Tacitus is probably attempting to convey the mood of the senators, whatever the emperor's real intentions were. They could not believe that the emperor sincerely intended to reward merit as it deserved. Appointments to commands seemed to be cap-ricious and sometimes in the hands of freedmen.[46] In this reign it was best to do nothing. M. Vinicius saved his life in this way, for a time.[47]

The high hopes raised by Nero's appointment of Corbulo were soon dispelled. As early as 58 a governor could veto a useful canal project with the excuse 'that it might worry the emperor'.[48] Suspicion was rife. The long inactivity of the German armies made men think that the commanders had been deprived of the right of acting against the enemy.[49] In this reign too, wise men laid low. The eminent Memmius Regulus survived 'protected by inactivity'.[50] Galba adopted a torpid and indolent demeanour during his governorship of Spain; no one could be forced to render an account of his spare time.[51] This illustrates vividly the hatred and fear among senators of an emperor who despised or neglected merit. Vespasian was also moved to reprimand Nero for his

[43] A 11.19.
[44] 61.30.4 ff.
[45] A 11.19: 'formidulosum paci virum insignem'.
[46] Suet., Vesp. 4.1. Vespasian got a legionary command through the influence of Narcissus.
[47] Dio, 60.27.4.
[48] Tac., A 13.53: 'formidulosum id imperatori'.
[49] 13.54.
[50] 14.47; cf. Ag. 6.3: 'inertia pro sapientia fuit'.
[51] Suet., Galb. 9.1.

slowness to reward ability. In praising Plautius Silvanus, he said: — 'He governed Moesia so well that the distinction of triumphal ornaments should not have been postponed for me to grant.'[52]

Naturally in 68–9 the personal security of the emperor was a paramount concern. Galba sent Vitellius to govern Lower Germany 'because a man who thought about nothing but food was least to be feared'.[53] Tampius Flavianus and Pompeius Silvanus, governors of Pannonia and Dalmatia respectively in 69, are described as rich old men.[54] Obviously they were thought to be quiet men of no ambition. Hordeonius Flaccus, governor of Upper Germany in 68, was feeble from advanced age and gout, without courage or authority.[55] Once again in this period the wise sought obscurity, safety rather than power.[56] But there was sometimes as much danger in avoiding office as there was in holding it.[57]

Domitian is the prime exemplar of an emperor who was held to suspect the meritorious. Agricola, so Tacitus alleges, incurred grave suspicion because of his success in Britain, which cast a bad light on Domitian's supposed failures in Germany. 'He was anxious because the name of a man in private station had been raised above the emperor's.'[58] The emperor was hostile to good qualities, and glory won by merit meant a quick death.[59] The denial of a second consular province and a proconsulate to Agricola are invoked to illustrate Domitian's suspicion. The accuracy or otherwise of these allegations is less important than the fact that, justifiably or not, Tacitus believed that Agricola was hated and distrusted by Domitian because he was a good man and a successful commander.[60] This was surely a genuine emotion among senators because the emperor was thought to be

[52] *ILS* 986.
[53] Suet., *Vit.* 7.1.
[54] Tac., *H* 2.86.
[55] *H* 1.9; cf. 1.56.
[56] 4.48.
[57] 1.2: 'omissi gestique honores pro crimine'.
[58] *Ag.* 39.2: 'formidulosum privati hominis nomen supra principem attolli.'
[59] *Ag.* 41.
[60] See T.A. Dorey, *Greece and Rome* 7 (1960), 66; Ogilvie and Richmond, *Tacitus: Agricola* (1967), 283 ff.

hostile to outstanding men and because of his attitude to the Senate. Pliny dramatically contrasts the reigns of Trajan and Domitian in this respect: 'Now men enter into offices by their merit, not, as before, into danger.' The danger was greatest for army commanders — 'when merit is an object of suspicion and inactivity is at a premium, the commanders have no authority, no power, and no obedience'.[61] The opinions of the upper classes are clear. 'Bad' emperors, that is, those who quarrelled with the 'best people', suspected and envied virtue. However it is too simplistic to argue that all emperors approved of by the Senate rewarded men of ability, while those whom the Senate hated suspected such men. Hostile senatorial sources might be prone to take the worst view of the character and appointments of an emperor whom they detested for other reasons. And there is, by accident, a plentiful supply of evidence about emperors who might *a priori* suspect men of talent, but not so much about those respected by the Senate. All emperors to some extent had to consider the demands of security. Even Marcus Aurelius was not free from military rebellion.[62] Moreover, an emperor who set out to win the support of the upper classes could find that they had been so cowed and terrified by the previous regime that the old fears lived on.[63] Nevertheless, the sources are perhaps right in the general supposition that the idea of proper reward of merit was most often ignored when an emperor failed to find a cordial relationship with the senatorial class.

The demands of the empire's defence were scarcely a less pressing problem than that of the ruler's security. Large concentrations of troops under one commander might be

[61] *Ep* 5.14.6; 8.14.7. The theme of emperors' suspicions about their commanders appears also in the second century; note Dio on Pescennius Niger — 75.6.1-2a; Cf. Tacitus on Galba — 'magis extra vitia quam cum virtutibus' (*H* 1.49). Macrinus — Dio, 78.13.2 ff.; Elagabalus — Dio 80.4.3.

[62] See p. 91.

[63] Pliny (*Ep.* 8.14.9), referring to the reign of Domitian, says 'quibus ingenia nostra in posterum quoque hebetata fracta contusa sunt'; cf. Tac., *Ag.* 3.1: 'sic ingenia studiaque oppresseris facilius quam revocaveris'. And note that when Pliny as governor of Bithynia received a charge involving 'crimen maiestatis' against Dio of Prusa, he did not have the confidence to reject this out of hand, but referred the matter to Trajan. The emperor was clearly angry: 'cum propositum meum optime nosses, non ex metu nec terrore hominum aut criminibus maiestatis reverentiam nomini meo adquiri' (*Ep.* 10.81-2).

dangerous, but they were also unavoidable if the empire was to be adequately protected. In the early imperial period there were eight legions in the Rhine area, four in Syria, and large forces on the Danube frontier. Syria retained three legions up to the time of Septimius Severus. Upper Pannonia also acquired a garrison of three legions although it was well placed for advances on Italy; beside it the two Moesian provinces contained four legions. Even when the large garrisons in Syria and Pannonia were eventually broken up, the number of troops facing the enemy was the same; merely their disposition had been altered. Syria was divided into two provinces, Coele retaining two legions; one legion was moved from Upper to Lower Pannonia, which, with two legions, now acquired consular status. This was the minimum change, consistent with national defence, needed to split up the big commands which had helped to launch the claimants for the purple in 193.

Furthermore, even a capricious or cruel emperor who suspected senators could not afford to allow the frontiers to be overrun, for that would create resentment and hostility on a wide scale and might bring about the collapse of discipline and loyalty in the army. Moreover, some emperors — Tiberius, who had considerable achievements to his credit, Claudius in his better moments, and Domitian — although they came to be hated by the Senate, were conscientious in attempting to provide for the welfare of their subjects and the efficient administration of the empire.[64] Any emperor who was concerned for national defence and the good of the empire must be prepared to appoint men of honesty and ability. In that event, an emperor like Domitian, who could have few real friends in the senatorial or equestrian order, would have to appoint men who could at least be surmised to be covertly hostile to him. He must judge their ambition and determination very carefully, and protect his position by other measures.[65] Of course, it is demonstrable that men of ability and standing were prepared to serve under an emperor hated by the Senate, whatever the risks. They might seek the

[64] Tac., A 4.6; Suet., Tib. 32.2; Dom. 8.2.
[65] See pp. 32ff; 385–401; 424–6.

emoluments of office, or find it dangerous to retire. A ready defence was at hand: a senator must think of the good of the state; obedience and restraint were praiseworthy if accompanied by energy and vigour.[66]

It stands to reason that an emperor could not know personally all senators and their background. When he wished to appoint a consular governor, no doubt he consulted his friends and advisers who knew something of the man to be considered. To some extent an emperor was at the mercy of those who advised him, though a prudent man would take opinion from several sources. The practice of commendation was widely accepted by the Romans, and there was great scope in this for the use of patronage. The advance of a man in his early career could depend on his having a strong patron and on the emperor's attitude towards his family, rather than on his presumed ability. His performance in several posts would then indicate if he was competent and reliable enough to accept wider responsibilities in various spheres of the administration. Inevitably, men whom an emperor specially favoured for whatever reason would be pushed on quickly to high honours, if they were willing to serve. It might be argued that an emperor of good character who got on well with the Senate would have excellent friends and favourites and therefore would be better able to choose the right man for each post. This was the view of Dio of Prusa, and is also suggested by Cassius Dio.[67] The idea, however, was but rarely achieved. Obviously an emperor might be mistaken in his judgements and it was difficult to predict how people would turn out.[68] Provincial misgovernment went on throughout the imperial period whatever the character of the ruler.[69] In the same way, it does not follow that the friends of those emperors hated by the Senate were

---

[66] Tac., *Ag.* 42.5; cf. *H* 1.1.

[67] Dio of Prusa, 3.8; Dio, 52.34.2; 39.2 ff.

[68] As Tiberius pointed out in the Senate (Tac., *A* 3.69).

[69] See the fundamental article by P.A. Brunt, 'Charges of Provincial Maladministration under the Early Principate', *Hist.* 10 (1961), 189. Note that P. Mummius Sisenna and Sedatius Severianus, who were consular governors under Antoninus Pius and Marcus Aurelius, are violently criticised by Lucian (*False Prophet* 27, 30, 57).

all bad men, detrimental to the welfare of the empire, and corrupt in their advice.[70]

Down to the end of the Severan dynasty at least, senators continued to hold most of the great provincial commands. Emperors accepted that it was right for these posts to go to senators, and this meant that in their appointments they were faced by the restrictions imposed by the *cursus honorum*. This conveyed men to the consulate only after they had reached a certain age and level of experience and prestige. It would be difficult for an emperor to thrust young men of no status and untried in public office into important commands; the Romans believed that ability to cope with responsibilities came with experience and age. But a problem also faced the emperor who wished to use the military ability and experience of a man of equestrian rank. He would have to be promoted to senatorial rank before he could hold a command usually reserved for senators. This is a sign of the importance of social status in Roman society and also of the idea that the man who commanded an army needed the greatest prestige and authority. Indeed many *equites* who were promoted to senatorial rank began low on the *cursus*. M. Statius Priscus was adlected by Antoninus Pius and began his career as a *quaestor*.[71] He went on to govern three consular provinces. Pertinax was adlected among the praetors and at once held the post of *legatus legionis*.[72] C. Vettius Sabinianus held eight posts in his praetorian career after being adlected.[73] Macrinius Catonius Vindex was a praetorian curator after his adlection to the senatorial class.[74] It seems that in a way these *equites* had to serve their time as senators before they were completely acceptable for the highest senatorial posts. The jealousy of the senators was sometimes hard to keep in check. Some of them hated Lusius Quietus, the commander of Trajan's Moorish cavalry, who was

---

[70] Note, for example, M. Aemilius Lepidus under Tiberius (Tac., *A* 4.20; cf. 3.22; 35; 50). Under Nero Seneca and Burrus flourished for a time; Burrus was well liked 'per memoriam virtutis' and because of the conduct of his successors (Tac., *A* 14.51). Seneca was seen by Tacitus as a restraining influence on the emperor (*A* 14.52). For patronage in Roman society, see E. Champlin, *Fronto and Antonine Rome*; R.P. Saller (n. 19).

[71] *JRS* 1975, no. 65.

[72] no. 28.   [73] no. 33.   [74] no. 12.

adlected among the ex-praetors and eventually became
governor of the prestigious province of Syria.[75] Although
Dio liked Helvius Pertinax, there were some who resented his
advancement because of his low birth.[76] Dio himself bitterly
resented Macrinus' appointment of men of questionable
social background.[77] It was widely believed that the tenure
of high office was the prerogative of men of eminent rank
and distinction; an emperor who desired an amicable relationship with the Senate would need to respect this, even if
senators were not always keen to take on such responsibility.

It must be assumed that a combination of all these variable
factors — reward of merit, personal security, the needs of
national defence, patronage, social status — influenced the
appointments to provincial governorships. The personality
of the emperor, the events of his reign, his relationship with
the upper classes, and the quality of his advisers determined
which factors were uppermost in his mind when he chose
his consular governors. Unfortunately we do not know
enough about the background to the appointment of senators
in individual reigns to see how all these factors worked in
practice. For that we would need the records and memoirs of
the senators who held important posts and the diaries of the
emperors who appointed them.[78] Although we know that
senators continued to hold the main provincial posts, we do
not know how difficult it was for an emperor to fill these
appointments from senators. What choice did he have? What
was the quality of the men who aspired to such posts?

Many major questions about this aspect of Roman
'government' remain obscure. For example, there is still no
satisfactory explanation of the long commands in the reign
of Tiberius,[79] and the extraordinary retention of Aelius
Lamia, governor of Syria, and L. Arruntius, governor of
Tarraconensis, in Rome for ten years. Tacitus suggests that
long tenures of provincial commands occurred because the
emperor did not like making decisions, was jealous, and was

[75] Dio, 68.32.5.
[76] Dio's view — 74.1.1; view of others — 71.22.1.
[77] Cf. Millar, *Cassius Dio,* 161-2.
[78] Note the cautionary comments of A.J. Graham on the limitations of
prosopography (*ANRW* II.1, 136-57).
[79] B. Levick, *Tiberius the Politician* (1976), 125 ff.

worried about whom to appoint.[80] Tacitus clearly was not sure of the explanation himself, and of his suggestions the first two seem feeble; furthermore, a long tenure could be injurious to an emperor's security since it would give the governor time to establish a rapport with his troops. Josephus quotes an anecdote about flies on a wound, suggesting that Tiberius thought that oppression would in the end be less damaging to his subjects if the governor had the leisure to practise it gently over a long period, and if the victim were not attacked by a new governor.[81] It is hard to believe that this was a serious policy on the part of Tiberius. The story of the flies was surely a bitter joke made by the emperor when he had discovered how badly some of the senators he had to employ discharged their duties. It makes little sense to see motives of security in the treatment of Lamia and Arruntius. If that was a reason for keeping them in Rome, it is very odd that Tiberius took the risk of appointing them in the first place.[82] The idea that Tiberius was trying to establish a centralized bureaucracy to administer the provinces from Rome has rightly been dismissed.[83]

Another line of approach is possible. Tiberius in AD 34 wrote to the Senate complaining that all the men of note who were suitable for taking an army command declined the duty, and that he was therefore reduced to entreaties to persuade someone of consular rank to accept a province.[84] He also had difficulty in distinguishing quiet men of talent from the ambitious or the plain incompetent.[85] And although he recognized that some men did not turn out according to expectations, he was reluctant to take any action to deal with corrupt and incompetent governors until

---

[80] *A* 1.80: 'causae variae traduntur: alii taedio novae curae semel placita pro aeternis servavisse, quidam invidia, ne plures fruerentur; sunt qui existiment, ut callidum eius ingenium, ita anxium iudicium; neque enim eminentis virtutes sectabatur, et rursum vitia oderat: ex optimis periculum sibi, a pessimis dedecus publicum metuebat.'

[81] *AJ* 18.172-7.

[82] It may be that Sejanus disliked the two senators, but it is very odd that his influence was strong enough to stop them from being sent to their provinces, but not strong enough to stop their appointment in the first place.

[83] Levick, *Tiberius*, 127 f.

[84] Tac., *A* 6.27.

[85] See above, n. 80.

after they had committed offences.[86] Perhaps then it was not easy for Tiberius to find competent senators whom he felt he could rely upon. Both L. Arruntius (whom Augustus had reportedly judged as both worthy and capable of being emperor)[87] and Aelius Lamia were very distinguished men. Lamia proceeded to be Prefect of the City after his governorship of Syria, and presumably had retained the trust of Tiberius.[88] It is possible that these eminent men desired the prestige and honour of a great governorship without the trouble of formally carrying out the duties on the spot. Because of their status and their standing with Tiberius they were able to gain this concession from him. It is easy to see how this could have been misinterpreted by hostile sources. The two absent governorships and also the long tenures may then have been a symptom of the increasing difficulty Tiberius was to find in getting men of rank to accept the prestigious, but possibly onerous, governorships.[89] It can hardly have fitted in with Tiberius' declared intention to make the Senate and individual senators play a full part in government; but he had to modify this ideal in other ways, under the pressure of circumstances.

These considerations may be relevant to another problem of the early principate. Security is usually invoked to explain Augustus' appointment of an *eques* to be prefect of Egypt. A senator in such a province might have dangerous ambitions; and the governor of nearby Syria commanded four legions. There is some justification for this view in Tacitus, who thought that Augustus wished to control closely a province which was rich in grain and easily defended by a small

---

[86] *A* 3.69.

[87] *A* 1.13. Some thought, however, that Augustus had mentioned not Arruntius, but Cn. Piso; cf. Crook, *Consilium Principis* (1955), p. 152, no. 34.

[88] *A* 6.27. By 37 Arruntius may have fallen from the emperor's favour. He was accused of an adulterous liaison with Albucilla, who had been denounced for *impietas* towards Tiberius. But Tacitus suggests that Tiberius did not know what was going on; no instructions had been received from him (Tac., *A* 6.47).

[89] For a slightly different explanation, see Levick, *Tiberius*, 128. Note that long commands were also a phenomenon of Nero's reign. Galba governed Spain from 60-8 *RE s.v.* Sulpicius 772.63); Flavius Sabinus spent seven years as governor of Moesia (*PIR*[2] F352); Plautius Silvanus was in the same province for about five years (*ILS* 986); the aristocratic Scribonii brothers simultaneously governed both German provinces for a long period (Dio, 63. 17.2; Tac., *A* 13.48; *H* 4.41).

force.[90] But Tacitus' account is partly anachronistic. It is unlikely that Rome can have received a major portion of her grain supply from Egypt c.31 BC while Antony was in control; there were other major sources in Africa and Sicily. Nor was Egypt impregnable now that Augustus had complete control of the seas. Dio, in a passage which seems to have been heavily influenced by Tacitus, pointed to the populousness, wealth, and grain supply as reasons why Augustus could not entrust Egypt to a senator.[91]

It was, of course, an important province and Augustus will have wished to choose his governor carefully. But after the turmoil of the civil wars and the example of his own career, could he be sure that an *eques* would not aspire to a leading position? Both senators and *equites* were prohibited from entering Egypt without Augustus' specific permission. If the mere presence of *equites* in Egypt was as worrying to the emperor as that of senators, why should *equites* be any more trusted as governors? Furthermore, the governor of Egypt might be intimidated and suborned into supporting a consular commander, as Tiberius Alexander did in 69. The first prefect, Cornelius Gallus, was accused of treason and committed suicide in 26 BC.[92] Despite this poor advertisement for the use of *equites* in posts of great responsibility, Augustus continued to appoint them. Finally, if the emperor thought that the appointment of *equites* to command troops was desirable for security reasons, it is difficult to see why he left senators in command of armies in Illyricum and Macedonia, which, by their proximity to Italy, were a more direct threat to him.

Another explanation may be suggested. Perhaps there were no suitable senators for the governorship of Egypt, or none willing to accept the post. The situation after the downfall of Antony and Cleopatra was particularly difficult for the new governor; the province itself was relatively unattractive, as Tacitus pointed out, and inhospitable apart from the Nile valley; it had no extensive infra-structure of cultured city life,

---

[90] *A.* 2.59; *H* 1.11 — 'provinciam aditu difficilem, annonae fecundam, superstitione ac lascivia discordem et mobilem, insciam legum, ignaram magistratuum. . .'
[91] 51.17.1.
[92] Dio, 53.23.5-7.

and probably little sophisticated judicial business; its violent and turbulent population was much given to religious fanaticism. Despite the presence of three, and later two legions, and some early military activity, the military responsibilities to be expected might be limited.

As an *ad hoc* solution Augustus chose Gallus not because he was an *eques*, but because he was a personal friend and hopefully loyal, as well as competent and willing to accept the post. When he proved unsuitable, another *eques* was appointed largely for the same reasons, and this temporary solution eventually became an accepted convention.[93] Augustus to start with had no definite intentions, although he will have had security in mind whatever the rank of the governor. The general exclusion of senators and *equites* may be explained on the hypothesis that Augustus was particularly sensitive about Egypt (which had been the centre of opposition to him) while it was being reorganized. He would be anxious to keep a check on where the upper classes were. In time this also became an accepted rule.

It may be supposed that normally the mechanism of appointment to praetorian and consular posts will have ticked over easily enough. The greatest difficulties arose when an emperor's relations with the senatorial class were strained; then suitable men might be unwilling to serve. It is likely that emperors were happy enough with the traditional, amateur, unsystematic methods of selecting army commanders, provincial governors, and other office holders. It was a personal preference, for they came in general from the same class and knew the traditions of Roman office holding. Moreover, it was very convenient. For there was no military oligarchy or coterie of 'marshals' in the Roman empire, with traditions, ideas, and aspirations of their own, and who might threaten the emperor or undermine the loyalty of the soldiers. 'Each post was an individuality and implied no formal position in the emperor's counsels or in any military hierarchy.[94]

---

[93] The *ad hoc* development of the post is also suggested by Ulpian's imprecise definition of the prefect's powers (*D* 1.17.1) – 'imperium quod ad similitudinem proconsulis lege sub Augusto ei datum est'; cf. Tac., *A* 12.60.

[94] *JRS* 1975, 27.

It is interesting that where evidence exists there is little sign that the governors of the great consular provinces were particularly influential in imperial counsels, or that, if they were, this was because of their military accomplishments. For the period between AD 14 and 96, it is worth noting that when Tiberius left Rome for Capri, the jurist Cocceius Nerva was the only senator to accompany him.[95] L. Vitellius, who had very strong influence with Claudius and who rivalled the imperial freedmen in importance in the emperor's counsels,[96] can hardly have owed this to his successful tenure of the governorship of Syria ten years before. Up to 62 Seneca, who had no military pretensions whatsoever, occupied with the commander of the Guard, Burrus, the most influential position with Nero.[97] It seems that Mucianus was the most important figure outside the imperial family in the early years of Vespasian. This will have been due in large measure to his role, as governor of Syria, in helping Vespasian to attain the purple. But he was certainly not a great military man; although he may have been legate of a legion with Corbulo, he subsequently governed the unarmed province of Lycia, and was known as a writer.[98] Vibius Crispus and Eprius Marcellus can also be recognized as intimates of Vespasian. But Tacitus ascribes their influence to their ability in eloquence.[99] Of the eight or perhaps nine senators who appear as Domitian's counsellors in Juvenal's fourth satire, only Rubrius Gallus is known to have been a military commander.[100] At least Juvenal did not think it necessary to mention any military attributes of the counsellors; his pen portrait of each man is based on quite different qualities and abilities that might serve an emperor. Under Trajan, many of the consular legates about whose interests something is known were men of culture and learning, orators and jurists. If they did acquire particular influence with Trajan (and it is far from clear that as a group they did), it need not be due to specifically military qualities or their tenure of a consular province.[101]

---

[95] Tac., *A* 4.58.
[96] 11.2 ff.; 33 ff.; 12.5 ff.; 12.42.
[97] *A* 13.2. See M. Griffin, *Seneca, A Philosopher in Politics* (1976), part I.
[98] *PIR²* L 216.
[99] *Dialogus* 8.   [100] 4.105.   [101] *JRS* 1975, 14–15.

The *Tabula Banasitana* contains two imperial letters, the first written by Marcus Aurelius and Lucius Verus in 168, the second by Marcus and Commodus in 177.[102] To the second are affixed the signatures of twelve men, presumably the emperors' counsellors on this occasion. Among them are the Praetorian prefects, Bassaeus Rufus and Taruttienus Paternus, Varius Clemens the *ab epistulis*, Cervidius Scaevola, *praefectus vigilum* in 175, Larcius Euripianus, the *a rationibus*, and Titius Piso whose function is unknown.[103] These *equites* probably sat on the council *ex officio*. It is worth noting that Scaevola and Paternus were also renowned as jurists. Of the five senators on the council, none is known to have governed a consular province. The known praetorian career of Acilius Glabrio was spent entirely in civil posts.[104] In addition, three of the senators had been consul by 154, which means that they would have been rather elderly by 177, with any governorships presumably well behind them.[105] Of the other two Gaius Severus was proconsul of Africa in 174,[106] which suggests that he had reached the end of any military career he may have had.

Of course when military or provincial matters were being discussed, no doubt *amici* with some experience in governing provinces were asked for advice,[107] and on imperial campaigns the *comites* could be called upon. But the consular legates, either during or after their active careers, do not seem to have had a permanent role among the imperial advisers, and if they were influential with the emperor it was on an individual basis, because they had his favour and because of the prestige gained from the successful performance of their duties in several spheres of activity. Their advice will have been given on the basis of the whole complex of their administrative experience, to help the emperor govern the empire efficiently, and not as 'military men' or 'marshals'.

[102] For the text, see A.N. Sherwin-White, *JRS* 63 (1973), 86.

[103] One name has been erased; it was probably that of Perennis.

[104] *PIR²* A 73.

[105] Gallicanus (*PIR²* G 114); Glabrio (n. 104); Sextius Lateranus (*RE Zweite Reihe* IV, col. 2046 no. 26).

[106] A.R. Birley, *Septimius Severus,* Appendix I, no. 34. P. Iulius Scapula Tertullus (*PIR²* I 556) was consul *c.*160-6.

[107] As Tiberius is said to have done – Dio, 57.17.9.

4. THE UPPER CLASSES AND THE SCOPE FOR MILITARY ACTIVITY AND GLORY

For those senators who wished to hold provincial governorships and enjoy the responsibilities and pleasures of commanding men, the field in which they could display their *virtus* was disappointingly small. The emperor was master of his army, virtually monopolized the celebration of military achievements, and controlled the foreign policy of the State, determining where Roman arms should go and whether campaigns should be fought or not. Military operations were often directed by the emperor himself, or members of his family, and the opportunities for an independent command with large numbers of troops directed by a senator were infrequent.

It was in every emperor's interests to exercise a strict supervision over his governors. Probably from the start of the imperial period, all imperial *legati* and proconsuls received *mandata* from the emperor,[1] and it may be surmised that they contained instructions on the use of the army. According to Suetonius, Augustus detested rash commanders and 'he always said that a war or a battle should not be undertaken at all, unless it was clear that the expectation of profit was greater than the fear of loss.'[2] How often an emperor wrote to his governors will have depended on his character and preoccupations,[3] the time available, and the circumstances of his reign.[4]

On the other hand, governors will presumably have reported regularly to the emperor on their activities,[5] including how they intended to use the troops at their disposal. On the death of Herod, both Quinctilius Varus, the governor of Syria, and the procurator wrote to Augustus making accusations about the situation in Judaea.[6]

---

[1] F. Millar, *JRS* 56 (1966), 157; *ERW*, 313 ff. For the issuing of *Mandata* to proconsuls, see G.P. Burton, *ZPE* 21 (1976), 63.

[2] Suet., *Aug.* 25.4.

[3] Tac., *A* 11.19 — Claudius worried by Corbulo.

[4] Herodian, 1.10.2-3 — Commodus wrote to several provincial governors criticizing them for their failure to deal with bandits.

[5] Examples of such despatches: Tac., *Ag.* 18.6; 39.1; *A* 15. 3; 15.8; 15.25; Plin., *Ep.* 10.20-1; 22-3; Josephus, *AJ* 15.10; Pliny, *NH* 9.4.9; Arrian, *Periplous*, 6.2; 10.1-4.

[6] Josephus, *AJ* 17.45.

Caesennius Paetus, during his governorship of syria in 72, wrote to Vespasian asking for permission to make war.[7] In the reign of Septimius Severus a legate of Britain wrote to inform the emperor of the dangerous military situation.[8] He probably wanted Severus to send further instructions or come in person. However, there is little explicit evidence for the nature of these reports. How regularly did an emperor expect them? Was the governor obliged to report every military action? Much will have depended on the character and diligence of the individual emperor; the careless or the frivolous may not often have bothered with what was happening in the provinces. It may be suggested that governors were expected to take no decisive action without consultation with the emperor.

Proconsuls were chosen by lot by the Senate and in the reign of Augustus several still commanded armies, in Macedonia, Illyricum, and Africa. By the time of Tiberius, the only proconsular province with troops (one legion) was Africa. It could be argued that proconsuls with troops in their charge had an independent *imperium* and therefore commanded under their own auspices (*auspicia*), in contrast to the *legati Augusti pro praetore*, who held power delegated by the emperor and acted under his auspices.[9] But it is far from certain that Augustus respected the legal niceties, even if these were clearly defined. Licinius Crassus, proconsul of Macedonia, was awarded a triumph, which was usually given to those acting under their own *auspicia*, for his success in pacifying Thrace in 29 BC. But he was denied the *spolia opima* (awarded for killing an enemy leader in battle) on the grounds that, as Augustus himself apparently alleged, only a man acting under his own auspices could claim such an honour.[10] What is more, Dio says specifically that Crassus was not in supreme command, and that Augustus refused to allow him to accept the acclamation as *imperator,* which was instead added to his own titles.[11]

[7] *BJ* 7.220 ff.
[8] Herodian, 3.14.1.
[9] Note the inscription from the arch of Titus celebrating his defeat of the Jews under the auspices of his father Vespasian — *ILS* 263.
[10] R. Syme, *Roman Revolution* 308; cf. H.S. Versnel, *Triumphus* (1970), 164 ff.; 313 ff.   [11] 51.24.4-25.2.

Augustus could not afford to allow a senator to accumulate so many prestigious military honours. Yet it must have been awkward when the question of the proconsuls and their *auspicia* was brought out into the open in this way. How could independently appointed proconsuls be acting under Augustus' supreme authority? The trial of M. Primus in 23 BC, another proconsul of Macedonia, was also embarrassing for this reason among others. For Primus claimed in his defence that he had instructions from Augustus which justified the operations he had carried on outside his province. Augustus appeared in court to deny that he had given instructions.[12]

It is perhaps true to say that in the early part of his regime Augustus did not wish to make clear formally whether proconsuls, appointed by the Senate and selected by lot, operated under their own *auspicia* or under his in military matters. In practice the proconsuls probably often acted on their own initiative under Augustus' general guidance; but the emperor could interfere in any province when he wished,[13] and could direct, curtail, or end any military operations if he chose; and so the proconsul in reality did not have full authority, though this could probably escape notice except on contentious points like military honours. It is likely that Augustus distributed these honours on an arbitrary basis to men whom he especially favoured or trusted, regardless of the legal status of their command.[14]

An inscription of Cossus Cornelius Lentulus, proconsul of Africa AD 5-6, distinguishes between the proconsul's leadership in a military campaign against the Gaetuli, and the overall direction and authority of Augustus ('auspiciis Imp. Caesaris Aug. . . . ductu Cossi Cornelii Lentuli').[15] This may indicate that by this date it was clearly accepted that Augustus with his *maius imperium proconsulare* was in control of the *auspicia*. On the other hand, the terminology could be explained on the hypothesis that Lentulus had not been chosen by lot by the Senate, but had been personally

---

[12] 54.3.1 ff.

[13] F. Millar (n. 1).

[14] L. R. Taylor (*JRS* 26 (1936), 168) argued that *triumphalia* were necessary because after 19 BC no senator held an independent command. See pp. 358-9.

[15] *AE* 1940.68.

appointed by Augustus to deal with the crisis of the difficult war in Africa.

The position of the proconsuls may have remained slightly ambiguous; in any event the question of *auspicia* became less relevant as the number of proconsuls with troops to command declined. Tiberius is found writing to L. Apronius (proconsul of Africa, 18-21 AD), chastising him because he had not bestowed the *civica corona* on a deserving soldier, 'by virtue of his right as proconsul'.[16] It is not clear what Tiberius meant by 'ius proconsulis'. It need not imply that the proconsul was acting under his own *auspicia*; he may have had certain limited rights to take actions concerning the army on his own initiative. It is in character for Tiberius to have insisted that senators carry out their responsibilities to the full. Another proconsul of Africa, Junius Blaesus, was granted the title *imperator,* again an honour usually given to commanders acting under their own *auspicia.*[17] But this too is not decisive since Licinius Crassus had been granted a triumph when he was apparently not acting under his own auspices. And Tiberius particularly desired to honour Blaesus, who was the uncle of Sejanus.

These technicalities will have mattered less to proconsuls than the responsibilities and prestige of their office. Africa was the last area where a senatorial proconsul could enjoy a command of troops that was in some sense independent, no matter how limited that independence was. This could be permitted since there was normally only one legion in Africa, and it was not a streategic threat. The long war in Africa from AD 17 onwards against Tacfarinas, leader of the Musulamii, brought military distinction to several proconsuls, and also the suggestion that not all the honours had been genuinely earned.[18] M. Furius Camillus (17), L. Apronius (18-21), and Junius Blaesus (22) all won triumphal ornaments.[19] The war was eventually terminated

[16] Tac., *A* 3.21; Suet., *Tib.* 32.1.
[17] Tac., *A* 3.74.
[18] Tac., *A* 4.23: 'Nam priores duces, ubi impetrando triumphalium insigni sufficere res suas crediderant, hostem omittebant; iamque tres laureatae in urbe statuae et adhuc raptabat Africam Tacfarinas . . .'
[19] See in general, R. Syme, 'Tacfarinas, the Musulamii, and Thubursicu', *Studies in Honour of A.C. Johnson* (1951), 113 = *Roman Papers*, 218.

in 24 by P. Dolabella, whose request for triumphal ornaments was refused.[20]

In dealing with Tacfarinas the Roman commanders had some difficulty in that the heavy infantry of the legion was not well suited for an enemy who employed guerrilla tactics, avoided set battles, and had few centres of civilization that could be knocked out.[21] Nevertheless, there is still an impression that the proconsuls made more out of Tacfarinas than was necessary and sought to exploit to the full the rare chance to command in their own campaign. Tiberius was happy to encourage these feelings,[22] in an area where it could do no harm to him.[23]

After Gaius transferred the legion in Africa from the control of the proconsul to that of a legionary legate appointed by himself, it was only as *legati Augusti* that senators could enjoy military command. In this capacity major independent commands were rare. Aulus Plautius was apparently allowed a fairly free hand by Claudius in the invasion of Britain, although he was obliged to summon the emperor for the climax of the campaign.[24]

One of the most distinguished commanders of the first century was Domitius Corbulo, who won particular renown for his conduct of his governorship of Syria and the war against the Parthians in Nero's reign. Recent studies have confirmed that for all the grandeur and power of Corbulo's command, the policy he followed was that of Nero and his advisers, although it is reasonable to suppose that throughout

---

[20] Tac., *A* 4.26. Tacitus says that this was because Tiberius did not want to offend Sejanus, the nephew of Blaesus.

[21] See the interesting comments on the difficulties the Roman army faced in certain types of campaign, in E.N. Luttwak, *The Grand Strategy of the Roman Empire* (1976), 40 ff.

[22] Tac., *A* 2.52: 'eo pronior Tiberius res gestas apud senatum celebravit.'

[23] The Senate, however, was not up to deciding who should govern a province with military responsibilities. Tiberius wrote to the Senate pointing out the military trouble in Africa and suggesting that they make sure that someone who knew something of military affairs and was physically capable of taking on a war, should be appointed (Tac., *A* 3.32). The Senate referred the matter back to the emperor without making any decision; Tiberius chastised the senators for referring all their difficulties to him and sent them two names from which to choose (3.35).

[24] Dio, 60.19-22.

he offered advice.[25] Perhaps the most striking point is Corbulo's firm refusal to act without the emperor's orders, and his consultations with the government in Rome.[26] Still, the *Annales* give a rather misleading general picture of the independence allowed to the commander. Tacitus wished to add colour and vigour to a narrative which at times may have seemed to him narrow and inglorious;[27] and the theme of a senator's military success will have brought pleasure to many of his class.

Possibly the same motives influenced Tacitus' description of his father-in-law Agricola's governorship of Britain. The biographer allows no mention of Domitian to impinge upon Agricola's achievements. That is misleading. Agricola would not invade Ireland, although he believed it both feasible and necessary.[28] Plainly he would not act without specific instructions from the emperor. Furthermore, the forward movement in Britain had been carried on by two previous governors, Frontinus and Cerialis, and it is likely that Agricola received general instructions in his *mandata* to proceed with this policy. The major campaigns in the fifth and seventh seasons perhaps reflect the initiative of the new emperor, Domitian.[29] Since neither Titus nor Domitian had any experience of Britain, they presumably relied a great deal on the advice of the man on the spot. What Tacitus' account does not reveal is the number of times Agricola reported to Domitian, and whether, having general permission to advance, he reported on his intended campaigns for the next summer and sought the emperor's formal approval.

At least Agricola had seven years in one province and distinguished himself with his careful tactics and victories that

[25] The basic account is still that of Schur (*Klio, Beiheft* 16 (1923)). Hammond, *HSClPh* 45 (1934), 81, argued that Corbulo initiated most of the policy followed in the East. This view is now generally discounted; see B.H. Warmington, *Nero: Reality and Legend* (1969), 85; M. Griffin, *Seneca, A Philosopher in Politics* (1976), 222 ff.; on the family of Corbulo, see R. Syme, *JRS* 60 (1970), 27 = *Roman Papers*, 805.

[26] Tac., *A* 15.3; 5; 17 (Corbulo's response when Paetus proposed a joint invasion of Armenia — 'non ea imperatoris habere mandata').

[27] See Syme, *Tacitus*, 493 ff.; *Roman Papers*, 223; Tac., *A* 4.32.

[28] *Ag.* 24.1 f.

[29] Cf. Ogilvie and Richmond, *Tacitus: Agricola*, 59 ff.

added new territory to the province. Usually senators would have to be satisfied with limited defensive or offensive operations.[30] An excellent example of the military tasks that a senator might perform is found in the governorship of Flavius Arrianus in Cappadocia c.132-7[31] during which he had to repel the invasion of the Alani.[32] Arrian wrote an account of the preparatory dispositions he made for this campaign — *Ectaxis contra Alanos*.[33] This unique work, in which Arrian represents himself as the famous Greek commander Xenophon, sets out the commands of the governor as if he were actually giving them. He had two legions, the *XV Apollinaris* and the *XII Fulminata*, and a number of auxiliary units under his control, in all about 20,000 men. Arrian himself took charge of the dispositions, and recognized the need for personal leadership. 'The commander of the entire army, Xenophon [i.e., Arrian], should lead from a position well in front of the infantry standards; he should visit all the ranks and examine how they have been drawn up; he should bring order to those who are in disarray, and praise those who are properly drawn up.'[34] To carry out his orders Arrian could look to the legionary legate (one of the *legati legionis* seems to be absent), the military tribunes, centurions, and the decurions of the auxiliary units.

Arrian devoted a lot of attention to a meticulous organization of the marching order, which was designed to foil any surprise attack. The mounted scouts and archers preceded the column, which was led by several units of auxiliaries; Arrian himself followed with the *XV Apollinaris* and then the *XII Fulminata*, foreign troops, baggage, and rearguard. The flanks were protected by the cavalry units.[35]

---

[30] Note the campaign of Julius Severus to suppress the Jewish revolt c.132 — Dio, 69.13.2 ff.

[31] For his background see P.A. Brunt, *History of Alexander and Indica* (*Loeb*, 1976), ix ff.; A.B. Bosworth, *Commentary on the Anabasis of Arrian I* (1980), 1-7; P.A. Stadter, *Arrian of Nicomedia* (1980), 32-49.

[32] Dio, 69.15.

[33] See A.B. Bosworth, 'Arrian and the Alani', *HScPh* 81 (1977), 217; and above, p. 327.

[34] *Ectaxis* 10; cf. 22-3.

[35] 1-9.

The preparations for battle were a model of careful, well-planned tactics. The scouts moved to high ground to watch for the enemy while the cavalry circled round the main body of infantry as they took up position. It is clear that Arrian was thinking about the exploitation of natural advantages of terrain, the strengths and weaknesses of the enemy, and the correct timing and discipline of the Roman army's attack. He adopted special tactics: legionaries with long spears were placed in the front rank, backed up by archers as a screen for the rest of the infantry. This was presumably intended to deal with the shock of a massed cavalry charge.[36] Arrian had also considered several possible eventualities in the battle itself. If the enemy fled, some of the Roman cavalry was to move through the ranks and charge, while the rest followed more slowly with fresh horses, and to offer resistance if their side met a reverse. Behind them the legionaries were to advance steadily. But if the enemy did not break immediately, and tried an encircling movement, the Roman ranks were to extend, but not so as to weaken the lines, and the cavalry was to provide extra support on the flanks. The emphasis throughout is on good order and discipline, and a well-planned approach to the battle. Arrian insists that perfect silence is to be maintained until the enemy come within range, and then a huge war cry must be raised.[37]

The tactics are safe and simple, competent rather than brilliant. But they are the complete responsibility of Arrian, who on a limited scale has command of a sophisticated fighting machine, could serve the empire, and also perhaps indulge his own inclinations towards the military arts, and his romantic imagination. For the senators who governed the consular provinces, this will have been the extent of their independent military activities; many will not even have had this limited opportunity.

Of course senators also had a role to play on campaigns directed by the emperor. Some of those men who were officially designated as friends (*amici*) of an emperor would be asked to accompany him when he went to the provinces

[36] 11 ff.; especially 16–19.
[37] 25. The account breaks off before battle was joined.

or on military expeditions. On these occasions the official title of *comes* was employed.[38] For example, Bruttius Praesens was 'comes Impp. Antonini et Commodi Augg. expeditionis Sarmaticae'.[39] The position of *comes* was quite distinct from any other post held, as may be seen from the inscription of Plautius Silvanus Aelianus, who is described as 'legatus et comes Claudii Caesaris in Britannia'.[40] A large number of the known *comites* are men of great seniority and prestige. Many had been consul and had already governed a consular province. Obviously on military expeditions a provident emperor would tend to seek advice of those senators who had experience of a variety of posts in the *cursus* and who knew something about the command and organization of armies. This would be useful, and necessary if the governors of those provinces affected by military action were not themselves men of great talent or effective military experience. But the advice of the *comites* would be valued by a conscientious emperor in other matters too, and there is no sign that they formed a kind of 'high command'. The consultation by magistrates and others of men who could give suitable advice was a feature of Roman life. When an emperor left Rome on campaign he might continue to deal with the problems of administration, if he chose to interest himself in this. His *comites* could be called upon to give advice on a wide variety of questions. Even while occupied with a military campaign, some emperors received embassies, heard legal cases, and proceeded with the routine administration of the empire by letter; they might also receive petitions from local communities.[41] And of course some time was devoted to pleasure and relaxation — literary and other cultural interests, physical pursuits, and sight seeing.[42] Hadrian went to see the sun rise in Sicily, and while in Egypt visited the statue of Memnon, on whose foot was

---

[38] Crook, *Consilium Principis* (1955), 24-5; a list of *comites* compiled by H.G. Pflaum can be found in *Bayerische Vorgeschichtsblätter* 27 (1962), 90.

[39] *ILS* 1117.

[40] *ILS* 986.

[41] See in general, Millar, *ERW*, 3 ff.; 28 ff.; 229 ff.; 375 ff.; 420 ff.

[42] For declamations before Marcus Aurelius and Caracalla, see Millar, *ERW*, 6; for Caracalla's physical pursuits, see Herodian, 4.7.2; Dio, 78.17.4; 18-19.

carved an inscription describing how the emperor, his wife, and a lady companion had heard it 'sing' at dawn.[43]

Doubtless life could at times be quite pleasant for the *comes* of an emperor. Velleius has an excellent story of the solicitude of Tiberius for his companions during his commands in the reign of Augustus in Germany and Pannonia; he made a horse-drawn carriage available for those who required it, and also offered the use of his doctor, his kitchen equipment, and his own portable bath tub to anyone who was ill. 'All they lacked was their own home and servants.'[44]

Velleius, who began his career as an *eques*, expresses some of the feeling of reward he experienced while serving under Tiberius as prefect of a cavalry unit and then as *legatus* after he had been designated *quaestor*; subsequently, on the instructions of Augustus, he led part of an army to Tiberius in Pannonia.[45] It is difficult to say, however, how much scope was left to the higher officers when an emperor or a member of the imperial family was present on expeditions. The ideal was that the emperor's commanders should not feel intimidated, or overawed and restricted by the presence of an emperor or a prince.[46] But how often was this ideal achieved? The senatorial commanders who acted under the supreme command of Tiberius in Germany and on the Danube seem to have had considerable responsibility and initiative, and several won the triumphal ornaments. But Velleius, in his desire to show the perfect harmony between Tiberius and his commanders, may give a misleading picture. It is worth noting the cases of Sentius Saturninus, to whom Tiberius gave 'less risky tasks' while he took the difficult ones himself, and Aelius Lamia, who served with distinction in Germany, Illyricum, and Africa, but who lacked the opportunity, not the ability, to win triumphal honours.[47] It is

---

[43] *Vit. Had.* 13.3; *IGR* I. 1186; 1187.   [44] 2.114.2.
[45] 2.104.3; 2.111.3.   [46] Pliny, *Ep* 5.14.6; 8.14.7.
[47] Cf. Marcus Lollius (2.97.1); Lucius Piso (2.98.1); Marcus Vinicius (2.103.2); Sentius Saturninus (2.105.1); Marcus Valerius Messalla Messallinus (2.112.2); Aulus Caecina, Plautius Silvanus (2.112.4); Marcus Lepidus (2.114.5); Vibius Postumus (2.116.2); Aelius Lamia (2.116.3). And note the role of A. Caecina Severus in the campaigns of Germanicus (Tac., *A* 1.31 ff.).

possible that, despite the restricted scope of operations, the lack of really independent commands, and the increasingly frequent presence of emperors on campaigns, there were still opportunities for those senators who inclined to the military arts. But everything was controlled by the emperor, and it was not the same as the good old days of the Republic, as Corbulo nostalgically reflected when ordered back across the Rhine by Claudius: 'How lucky the old Roman commanders were!'[48]

In the Republic senators vied with their peers for military glory, and success brought public recognition of military *virtus*. Augustus had won power by eclipsing the other military dynasts in armed combat; it was expedient that there should be no other who might surpass him in military glory or reputation. This is reflected in the honours he received, his nomenclature, and his control over the laurels of military victory. It would not do for senators or *equites* to boast too openly of military renown; this was part of the reason for the fall from favour in 26 BC of Cornelius Gallus, the prefect of Egypt. He inscribed a list of his achievements on the pyramids, and set up at Philae a grandiloquent inscription proclaiming that he had led the legions further than any other Roman commader or the kings of Egypt; nowhere was there a mention of Augustus.[49]

We may trace part of the process by which the recognition of military success achieved by senators was restricted. The last full-scale triumph for a senator is recorded on the Capitoline *Fasti*; it was won by Cornelius Balbus in 19 BC. After this date successful commanders received *triumphalia*, which consisted of the ornaments and dress usually associated with a *triumphator*, but excluded the grand parade. It has been suggested that proper triumphs were discontinued because after 19 BC all important commands not held by members of the imperial family were in the hands not of proconsuls, but of *legati Augusti pro praetore*, who acted under the imperial *auspicia* and therefore had no claim to a triumph. However this idea does not fit the

---

[48] Tac., *A* 11.20.
[49] *Ehrenberg and Jones*, no. 21; Dio 53.23.5-7.

evidence.[50] According to Dio, Agrippa was granted a triumph by the Senate in 19 BC, but refused to hold it.[51] In 14 BC he again refused a triumph and Dio believed that this was the reason why no other senator was given a full triumph after this date.[52] In addition, Suetonius records that Tiberius was the first to receive the honour of *triumphalia*. This can be dated to 12 BC.[53] The train of events can plausibly be reconstructed as follows. Augustus who had himself declined a proper triumph in 25 BC, had decided by 19 BC that no more senators should hold a full triumph, and he used Agrippa and Tiberius to impress this point as politely as possible on the senatorial class. The ostentatious refusal of two separate grants of a triumph by Agrippa, and a hint that his *dignitas* demanded that others do the same, would serve to convince senators that it would not be in their best interests to apply for a triumph. And it may be that the new and unprecedented honour of *triumphalia*, designed to replace the traditional triumph for men in private station, was first given to Tiberius, a member of the imperial family, to add dignity and respectability to it. In this way it would be gradually accepted that the *iustus triumphus* with its surpassing glory was the prerogative of the emperor or a member of his family.

The award of triumphal ornaments was the highest military honour a senator could aspire to; they marked a man out in society and originally were held in great respect. P. Plautius Pulcher, the son of M. Plautius Silvanus, who had won triumphal honours from Augustus for his successes in Illyricum, is described on an inscription as 'triumphalis

---

[50] For Balbus, see Degrassi, *Fasti Capitolini* (1955), 90 ff.; for the question of *auspicia*, see above p. 350 (n. 14); and note V.A. Maxfield, *The Military Decorations of the Roman Army*, 101 ff.

[51] 54.11.6-12; cf. 53.26.5 — Augustus' refusal of a triumph in 25 BC.

[52] 54.24.7.

[53] Suet., *Tib.* 9.2; Dio, 54.31.4. A.A. Boyce (*Class. Phil.* 37 (1942), 130) thought that Augustus instituted a new triumphal cult in the temple of Mars Ultor, where *triumphalia* could be dedicated. Augustus himself, she claims, was awarded *triumphalia* in 20 BC. But the evidence she cites proves only that Augustus enjoyed certain honours associated with the triumph because he voluntarily declined a full triumph, not that he was formally granted *triumphalia*. If such a grant did take place, it is very odd that neither Dio nor the *Res Gestae* mention it.

filius' ('the son of the man who held triumphal honours').[54] Indeed the inscription of another member of the family, M. Plautius Silvanus Aelianus, recording the achievements of his career, shows that fulsome praise for the military ability displayed by a senator was still possible in the imperial period, especially after he was dead:

In honour of Tiberius Plautius Silvanus Aelianus, *Pontifex, Sodalis Augusti, III vir,* questor of Tiberius Caesar, legate of the fifth legion in Germany, praetor *urbanus, legatus* and companion of Claudius Caesar in Britain, consul, proconsul of Asia, *legatus pro praetore* in Moesia; in this post he brought over more than 100,000 of the people who live across the Danube to pay tribute to Rome, along with their wives and children, leaders and kings. He suppressed an uprising among the Sarmatians, although he had sent a large part of his army to an expedition in Armenia; he compelled kings who had previously been unknown or hostile to the Roman people to worship the Roman military standards on the river bank which he was protecting. He sent back to the kings of the Bastarnae and the Rhoxolani . . . their sons who had been captured or taken from the enemy. From some of them he took hostages and in this way strengthened and extended the peaceful security of his province. And the king of the Scythians was driven by siege from Chersonesus, which is beyond the Borysthenes. He was the first to help the corn supply in Rome by sending from his province a large amount of wheat. After he had been sent to be governor of Spain he was recalled to be Prefect of the City [?] , and during this office the Senate honoured him with the triumphal ornaments on the authority of the emperor, Caesar Augustus Vespasianus; an extract from his speech is set out below:
'He governed Moesia so well that the honour of triumphal ornaments should not have been postponed for me to confer on him. However, because of the delay, now a greater title of honour has fallen to him during his prefecture of the city.'
While he was Prefect of the City, the emperor Caesar Augustus Vespasianus made him consul for the second time.[55]

Old traditions were also respected in that, as in the case of Plautius Silvanus, the Senate was invited to confer the *triumphalia* on the advice of the emperor.[56] In these ways

---

[54] *ILS* 964; cf. Tac., *A* 13.45; 15.72; Dio, 55.10.3; 68.16.2; Suet., *Cl.* 17.3; Vell. 2.121.3.
[55] *ILS* 986.
[56] Cf. Pliny, *Ep.* 2.7.1.

emperors did attempt to accommodate the ambitions of the upper classes. But triumphal ornaments were only a substitute for the real thing. Tacitus, describing the triumphal honours of Agricola, says 'and whatever is given in place of a triumph'.[57] And the liberal grants of the honour by emperors whom senators despised eventually reduced its value, and gave rise to the rumour that not much had to be done to earn it.[58] Claudius is said to have given *triumphalia* to everyone who accompanied him on the British expedition.[59] Nero awarded the honour to two senators and the Praetorian prefect after the suppression of the conspiracy of Piso; he also gave *triumphalia* to men of low rank.[60] *Triumphalia* were the remnant of senatorial military honour and they mark how far that tradition had been eclipsed by the supreme *imperator*. But senators obstinately clung to the concept of the public recognition of military *virtus*, and although *triumphalia* disappear possibly from the time of Hadrian, statues in military dress continued to be given to senators who distinguished themselves in command of troops.[61]

It should be emphasized that all other military honours, with the exception of decorations, had been severely curtailed or removed. After AD 22 there were no more acclamations of men in private station as *imperator*.[62] After Crassus, there is no hint that any senator was ever considered for the *spolia opima;* either the opportunity did not

---

[57] *Ag.* 40.1.

[58] See n. 18; and cf. the story in Tacitus (*A* 11.20) where Curtius Rufus was awarded *triumphalia* by Claudius apparently for sinking a mine. The exhausted soldiers, who had had to dig it, appealed to the emperor to grant *triumphalia* in future to commanders before they got their commands. Note also *A* 13.53.

[59] Dio, 60.23.2.

[60] Tac., *A* 15.72; Suet., *Ner.* 15.2. Grants of *triumphalia* for political reasons — Suet., *Cl.* 24.3; Tac., *A* 12.3; *II* 4.4.

[61] For a list of those who received *triumphalia*, see A.E. Gordon, *Quintus Veranius, Consul AD 49* (1952), 312 ff. The last recorded examples of *triumphalia* were won by Iulius Severus (*PIR*² I 576) and Haterius Nepos (*PIR*² H 30). Nepos may have won his under Antoninus Pius. See Gordon, ad loc. For examples of honorary statues, see *ILS* 1098, 1100, 1112.

[62] Tac., *A* 3.74: 'Tiberius . . . id quoque Blaeso tribuit ut imperator a legionibus salutaretur, prisco erga duces honore qui bene gesta re publica gaudio et impetu victoris exercitus conclamabantur; erantque plures simul imperatores nec super ceterorum aequalitatem. Concessit quibusdam et Augustus id vocabulum ac tunc Tiberius Blaeso postremum.'

arise, or this honour had been quietly forgotten about. Only two senators in the imperial period are recorded with a *cognomen* proclaiming military fame.[63] Nevertheless, for his campaign in Britain Aulus Plautius was granted the honour of an *ovatio*, less prestigious than a full triumph, but better than *triumphalia*.[64] This was a signal distinction for a man in private station.

Emperors sought to direct the military ambitions of senators into service of the State with limited possibilities of independent action and severely restricted recognition of military ability. They had to use senators in military commands and were prepared to go some way to preserve the balance between their own dominant position and the need to satisfy the desire of the upper classes for honour and prestige, especially since the avenue to these by political activities had been closed down. The award of *triumphalia*, a statue in military dress in the forum, and the military decorations, rigidly graded according to the rank of the senator or *eques* who received them,[65] were the summit of senatorial ambitions. And even these honours, although perhaps voted by the Senate, were entirely at the discretion of the emperor. A senator would find it very difficult to reach by military honours and reputation alone that point of prestige and standing where he could be considered 'capax imperii'.

---

[63] Lentulus Gaetulicus — Vell. 2.116.2; Syme, *Roman Papers*, 222; Gabinius Secundus Chaucicus — Suet., *Cl.* 24.3.

[64] Suet., *Cl.* 24.3: 'Aulo Plautio etiam ovationem decrevit ingressoque urbem obviam progressus et in Capitolium eunti et inde rursus revertenti latus texit'; see Versnel, *Triumphus*, 166.

[65] P. Steiner, 'Die Dona Militaria', *BJ* 114 (1906), 89; Maxfield, *The Military Decorations of the Roman Army*, 145 ff.; 158 ff.

PART FOUR
EMPEROR, ARMY, AND *RES PUBLICA*

IX

THE ARMY IN POLITICS

1. INTRODUCTION: EMPEROR AND ARMY IN CRISIS

In his analysis of the careers of men who became princes by good fortune, Machiavelli had in mind some examples from Roman history: 'They make the journey as if they had wings; their problems start when they alight . . . This was also the case with those who from being private citizens became emperors by corrupting the soldiers. Such rulers rely on the good will and fortune of those who have elevated them, and both these are capricious, unstable things.'[1] This touches on an important theme, which is amply illustrated by Tacitus' account of the events of 68-9. Syme has argued convincingly that in the *Historiae* Tacitus used a variety of sources, including eye-witness reports and official records, and achieved an independent historical description that includes the historian's own views and comments on the crisis.[2] Tacitus was interested in what happened when the stable and organized relationship between emperor and army broke down and the restraints of discipline were removed. He was appalled at the violence and brutality of the troops, and the description of the murder of Galba early in the *Historiae* is designed to create the worst possible impression of them. Galba, defenceless, old, and isolated in his own capital, was savagely butchered in the Roman forum in front of the

[1] *Il Principe* — G. Bull, Penguin Translation, 1961, p. 53.
[2] *Tacitus*, 176 ff.; Appendix 29.

temples of the gods.[3] Traditional discipline collapsed —
'where once there had been a rivalry in courage and
discipline, now the contest was in insolence and abuse'.[4] This
culminated in the murder of Hordeonius Flaccus, governor
of Upper Germany.[5] A long catalogue of the violence and
destruction in Italy itself shows the effect of the uncontrollable soldiery;[6] appeals for restraint were brushed aside.[7]

The importance of the greed and licence of the troops as
one motive for the convulsions of 68-9 also appears in other
sources. The following points seem particularly significant.
The army of Verginius Rufus attacked the Gauls led by
Vindex without orders and entirely in the hope of pillage.[8]
The Praetorians finally abandoned Nero only on the promise
of an immense donative,[9] and then supported Otho because
Galba failed to pay the largess and had a reputation as a
strict disciplinarian.[10] The legions of the Rhine proclaimed
Vitellius because they hoped for enrichment and a relaxation
of discipline, and because they resented Galba's favours to
the supporters of Vindex.[11] The Illyrian legions supported
Vespasian partly because they wanted to get their own back
on the Rhine legions, the eastern legions because they
resented the way in which the other troops had promoted

---

[3] *H* 1.40-3. I am not here primarily concerned with the motives of the various
leaders who attempted to seize power in 68-9. This theme has been thoroughly
investigated by other scholars: C.M. Kraay, 'The Coinage of Vindex and Galba,
AD 68, and the Continuity of the Augustan Principate', *Num. Chron.* 9 (1949),
129; G. Chilver, 'The Army in Politics, AD 68-70', *JRS* 47 (1957), 29;
P.A. Brunt, 'The Revolt of Vindex and the Fall of Nero', *Latomus* 18 (1959),
531; contrast R.J.A. Talbert, 'Some Cáuses of Disorder in AD 68-9', *American
Journal of Ancient History* 2 (1977), 69; and note also, K. Wellesley's commentary in *Histories III* (1972) and G. Chilver, *A Historical Commentary on
Tacitus' Histories I and II*, (1979).

[4] 3.11; cf. 2.18-19; 27; 39; 99.

[5] 4.36.

[6] 1.51 (general hostility of the troops to local communities); 1.63 (4,000
killed at Divodurum); 2.12-13 (attack on Intimilium); 2.56 (destruction in Italy
by the Vitellians); 2.87-8 (slaughter of civilians outside Rome by the Vitellians);
2.88 (chaos in Rome itself); 3.25 (a son kills his father in battle); 3.33-4 (sack
of Cremona by Flavians); 3.80-1 (attack on senatorial envoy); 3. 83-4 (battle in
Rome as the Flavians enter).

[7] 3.81.

[8] Dio, 63.24.3.

[9] Dio, 64.3.3; Tac., *H* 1.5.

[10] 1.5; 18; 37-8; Dio, 64.4.1 ff.

[11] Tac., *H* 1.51.

their own candidates, and the Syrian legions in particular because they feared that they would be moved from their accustomed station.[12] All the troops who supported the various military leaders plundered the civilian population ruthlessly, especially the rich.[13] Tacitus had good reason to remember this, since his father-in-law's mother had been killed by a band of marauding sailors during the attack on Intimilium in 69.[14]

Furthermore, when the armies were used for personal aggrandizement, their only proper function, the defence of the empire, was neglected.[15] For Tacitus, military disaster on the frontiers was a danger to be apprehended from the continuation of civil wars.[16] There was some justification for this view, since during the revolt of Civilis Roman soldiers actually took an oath of allegiance to a foreign state and so completed Rome's humiliation.[17] Their action is an 'unheard of outrage'; the oath taken by the troops to the enemy is described by the phrase 'in verba iurare', which normally expresses the oath of loyalty to the emperor, and here emphasizes the enormity of the deed. Tacitus provides Dillius Vocula, the *legatus legionis*, with a traditional commander's speech in which he stresses the glory of the Roman army and urges the troops not to desert. The unreality of this rhetoric and the collapse of accepted values are brought out by the juxtaposition of this speech with Vocula's immediate murder by a deserter.[18]

Although Tacitus gives the impression that the soldiers initiated some events in 68-9,[19] he was well aware that they

---

[12] 2.74; 80; 85. [13] See n. 6. [14] *Ag.* 7.1.

[15] *H* 3.46; 4.13; cf. 1.79 — 'conversis ad civile bellum animis externa sine cura habebantur'.

[16] Cf. Livy 9.19.17. Romans might remember the success of Mithridates in 88 BC, and the Parthian invasion of 40 BC.

[17] *H* 4.24 ff.; 54; 57; 62.

[18] 4.58-9.

[19] Cf. 1.25 where two minor officers help to organise the coup of Otho. Although the 'furor principum' was ultimately responsible for the destruction of the Capitoline temple, it was the soldiers who actually did it — 'furens miles aderat, nullo duce, sibi quisque auctor' (3.71-2). In several other passages Tacitus pursues a similar theme — 1.46; 51; 83; 2.94. He makes a particularly vivid contrast between the lazy and indifferent Vitellius and his troops eager to march on Rome at once (1.62).

needed leaders. Armies, inspired with a lust for booty and rapine, were ready for anything; but they were led on by the 'furor principum', the 'madness of the leading men'.[20] The revolt against Nero could not have succeeded had not Galba been prepared to offer his leadership, for Vindex himself knew that he would never be accepted as emperor. Again, it was Otho who procured the assassination of Galba. The chief event of 69, however, was the revolt on the Rhine, and here it is clear from the failure of the Rhine legions to persuade Verginius Rufus to assume the purple in 68, that their seditious behaviour would not have ended in open insurrection but for the ambitions of Vitellius and his lieutenants.[21] Similarly, Vespasian clearly organized revolt in the East and exploited the legions' resentment and fears, with the help of other governors and men of note.[22] Tacitus, although he believed that in the end Vespasian's victory was good for Rome, had little sympathy for the conduct of the Flavian leaders. He depicted Mucianus in a sinister light and claimed that the leaders worked on the troops by disreputable means and were influenced by a 'lust for booty'.[23] Indeed Tacitus is contemptuous of the conduct of senators in general during 68-9. He hints that the prevalence of indiscipline and disobedience was often due to mistrust of the officers' loyalty; and this was rarely unreasonable and frequently well-founded.[24] The civil wars, it could be argued, were prolonged because the soldiers found men willing to exploit their disobedience and lead them in rebellion.

These ideas are summed up in Tacitus' comments on a story about the first battle of Cremona. It was rumoured that the soldiers of the armies of Otho and Vitellius thought of concluding a truce and agreeing on a choice of emperor. But Tacitus contemptuously dismisses such an idea; the troops had too much to gain from war to desire peace, and their equally disreputable officers and generals had nothing

---

[20] 3.72.

[21] 1.52.

[22] Josephus' story that the troops in Judaea were incensed by what they heard of the misdeeds of the Vitellians is certainly Flavian propaganda. See J. Nicols, *Vespasian and the Partes Flavianae* (1978), 87 ff., especially 92 ff.

[23] 2.5; 7.

[24] Cf. 2.23; 33; 99; 3.4; 9-10; 61; 4.19; 24; 25; 27; 35-6; 57.

to gain from peace and order; they wanted an emperor who would be under an obligation to them for their support.[25] As the desire for personal power grew unabated, leading men were prepared to exploit military force for selfish interests. This was nothing new. Marius and Sulla had overthrown the government and replaced it with personal domination. Pompey's methods were more stealthy but no better, and after him autocracy was the paramount objective. And so wars continued; the same rabid ambitions and the same evil motives produced civil strife.[26]

In this sombre and pessimistic digression Tacitus expresses his belief that there was always a danger of military anarchy in a state where political power depended on an autocrat's control of the army. Once a successful military revolt occurred, it brought out into the open the importance of the army's personal loyalty and encouraged the development of all the most unscrupulous means of winning the support of the troops — flattery, open bribery, and subservience to their wishes.

Galba and Piso, although they abhorred the use of flattery ('favor') or bribery ('largitio'), nevertheless decided that the first public announcement of the latter's adoption should be made before the Praetorian Guard, since 'that would be a mark of respect to the soldiers'.[27] Otho won the troops' support by promising them a large donative and criticizing the strict ideals of Galba.[28] It seems that Otho deliberately made himself subservient to them — 'he said that he would have nothing more than whatever they had left to him'.[29] The presumption of the soldiers increased, but imperial prestige, and with it the ability to control the army, declined. Otho's troops, fearing a plot, burst into a state banquet; the guests scattered in panic to various ignominious hiding places throughout the city, while the emperor was forced to climb on a couch from which he tearfully begged his soldiers to leave. Otho did not dare address the troops formally in the camp until a donative had been distributed; he restored a measure of order, but only two men were punished and the

---

[25] 2.37.   [26] 2.38.   [27] 1.17.   [28] 1.18; 46.
[29] Suet., *Otho* 6.3; Tac., *H* 1.46.

atmosphere in the city remained fearful and suspicious, with the streets empty and the houses of the great shuttered.[30] During Vitellius' brief reign the troops were even allowed to choose their own commanders and the units they wished to join.[31]

In Tacitus' view, the apparent success of such methods provoked similar attempts from others and so produced a cycle of violence and intrigue. He makes Otho reflect sadly that a man who wins the purple by violence cannot suddenly impose strict discipline again. The inevitable futility of all this is summed up in Tacitus' comment on the murder of Galba — 'a crime which is always avenged by the murdered man's successor'.[32] His thoughts have moved from the particular to the general and suggest the usurper inextricably caught up in the implications of his own methods. Moreover, about Vitellius' action in putting to death those who had presented petitions to Otho claiming some service on the day of Galba's death, Tacitus says: 'This was not a mark of respect to Galba, but in the accepted practice of emperors was a protection for the present and an act of vengeance for the future.'[33] By this epigram Tacitus seems to mean that usurpers were so unsure of their position that they not only sought protection for the present in such measures, but also avenged in advance their own anticipated violent deaths. In 69 there was perhaps a danger that the empire would degenerate into the kind of military anarchy that had existed before Actium and was later to plague the third century. It was obviated by the very different policy of Vespasian, who restored military discipline, by the exhaustion of the other military leaders, and by the general desire for peace.[34]

But the underlying problem remained. The preservation of good discipline and at the same time the affection and loyalty of the armies was all the more difficult after 69. And the latent power of the army for destruction was always there; Tacitus no doubt saw further evidence for this when he

---

[30] 1.81-3.   [31] 2.93-4.   [32] 1.40.

[33] 1.44 — 'sed tradito principibus more munimentum ad praesens, in posterum ultionem'.

[34] 2.82 — 'egregie firmus adversus militarem largitionem eoque exercitu meliore'.

came to write the history of the mutinies in AD 14, when
once again disloyalty and licence were rife, officers were
disobeyed and assaulted, and the imperial family itself was
threatened and humiliated as the soldiers abandoned all
traditional marks of respect.[35] It is indeed significant if some
soldiers were prepared to establish Germanicus as a rival
emperor to Tiberius, despite the latter's hereditary claims to
their allegiance and the prestige he had acquired earlier in
command of these German legions. The disturbances of 14
took place when Tiberius was most vulnerable, as he was
attempting to ensure a smooth transition from the principate
of Augustus. They were terminated by timely concessions
from the emperor and his sons. However, concessions made
in the face of pressure might bring the danger of endless
sedition with damaging consequences for the emperor's
prestige and ability to control his army. Tacitus explains
this in his bitter description of how Germanicus, having
promised in Tiberius' name concessions in pay and service
conditions, was forced by the soldiers to pay the money at
once; it had to be collected from Germanicus' own travelling
expenses and the resources of his friends — 'in this disgraceful
column the cash stolen from the commander, the standards,
and the eagles were all carried along together'.[36] What is
more, Drusus was forced into very questionable conduct.
Tacitus recounts and does not explicitly deny the story that
he had the ringleaders butchered and buried in his own
tent.[37] It was perhaps the repressive measures against the ring
leaders[38] and the failure of the mutineers to find adequate
leaders that quietened the convulsions of AD 14.

For the civil wars of 193-7 and the deterioration of
ordered government after the death of Caracalla in 217,
there is no account comparable, in depth of analysis or

[35] *A* 1.16-39. The troops did not come out to meet Drusus in full dress
uniform as usual (24); they refused to stand in their proper order for the speech
of Germanicus (34); insulting remarks were made and when he threatened to stab
himself, a soldier offered his sword (35); Germanicus' life was threatened by the
troops (39). In 1.40-1 Tacitus stirs up pity for Germanicus' family with careful
use of language — 'muliebre et miserabile agmen'; 'profuga ducis uxor'; 'cum fletu
complexus'; 'lamentantes'; 'tristes'.
[36] 1.37.
[37] 1.29; cf the conduct of Germanicus — 1.44.
[38] Velleius, 2.125; Tac., *A* 1.78.

detailed evocation of atmosphere, to that of Tacitus for the earlier period. Dio has some helpful comments, preserved in the excerptors, but his general survey of the trends of the period, if he wrote one, is lacking. He mentions the disquiet caused by the activities of Septimius Severus in 193: 'He did many things that we [the senators] did not approve of; he was blamed for making the city unruly by bringing in so many soldiers, for exhausting the public treasury with a huge outlay of funds, but most of all for placing his hopes for survival in the strength of his army rather than in the good will of those around him.'[39] Because he became emperor by military force, Severus was perhaps compelled to rely more openly on the support of his troops, and Dio thought that this was ominous for the emperor's relationship with the other elements in the Roman state, particularly the upper classes.

A short excerpt is preserved from Dio's history of the reign of Elagabalus: 'The false Antoninus was despised and disposed of by the soldiers. For whenever people, and especially the soldiers, have become accustomed to be contemptuous of their rulers, they feel that there is no limit to their power to do whatever they want; and indeed they use their weapons against the man who gave them that power.'[40] This comment resembles Tacitus' sentiments on the civil war of 68-9; Dio indeed thought that the problem of the emperor's relationship with the army went back to the start of the principate. He dismissed Augustus' protestations about surrendering any of his power; and after a long speech attributed to Augustus in which the emperor depreciated autocracy, Dio goes straight on to report the establishment of special emoluments for the Praetorians. 'Therefore it is clear that he certainly was eager to establish a monarchy.'[41] Furthermore, elsewhere in this speech,[42] and in the one put into the mouth of Tiberius at the funeral of Augustus,[43] Dio frequently returns to the theme of the emperor's assoc-

---

[39] 75.2.3. For this interpretation of the passage, see Campbell, *JRS* 1978, 166, n. 90.

[40] *Loeb*, vol. ix, p. 470.

[41] 53.11.5. See Millar, *Cassius Dio*, 93.

[42] 53.4.2; cf. 4.3; 5.4; 8.1; 10.6.

[43] 56.39.1-40.

iation with the troops and the importance of strict discipline.[44]

Although Herodian, the other contemporary historical source of the Severan era, may not have been a senator, he shares the viewpoint of the upper classes.[45] Since he had lived through a period of violence and prolonged civil war, it is not surprising that he should pass severe judgement on the troops. His immediate experiences, or those of his sources, had convinced him that military anarchy was not far from the surface and that the soldiers were potentially disruptive, interested only in their own gain, and prepared to do anything for money.[46] Most of the instability and disorder could, in Herodian's view, be traced to the troops, especially the Praetorian Guard, and the ease with which they could be incited to rebel. Things that pleased everyone else did not please them; they resented well-ordered regimes that prevented them from following their usual practices of looting and violence against the civilian population.[47] Herodian also noted the wider implications of a virtually uncontrollable soldiery allied with disreputable leaders:

Then for the first time [after the murder of Pertinax] the character of the soldiers was corrupted and they learned to have a disgraceful and unbounded craving for money and they despised any feelings of respect for their emperors. Since no one took any action against the soldiers who had cold bloodedly murdered an emperor, or prevented the outrageous auction of the imperial power, this was a major reason for the disgraceful state of disobedience that was to persist in the years to come. The soldiers' increasing lust for money and disrespect for their leaders had culminated in the shedding of blood.[48]

Although Herodian is inaccurate in stating that the accession of Didius Julianus was the first time the soldiers were corrupted,[49] he has understood the ease with which the

[44] See in general, for Dio's political views, Millar, (n. 41), Chapter III.
[45] The best discussion of Herodian is that of C.R. Whittaker, *Loeb*, vol. 1 (1969), pp. ix ff.
[46] 2.6.10-11, 6.14; 5.4.1-2, 8.1-3; 6.7.10, 9.4 ff.; 8.7.3, 8.1 ff.
[47] 2.4.4-5; 5.1.
[48] 2.6.14; cf. 6.5: οὔτε προσῆλθον τῷ τείχει οὔτε ἀπρεπῆ καὶ ἐπονείδιστον χρήμασι κτήσασθαι τὴν ἀρχὴν ἠθέλησαν.
[49] Cf. his statement that Septimius Severus was the first to undermine discipline: 3.8.5.

empire could slip into military anarchy, especially when the army was suborned by bribes and flattery to commit crimes against authority. His mistake is understandable since the events of 193 were the most vivid example in recent years of the consequences of the political association between an autocrat and his army.[50]

Most of the upper classes will, like Tacitus and Dio,[51] have accepted the need for autocracy of some sort as the only way to achieve political stability. The army was an inevitable partner of this autocracy, but hopefully it might be unobtrusive if the delicate balance of the various elements in an emperor's regime could be preserved. This balance was most obviously undermined by military revolts. It was in fact no secret that emperors could be made outside Rome.[52] Everyone who had won power in the Republic by force of arms had done so by marching on Rome from outside — Sulla, Marius, Pompey, Caesar, and Octavian. It was the further demonstration of this truth by a successful military coup against an established emperor that was important. The *status quo*, the power of inertia, and inherited traditions of loyalty were strong elements of political stability. But whoever took the initiative and overthrew them demonstrated how fragile the power base of an autocracy could be, despite all the devices for cementing the army's loyalty. And the task of building this base up again and restoring respect and discipline was so much more difficult for future emperors.

2. MILITARY SANCTION OF THE EMPEROR'S RULE

It remains to consider what formal role, if any, soldiers played at the accession of emperors in more peaceful conditions. Mommsen's contention that every soldier had the right to make someone else emperor[1] is now generally discounted. He was presumably influenced by the fact that most

---

[50] Note the speech he invents for Severus on the disbanding of the Guard which had killed Pertinax — 2.13.5 ff.; cf. 2.10.4.

[51] For Tacitus, see Syme, *Tacitus*, 547 ff.; for Dio's views, see Millar, *Cassius Dio*, 74 ff.

[52] Tac., H 1.4.

[1] *Römisches Staatsrecht* (1877), II.II, 814.

emperors, whatever the circumstances of their accession, would normally first address the Praetorians or those legions accompanying them, and receive an acclamation.[2] For all practical purposes this recognition by the soldiers served to make a man emperor, before any discussion had taken place in the Senate. However, that the troops had the practical power to make a man emperor, by fighting for him or by promising to do so, does not mean that they had the legal right to create emperors; and it is highly unlikely that the acclamation was considered a legal justification of an emperor's position. Those who sought the purple must have recognized that they needed an expression of support from the soldiers, but they would never have thought in terms of the soldiers having a legal right to be asked for their support and to confer power. What is more, the fact that Ulpian in the third century could contend that an emperor held his *imperium* by virtue of a *lex* passed by the people,[3] indicates that when he came to define the legal basis of imperial power, he did not think in terms of military backing.

A papyrus letter from an emperor or usurper announcing benefits to the people of Alexandria is relevant to this discussion. It has been convincingly ascribed to Avidius Cassius on the occasion of his revolt against Marcus Aurelius in 175.[4] The author writes as follows: 'Having been elected emperor by the most noble soldiers, I shall auspiciously enter upon my rule among you.' It is possible that there is a distinction here between the proclamation by the troops and the assumption of supreme power.[5] However, it can be argued that the two phrases are rhetorically balanced, indicating that the general grant of favours to Alexandria will be tantamount to the writer's first official act as emperor. The phrase 'entering upon my rule' will then have no technical or constitutional significance for the assumption of imperial power.[6]

---

[2] See above, pp. 126-7. [3] *D* 1.4.1.

[4] A.K. Bowman, 'A Letter of Avidius Cassius?', *JRS* 60 (1970), 20.

[5] *Ibid.* 24-5. The letter reads: κεχειροτονη<μένος> μὲν αὐτοκράτωρ ὑπὸ τῶν γενναιοτάτ<ων> στρατιώτων 'επὶ δὲ τὴν ἀρχὴν παρ' <ὑμῖν> αἰσίως παρελευσόμενος.

[6] For this suggestion I wish to thank Dr. Z. Rubin, who gave me permission to consult his unpublished Oxford D. Phil. thesis, *Supernatural and Religious Sanction of the Emperor's Rule AD 193-217*, 77 ff.

This interpretation of the letter attributes more importance to the soldiers. They alone are cited by the writer as the justification for his power; it is notable that he is prepared to state so openly and effusively his absolute reliance on the troops. Although the letter serves to illustrate the practical power of the army in imperial politics, it does not show that soldiers had the right to nominate or create emperors, or that such a right was recognized by the provincials.[7] It merely shows that the writer had persuaded his soldiers (the idea of being elected by them is surely propaganda) to support him in a personal bid for power, and that allowed him, in the East at least, to exercise the functions of an emperor. The Alexandrians would normally support the person who had the greatest military force at his disposal, and it would matter little to them what the Senate and the people thought or what the legal rights of the situation were.

The man who was saluted by the troops was *de facto* emperor if he could enforce his claim with enough of the army, but this acclamation was only an informal indication of the acceptability of the contender for the purple. Because of the army's great practical power, it was expedient and necessary for the new emperor to obtain a demonstration of military support to strengthen his hand with the Senate and upper classes, who might at the outset doubt his capacity to rule and wonder if he had the whole-hearted support of all the army. Tacitus' description of the accession of Nero illustrates this procedure exactly: 'Nero was brought into the Praetorian camp, and when he had said a few suitable words and offered a donative on the scale of his father's generosity, he was hailed as *imperator*. The decree of the Senate followed the decision of the soldiers, and there was no hesitation in the provinces.'[8] When Nero presented himself to the Praetorians as prospective emperor, they yelled their approval in the form of a salutation, and this was informally taken as an indication that he would be emperor. Later in the Senate, Nero could speak of the 'auctoritas patrum' and

---

[7] This was suggested by Rubin.

[8] *A* 12.69: 'Inlatusque castris Nero et congruentia tempori praefatus, promisso donativo ad exemplum paternae largitionis, imperator consalutatur. Sententiam militum secuta patrum consulta, nec dubitatum est apud provincias.'

the 'consensus militum', which implies that the positive agreement of the soldiers was vital, but also that the influence and formal backing of the Senate were not negligible factors.[9] But the role played by the Senate should not be elevated into any formal *right* to confer *imperium* and legitimacy, a right that was merely overriden by the practical power of the troops.[10] It is indeed true that emperors generally sought recognition from the Senate, and requested that it formally confer the prerogatives and powers that traditionally were the basis of autocracy in Rome. Gaius and Ulpian, however, state that the legal basis of the emperor's power was a *lex* passed by the people.[11] If the Senate had the legal right to confer the imperial powers, it is odd that the jurists do not mention the *senatus consultum,* since this too had the force of law.[12] It is likely that, as in the Vespasianic *lex de imperio,* the *senatus consultum* normally formed the basis of the *lex* without substantial change.[13] The formal *rogationes* would be submitted to the people some time later than the date of recognition by the Senate. Therefore in theoretical and constitutional terms the legitimacy of an emperor rested on conferment of powers by the people. However, since in practice the legitimating votes of the people were taken on the recommendation of the Senate, it is in a sense true that the vote of the Senate conferred legal recognition. But that is far from saying that the Senate had the *right* to confer legitimacy. There is no real sign that any ancient writer thought of the Senate as having any formal right or 'choice' in the creation of a new emperor. Tacitus everywhere emphasizes the role of individuals and the power of the

---

[9] *A* 13.4.

[10] This was suggested by O. Schulz, *Das Wesen des römischen Kaisertums der ersten zwei Jahrhunderte* (1916), 28 ff.; see also, *Vom Prinzipat zum Dominat* (1919); for a more balanced but still too legalistic view, see M. Hammond, 'The Transmission of the Powers of the Roman Emperor 68-235', *MAAR* 24 (1956), 63 ff.; and note the comments of B. Parsi, *Désignation et Investiture de L'Empereur Romain* (1963), 144-68.

[11] *D* 1.4.1; Gaius, *Inst.* 1.5.

[12] *Inst.* 1.4: 'Senatus consultum est, quod senatus iubet atque constituit idque legis vicem optinet, quamvis fuerit quaesitum.'

[13] See O'Brien-Moore, *RE* supp. vi col. 809; P.A. Brunt, *JRS* 67 (1979), 95; cf. n. 28 below.

soldiers; approaches to the Senate were based on mere expediency, and there is sarcasm in his description of the accession of Nero, with the careful juxtaposition of words.[14] He aims to show that any decision made by the Senate was consequent and dependent upon the approbation of the troops.

The behaviour of the Senate in 41 does not imply any senatorial rights in the bestowal of power. An emperor had been murdered and for the first time no obvious successor had been marked out. As the Senate was still the great council of state and there was no other constitutional body that could properly and effectively discuss the problem of how best to ensure the stable administration of the State in the crisis, the senators acted in an *ad hoc* fashion to safeguard the interests of their class; they were not claiming or defending any constitutional rights. While the Senate talked, the Praetorians accepted Claudius as the most likely member of the imperial family to which they had grown accustomed, to sustain their privileges and emoluments.[15] Claudius was then *de facto* emperor and there was nothing the Senate could do about it. This merely confirmed what had always been the case – the Senate was completely subject to external factors.

The *Historia Augusta* alleges that Hadrian wrote to the Senate apologizing because he had not given 'the decision concerning his power' ('de imperio suo iudicium') to it, but had been saluted at once because the State needed an emperor.[16] No confidence can be placed in this detail, which is likely to be part of the *Historia Augusta's* pro-senatorial bias. In any event the passage shows only that Hadrian made a show of conventional politeness to the Senate after his proclamation in the provinces.

Dio criticises Didius Julianus and the manner in which he first appeared in the Senate. He was surrounded by Praetorians complete with armour and standards, 'in order that, by terrifying us and the people, he might win our

[14] See n. 8.
[15] See Schulz (n. 10), 36, who finds constitutional significance in the behaviour of the Senate. For the events of 41, see above, p. 81.
[16] *Vit. Had.* 6.1 ff.

support'.[17] But this is surely hostile propaganda against Julianus and does not imply any constitutional principle that the Senate had a right to confer power. Again, Dio expresses anger because Macrinus assumed the imperial titles before they had been voted by the Senate.[18] This however merely reflects the usual senatorial prejudice that the dignity and the appearance of its participation in important affairs of the empire should be maintained. Dio's phraseology reveals the truth; it was 'fitting' or 'proper' for the Senate to vote titles and powers before an emperor used them, but it was not legally necessary. Indeed Macrinus' letter to the Senate had revealed a sure grasp of realities: 'I was well aware that you agreed with the soldiers, since I knew that I had benefited the state in many ways.' Nevertheless, it is important that senators did feel even at this date that an emperor should approach them for the formal grant of his titles and powers.

Herodian believed that Maximinus was a cruel tyrant who relied entirely upon the support of his army, which he regarded as a citadel where he could hide himself.[19] Eutropius commented: 'Maximinus was the first man from the body of the army to assume imperial power, and with the approval of the soldiers alone, since the authority of the Senate was not involved.'[20] Aurelius Victor stated that the senators considered it dangerous to resist a man supported by the army when they had no force at their disposal. That, however, could have been said of many earlier accessions, and Victor does make it clear that Maximinus was recognized by the Senate and had his powers voted by it.[21] This is confirmed by the entry of the emperor's name among the *Sodales Antoniniani* by decree of the Senate.[22] The fact that the emperor did not come to Rome is not an indication of

---

[17] 74.12.1; *Vit. Did. Jul.* 4.2; Herodian, 2.6.11 f.

[18] 78.16.2. ἐνέγραψεν δὲ ἐν τῇ ἐπιστολῇ Καίσαρά θ' ἑαυτὸν καὶ αὐτοκράτορα καὶ Σεουῆρον, προσθεὶς τῷ Μακρίνου ὀνόματι καὶ εὐσεβῆ καὶ εὐτυχῆ καὶ Αὔγουστον καὶ ἀνθύπατον, οὐκ ἀναμένων τι, ὡς εἰκὸς ἦν, παρ' ἡμῶν ψήφισμα.

[19] 7.1.2. Schulz used this and the other source material quoted below to argue that the reign of Maximinus was the first break with the concept that only the Senate had the right to confer legality on an emperor (p. 51).

[20] 9.1.

[21] 25.1.

[22] *CIL* VI, 2001; 2009; cf. G. Bersanetti, *Studi sull' Imperatore Massimo il Trace* (1965), 9 ff.; C.R. Whittaker, Herodian, *Loeb* vol. II, p. 151.

disdain for the Senate; he was involved in a major military campaign. Therefore there is no reason to think that the reign of Maximinus marked a break in the usual tradition by which the acclamation of the soldiers was automatically followed by the vote of the Senate.

When Gordian I and his supporters in Africa rose in revolt against Maximinus, the Senate showed remarkable courage and energy in stripping the emperor of his powers and titles and apparently declaring him a public enemy.[23] The Senate then proceeded to declare Gordian and his son emperors. It is unlikely that anyone worried about the legal basis for these actions; but it could presumably be argued that since the Senate and people did formally grant powers and titles, they could revoke them, on the grounds that Maximinus was an unnatural tyrant whose conduct had made all legal enactments and oaths of loyalty irrelevant.[24] This had happened in the case of Nero and Didius Julianus. But in 238 the action was much more striking because the man whom the Senate declared against was still in a strong position.

When Gordian and his son were killed by Capellianus, the legate of Numidia who was loyal to Maximinus, the Senate, being already committed, had to establish an emperor of its own choice, in the apparent absence of any other governor willing to resist Maximinus. In the event they chose two, Pupienus and Balbinus, from a short list of candidates, and by decree voted them all imperial powers and honours.[25] Subsequently the two emperors were forced by popular demonstration to have the title 'Caesar' voted to the son of Gordian's daughter. After the death of Maximinus he was to emerge as the soldiers' choice as emperor.[26] These events show not that the Senate had the right of conferring the imperial powers, merely that by 238 the avenues to the purple had widened considerably and the Senate was prepared to field its own candidates. But in the end success depended not on legal enactment but on military power, and the Senate as a body had no access to the regular armies.

[23] 7.7.2 ff.; see in general, P.W. Townend, *YCS* 14 (1955), 49.
[24] An inscription refers to the 'saevissima dominatio' of Maximinus — *AE* (1935), 164.
[25] 7.10.3 ff.   [26] 7.10.7; 8.8.2-8.

So Balbinus and Pupienus died at the hands of the soldiers who instead acclaimed Gordian III, and the Senate had to acquiesce.

The general picture that emerges is clear enough. It was customary to seek the support of the Senate, and because of the traditionally high reputation of that body as the supreme council of state, the importance of a good relationship with the upper classes, who set store by the concepts of legality and legitimacy, and the decline of the *comitia*, it was useful for the new ruler to have the Senate's formally expressed approval; this would help him persuade other army commanders that stable government was possible. It was politically expedient to claim that power was based on law, and technically the vote of the Senate approximated to a legal sanction to exercise power; this was important since it was the only constant factor in a situation where there were no formal criteria for designating a successor. It also made good sense for the new emperor to claim a large measure of support, and the Senate and people (through the *comitia*), it could be argued, represented a wide body of significant opinion. And so Otho, as he left to fight Vitellius, invoked the 'majesty of Rome and the approval of people and Senate'.[27]

Such emphasis on legality and widespread support concealed the helplessness of the Senate and the Roman people, but emperors could hope to get away with it. Civil war, however, brought the realities of the situation into a harsher light. It is well known that Vespasian placed his *dies imperii* on 1 July 69, the date on which he had been acclaimed by his soldiers, rather than the day somewhere between 20 December 69 and 1 January 70 when his powers were formally voted by the Senate. In effect he was emperor from the moment he had his army's support and was prepared to back up his intentions with force; the political niceties could be sorted out later.[28] The suggestion that

---

[27] Tac., *H* 1.90: 'maiestatem urbis et consensum populi ac senatus pro se attollens'.

[28] The last clause of the *Lex de Imperio* states: 'utique quae ante hanc legem rogatam acta gesta decreta imperata ab imperatore Caesare Vespasiano Aug[usto] iussu mandatuve eius a quoque sunt, ea perinde iusta rataq[ue] sint, ac si populi

Footnote 28 continued at foot of page 382

'an emperor did not become such until recognized by the Senate but that, once recognized, he could date his *imperium* from his salutation by the troops'[29] seems too legalistic. What would have happened if the Senate had refused to confer power on Vespasian? Would he have stopped being emperor? Of course it was unthinkable for the Senate to do such a thing, and so it was never tested. But, if the vote of the Senate was only a formality depending entirely on the instructions of an already proclaimed emperor backed by force, it seems irrelevant to talk of 'constitutional principle' or the 'rights' of the Senate. The vote of prerogatives and powers conferred legitimacy and recognition only in so far as the Senate did not have a free choice, and could not enforce its decision if the new emperor failed to persuade the other army commanders to accept him. It was more important for him to make his rule unchallengeable; for a lengthy incumbency would form a habit of obedience, and respect for the *status quo*. The concepts of legitimacy and legality in the Roman context belonged not to constitutional history, but to the façade built up by Augustus to make absolute monarchy more palatable; they had no real meaning except as propaganda for the victor.

3. WINNING SUPPORT

In Rome a man became emperor by his ability to master certain external factors. Augustus' propaganda suggested that no man or family had a right to rule the empire; his own pre-eminence was unique, to deal with a special situation. To have appointed a successor would have proclaimed the monarchical character of the government. Therefore from

Footnote 28 continued from page 381

plebisve iussu acta essent.' See in general P.A. Brunt, 'Lex de Imperio Vespasiani', *JRS* 67 (1977), 95 ff.; especially 106-7. The drafter of the bill presumably intended this omnibus clause to cover all possible legal loopholes in the period between Vespasian's acclamation and the formal vote of powers. It shows how Vespasian had been exercising all the functions of an emperor in that period. Brunt has suggested another interpretation of the clause: 'it could be held to mean that he had really been the legitimate Princeps from the very moment of his pronunciamento, and no disrespect for the constitutional rights of senate and people was involved' (p. 107).

[29] Hammond (n. 10), 77.

the start of the imperial period no formal criteria for legitimate succession were established, and there was rarely any settled dynastic policy. It was consequently all the more important for the man who sought the supreme authority to influence important men and groups. In this process the most powerful factor (apart from the use of force with all its attendant difficulties) was connection by birth with, or adoption by, the previous ruler or divine ancestors. The chosen heir of a ruling emperor would start from a position of strength, but he would still need to be accepted by the Praetorian Guard and enough army commanders to make it impossible for any other man of note to stand against him. In addition, he could hope that a reputation for service to the state in military and civil duties, his experience, wealth, status, demeanour, and upbringing would be influential with both the troops and the upper classes. The soldiers, however, must have absorbed much of a new emperor's attention. He would like to know their political views and what they expected of him.

The ordinary soldiers, or even the soldiers and the centurions together, had neither common political aims nor the experience and ability to realize them by concerted action. There was almost a total lack of political consciousness among the troops. The price of their political support was money and rewards of various kinds, not political change or any formal share in power.[1] They naturally wanted to see the empire ruled by a man who needed their support and who recognized the payment of their emoluments as an obligation upon him. It little mattered whether the emperor was a Nero or a Marcus Aurelius in his treatment of his government of the state; the soldiers would support him loyally. There is no force in the argument that in the first two centuries the troops had a strong sense of loyalty to the State and resented 'incompetent' emperors like Nero or Commodus.[2] Nero ruled for fourteen years before any disloyalty manifested itself, and even then the soldiers needed

---

[1] For the attitude of Caesar's veterans, see in general. H. Botermann, *Die Soldaten und die römische Politik von Caesar's Tod bis zur Begrundung des zweiten Triumvirats* (1968).

[2] As suggested by M. Hammond, *The Antonine Monarchy* (1959), 168 ff.

to be prompted by prominent men. When the army of Upper Germany threw off its allegiance to Galba in January 69, it left the choice of a new emperor to the Senate and people. This was merely to create a good impression, as Tacitus perceived, 'so that the rebellion would be more agreeably received'.[3] And when they subsequently swore loyalty to 'senatus ac populus', that was not an act of devotion to the Roman state; it was a specious attempt to cover their real object — support for Vitellius in his bid for power.[4] Indeed no good motive can be discerned in the behaviour of the troops in 68-9.[5]

Early in the reign of Nerva the Praetorian Guard successfully demanded the execution of the murderers of Domitian. But this demand did not come about because of a respect for law and order. The troops probably thought that their interests were threatened by this change of emperor and attempted to reassert themselves and protect their privileges. Under the Antonine monarchy the only recorded intervention of the troops in the affairs of the state was an appeal to Marcus for a donative after a victory in the northern wars.[6] Some troops, however, were prepared to support Avidius Cassius against their emperor. Commodus, despite his 'excessive' behaviour, ruled for twelve years, and after his murder Pertinax was compelled to lie to the loyal Praetorians that he had died accidentally.[7] The soldiers who marched to Rome from Britain apparently wished merely to complain about their own conditions, or warn the emperor about a plot by Perennis.[8] In 193 the Guard overthrew Pertinax because his donative was not generous enough and because he enforced discipline.[9] It is true that the manner of Didius Julianus' accession cast doubt on his ability to govern effectively and provoked a hostile reaction from two senators in provincial commands, who despised him and thought that they could exploit the mood of the troops, no doubt

---

[3] *H* 1.12.
[4] 1.55-7.
[5] 1.51; 80; 2.6; 80. See above, pp. 365ff.
[6] Dio, 71.3.3.
[7] Herod., 2.2.5 f.
[8] See above, p. 193, n. 67.
[9] Dio, 74.8.

perplexed by the rapid demise of two emperors. But the soldiers who supported Septimius Severus against Didius Julianus hardly shared this concern at the way he had aquired power or the way in which the empire was being governed, however much Severan propaganda may have suggested this. They were no doubt won over by his offer of rewards consequent upon victory, and probably by a promise of service in the Praetorian Guard.[10] At the first meeting of the Senate in Rome the troops did intervene, but with a demand for an immediate donative.[11]

Herodian claims that the soldiers were offended by Macrinus' effeminate and un-Roman habits and therefore acquiesced in his overthrow.[12] It is true that the soldiers might be resentful if Macrinus lived in a luxurious fashion while they laboured during the campaign. But most of their resentment came from the emperor's attempts to reduce pay and benefits;[13] and they did accept Elagabalus, who dressed and behaved outlandishly.[14] Herodian indeed alleged that it was the troops' disgust at the peculiar antics of Elagabalus that led them to support Severus Alexander. There may be something in this, but he also stressed the importance of bribing the army, money being the most effective inducement for the men.[15] Severus Alexander was the first emperor to be overthrown by purely military discontent on a wide scale, and this was based partly on his poor showing in the military duties of the emperor's role. But the tumultuous interference of the troops in various aspects of the government in his reign shows only the indiscipline of a truculent soldiery.[16]

It was one of the advantages of an emperor's association with the army that it provided powerful support with no corresponding demands for political concessions, and with few conditions or restrictions in his conduct of the state's affairs. Mutinous and discontented soldiers could disrupt the

[10] See above, p. 30.
[11] Dio, 46.46.7.
[12] 5.2.4.
[13] Dio, 78.9.2.
[14] Herodian, 5.5.5.
[15] 5.4.2.
[16] See above, pp. 196–7.

defences of the empire, but they could not directly threaten the fabric of the state or society, and there is no evidence that they used their privileged position to help the class from which they had come.[17]

It remains true that an emperor's personality and conduct could have some effect on the troops, especially if, as in the case of Macrinus, they could actually see him living luxuriously on campaign and not seeming to care about their hardships. It is likely that emperors who identified themselves with their soldiers, and displayed obvious concern for them, could gain affection and respect. But generally, most soldiers would see little of their emperor during his reign and would perhaps learn of his demeanour from reports or gossip. And at the accession of an emperor, nothing could be known about how he intended to conduct himself. Possibly, then, a man's previous record or reputation would weigh heavily with the army. Trajan may have seemed impressive with his long service as a military tribune and his tenure of the higher military commands. But did the average soldier want a great warrior who might fight many campaigns and produce booty and glory, but at much greater risk to the army, or a less ambitious ruler who preserved peace and stability and did not exercise the troops too much? Indeed was there any common feeling among the rank and file? It is perhaps safe to say that if the soldiers shared a general opinion, they will have supported a man of standing, a man who looked as if he could preserve his regime, a man who was strong enough to avoid civil conflict with all the attendant dangers of war against other Roman troops, and a man who could guarantee all their emoluments and privileges. In this sense the prospective emperor's previous reputation and record, in so far as it could be made known to them, could have been important. But immediate motives and self-interest ultimately dictated what the troops did. It was so much the better if an emperor visited his men, showed respect for them, and seemed to identify with his army. This behaviour, if properly managed, could increase his support and cement loyalty, though of itself it could not guarantee such loyalty.

[17] For this idea see Rostovtzeff, *SEHRE*[2], Chapter IX.

On the other hand, in certain circumstances, thoughtless or arrogantly ostentatious conduct by an emperor in front of his soldiers could lose him support. The close proximity of an emperor to his soldiers over a longer period of time, or the advent of persistent warfare, will certainly have increased the importance of his military reputation with the troops.

The soldiers must also have been influenced by the attitude of their immediate commanders, who were generally senators, and whose acquiescence the new emperor had to win. In some ways this was just as difficult as dealing with the army. The apparent approval of the Senate may have helped to persuade the commanders. But even if most senators accepted autocracy as inevitable, in a body of some six hundred members opinions will have been multifarious; some will have maintained high principles, others were careerists, still more will have hoped for a quiet life and relapsed into torpor, some were perhaps plain frightened. What kind of emperor could win the general support and co-operation of the upper classes?

Emperors were not slow to exploit the prestige to be gained from military honours (p.120). Nevertheless, those men who appear in the senatorial sources as 'good' or 'model' emperors owe this laudation to a variety of achievements, and certainly not just to their ability in the military arts. It is clear that in the first century Augustus stood as the model to which conscientious emperors aspired. Dio's summary of the emperor's character is very favourable, emphasizing the benefits to the empire.[18] His successors honoured his achievement and his memory. A private festival begun in Augustus' honour by Livia was carried on by emperors even down to Dio's time.[19] The revered name 'Augustus' was retained in the nomenclature of all emperors. The ritual acclamation of the Roman Senate ran: 'May you be even more fortunate than Augustus, and even better than Trajan.'[20] In Dio's view, the praise of Augustus was based on his bringing of peace and stability, his courteous conduct of the government, and his treatment of the Senate. According to Tacitus, one of the main reasons for Augustus'

[18] 56.43–45.3.   [19] 56.46.5.   [20] Eutrop. 8.5.3.

success was that he charmed everyone with the 'sweetness of peace'.[21] And those who took a favourable view of the emperor thought that his greatest achievement was the creation of a system of ordered government. His equitable administration of the provinces, the beautification of Rome, the maintenance of the law, and the minimum use of force were also remembered. In all this the military victories of Augustus were sound and genuine, if not spectacular. 'The empire was fenced in by the Ocean or distant rivers; the legions, the provinces, the fleets were all connected together.'[22] This efficient military activity played a part in establishing the reputation of Augustus, but the emperor's *virtus* embraced all his qualities and achievements.

By the third century the canon of ideal emperors included Trajan, Antoninus Pius, and Marcus Aurelius.[23] Trajan was a great soldier and later sources like the *Historia Augusta* and Eutropius are much influenced by his military achievements.[24] But Trajan was admired for other qualities in addition to military excellence. The senatorial acclamation quoted above implies qualities of character, not military prowess. And the title 'Optimus Princeps' was intended to convey praise of the emperor's general demeanour and conduct. Indeed Trajan prided himself above all on this title because it referred to his character rather than his abilities as a commander.[25] Dio's source recognized Trajan's courage and military excellence, but the greatest praise was reserved for his justice and his dignified and courteous conduct towards the Senate, because of which he was 'well loved by everyone'.[26]

Antoninus Pius did not leave Italy during his reign and could hardly be described as a military figure; no major wars were fought during his reign, although there was a forward push through the Scottish lowlands and the Antonine wall was established. His outstanding reputation was due to his

---

[21] *A* 1.2.
[22] 1.9. See further below, n. 48.
[23] R. Syme, *Emperors and Biography* (1971), 93 ff.
[24] *Ibid.*
[25] Dio, 68.23.2.
[26] 68.6–7. Cf. Aurelius Victor, 13.3 ff.; *Epitome* 13.1 ff.

high moral character, his moderation, his desire to reward
merit, and his excellent relationship with the Senate.[27] In
fact it was recorded as one of his virtues that he fought no
war, but intimidated the enemy by his reputation.[28]

Marcus spent a large part of his reign fighting crucial wars
and he was respected for his determination to meet his
military responsibilities despite his weak health, and for the
qualities he displayed on campaign.[29] But this was not the
most important reason for his fame. His character, justice,
consistency, and conduct towards the Senate and the government of the empire were among the main reasons for the outstanding respect in which he was held. 'He not only possessed
all the other virtues, but also was a better ruler than anyone
else who had ever been emperor.'[30]

In the third century Severus Alexander became an
exemplar of what an emperor should be. The *Historia
Augusta* produces a picture of a great military man and a
strict disciplinarian. This is completely false.[31] The favourable account of Alexander in Herodian surely derives from
the fact that the thirteen years of relatively consistent
government under Alexander, despite his inability to control
the army, must have seemed like a golden age to senators
and the rest of the upper classes in contrast to the years of
violence and anarchy which followed. Furthermore,
Alexander treated the Senate kindly and tried to give the
impression that it was involved in the government of the
empire.

No one would have disputed that military *virtus* was
indispensable and that defence of the empire was one of the
chief concerns of every ruler. Senators would certainly
expect that an emperor should show himself capable in these
requirements or at least appoint men competent to deal with
them. The fictitious picture of Alexander in the *Historia
Augusta* emphasizes this point. However, although military
prowess could win an emperor respect, it seems that by

---

[27] Victor, 15.1 ff.; *Epit.* 15.1 ff.; Marcus Aurelius, *Meditations* 1.16.
[28] Victor, 15.5; *Epit.* 15.3.
[29] Dio, 71.36.3; *Vit. M. Ant Phil.* 8.1 ff.; 10.
[30] Dio, 71.34.2; cf. Herod. 1.2.1.
[31] Syme, *Emperors and Biography*, 98 ff.

itself it would not suffice to win the affection of senators.[32]
Although an incompetent ruler who allowed Roman military
strength to be undermined would not win favour, an emperor
did not have to do anything of note militarily or show himself a great commander, in order to enter the canon of 'good'
emperors, as the example of Antoninus Pius shows. On the
other hand, several emperors who looked after the army carefully, saw to the empire's defence competently, or indeed
annexed new territory, could not find favour because they
had offended the senatorial class in some way and were disliked on that account.

In Rome there was no primacy of the military arts and
emperors could not necessarily win support by assuming the
role of the great military man. It is worth pointing out that
it was comapratively rare for a Roman emperor to use the
army in a manner dictated more by his personal motives than
by strategic needs or hostile action by the enemy. Augustus
perhaps allowed the upper classes to think that he was more
belligerent than he really intended to be. At any rate, he
faced special problems in establishing the extent and defence
of an empire torn apart by civil war. The campaigns conducted by Domitian in Germany and Dacia, by Trajan in
Dacia, by Marcus Aurelius, by Septimius Severus in Britain,
by Caracalla in Germany and on the Danube, by Severus
Alexander, and by Maximinus, can all be plausibly explained
on the grounds of the strategic and security requirements of
the empire.[33]

Claudius' invasion of Britain, however, was probably
intended primarily to enhance his prestige for political
reasons. Nero was said to be planning an expedition to the
Caucasus just before his death. The strategic motive was

[32] Note that Pliny devotes about eight sections of the *Panegyric* to Trajan
the soldier, the majority of the speech to his general character and conduct.

[33] For Augustus, see n. 48. For Domitian's campaigns, Syme, *CAH* XI (1936),
168 ff., is still fundamental, though some may dispute the success achieved by
the emperor. For a full bibliography, cf. A. Garzetti, *From Tiberius to the
Antonines* (1974), 655 ff. And see above, p. 142, n. 101. For Trajan's Dacian
wars, see Garzetti, 676–8. Marcus – Dio, 71.36.3; Septimius Severus – A.R.
Birley, *Septimius Severus* (1971), 244 ff.; Caracalla – see Whittaker, Herodian
(*Loeb*) I, pp. 409; 414; Severus Alexander – Herodian, 6.2.1 ff.; 6.7.2 ff.;
7.2.1 ff.

perhaps to prevent raids by tribes like the Sarmatians and Alani. But the emperor had raised a new legion of specially chosen Italian recruits all at least six feet tall, and he called it 'Alexander's Phalanx'.[34] He was apparently more interested in the romantic aspects of a victorious campaign in the East like that of Alexander.

Furthermore, the best explanation for Trajan's Parthian war still seems to be a 'desire for glory', as suggested by Dio.[35] The Parthians were prepared to negotiate in the usual way about Armenian sovereignty,[36] and although they could cause sporadic trouble to the governors of Syria and Cappadocia, they were not a serious threat to Roman control of the Eastern provinces at this time. The acceptable and defensible frontiers established by the Flavians in the East could provide no excuse for the annexation of Armenia or the establishment of Mesopotamia as a new province. Punitive expeditions or the sacking of Ctesiphon were unlikely to be effective in view of the loose organization of the Parthian empire and its ability to recover quickly. It is possible that Trajan, whose political position was unchallenged and who had a good relationship with the Senate, liked the role of the great conqueror and had been inspired by the glory of the conquest of Dacia. Parthia, a traditional if relatively quiescent enemy of Rome, was a suitable area in which to acquire renown among the battlefields of Alexander.[37]

Dio also ascribes the first Parthian war of Septimius Severus, which saw the creation of the new province of

[34] Suet., *Ner.* 19.2. B.H. Warmington, *Suetonius: Nero* (1977), 77-8, doubts that Nero was much interested in Alexander. See too *Nero: Reality and Legend* (1969), 98-9.

[35] The controversy carried on by J. Guey, *Essai sur la Guerre Parthique de Trajan (114-117)* (1937), F.A. Lepper, *Trajan's Parthian War* (1948), and Henderson, *JRS* 39 (1949), 121, is still largely unresolved. See Garzetti (n. 33) 678-81 for a bibliography. Both the arguments for an economic motive and for 'frontier rectification' depend to some extent on the chronology, which cannot be proved.

[36] Dio, 68.17.2.

[37] For the *imitatio Alexandri* in Roman thought, see Syme, *Tacitus*, App. 72; cf. A. Bruhl, 'Le Souvenir d'Alexandre le Grand et les Romains' *MEFR* 47-8 (1930-1), 202. Syme himself depreciates the idea of the *imitatio* in the case of Trajan.

Mesopotamia, to a 'desire for glory'.[38] The enemy were
willing to negotiate and there were valid strategical objections
to the addition of a new province. The war probably owed
more to political motives, namely to direct attention away
from the defeat of Niger in civil strife to a war against
traditional enemies of the Roman state.[39] The immediate
pretext for the second war was a Parthian invasion of
Mesopotamia,[40] and it could be argued that if Mesopotamia
was to be retained, a convincing demonstration of Roman
power was necessary. But the full-scale invasion of Parthia,
and the fact that Ctesiphon was stormed precisely on the
hundredth anniversary of Trajan's accession, suggest that
military glory was the main objective.[41] This would also
counterbalance the opprobrium created by the violent
campaign against Albinus and the slaughter of Roman
soldiers to satisfy the ambition of powerful men. In addition,
Severus, like Trajan, was apparently influenced by the reputation of Alexander. He visited the king's tomb and ordered
that it should be locked up so that no one should see his
body in future.[42]

For his travels in the East Caracalla chose a route modelled
on that of Alexander;[43] he also offered to marry the
daughter of the Parthian king, used cups and weapons
supposed to have belonged to Alexander, and enrolled a
phalanx of Macedonians.[44] It seems that his vivid imagination
and desire to be seen as the great soldier had caused him to
seek military glory against Rome's old enemy, conveniently
in an area where Alexander had conducted some of his
campaigns.

It is of some significance for the desire of several emperors
to acquire military glory, and for the resilience of the
concept of military excellence in Roman society, that there
were six wars in 120 years after AD 114 against Rome's
traditional enemy in the East. Of these campaigns, only that

[38] 75.1.1.
[39] See A.R. Birley (n. 33), 181-2.
[40] 75.9.1.
[41] Birley, op. cit., 202 ff.
[42] 75.13.2.
[43] B.M. Levick, 'Caracalla's Path', *Hommages à M. Renard* (1969), 426.
[44] Dio, 78.1.1; Herod., 4.8.2.

of Lucius Verus in 162 and that of Severus Alexander against the more dangerous Persians, who had replaced the Parthians as the dominant racial group, were, so far as we can tell, fully justified by strategic or military requirements.[45] Was Parthia seen as an area where the laurels of victory could be earned without too much risk or expense to the empire? Nevertheless, on a wider view, from the close of Augustus' reign up to 238 only five campaigns can be ascribed in any sense to a gratuitous exercise of the imperial will which did not necessarily put the interests of the empire first; although client kingdoms came under Roman control and some territory was added to existing provinces, only three emperors added a new province to Rome's dominions by major military action.[46] On the whole emperors used the army responsibly and carefully and did not exploit the fact that it was virtually a private mercenary force. Furthermore, the army was rarely vaunted for its own sake in imperial propaganda; the security and glory of the empire of the Senate and Roman people, enhanced by the intelligent direction of its ruler, are the dominant themes.[47]

The restraint of emperors in the use of the army is not surprising. Although, as Strabo said of Augustus, the ruler was 'lord of war and peace', and although he could himself decide questions of strategy, foreign policy, the annexation of territory, and the organization and use of the army, he would in practice consult his advisers and confidants, who were drawn mainly from the upper classes. And so the emperor would tend himself to limit his absolute power according to his willingness to accept the traditions, prejudices, and opinions of men of note, whose advice and support he needed and from whom the military commanders, who helped to execute decisions, were selected. Once again it was a delicate balance; he needed to win and maintain the good will and support of public opinion and his commanders; he

[45] In 162 Vologaeses, the Parthian king, had entered Armenia and placed Pacorus, a Parthian prince of the royal house, on the throne. Severianus, the governor of Cappadocia, was subsequently defeated and killed by the Parthians with the loss of two legions. Roman prestige, and her ability to impose diplomatic solutions on the basis of her known strength, required decisive action.

[46] Claudius, Trajan, and Septimius Severus.

[47] See above, pp. 133ff.

needed to build up a rapport with his troops, and that could involve the establishment of a suitable military reputation; in any event he had to show himself competent in the military aspect of his role, but at the same time not neglect his civil and other responsibilities. And when policies went wrong and embarrassing losses occurred, it was the man with supreme authority and responsibility who took the blame, not his subordinates.

It is plausible to suggest that emperors were to some extent influenced by senatorial opinion about Rome and her relations with outside powers, not least because emperors in general themselves shared the feelings of the upper classes. It was doubtless a difficult task to ascertain what the main body of senators thought on particular occasions. Of the consular governors, some perhaps wanted the prestige of a mighty command without the dangers of fighting a war; others may have genuinely desired a great military reputation and so favoured the forward march of Roman arms.

In fact it is unclear what attitude the Romans after Augustus had to the expansion of their power abroad.[48] At the most basic level two hypotheses can be put forward. Firstly, senators believed in world conquest; this might take place by degrees and with due caution, or indeed only on just pretexts. The handbook of Roman history written by L. Annaeus Florus in the second century AD may be taken to express some of the conventional ideas likely to be familiar to an upper-class audience. Florus displays an intense contempt for foreign peoples;[49] anyone who dared to oppose Rome was clearly an incorrigible savage with no understanding of the benefits of the Roman peace. He complains that after the defeat of Varus in AD 9 Roman power, which an ocean had not stopped, should come to a halt on the

[48] For the attitude of contemporaries to Augustus, see P.A. Brunt, review of Meyer, *Die Aussenpolitik des Augustus und die Augusteische Dichtung* (1961) in *JRS* 53 (1963), 170; C.M. Wells, *The German Policy of Augustus* (1972). Whatever Augustus' ultimate intentions were — world conquest or limited offensives for strategic or economic objectives — for political reasons he would want to be seen as something more, militarily, than the mere victor in a civil war. It is relevant that upper-class opinion needed to be stirred up to the idea of widespread conquest (Brunt, 171).

[49] 2.21.12; 27.17; 30.27.

Rhine.[50] New conquests could be defended simply on the grounds that they brought more glory to the empire.[51] The empire was like the human life-cycle; youth and energetic maturity had gone and the sluggishness of old age prevailed, the 'inertia Caesarum'. Then, under Trajan, the empire flexed its muscles and beyond all expectation new vigour supervened.[52] Yet, despite his belligerent tone, Florus was prepared to see nations remain outside the empire; wars could strain the empire's resources, and caution was better than the disgraceful surrender of a province.[53] But these people outside the empire should revere Rome and the Roman people, 'conqueror of the nations'.[54]

Secondly, there was the argument that the empire should be kept inside reasonable limits that were not beyond its strength to conquer, hold, and administer.[55] This would involve the defence of Roman territory and interests, and might include limited offensive wars with specific objectives and with *iustae causae*. Pliny seems to espouse this view in his *Panegyric*. He rejoices that the barbarians go in fear of Rome, offer hostages, and beg and supplicate 'in line with the majesty of Roman power'.[56] He applauds Trajan's moderation in not beginning hostilities; it is a sign of true glory if an enemy's obedience is so great that no one needs to be conquered. But any barbarian who displayed insolence or wildness and earned Trajan's just anger will experience the full force of the emperor's *virtus*.[57] Pliny was presumably adapting what he says to suit Trajan's activities at the time;[58] but he surely intended his comments to be consistent with accepted ideas and policy on foreign relations.

[50] 2.30.39; cf. 30.27.
[51] 1.47.4–5.
[52] 1.Introd.5–8.
[53] 2.30.21.
[54] 2.34.61.
[55] Augustus' final advice to Tiberius — Tac., *A* 1.11.
[56] 12.1 ff.
[57] 16.1; 5.
[58] Pliny delivered the speech in 100, but edited it afterwards for publication. If it was published after 102 and the start of the Dacian wars, we might expect more explicit references to the emperor's military prowess and warlike policy. Perhaps Pliny knew Trajan's military background and that he had visited the northern frontiers, but had taken no decisive action. See Sherwin-White, *Letters of Pliny*, 250 f.

Tacitus seems to approve of energetic commanders and the advance of Roman arms;[59] he adverts to the deleterious consequences of long peace, which in itself could be dishonourable.[60] In a moment of sadness the historian is moved to lament the poverty of his theme; in the old days Rome was on the move and history was worth writing; but for the historian of the early empire, torpid and uninterrupted peace prevailed, and an emperor (Tiberius) indifferent to expansion. Yet at the same time Tacitus accepts that negotiation and even trickery might be necessary, and as effective as war in securing Roman interests.[61] And he gives considerable weight to Tiberius' statement of his preference for diplomacy rather than force in dealing with the Germans.[62] He also approves of the negotiations that ended the dispute with Parthia in Nero's reign.[63] These few hints suggest that Tacitus thought that diplomacy and negotiation were acceptable as long as they were based on Roman strength and the threat of offensive action. Nowhere does he say, except perhaps in one rhetorical passage, that Rome's policy should be expansion and conflict.

Although Suetonius rarely reveals any of his own views in his imperial biographies, a few scattered comments indicate recognition that some expeditions were essential, but disapproval of others carried on at the imperial whim for no obvious strategic reason.[64] Suetonius, or his source, apparently represents a view that depreciated further expansion of the empire and unnecessary campaigns for imperial glory; while the empire should be preserved from insult, there was much to be said for moderation and even retrenchment.[65]

---

[59] In his review of the governors of Britain, he concentrates on their enthusiasm for military affairs and their efforts to extend the province (*Ag.* 14–17; cf. 18). Those advisers of Agricola who urged a cautious strategy get little respect (25.3; 27.2). In the *Annals* it is possible that the campaigns of Domitius Corbulo have an over-generous allotment of space (R. Syme, *Tacitus*, 494 ff.).

[60] *A* 15.25.

[61] *A* 4.32; negotiation — *A* 12.48.

[62] 2.26.   [63] 15.29–31.   [64] *Dom.* 6.

[65] *Iul.* 24.3 (Caesar never let slip any pretext for war even if it were 'iniustum' or 'periculosum'); *Iul.* 25 (there is no praise for Caesar's activities in Gaul; the tone is factual and neutral); *Iul.* 47 (he depreciates Caesar's motives in invading

Footnote 65 continued at foot of page 397

Cassius Dio seems uniformly hostile to campaigns that involved the extension of the empire.[66] He comments bitterly on Severus' campaigns in the East in 195. The new conquests, he claims, cost far more to maintain than they yielded in return, and were a constant source of instability since they brought the Romans into contact with people who were neighbours of the Parthians. Perhaps political hostility has coloured Dio's view. But the objections are reasoned and convincing; they may represent an accepted alternative view, that is, the avoidance of expensive new provinces with fresh obligations. Dio is also strongly critical of the British campaign launched by Severus. The cost was heavy in both money and men, and, as Dio implies, the British were not worth conquering.[67] Finally, the campaigns of Caracalla had no discernible purpose beyond the indulgence of the emperor's whim.[68] Nevertheless Dio is adamant that the frontiers must be vigilantly guarded, and he has no criticism for the long wars waged by Marcus Aurelius, which could be seen as essential for the preservation of the empire.[69]

It can be conjectured that many of the upper classes, while paying lip service to the idea of world conquest, preferred to see the *status quo* honourably maintained and peace secured by diplomacy, provided that it was based on Roman strength. Slights to the empire's majesty could be dealt with by limited, punitive expeditions. If this was a prevailing opinion, then an emperor who sought to win widespread support would have to consider it. He could, of course, hope to work

---

Footnote 65 continued from page 396

Britain); *Aug.* 20 ff. (He devotes little time to the conquests of Augustus); *Aug.* 21.2 (Augustus is vigorously commended because he allegedly did not make war on any nation without due cause, and for his lack of desire to expand the empire or increase his own glory); *Cal.* 43 (Suetonius is sarcastic at Gaius' military posturing); *Cl.*17 (he criticizes the motives for the invasion of Britain); *Ner.* 18 (he says that Nero had no desire to expand the empire and even thought of withdrawing the troops from Britain; this is registered among the emperor's good acts). The criticism of Tiberius at 37.4 and the praise of Germanicus' victories (52.2) may reflect political propaganda against Tiberius.

[66] 67.4.1 (Domitian); 68.7.5; 33.1 (Trajan); 75.3.3; 76.13.2; 78.1.1 (the Severi). See Millar, *Cassius Dio*, 142–3.

[67] 75.3.2 ff; 76.11.2; 12.1; 13.2.

[68] 78.1.1.

[69] 71.36.2 ff.

on public opinion and convince it that another policy was necessary.[70]

An emperor would also have to bear in mind that military incompetence, real or imagined, could be a useful weapon of political propaganda against him. To mock the military activities of the man with supreme authority, and to criticize his celebrations of supposedly genuine military success, could be tantamount to doubting his general capacity for the burdens of empire. It is well known how a hostile senatorial tradition has held up to criticism and ridicule the achievements of Tiberius, Claudius, and Domitian in military and foreign policy.[71] The judgement of the senators is suspect. Were they influenced too much by the failure of these emperors to find an equitable relationship with the Senate? From this came sullen disapproval of whatever they did; a military set-back or grandiose posturing as the military man were easy targets.

This theme is further illustrated in the attitudes of senators to Trajan and Hadrian. Trajan was popular with the upper classes for his general conduct; he also brought expansion and military glory. Hadrian had an ambiguous reputation (the execution of four consulars cast a shadow) and did not continue Trajan's belligerent policy. Yet the senatorial tradition on the two men was by no means clear cut. Dio praises Trajan for his bravery, but his comments on the conquests are very guarded, implying that an emperor who 'loved war' was dangerous.[72] Elsewhere Trajan's policy comes in for more open criticism: Dio highlights his ultimate failure in the Parthian war by juxtaposing notice of the emperor's grandiloquent despatches to the Senate with the sarcastic comment that he could not even hold the territory he had captured.[73]

---

[70] For example, after the invasion of Britain, if the province were not to be surrendered, it was prudent to seek the most defensible frontiers on the island. The forward policy of the Flavians in Britain, which is not paralleled elsewhere, is therefore perfectly explicable in terms other than the glorious expansion of Roman power.

[71] Tac., *A* 4.32; 6.31 (Tiberius); 13.6 (Claudius); cf. Suet., *Cl.* 17.1ff; Dio, 60.23.1. Domitian — Tac., *Ag.* 39.1; *Ger.* 37.6; Plin., *Pan.* 16; 11.4; Dio, 67.4.1; 3.5 (The strange story that Domitian repented of his pay increase and reduced the number of soldiers in the army).

[72] 68.6.3; cf. 7.5.

[73] 29.1.

Trajan's vaunting claims may have displeased senators, Dio emphasizes strongly the loss of all the new acquisitions in the East, the massacre of garrisons, the destruction in the provinces and the fact that all the toils and dangers endured were for nothing.[74]

By contrast it was a specific point of praise for Hadrian that he provoked no wars and ended those in progress.[75] He imposed strict discipline and training on the legions; and foreign nations, fearing his preparedness and the toughness of the Roman forces, stood in fear of him.[76] This may represent a view among senators in Hadrian's day, and it has been suggested that Tacitus also expresses approval of Hadrian's policy, through a parody, concealed in his account of Corbulo, of the campaigns of Trajan.[77] This cannot be proved, but some of Tacitus' comments elsewhere in the *Annals* suggest that he would not have been out of sympathy with what Hadrian did.[78]

Cornelius Fronto is a dissenting voice. He comments sourly that Hadrian preferred to give up rather than 'retain by force' the provinces won by Trajan, and alleges that he actually surrendered Dacia, a scandalous falsehood repeated in the hostile Eutropius.[79] Fronto's argument is that Hadrian's devotion to peace diverted him from necessary and justifiable military actions. This may echo a contemporary debate on the respective value of the policies adopted by Trajan and Hadrian. Were Trajan's conquests really justified? Did the policy of Hadrian safeguard the welfare of the empire and Roman honour, or was it an excuse for doing nothing? Hadrian's boast (if correctly quoted by the *Epitome*), 'I have achieved more by peace than others by war',[80] may be his defence of his policy. From the evidence available, it appears that although there was little open criticism of

---

[74] 29.4-33.1.

[75] General praise for Hadrian — 69.23.2; cf. 5.1; 7.1; 69.2.5 — Dio seems to ascribe the criticism of the execution of the four consulars to others, and disassociates himself from it. Praise for ending wars in progress — 69.5.1.

[76] 9.4-5.

[77] Syme, *Tacitus*, 494 ff.

[78] See above, p. 396.

[79] Haines (*Loeb*) II, p. 206; Syme, *Tacitus*, 489; *JRS* 36 (1946), 164. Eutropius, 8.6.2.

[80] 4.10 'plus se otio adeptum quam armis ceteros'.

Trajan, many senators welcomed the less exciting, but more stable and sound policies of Hadrian, who maintained the empire's military strength at a peak. Trajan's reign had been glorious for a time, and no one could deny him praise for his *virtus*. But he made a fatal mistake: he lost. Chaos, instability in the eastern provinces, vast loss of money and life, and the humiliation of the Roman name ensued.[81] It is indeed interesting that the criticism of this fiasco was less openly expressed than it might have been and did not dim the splendour of Trajan's memory in general for future generations. In this case an emperor's undoubted popularity with the senatorial class has served to disarm some of the hostility and ridicule which might otherwise have occurred after such a serious set-back.

The absolutism of the Roman emperor was hedged in by many conventions and limitations, if he chose to respect the ideals of the class from which he came. The army was a source of strength and comfort to the holder of the supreme power. It was also an anxiety,[82] and he was not often free to use it entirely as he wished. The soldiers could never be taken for granted, no matter how safe the ruler felt he was. Generalizations, however, are difficult in the history of the emperors since individual character and inclinations prevail over policies. Nothing could stop Trajan leading the Roman legions to disaster in Parthia if it suited him, nor Septimius Severus from expending more Roman lives to add a respectable façade to the carnage of civil war. But it is not surprising that Roman emperors were more likely to follow a conservative approach, fighting when they had to and celebrating in the main only genuinely earned success. It was safer to preserve what they had. In winning support, qualities as a military leader, though important, could often take second place to the ability to manage men, the Senate, and the duties of administration,

---

[81] For a hostile estimation of Trajan's activities in the East, see Syme, *Tacitus*, 495 ff.

[82] It is significant that after the revolt of Avidius Cassius against Marcus Aurelius, a law was passed to prevent anyone serving as governor in his native area; Avidius Cassius had been governor of Syria, which included his home (Dio 71.31.1).

with efficiency, dignity, and consistency. It was the combination of skills that brought approval, as can be seen in a late source's judgement on Trajan: 'He displayed integrity in domestic affairs, and courage in military matters.'[83]

4. THE SEVERAN DYNASTY AND THE ARMY

The year 193 has often been seen as a great watershed in the history of the empire, marking the way to its subsequent decline.[1] In particular, Septimius Severus was the emperor who corrupted military discipline, militarized the principate, and 'intended gradually to open to the common soldiers the highest posts in the imperial administration'.[2] The extreme statement of these views is now generally discounted.[3] There is no reason why Severus should have had any personal inclination towards military autocracy; he was in no sense a military man, had had some training in the law,[4] and had arrived as governor of Upper Pannonia with less military experience than many other governors.[5] It is still possible, however, that the manner of his accession forced him to make a fundamental change in the government of the state and the ways of winning support, and to pay less attention to the methods which had been consecrated by tradition and which gave little offence to the senatorial class. This question can be tested in five significant areas of the emperor's activity.

Septimius Severus and the Senate

Dio has three main criticisms: that Severus burdened Rome with large numbers of soldiers, made vast expenditures, and

---

[83] *Epitome*, 13.4.

[1] Gibbon, *Decline and Fall of the Roman Empire*, chap. 5; S.N. Millar in *CAH* XII (1939); J. Hasebrock, *Untersuchungen zur Geschichte des Kaisers Septimius Severus* (1921), 99; A. Piganiol, *Histoire de Rome*[4] (1954), 356.

[2] M. Rostovtzeff, *SEHRE*[2] chap. IX, especially 402 ff.

[3] E.B. Birley, 'Septimius Severus and the Roman Army', *Epig. Stud.* 8 (1969), 63; Birley, *Septimius Severus*, 279 ff.

[4] M. Hammond, 'Septimius Severus, Roman Bureaucrat', *HSCPh.* 51 (1940), 150; for the question of the extent to which Severus' origins influenced his ideas, see R.M. Hayward, 'The African Policy of Septimius Severus', *TAPA* 71 (1940), 175; 'A Further Note on the African Policy of Septimius Severus', *Hommages à A. Grenier* (1962), 786 = *Collection Latomus* vol. 58; T.D. Barnes, 'The Family and Career of Septimius Severus', *Hist.* 16 (1967), 87.   [5] See above, pp. 328ff.

placed his hopes of safety on the strength of the army and not the good will of those around him.[6] Dio's first criticism is an immediate reaction to a particular situation, the entry of Severus into Rome with his full army in 193. As for the second, Dio in a later judgement says that Severus managed the finances well.[7] The third criticism does suggest that the emperor was forced to rely more openly on his soldiers, at the expense of the other factors in his position.[8] But it should be remembered that Dio is referring to the period just after the coup of 193, when the uncertainty and the huge number of soldiers in Rome may have caused many senators to have misgivings about the emperor's intentions. It is possible that Dio is describing his feelings at the time (he may have jotted them down) and not producing a considered final judgement. Moreover, although Dio is in general hostile, he has some good things to say about Severus, and his summary of the reign hardly suggests that he viewed the emperor as a military autocrat who had dealt the empire a fatal blow.[9] And yet Dio had an excellent opportunity to evaluate the impact of the reign, since he lived to see almost the end of the dynasty.

Herodian believed that Severus sought his own advantage by deceit and hypocrisy, and that his early favourable attitude to the Senate was a sham.[10] His view that Severus corrupted the army's discipline is exaggerated.[11] There may be something, however, in Herodian's claim that the emperor's rule was based on fear, not good will.[12] This suggests that Severus did not fully gain the confidence or affection of senators, not that he deliberately developed a militaristic type of government. The *Historia Augusta* makes no significant comment on Severus' conduct of the government,[13] and apparently repeats the opinion of the Senate

[6] 75.2.3

[7] 76.16.1.

[8] See p. 372.

[9] 76.16-17.

[10] 2.14.4.

[11] 3.8.5; cf. 2.6.14. And see above, p. 194. Herodian also claims that Severus gave the soldiers the right to wear gold rings. But this does not mean that he made them *equites*. They were simply permitted to wear a ring, if they could afford it.

[12] 3.8.8.

[13] *Vit. Sev.* 8.1 ff.

that he was 'exceedingly cruel and exceedingly useful to the state'.[14] Probably little credence should be placed in this detail.

Of course there are many indications in the sources that Severus displeased the senatorial class by particular actions. He incurred resentment for his speech in the Senate after the defeat of Clodius Albinus, in which he praised the cruelty of Marius, Sulla and Augustus, and alleged that the behaviour of many senators was worse than that of Commodus, whom he defended.[15] This was followed by the execution of twenty-nine senators despite the fact that Severus had taken an oath in 193 not to execute any senators. Dio is very hostile at this point, commenting ironically that Julius Solon, who drew up the consequent *senatus consultum*, was himself executed.[16] But does this really show a determination to abase the Senate and make it an instrument of Severus' autocracy?[17] The speech, and the executions in 197, were probably provoked by the fact that there had been a strong current of support for Albinus in the Senate; Severus thought that he needed to make an example of some senators. Most of those executed were probably supporters of Albinus and guilty of high treason. What is more, Dio, with complete fairness, mentions that the emperor pardoned another thirty-five senators. Severus' policy was one of expediency, dictated by the manner of his accession and four years of civil war.

Nevertheless, it is clear from Dio that during at least some of the reign senators felt insecure, feared the use of informers, and suffered some embarrassing experiences in the senate house.[18] Perhaps the emperor found it difficult to be consistent enough to win the confidence of the senators. But he did make some attempt to accommodate some of their traditional fears and prejudices. We can see this in his moderate speech in 193,[19] in his attested desire to win the sincere affection of senators,[20] in his careful control of

---

[14] 18.7.

[15] 75.7.4 ff.

[16] 75.2.2.

[17] As suggested by H.M.D. Parker, *History of the Roman World AD 138–337*[2] (1958), 69.

[18] 74.9.5; 75.8.5; 76.8.1.   [19] 75.2.1.   [20] 75.15.2b.

his freedmen — this won special praise from Dio[21] — and in his concern to conduct legal business and government diligently.[22] Severus treated his senatorial counsellors with respect and allowed them time to speak.[23] He did not employ widespread confiscations and killed no one in order to get money.[24] Finally, Dio's account of Severus' daily routine could probably be applied to most emperors of the Antonine period.[25]

The stationing of a legion in Italy was not necessarily designed to overawe the Senate. The defence of Italy itself required such a measure in view of the ease with which Severus had captured Rome in 193, and the troublesome activities of Bulla and his band of robbers. In conclusion, there is no real evidence to support the idea that Severus deliberately set out to degrade the Senate and ignore all the conventions of the traditional relationship between Senate and emperor. On the contrary, he actively sought to win the favour of senators by correct and courteous behaviour, though it is true that he was not entirely consistent or successful in this, largely because of the circumstances of his accession and the prolonged civil war.

The Use of Equites in Place of Senators

It has been suggested that the increasing use of *equites* in the Severan era in various areas of the administration is evidence of Severus' suspicion of and hostility to the senatorial class.[26] The argument centres on the commanders of the three new legions formed by Septimius Severus, the governorship of Mesopotamia, and the replacement of senatorial governors by *equites*.

Equites were appointed to command the three new legions instead of the usual senatorial *legati legionum*. But one of the

---

[21] 76.6.1–3.
[22] 76.7.3; cf. Herod. 3.10.2; 13.1.
[23] 76.17.1.
[24] 75.8.4; 76.16.
[25] 76.16–17.
[26] O. Hirschfeld, *Die Kaiserlichen Verwaltungsbeamten*[2] (1905); C.W. Keyes, *The Rise of the Equites* (1915).

legions was stationed in Italy, and may have been placed under the command of the Praetorian prefect. In that case, since senators could not be asked to serve under an equestrian, the emperor would have to appoint an equestrian *praefectus legionis*. There was a long standing parallel for this in the province of Egypt. Furthermore, the tradition was that élite troops in Italy were commanded by *equites*. The other two legions to which *praefecti* were appointed were stationed in Mesopotamia, which was governed by an *eques*. Once again, the emperor's decision to appoint equestrian legionary commanders was a mark of respect for the traditional dignity of the senators.

However, that the governor of the new province of Mesopotamia was an equestrian prefect is significant, since it was the only major provincial governorship (with the exception of Egypt) that was permanently in the hands of an *eques*. Like Egypt the post entailed the command of two legions. Was the emperor worried about his personal security and the loyalty of his senatorial governors? There were five armed provinces near by, all under senators (Syria Coele with two legions; Syria Phoenice with one legion; Syria Palestina (Judaea) with two legions; Cappadocia with two legions; Arabia with one legion). Together with Mesopotamia these provinces provided a formidable force of ten legions. The division of both Britain and Syria, where his rivals for power had been governors, into two separate provinces, and the consequent reduction in the size of the army concentrated in the hands of one governor, seem to confirm that Severus was worried about security.[27] But this argument is not a convincing explanation for the treatment of Mesopotamia. The social identity between the two leading classes in the state was such that it is doubtful whether an *eques* would have been any less likely than a senator to support rebellious imperial governors if he disliked an emperor, or indeed whether he could have done anything to prevent them if force and threats were applied to him. Moreover, it is unlikely that an emperor who had executed Plautianus, his

---

[27] For Britain, see S. Frere, *Britannia*[2] (1974), 203 ff.; for Syria, Birley, *Septimius Severus*, 180.

powerful Praetorian prefect, ostensibly for disloyalty, will have been particularly trusting of *equites*. It is worth noting that Severus' son was overthrown by an *eques* who became emperor in his place.

It is plausible to suppose that an *eques* was appointed governor of Mesopotamia because Severus was finding it difficult to get enough senators to fill posts that traditionally required men of that status. Many were possibly less inclined to go abroad, especially after the upheavals of the civil wars which showed how dangerous it might be to hold a command. In addition, the number of consulars available and entirely acceptable to Severus may have been small after the civil conflict. If Severus was obliged to appoint an *eques*, he may well have chosen a close friend and partisan with a personal knowledge of the area, in much the same way as, in my view, Augustus came to appoint Cornelius Gallus as the first prefect of Egypt.[28]

There are about seven cases of *equites* who served in place of the usual governor ('vice praesidis') in the reign of Septimius Severus: two in Dacia, one in Africa, one in Asia, one in Syria Coele, one in Galatia, and one other.[29] It is worth noting the case of Antius Calpurnianus, the senatorial *iuridicus* of Britain, who acted in place of the governor, possibly in the reign of Commodus.[30] This is good evidence that towards the end of the second century there was no principle of replacing with *equites* all senatorial legates who could not fulfil their duties. Of the seven examples, at least one happened in a crisis, on the sudden death of the governor – 'Hilarianus, procurator who then received the right of capital jurisdiction in place of the proconsul who had died'. The usual title of these men – 'vice' or 'loco praesidis' – implies a purely temporary arrangement, and there is no evidence for two or three equestrian *vicarii* holding a post consecutively. And only one of the known *vicarii* was in charge of a province involving the command

[28] See pp. 343–5.
[29] Keyes (n. 26), 3 ff.; updated list in Pflaum, *Les Procurateurs équestres*, 134; note also J.F. Gillian, *AJP,* 79 (1958), 230. There are four other certain examples of *equites* 'vice praesidis agentes' from 212 down to 235 (Pflaum, 135).
[30] A.R. Birley, *Fasti of Roman Britain* 137–8.

of troops. What is more, the number of known *vicarii* of equestrian rank in Severus' reign is hardly significant, and there were precedents for the use of *equites* in this way. There is an example from Asia, after the proconsul had been executed by Domitian.[31] This emperor also employed Cornelius Fuscus, his Praetorian prefect, in an independent command in Dacia.[32] Under Trajan an equestrian procurator served 'in place of a legate' ('pro legato') in Mauretania Tingitana; presumably he was in charge of legionary troops.[33] In 118 Hadrian employed Marcius Turbo in a temporary capacity in Dacia; to add to his authority he may have had a status equivalent to that of the prefect of Egypt.[34] His mission was probably to organize the province of Dacia as quickly as possible, but the appointment was highly unusual. Most interesting is the inscription of Cl. Paternus Clementianus, which should probably be dated to the mid-second century: 'Cl Paternus Clementianus proc[urator] Aug[usti]   provincia<rum>   Iud[aeae]   v[ice]   a[gens] l[egati],   Sar<din[iae]>,   Africae   et   <Norici>   ...'[35] Clementianus, from his duties as procurator of Judaea, had taken over the responsibility for the legionary troops and the government of the province. It is remarkable that the abbreviation *v a l* is used on an honorary inscription to express 'vice agens legati' ('acting in the place of the legate'), with the expectation that people would understand it. This implies that the use of equestrian *vicarii* was well established by the second century.

In using *equites* to do the job of senators in a temporary capacity, Septimius Severus was following the example of his predecessors. It was not a systematic attempt to undermine the power of the Senate. The emperor responded in an *ad hoc* fashion to immediate crises, and perhaps to a general shortage of senators for the available posts. At least as early as Tiberius' reign there had been difficulty in finding

---

[31] *CIL* V.875; cf. III. 5776.

[32] H.G. Pflaum, *Carrières*, vol. 1, 77 ff.

[33] *ILS* 1352; cf. 1348 (dated by Pflaum, *Les Procurateurs équestres*, 10, to Caligula and Claudius; it may refer to Marcus Aurelius and Lucius Verus).

[34] *Vit. Had.* 6.7–8. See R. Syme, 'The Wrong Marcius Turbo', *JRS* 52 (1962), 87 = *Roman Papers*, 541 ff.

[35] Pflaum, *Carrières*, vol. 1, 354 ff.; *ILS* 1369.

enough senators willing to serve; the long wars and civil strife of the late second century had perhaps exacerbated this trend.[36]

The Use of Military Personnel in Government

Was there a significant development under Severus of the use of promoted centurions in equestrian posts? Pflaum lists eighty-eight procurators in the Severan age whose careers are known fully or in part. Of these, sixty-eight are known to have held some military posts in their previous career. Of these sixty-eight, thirty-nine had served in the traditional equestrian *tres militiae*, eleven had been *primi pili* in the legions, and eleven *primi pili bis* with service in the tribunates in Rome.[37] These figures mean that promoted centurions comprise only *c.*32 per cent of known equestrian procurators in the period who held some military posts in their career. Moreover, from Hadrian to Commodus promoted centurions comprise *c.*30 per cent of procurators who had held one or more military posts in their career.[38] Clearly, there was no significant increase in the use of promoted centurions in the Severan period. On the contrary, we may speak in terms of the gradual continuation of a process already well established.

It is true that in the Severan period the number of centurions promoted from the legions is equal to the number of *primi pili bis* who had served in the Guard. In the preceding period only five out of twenty-five centurions were legionary centurions who had not served in the tribunates at Rome.[39] However, this in itself shows that the trend did not begin with Severus, and it can be argued that, since in his

[36] Aurelius Victor (*De Caes* 33.33) claimed that Gallienus deliberately excluded all senators from commands; cf. Keyes, 49. It is more likely that the emperor gave formal recognition to the increasing unwillingness of senators to hold the great commands.

[37] Pflaum, *Les Procurateurs équestres*, 186 ff. Fifty-one other inscriptions are too mutilated to be of any value in interpretation. Note that there are twenty procurators who are known to have held no military posts at all.

[38] Pflaum, 179 ff.

[39] Pflaum, ad loc.

reign Guardsmen were more often recruited from the legions, in practice the distinction between *primus pilus* in a legion and an officer in the Guard was less meaningful. It is also true that promoted centurions in the Severan period tended to hold more and more important equestrian posts – the Praetorian prefecture, the prefecture of the fleet, and the governorship of equestrian provinces.[40] But this process too had begun as early as the reign of Hadrian.[41] The advance of ex-centurions to such posts is not a sign of militarism, but the use of the more educated and intelligent soldiers to fill gaps in the administration.[42]

The Association between Emperor and Soldier

The soldiers were materially better off under the Severi than at any time in the second century, and they enjoyed the right of marriage for the first time. There may have been some deterioration in discipline, but most of the trends for which we have evidence in the Severan era had their origins in the second century or earlier. The basis for the emperor's association with the army was firmly established by Augustus, and subsequent emperors preserved and enhanced his ideas. The concept of the emperor as *commilito* probably evolved in the first century, but received its main impetus in the second; the other devices for bringing the reigning emperor's name before the troops at every opportunity were all well established in the early imperial period. His pay rise for the army was generous, but should be seen in its context. Rates of pay in themselves were not generous and there had been no increase since Domitian. Moreover, Severus seems to have been moderate in his use of donatives, which of course had always been politically important. Virtually all the legal privileges granted to soldiers originated in the

[40] Pflaum, *Carrières*, nos. 263; 313; 316; 332.

[41] Five reached the great prefectures – *Carrières*, nos. 94; 100; 109; 162; 165; four reached Ducenarian governorships – nos. 143; 162; 173; 182; three became prefect of the fleets – nos. 102; 107; 211.

[42] See above, pp. 102ff; Appendix 1; and note Dobson, *ANRW* II.1, 420 ff. I can see nothing sinister in the increasing use of soldiers on a provincial governor's staff (MacMullen, *Soldier and Civilian*, 67 ff.) The more educated soldiers were a natural choice for these minor clerkships, and were readily available.

first or second century, and the benevolent attitude of emperors and imperial officials, and even the effusive language of some rescripts, can be paralleled from public documents in the second century. In addition, there are grounds for thinking that Severus preserved the general discipline, morale, and fighting qualities of the army, and did not dramatically alter the relationship between emperor and troops.[43]

The Legal Basis for Septimius Severus' Power

It has been alleged that in his 'policy of senatorial oppression' Severus had the support of the lawyers, who suggested that the Senate and people had surrendered rather than delegated their power to the emperor.[44] This implies a deliberate change in the legal basis of the principate. Some support for this has been found in a passage of Dio, where the historian describes the passage of power from Senate and people to Augustus. 'And so the power of the people and the Senate was entirely transferred to Augustus, and from this time it is accurate to say that a monarchy was established.' This part of the history was probably written after the death of Severus,[45] and may be an anachronistic reflection on the increasing autocracy in Dio's own day. But he is commenting on the particular fact that power had passed from those who had traditionally exercised it, the Senate and people, to Augustus; and this was the case from the beginning. He thought that the accumulation of powers meant *de facto* monarchy, no matter what it was dressed up to look like, since the emperor directed affairs, commanded the military force, and could block any initiative from Senate, people, and magistrates. There is nothing to suggest that Dio was referring to any specific legal change under Severus.

In fact the main evidence for this view is a passage of Ulpian: 'Whatever the emperor has decided has the force of law; in as much as through the law which was carried concerning his power, the people confers all its power and

---

[43] See pp. 194–5.

[44] Parker (n. 17), 75. Hammond (n. 4), 169 ff.

[45] 53.17–18; for the date of this passage, see Millar, *Cassius Dio,* 38, 119, 194.

authority on him and in him.'[46] Ulpian is writing rather care-
lessly here. He surely means that the Senate and people
conferred on the emperor all the power that they already
enjoyed, that is, gave him the right to exercise the same
power they had. He does not mean that they actually gave up
all power to the emperor. This interpretation is supported
by another statement of Ulpian: 'It is not in dispute that the
Senate can make law.'[47] That the emperor can make law
does not remove the power of others to do so.

Furthermore, since Ulpian lived until 223, it is by no
means certain that the passage in question was written during
the reign of Septimius Severus. Finally, Ulpian was not
necessarily the first to define the validity of imperial constitutions in this way. In fact Gaius, writing in the 160s, gives
much the same type of explanation: 'The constitution of an
emperor is what he decided in decree, edict, or letter; and it
has never been in doubt that that has the force of law, since
the emperor himself receives his power by a law.'[48] Therefore, neither Dio nor the legal texts give any reason to believe
that Septimius Severus used the army's support to change the
legal basis of the principate along more absolutist lines. From
the start it had been an absolute monarchy in a framework
of constitutional formality and legality.

Septimius Severus did not deliberately intend to advance
militarism. Like all emperors he based his position on
military support, but he also recognized the need to accommodate the wishes of the upper classes. Despite this, he
could not conceal the fact that for the first time in over one
hundred and twenty-four years a military commander had
captured Rome with his army. Inevitably the power of the
army and his reliance on it were made more obvious to
everyone. The prolonged disorder of 193-7 and the consequent executions of the supporters of the various factions
will have made senators less confident and less willing to

---

[46] *D* 1.4.1: 'Quod principi placuit, legis habet vigorem; utpote cum lege regia,
quae de imperio eius lata est, populus ei et in eum omne suum imperium et
potestatem conferat.'

[47] *D* 1.3.9: 'Non ambigitur senatum ius facere posse.'

[48] *Inst.* 1.5: 'Constitutio principis est quod imperator decreto vel edicto vel
epistula constituit; nec umquam dubitatum est quin id legis vicem optineat, cum
ipse imperator per legem imperium accipiat.'

play a part in the Senate. They will have been unable to trust Severus fully because of what he had done and his ruthless reliance on armed might. And so the Senate as a body may have tended towards a more self-effacing role, leaving the way open for emperors to pay less attention to it. In the same way, individual senators may have been less willing to accept responsibility and seek the great commands with their consequent dangers. Therefore it could come about that senators would gradually disappear from posts that it had been their prerogative to occupy from the start of the imperial period. In this indirect way, the rule of Severus, by dealing another blow at the self-confidence and will to participate of the senatorial class, contributed to making that class, which had been one of the major factors in the imperial state, more effete and helpless. In this period there will have been less need to cater for senatorial traditions and prejudices, less need to seek its help and support, and indeed less point in doing so. This is illustrated by Septimius Severus' last advice to his sons: 'Be harmonious, enrich the soldiers, and despise all the rest.'[49] As a private statement of the 'secrets of ruling', this was unexceptionable. Augustus would have understood. The difference was that it was becoming increasingly difficult to conceal the reality of an autocracy backed by military force. That these developments were not part of a deliberate policy renders them hardly less significant.

Caracalla followed his father's advice too well. We may note his occasional willingness to grant a legal privilege, his extravagance in money benefits for the army, his total identification as 'fellow-soldier', his depreciation of the senators and their role, his outspoken praise of the troops. His reign certainly played a part in the undermining of military discipline, the decline of imperial prestige, and the further degradation of the Senate. Dio's dislike of Caracalla, however, is based on his attempts to get money for the soldiers,[50] his discourteous treatment of the senators and failure to consult them,[51] his inconsistency,[52] his exe-

---

[49] Dio, 76.15.2.
[51] 77.13.6; 17.3-4; 18.4; 20.2; 11.5 ff.

[50] 77.10.1 ff. See also p. 175.
[52] 77.5.2.

cutions,[53] and his use of freedmen and eunuchs.[54] These seem like the traditional criticisms of the 'bad' emperor and derive from particular incidents rather than any deliberate policy. Moreover, Caracalla was capable of acts of good judgement and often hit upon a happy phrase.[55] From Antioch he wrote criticizing the senators because they did not assemble enthusiastically and give their votes individually;[56] apparently he wanted the Senate to be seen to play a part. And a story in Dio shows that he was capable of polite social contact and pleasantry with senators.[57] Even Caracalla, therefore, made some attempt to carry on the traditional relationship with the Senate and did not set out deliberately to establish an open military absolutism. He faced the immediate need of reconciling the troops to the murder of his brother Geta, and had to exploit to their logical conclusion the methods successfully employed by his father. The emperor was, it seems, naturally effusive and subject to childish whims. Although he did not totally abase the Senate, he perhaps despised the dull and boring senators and found it easier and more congenial to be on campaign with his troops with an easy mastery of men and events, rather than to deal with the Senate and the intricacies of administration; some of this he indeed preferred to leave to his mother while he was on campaign.

The nemesis of a victory in civil war by the founder of the dynasty finally claimed for its victim the last member of the Severan family, Severus Alexander, who was overthrown largely by military discontent because he seemed feebly incapable of impressing his troops and keeping discipline. By 235 the balance between emperor, army, and State had shifted considerably from that established by Augustus, or even that in the second century. The soldiers themselves were more easily exploited for seditious purposes, expected more from their emperor, and were perhaps more ready to take the lead in overthrowing him. The ruler was now virtually obliged to meet the troops and take personal charge of campaigns; his capacity to rule was dangerously associated with his military ability.

[53] 77.11.5; Herodian 4.6.1.   [54] 77.17.2.
[55] 77.11.2; Herodian 4.7.2.   [56] 77.20.1.   [57] 78.8.4.

But convenient generalizations should be avoided. It was still the case that the tenor and direction of the government depended to a large degree on the character of the individual emperor and the immediate circumstances. The upper classes and the senators in particular still held the most important posts in the administration of the empire. The conventional formalities and traditions remained, to be resurrected with honour or ignored, as it suited. It is notable that at the end of the dynasty Severus Alexander could still proclaim in a rescript his intention 'to live according to the laws'.[58]

---

[58] *CJ* 6.23.3.

EPILOGUE

X

'HOLDING THE WOLF BY THE EARS'

That is how Tiberius described his tenure of power in the midst of difficulties and dangers threatening him from all sides; there was disaffection and sedition among the nobility, mutiny in the army, and the problem of the role of the Senate.[1] This emperor, who took his duties and responsibilities very seriously, could find no peace; if he let go the wolf might destroy him; to hold on required both courage and skill. The army was the most important problem with which every emperor had to deal. His close relationship with the troops meant that the ruler had a personal responsibility for most military affairs; he could be praised or blamed for everything. The Senate was not up to such matters, and its interference might be unwelcome; the emperor should go to trouble spots himself.[2]

The methods used to cement the loyalty of the soldiers to the ruling emperor and his house were simple and based on mutual self interest. Each soldier could expect moderate pay, which was guaranteed by the emperor, occasional donatives, and fairly generous discharge benefits. Discipline, though in theory strict, in practice was often more liberally interpreted; even before Septimius Severus removed the legal prohibition on marriage, soldiers could live with their women and produce children, for whom some concessions were made. Life in the camps will have been quite acceptable to many of the troops if they could avoid strict disciplinarians and difficult campaigns. The common soldier

---

[1] Suet., *Tib.* 25.1.
[2] It was suggested that Tiberius should go himself to deal with the mutinies in Germany and Pannonia — Tac., *A* 1.46.

certainly enjoyed a status higher than that of any of the lower classes of society in the imperial period. All this cost the empire a large proportion of its available revenue and created problems, especially in the context of the disorganized, hand-to-mouth economy of the Roman world. But the cost of the army was kept in check; there were only three pay rises in over one hundred years, and these significantly were largely for political reasons. Although individual emperors were sometimes put under pressure, the system was not exhausted by the army. Nevertheless, there is no doubt that acceptable emoluments and service conditions were the essential basis of the army's loyalty.

Service conditions were made more bearable by the legal privileges conferring on the troops substantial rights in making a will, owning and disposing of their own property, and in protecting their interests while absent in the army. In addition the anxieties of an appearance in court were smoothed over; the soldier had ill-defined but distinct advantages over civilian litigants, and it was difficult for a civilian to get a soldier into a court outside the military camp. Here again the soldiers were better off than the lower orders and in some respects were treated like the *honestiores,* even if they were not formally classed in this group. Yet they lacked the usual criteria of birth, wealth, and social standing for such privileges. They were vital, however, to the emperor's security and survival. Moreover, soldiers had a better opportunity of gaining access to their emperor with petitions on private matters, though in general these were treated by emperors with exemplary fairness. Finally, the soldiers could enjoy the power of their numbers, and the possible opportunity they had to supplement their pay by oppressing the local population, often without much apparent restriction.

As far as they could, many emperors attempted to preserve the principle of the law, the traditions and ideals of Roman society, and the interests of others. Nevertheless, the need to keep service conditions as attractive as possible and to encourage recruiting, since volunteers were more desirable than conscripts, the powerfully privileged position of the army, and the favourable attitude of emperors and their officials, meant that it was very hard to prevent discrimination against, and abuse of, sections of society. As usual it was mainly the lower orders who suffered, although the better off may also have occasionally fallen foul of the soldiers, since Juvenal's Sixteenth Satire, bitterly attacking the army's legal privileges and other advantages, was obviously aimed at an upper-class audience.

In addition to these measures a prudent emperor sought an 'ideal' relationship with his soldiers. The oath of loyalty and obedience expressed the commitment of the troops to their emperor, sanctified by the gods and Roman military tradition. It was not without effect if officers harped upon the dangers of perjury to a superstitious soldiery. The oath taken at the accession and renewed each year was a formal demonstration of an emperor's control of his troops; it was also excellent propaganda, and a ceremony at which the soldiers could be inspired with a sense of common loyalty. But oaths were broken, and the guilty often seemed to prosper. And so it was expedient to develop a rapport with the army and win its affection if possible; this would give the oath more meaning and make it more difficult for the seditious to undermine the army's loyalty. Therefore emperors adopted the role of 'fellow-soldier' of their men, and for many it was more than an empty term of address; true comradeship imposed real responsibilities, and real hardships, especially when an emperor was present with his legions. This relationship was symbolized by the frequent repetition of the reigning emperor's name in the camp, by the religious calendar, by the placing of his portrait with the military standards, and by the less common practice of bestowing the imperial name on individual legions. All this could be done in a manner that was restrained and inoffensive to senators. Only with Caracalla does there seem to be a desire for total identification with the troops.

The ruler of the Roman empire could not escape his military responsibilities. He was an *imperator,* and he received acclamation as a successful commander for the victories of his legates. This became a convention, involving no risk or obligation to take personal charge. The emperor's general responsibility, his control (*auspicia*), and advice (*consilia*),[3] had ensured the success. However, the emperor's personal connection with the army, and his position as effective commander-in-chief, meant that he was directly in charge of the disposition and organization of Roman forces, of strategy and tactics, of frontier defence, and of decisions on war and peace and treaties. And even if he delegated, the emperor took the blame if things went wrong. Since military operations were so important to the defence of the empire and the personal standing of its ruler, it is not surprising that many emperors were not satisfied with a general supervision but went on campaign in person, especially from the late first century onwards, and directed operations on the spot. Doubtless other motives influenced them as well; an interest in the military arts and the thrill of commanding men in battle; a desire to avoid the tedium of some of the administration in Rome; a fear of trusting their senatorial governors with independent commands; a realization that the true 'fellow-soldier' should be present on campaign sharing the toils of his men. By the early second century all major campaigns were led by the emperor himself. This military role was taken seriously. In general triumphs and honorary *cognomina* were accepted only for genuine military success won under the personal direction of the emperor. The increasing military role of the Roman emperor brought some advantages. Success, celebrated with pomp and splendour, increased his dignity and prestige and made it more difficult for lesser men to aspire to the purple. It may also have increased the affection and respect of the soldiers, who could profit by booty and increased opportunities for donatives. On the other hand, as the emperor became more closely associated with military success, he would find it harder to distance himself from military failure. And a tough campaign with heavy casualties might undermine the confidence of the soldiers.

The autocracy established by Augustus was flexible. It could accommodate men of such diverse habits and characteristics as Antoninus Pius and Caracalla. It was not

[3] For example, cf. the dedication on the arch of Titus in Rome which celebrates his victory over the Jews: 'quod praeceptis patris consiliisq. et auspiciis gentem Iudaeorum domuit' (*ILS* 264).

essential for the Roman emperor to command in person; therefore if the circumstances were favourable, he could play down the support of the army, leave the military machine ticking over, and confine himself to the conventional symbols of his association with the troops, since the customs and traditions of the upper classes accepted that a man could serve the State well in a variety of capacities. The measures to secure the army's loyalty at no time constituted a system conformed to alike by all.

At the same time no emperor could escape the central problem, which was that everyone knew the 'secrets of ruling' — how to work on the troops to gain their loyalty and affection. The same methods were consistently employed from the career of Sulla at least down to the end of the fourth century. Nothing new had to be invented. Sulla fought his way to supreme power with his army, and then tried to block ambitious men's opportunities for using army commands against the State and exploiting popular support. But his own example was too strong. The revolutionary career of Pompey was based on military strength, intimidation, dominant army commands, and popular support. After 59 BC Caesar, Pompey, and Crassus sought to control the important army commands and monopolize support in Rome. But this was difficult to sustain indefinitely against the interests of the upper classes. Julius Caesar, after his victory in the civil war, tried to find a solution; his close personal connection with the soldiers (whom he would address as 'comrades'), and his immense popularity with the people, could be combined with a permanent, dominant position for himself within the republican framework of government, with the co-operation of the upper classes, who could be conciliated and assimilated into the new system. He failed in his bid to conciliate the senators, and his army could not save him from death at the hands of his own friends from the class that detested him and his personal domination.

Augustus accomplished this difficult task by using the same methods as Caesar. He was luckier. The senators were exhausted and their numbers depleted by the constant civil strife; they were more ready to be conciliated. Augustus satisfied the soldiers, the populace, and the upper classes well enough to produce the stable, peaceful, and relatively consistent government for which everyone yearned. Whereas he recognized at least in his own mind that in the last resort he depended on the soldiers to protect him against senatorial revolt, he also desired to be free of military pressure and for this purpose was intent on restoring discipline and preserving a certain distance between himself and the army. He lived long enough for his system to become established and for all to learn its benefits. His successors, lacking his mystique and prestige, used the same methods, but had to develop and adapt them as the situation demanded. As the effects of civil conflict were forgotten and men of ambition could think again of bidding for the supreme power, the army took up more of the emperor's time and attention. But the Severi followed the same kind of policy as Augustus, and although the importance of the army was increasing at the expense of the other factors in the security of the imperial regime, it was only the more open expression of what had always been the case. Even the eccentric Caracalla was merely developing the well-tried methods of his predecessors for cementing the army's loyalty. The spirit, not the form, of the system had changed. Augustus would certainly have recognized the outward appearance of the government he had built up and which had fulfilled his hopes: 'I shall carry with me the hope that the foundations of the state which I have laid will remain unchanged.'[4]

In AD 311 Constantine is found writing to the military commander in Illyricum about further privileges for the army:

Since we are always eager to provide for the welfare and emoluments of our soldiers in keeping with their devotion and toils, in this matter also, my dearest Dalmatius, we believe that we must provide for the soldiers through the foresight of our measures. And so, as we observe the toils of our soldiers which they bear in their constant activities for the stability and good of the State, we believe that we must make provision and arrange so that during their military service they may rejoice in the

---

[4] Suet., *Aug.* 28.2.

enjoyment of the pleasant fruits of their labours in accordance with
our provision, and that after military service, they may obtain peaceful
repose and consequent tranquility.[5]

The emperor goes on to list in detail the privileges and
advantages the soldiers are to have. The effusive language,
the emphasis on their labours on behalf of the State and the
personal loyalty of the soldiers, and the insistence on wide-
ranging privileges, recall the methods and language of Trajan
in the early second century.

In 326 Constantine went to meet some of his veterans
personally.

When he had entered the army headquarters and had been saluted by
the prefects and tribunes and most eminent men, the acclamation arose,
'Augustus Constantine! May the gods preserve you for us! Your
salvation is our salvation. In truth we speak, on our oath we speak.'

The assembled veterans cried out, 'Constantine Augustus! To what
purpose have we been made veterans if we have no special privilege?'

Constantine Augustus said, 'I should more and more increase rather
than diminish the happiness of my fellow veterans [conveterani].

Victorinus, a veteran, said, 'Do not allow us to be liable for compulsory services and burdens in all places.'

Constantine Augustus said, 'Indicate more plainly. Which in
particular are the compulsory public services that insistently oppress
you?'

All the veterans said, 'Surely you yourself understand?'[6]

The emperor proceeds to confirm emphatically the veterans'
privileges. The personal interest of Constantine, the use of
the phrase 'fellow-veterans', his willingness to respond
directly to the soldiers' complaints in this remarkable
dialogue, their confidence in approaching the emperor face
to face, and their assumption that he was fully conversant
with their rights and privileges, all reflect the traditionally
close and personal association of emperor and soldier, which
had existed from the early empire. It is interesting to see
that the same attitudes and methods prevailed even after

[5] *FIRA*[2] I, no. 93.
[6] *Theodosian Code*, 7.20.2. The translation is that of Lewis and Reinhold,
Roman Civilization: Sourcebook II: The Empire (1966), p. 530.

the military reorganization of Diocletian and Constantine and the collapse of military discipline in the mid-third century, under the pressure of continuous civil and foreign warfare, and the willingness of ambitious commanders to profit from the unstable situation to which they themselves had contributed by military insurrection. In this period it became almost impossible to preserve the balance between the various factors in an emperor's rule, establish respectability, and gain acceptance and loyalty throughout the empire.

This balance was of paramount importance to an emperor's successful tenure of power and the administration of the empire. It was above all the function of the commanders and higher officers to maintain discipline in the army and defend the empire with the troops under their command. But it was also they who had the best chance of threatening the emperor himself. If an emperor could keep on good terms with the upper classes and find a working relationship with the Senate, his popularity would cause men to be less ready to overthrow him or feel less confident about obtaining widespread support for such an action. The emperor had to find a course between the need to reward and encourage the soldiery and the need to retain friendly relations with the class from which their commanders were drawn. And the senators were a critical audience, detesting pretension and unearned military celebrations, and despising the ordinary soldier, whose indiscipline and capacity for destruction they feared.

An emperor could of course take other precautions. He could reduce the risk of revolt by ensuring that only safe men were appointed to army commands; but here his judgement might be at fault. Then, by replacing army commanders at frequent intervals and by preventing any 'professional' army caste from developing, he could ensure that they had the least opportunity to gain the affection of the troops. But the events of 68–9 were a warning, when the Rhine legions were prepared to acclaim both Verginius and Vitellius, neither of whom had enjoyed a long command. Other factors operated on the emperor's side. Revolt was hazardous. No single army commander had forces large enough to hold out against all other armies. If he tried to win the support of other legates in advance, it was likely that the plot would be prematurely discovered. Even the governor's own higher officers and the procurators were the appointees of the emperor, and the governor could not therefore count on their support. He could perhaps hope to corrupt his troops since they were virtually mercenaries and the emperor could be outbid. But the troops might also be reasonably conscious that in isolation they stood small chance of success and that therefore their commander's promises were worthless. They might prefer to remain loyal to the man to whom they had sworn fealty and who consistently provided their rewards and privileges.

However it was a different matter if the reigning emperor were generally detested by the upper classes or if his power were not yet fully established, or both. In the former case a legate had more hope of support from his peers (like Galba), and in the latter, any 'ideal' ties between emperor and troops were likely to be looser. The soldiers might indeed be less enthusiastic about supporting an emperor who took no interest in them or failed to provide pay promptly, or who could be represented as being unable to maintain his position and their benefits. The infrequency of revolts, and still more of successful revolts down to the third century, shows how seldom such conditions were fulfilled, or at least how seldom men could reckon on their fulfilment.

At all times, it must be emphasized, the risk of revolts was minimized if the emperor could remain on good terms with the Senate and the upper classes, despite their variegated opinions. And we can see this point in another way. Of 'established' emperors whose conduct was detested, only Nero (before the third century) succumbed to military revolt. But Gaius, Domitian, Commodus, and Caracalla were murdered by plotters in the imperial entourage, or in the palace itself. The authors of conspiracies could hope that their acts would be so applauded by the upper classes that they would be secure under a new ruler, since it was likely that the new regime would be accepted by men of note and consequently by the leaderless troops. For if the soldiery could find no leaders, their resentment could be ignored. By contrast to all this, those emperors who had a good working relationship with the Senate, and who showed restraint and consistency, died in their beds.

Emperors perhaps readily accepted the need to conciliate senators and *equites* because many of them reached maturity in private station, had the traditional education, and shared the basic ideas of other senators. Their natural inclination would be to assure the loyalty of the army by methods that had been consecrated by tradition and gave little offence to the senatorial order.

Holding the wolf was a dangerous and often unenviable task. Even if a suitable balance were achieved, it was always at the mercy of external factors, like a sudden war or conspiracy. The *Historia Augusta* has a fictitious account of a conversation between Severus Alexander and a senator, 'Ovinius Camillus', who aspired to be emperor. The story is useful since it illustrates what an emperor's way of life was thought to be like, at least in the late fourth century. Alexander welcomed Camillus' desire to share the burden of ruling, proclaimed this in the Senate, and brought him back to the palace.

There he gave a banquet for Camillus at which he provided the imperial trappings, and indeed on a grander scale than he usually enjoyed himself. When an expedition against the barbarians was proclaimed, Alexander invited Camillus to go himself if he wished, or to accompany him. And when the emperor marched on foot, he encouraged Camillus to do the same; then after five miles Alexander told the flagging senator to ride on horseback; and when after two post-houses he was tired by even this, he placed him in a carriage. But Camillus could not put up with this, either genuinely or through fear, and abdicated from the imperial power. Although he was expecting to be executed, Alexander sent him away and commended him to the soldiers.[7]

The writer's imagination has produced a vivid picture of great power, grandeur, and a lavish style of living. But the problems of conspiracy, ambitious senators, the personal responsibility of the emperor for the direction of campaigns, the need to set an example by enduring the rigours involved,

---

[7] *Vit. Sev. Alex.* 48.1–6. For the fictitious context, see R. Syme, *Emperors and Biography*, 96.

and the looming power of the soldiers, will often have attenuated the undoubted pleasures which immense wealth and apparently absolute power conferred.

The Roman empire was a military autocracy, but the ruler was not a warrior and sometimes not even very military; nor could he always be autocratic. The nemesis of the system worked out by Augustus of an absolute monarchy backed by the army, but hedged in by various traditions and a worn-out republican framework, was that the emperor was subject to different constraints and obligations in order to accommodate all the groups and institutions that made the Roman empire work and his own position secure. He could rely exclusively neither on the upper classes nor the army. Hence in practice he himself tended to limit his absolute power. Tiberius had recognized what a daunting task all this was. Over 180 years later Septimius Severus, who had made himself master of the whole Roman world by military force and established his dynasty, perhaps had the same idea in mind as he reflected on the many vicissitudes of fortune that had brought him through scholarly pursuits and military offices to the highest power: 'I have been everything, and I have gained nothing from it.'[8]

---

[8] *Vit. Sev.* 18.11: 'Omnia fui et nihil expedit.'

APPENDIXES

BIBLIOGRAPHY

INDEX

APPENDIX 1
THE JUDICIAL ROLE
OF CENTURIONS

In the case imagined by Juvenal (16.7 ff.), a centurion acts as a judge appointed (*iudex datus*) by the praetor. The use of centurions in judicial roles may help to illustrate further the position of soldiers before the law and the extent to which trial by civilian and military judges became blurred. As early as the start of Gaius' reign we find a centurion appointed by a consular legate to act as *iudex datus* (*CIL* III.9832). Under Claudius, L. Arruntius Scribonianus appointed a centurion to fix the boundary line between the territory of the Sapuates and the Matini in Dalmatia (*CIL* III. 9864). An Egyptian papyrus *c*.41 records how the 'praefectus castrorum' of the *III Cyrenaica* appointed a centurion to adjudicate between rival claimants (both soldiers) for the property of a soldier who had died intestate (*FIRA*[2] III, pp. 190–1).

In Rome in the formulary system, the judges were drawn from the *album* of those with the given property qualifications, if the parties did not agree on someone else. But in the *cognitio* system the magistrate could determine the issue himself (*in iure*), or he could appoint a *iudex* to determine the issue (*in iudicio*) as defined (*in iure*). In this procedure the magistrate, or in the provinces the provincial governor, could choose whomever he wished as *iudex*. If most cases involving soldiers were decided in the military camp, the centurion, by virtue of his prestige and authority, would be a natural choice as judge, unless the case were particularly important, in which event the governor himself would take it.

Quite apart from this role of the centurion as *iudex datus*, a wealth of evidence in Egyptian papyri shows the centurion fulfilling a judicial role in the first instance. Mitteis held that the centurion did not have delegated power from the governor and could not decide a case in the civil legal process on his own authority unless the parties were in agreement. But the centurion could use his existing quasi-magisterial authority to conclude a provisional agreement and then refer the litigants to the governor, at the opening of the *conventus*. The centurion in fact exercised a kind of 'Justice of the Peace' function and could not give a legally binding decision on a question of law (L. Mitteis and U. Wilcken, *Grundzürge und Chrestomathie der Papyruskunde* (1912), II.1, 33 ff.; cf. Mitteis, *Hermes* 30 (1895), 567 ff.). Mitteis was referring to the strict legal position of the centurion. It is possible, however, that informally a centurion could exercise effective legal authority, as there were doubtless many reasons why a litigant would not wish to exercise his full legal rights (see below).

In fact the evidence of the papyri shows that the litigants frequently believed that the centurion would judge the case on his own initiative and make *de facto* legal decisions. The earliest known example is found in a papyrus of AD 31 (*P. Ox.* 2234; much of the evidence which illuminates the process by which centurions received petitions on legal matters is collected by S. Daris, *Documenti per la Storia dell'Esercito Romano in Egitto* (1964), 156 ff.). A fisherman, who has been assaulted and robbed by several civilians and a soldier, petitions a centurion directly for redress: 'I claim, if it seems appropriate, that the accused should be brought before you to pay the penalty to me.' It is particularly interesting that the centurion is judging a soldier who has committed an offence against a civilian. Another petitioner asks that a suspected thief be brought before the centurion 'to give an explanation to you ... so that I can get back my private property and obtain justice' (*Sammelbuch Griechischen Urkunden aus Ägypten 6952*). The return of the stolen property seems to be consequent upon the centurion's judgement.

The impression given by other petitions *P. Mich.* 3.175 (AD 193); *BGU* 515 (193); *P. Gen.* 3 (175-80); *Amherst Pap.* II.78 (184) is that the centurion had the power to summon the litigants, hold a hearing, and in practice often arrive at an effective judgement on his own authority. The petitions were probably drawn up with the assistance of a legal expert who knew the correct formulae and the basic principles of jurisdiction. They suggest that such persons knew that centurions often *de facto* provided the remedy desired.

One fragmentary petition is addressed to the *decurion* of the Arsionite nome in 167/8 (*Pap. Teb.* 2.304). Another petition addressed to the centurion of the area (ὸ ἐπὶ τῶν τόπων) in the second century begs for his benevolence (*BGU* 522). The formal title may indicate that these soldiers had an established position where they were stationed, probably in charge of small detachments of troops. In the light of these petitions, it is plausible to suppose that they exercised some minor jurisdiction in the area for which they were responsible. E. C. Baade has pointed out that many petitions addressed to centurions come from remote parts of Egypt where soldiers could be expected to be stationed; in these areas it would perhaps be difficult to find a competent civil official to judge a minor case (*Akten des VIII Internationalen Kongresses für Papyrologie* (1955), 26).

The cases heard by centurions cover a wide variety of issues: pure assault (*P. Rhylands* 141; *P. Teb.* 2.304); theft of goods and assault (*P. Ox.* 2234); assault and theft of common property (*P. Mich.* 3.175); assault and theft of goods left in a will (*P. Gen.* 3); theft from a yard and a house (*P. Osl.* 2.21; *Sammelbuch* 6952); robbery of a woman (*BGU* 157); dishonest actions against property held in common (*P. Amherst.* II.78); dispute over common grazing rights (*P. Gen.* 16); assault and robbery of the collectors of public corn (*BGU* 515). One papyrus provides a vivid illustration of how a centurion might conduct a case that came before him (*Sammelbuch* 9290). The centurion instructs one of the litigants not to disregard his summons, but to come to him and indicate who owns the fruits over which there is a dispute. The tone of the message is peremptory and shows that the centurion had the power to compel the presence of the litigants. His method on this occasion was to bring all the parties together to discuss the ownership of the disputed property.

If it is true that on many occasions centurions made effective judgements on the cases that came before them, the process may be explained on the following hypothesis. Centurions, and the soldiers they commanded, were frequently used in a police capacity to arrest and detain miscreants (MacMullen, *Soldier and Civilian*, 52 ff.; and note several papyri containing petitions to centurions in which the plaintiff notes that an injustice has been committed and that the guilty are accountable to him. The common feature of these petitions is that the identity of the alleged criminal is not known. It seems reasonable that it was the centurion's duty to find out who had committed the crime and detain him until a hearing could be arranged: *P. Osl.* 2.23 (*AD* 214); *Chrestomathie* II.2; no. 111 (192); 115 (216); *BGU* 454 (193); 275; *Sammelbuch* 9203 (Severus Alexander)). From this it was a short step to a grant of power to try the offenders with a view to ascertaining the facts of the case for trial by the provincial governor. It is easy to see that from this centurions could usurp *de facto* jurisdiction. In the same way as they could use their power and prestige to make illegal exactions, so they could employ these qualities to administer a kind of rough justice for which they had inadequate legal authority. No doubt the local population came to recognize this and probably found it easier to accept the *fait accompli*. Many would not be able to afford to raise official objections or exploit their full legal rights. And they might be frightened of the centurion's physical power and the troops he commanded. In time this *de facto* practice gradually assumed the status of an established convention. Other officials perhaps accepted this because they themselves were very busy with legal matters and were glad to have some of the burden removed. Moreover, in some areas the centurion was probably the only available official of the government; and to write to someone in higher authority would take time and money the litigants could not afford.

What significance is to be attached to the judicial roles of centurions? The appointment of soldiers as *iudices dati* is not odd in itself. They remained citizens and in principle there was no reason why they should not be appointed provided that it was compatible with their military duties. In addition many soldiers already exercised civil functions in the *officium* of the provincial governor. With regard to the development of the *de facto* jurisdiction exercised by centurions (at least in Egypt, the only province for which we have evidence, although I see no reason to doubt that the same practice was employed elsewhere), if the account given above is correct, then it indicates a natural process which was convenient to the emperor and his officials, and not a deliberate attempt to benefit soldiers by the appointment of favourable judges. However, although it is true that soldiers were citizens, it is also the case that there was a distinction between civilians and soldiers, which transcended common citizenship since the latter enjoyed privileges not enjoyed by the former. As the soldiers belonged to a privileged, closely knit group, it was in principle dangerous to set them in judgement either as *iudices dati*, or in their *de facto* jurisdiction, over one of their own number or over civilians. There were surely strong grounds for suspecting the imparitality of centurions in dealing with other soldiers, and civilians, whom they had the power to terrorise. In particular the centurion would be open to bribery from soldiers, with whom he might be acquainted and over whom his military rank gave him great powers of exploitation.

A rescript of Gordian III gives a tantalizing glimpse of the regulations and problems surrounding the use of military judges: 'If a military judge, appointed by someone who had no right to appoint him, judged an issue which ought to have been decided in civil proceedings, then even though the right of appeal was removed, whatever he decided does not have the force of a legal judgement' (*CJ* 7.48.2).

R. MacMullen thought that there was a significant increase under the Severi of cases heard by centurions exercising a *de facto* legal jurisdiction. He noted fifteen examples between 192 and 217, compared to nine in the whole period before the Severi (*Soldier and Civilian*, 53, and n. 11). There may be some significance in this, but it is incorrect to say, 'what was exceptional in the first two centuries and more of the empire, suddenly became the recognized procedure'. Indeed many of the pre-Severan examples date from the period 170–90, showing that there was no sudden development. Moreover, it cannot be affirmed that there was ever a recognized procedure. Other minor officials continued to hear the same type of case as centurions, who were never used exclusively. For example, a lady who petitioned a centurion concerning the possible death of her husband, states that she is presenting a similar petition to the *strategos* so that it may be entered on the register (*Chrestomathie* II.2, no. 115). No doubt the circumstances in the local area and the availability of other officials played a large part in how far centurions were employed in a judicial role. In any event, centurions usually decided very minor cases, and their employment in this way cannot be taken as a sign of a deliberate increase in militarism under the Severi.

APPENDIX 2
IMPERIAL RESCRIPTS

Table 1

This contains rescripts sent to individual soldiers or veterans, and some or all of whose contents are known; the date of the rescript is given in brackets.

HADRIAN

D 49.17.13 (?)

ANTONINUS PIUS

D 29.1.9 (?)
CJ 4.32.1 (?)

SEPTIMIUS SEVERUS
and *CARACALLA*

CJ 3.31.2 (200)
4.61.3 (?)
12.33.I (?)
(addressed to recruits?)
Frag. Vat. 295 (210)

CARACALLA

CJ 1.18.1 (212)
2.18.8 (217?)
4.32.6 (212)
4.32.10 (?)
5.16.2 (213)
5.53.3 (215)
5.65.1 (213)
5.72.1 (205)
6.21.1 (212)
6.21.2 (213)
6.46.3 (215)

7.53.4 (216)
9.16.1 (215)
10.53.1 (?)
10.55.1 (?)
12.35.1 (?)
12.35.2 (?)
12.35.3 (?)

SEVERUS ALEXANDER

2.12.7 (223)
2.12.12 (230)
2.27.1 (?)
2.43.2 (226)
2.50.2 (222)
2.50.3 (223)
3.36.4 (?)
3.37.2 (222)
3.42.1 (222)
3.44.5 (224)
4.34.1 (234)
4.39.4 (223)
4.39.6 (230) = 7.10.3
4.44.1 (222)
4.51.1 (224)
4.54.2 (222)
4.54.3 (?)
4.65.7 (227)

4.65.9 (234)
6.21.5 (224)
6.24.3 (223)
6.30.2 (223)
7.10.3 (230) = 4.39.6
7.35.1 (224)
(addressed to a veteran)
8.1.1 (224) cf. 8.10.3
8.16.4 (225)
9.23.5 (230)
10.44.1 (?)
(addressed to a veteran)
12.36.2 (224)
12.36.3 (224)
D 49.13.1

GORDIAN

CJ 2.3.14 (241)
     2.4.7 (238)
     2.4.8 (239)
     2.9.2 (238)
     2.12.13 (239)
     2.19.5 (239)
     2.22.1 (238) = 4.13.1
     2.22.2 (241)
     2.49.1 (239)
     2.50.5 (240)
     2.52.1 (238)
     2.52.2 (238)
     2.52.3 (238) = 3.32.4

3.32.4 (238) = 2.52.3
3.32.6 (239) = 4.34.3
3.33.7 (243)
3.36.6 (?)
3.42.5 (239)
4.13.1 (238) = 2.22.1
4.21.5 (240)
4.31.8 (?)
4.34.2 (238)
4.34.3 (239) = 3.32.6
4.34.4 (?)
4.35.6 (238)
4.48.4 (239)
4.52.1 (?)
4.52.2 (?)
4.54.5 (?)
4.64.1 (238)
5.65.2 (239)
(addressed to a veteran)
6.21.8 (238)
6.22.1 (243)
6.30.3 (241)
9.1.8 (238)
9.1.10 (239)
9.9.15 (242)
12.35.5 (?)
12.35.6 (?)
12.35.7 (?)
(addressed to a veteran)
12.36.4 (?)
FIRA[2] 2, p. 659, 3.6.1.

Table 2

This contains rescripts conerning soldiers, but not necessarily addressed to an individual soldier.

TRAJAN

D 29.1.24
49.16.4 pref.
49.16.4.5

HADRIAN

D 22.5.3.6

28.3.6.6
29.1.34; cf. 49.16.6.7
29.1.41.1
48.3.12
49.16.5.6
49.16.5.8
49.16.6.7

ANTONINUS PIUS

D 29.1.15

29.1.30

MARCUS AURELIUS

D 29.1.3

29.1.28

SEPTIMIUS SEVERUS

CJ 2.50.1 (197)

SEPTIMIUS SEVERUS AND CARACALLA

D 40.4.52

49.15.9.1

D 49.16.3.1

49.16.9

49.18.5

CARACALLA

CJ 6.21.3 (213)

9.47.5 (?)

SEVERUS ALEXANDER

CJ 2.12.9 (?)

3.28.9 (223)

6.50.7 (226)

12.35.4 (?)

12.36.1 (223)

GORDIAN

CJ 2.11.15 (239)

6.21.9 (238)

APPENDIX 3

THE PRIVILEGES OF MARRIAGE AND CITIZENSHIP ON DISCHARGE

The evidence for these privileges is contained in the discharge *diplomata* given to individual veterans. These exist for soldiers of the *auxilia*, the fleets, Praetorians, and members of the Urban Cohorts. A papyrus demonstrates conclusively that legionaries did not normally receive *diplomata* (A. Degrassi, *Aegyptus* 10 (1929), 242 = Lewis and Reinhold, *Roman Civilization II* (1966), 525). The reason for this is obscure. Nesselhauf suggested that the grant of citizenship to non-citizen soldiers required individual authorization. The grant of *diplomata* to the troops in Rome could then be explained on the hypothesis that it was a mark of honour (*CIL* XVI, pp. 147 ff.).

The traditional view of the discharge privileges given to soldiers, at least up to 144, is as follows. Veterans of the *auxilia* and the fleet received citizenship for themselves, their existing children, and their posterity. This did not exclude citizenship for children born before service or other than those which they had at the time of the grant. If the soldier's wife were already a citizen, their subsequent children would be automatically citizens, since the marriage would be valid on discharge. If the wife were not a citizen, the grant of *conubium* (the right of legal marriage and the effective consequences) would produce the same consequences for children subsequently born to the wife covered by the grant. The consensus of scholarly opinion is that the Praetorians and the urban troops, although receiving *conubium* with the women with whom they had lived in service (even if *peregrinae*), did not receive citizenship for children actually born in service. Although there are no *diplomata*, it is usually assumed that legionaries were treated in the same way as the urban troops (Nesselhauf, *CIL* XVI, pp. 147 ff.; H.M.D. Parker, *The Roman Legions* (1928) and reprint with corrections 1958), 242 ff.; P. Meyer, *Der römische Konkubinat* (1895), 108 ff.; E. Sander, *RhM* 101 (1958), 160 ff.; G.R. Watson, *The Roman Soldier* (1969), 134 ff.; P. Garnsey, 'Septimius Severus and the Marriage of Roman Soldiers', *CSCA* 3

(1970), 47). Yet it would be *a priori* very odd if the auxiliaries and the sailors of the fleet received more privileges than the citizen legionaries and the Praetorians, who were the only source of military strength at the centre of power, and who were indeed entrusted with the emperor's physical safety.

To explain this anomaly, Durry suggested that as the Praetorian Guard was an élite corps, discipline was more rigorously enforced in it than in the rest of the army. But it is strange to suppose that in matters of discipline the Praetorians were more harshly treated than the other troops, seeing that the Guard enjoyed special privileges in pay and conditions of service (note *Frag. vat.* 195 = *FIRA*² 2, p.503; see above, p.84.) Moreover this argument does not explain why the legionaries also received fewer privileges than the auxiliaries and the sailors of the fleets.

A fresh examination of the evidence can suggest that the Guard, the Urban Cohorts, and possibly the legionaries, received citizenship for children born in service. The formula on the Praetorian *diplomata* runs as follows: *CIL* XVI.21 (AD 76) 'Nomina speculatorum qui in praetorio meo militaverunt item militum, qui in cohortibus novem praetoriis et quattuor urbanis, subieci, quibus fortiter et pie militia functis ius triubo conubi dumtaxat cum singulis et primis uxoribus, ut, etiamsi peregrini iuris feminas matrimonio suo inuxerint, proinde liberos tollant ac si ex duobus civibus Romanis natos' With regard to the precise formula used, if the emperor had wished merely to grant citizenship to the Praetorians' children born after discharge, he could have accomplished this through the grant of *conubium* to their wives — 'ius tribuo conubi dumtaxat cum singulis et primis uxoribus etiam peregrinis'. For the 'ius conubi' meant that the subsequent issue of peregrine wives would be Roman citizens. Therefore the clause introduced by 'ut' seems to be superfluous, unless it is intended to add a further privilege. It is difficult to see what such a privilege could be if not a grant of citizenship to children born in service. The traditional view of the privileges conferred by Praetorian *diplomata* appears to depend on the unwarranted assumption that 'tollere' must mean 'to beget'. But the verb can also mean 'to raise', and it would be odd to say 'beget children just as if born to two Roman citizens'. If, however, 'tollere' is taken to mean 'to raise', the diploma reads: 'So that, even if they shall have joined to them in marriage women of peregrine status, they may raise their children just as if they have been born from two Roman citizens.' In the context, without any qualification, the word 'liberi' should refer to any existing children whom the soldier has; the *diploma* would then mean that children born to peregrine wives during service could be raised as Roman citizens from the moment of the soldier's discharge and formal marriage.

Against this it may be argued that, if the author of the *diplomata* had wished to make it clear that children of unions contracted during service received citizenship, he should have written 'iunxerunt iunxerintque'. But the future perfect is used presumably because the author is looking forward to the moment when, after discharge, the soldier will legally marry his concubine, and has in mind that the marital union will be in being when the two raise their children. Indeed the absence of 'iunxerunt' can be explained on the hypothesis that prior to discharge no legal union could have taken place (before the time of Septimius Severus). The language certainly does not rule out the possibility that the women eventually to be linked in marriage with the soldiers would be those with whom they had formed liaisons in service, and that any existing children of such liaisons could be raised as Roman citizens.

A passage of Gaius (*Inst.* 1.57) is also relevant:

Unde et veteranis quibusdam concedi solet principalibus constitutionibus conubium cum his Latinis peregrinisque quas primas post missionem uxores duxerint; et qui ex eo matrimonio nascuntur, et cives Romani et in potestate parentum fiunt.

And so in the decisions of emperors, certain veterans are usually granted the right of *conubium* with the women of Latin and peregrine status whom they first took as their wives after their discharge; and the children who are born to such unions, are both Roman citizens and in the legal control of their parents.

It is usually thought that Gaius is referring to the legionaries and the Praetorians in this passage, and that the phrase 'et qui ex . . . fiunt' proves that only children born in legal marriage after service could receive the citizenship (Parker, *Roman Legions*, 242). However, this is not a necessary conclusion. Firstly, Gaius wrote the *Institutes c.*160, and by this time the *auxilia* had lost the right of citizenship for those children born during military service (see Nesselhauf, *CIL* XVI, p. 147 f.). It is possible that Gaius is referring to the auxiliary troops and not the Guard or the legionaries. Secondly, it seems that Gaius is not quoting the formula of the *diploma* precisely; he has taken part of the usual wording — 'conubium cum his . . . duxerint' — and then added his own interpretation — 'et qui ex eo . . . fiunt'. He is particularly interested in the question of *patria potestas* and how children came under it. Gaius claims that children who were born to soldiers after discharge in legitimate marriage were 'in patria potestate' as well as being Roman citizens. This implies that children born to a soldier in service were not 'in potestate', but it need not imply that such children were not granted citizenship.

The implication, then, of what Gaius says is that children born after the grant of *conubium* were citizens and 'in potestate'. On the other hand, in default of specific provision in the grants, which is not found, the *liberi* already born during military service would not be 'in potestate'. And so, unless it is assumed that the grants of citizenship recorded in the *diplomata* were construed to mean that all *liberi* were 'in patris potestatem adducti', it must follow that the children born to soldiers before discharge were not in their legal control. Now Gaius is referring only to some veterans ('veteranis quibusdam'), and it was suggested above that he was in fact concerned with the *auxilia*. If this is correct, it may be conjectured that there were some veterans (not defined by Gaius) whose children born in service were held to be 'in patria potestate'. It is surely the Praetorians (and presumably the Urban cohorts) whom one would expect to be the most highly privileged in this respect, since they were better treated than the rest of the army.

To revert to the Praetorian *diplomata*, if it is correct that the 'ut' clause was intended to add an extra privilege, it may be suggested that its effect was not only to confer the citizenship on already existing children, but also to bring them under the veteran's *patria potestas*. It is possible to construe the phrase 'ut . . . inuxerint' to have a fairly wide reference not merely to a union that was in being when the soldier and his wife 'raised children', but a union that had been in existence during military service. In that event, the use of the term 'matrimonium suum' was perhaps intended to validate retroactively the previous concubinage as a marriage 'iure civili'; and as such the children would not only be Roman citizens, but also 'in patria potestate' (cf. Gaius, 1.56). Indeed the use of the word 'tollant' may be deliberately ambiguous since the intention was to apply the same rule to children already born who were not hitherto 'in patria potestate', and to children born after the union had been legally recognized, who would certainly be citizens and in the legal control of their father. This formulation may seem unnecessary indirect and ambiguous. But perhaps the author desired to state the privilege in as brief a formula as possible, seeing that it had to be produced on so many handy documents.

It is possible that the legionaries, like the Praetorian Guard and the Urban Cohorts, received citizenship for any children born in service, since it is hard to see why they should have been treated less well than the *auxilia*. I do not find convincing the argument that emperors wished, by withholding citizenship from soldiers' children born in service, to attract them into the army, where they would receive a grant of citizenship and legitimacy (Campbell, *JRS* 1978, 164-5).

It should be noted that there is some evidence to indicate that legionary veterans did have the same privileges as the *auxilia*. In 31 BC Octavian granted to all veterans citizenship for themselves if they did not have it already, their parents, children and wives — 'ipsis parentibus liberisque eorum et uxoribus qui secum erunt immunitatem omnium rerum dare, utique optimo iure optimaque lege cives Romani sint' (*FIRA*² 1, p. 316). The 'liberi' must be already existing children (i.e. born before or in service) because subsequent children would be citizens by birth from citizen parents and there would be no need to mention them specifically. The word 'liberi', used without any qualification, most naturally should mean all the veteran's children. These concessions doubtless represent a strong bid for the support of the troops and may not be typical.

A similar edict was published by Domitian in 88/9 conferring privileges on all veterans, and extending citizenship to those soldiers who did not have it already, their wives, children, and parents (*FIRA*² 1, p. 424). This is parallel to Octavian's grant in intention and wording, and for the same reasons 'liberi' must again refer to a veteran's existing children. This may have been an innovation introduced by Domitian. On the other hand, it is perhaps more likely that in the edict Domitian states in formal terms and links specifically with his own name a privilege that was already established, but may have been bestowed on an *ad hoc* basis.

The measure was apparently in operation in 94. One Marcus Valerius Quadratus, a legionary veteran of the *X Fretensis*, had copied down for himself the original constitution referring to his discharge, and the provisions of Domitian's edict (*FIRA*² 1, pp. 426–7). The text is defective and Parker (*Roman Legions*, 240 ff.) suggested the following restoration:' ⟨civitatem dedit eis v⟩ eteranorum cum uxoribus et liberis s[upra] s[criptis] in aere incisi⟨s⟩ aut si qui caelibes sint cum is quas postea duxissent dumtaxat singuli singulas, qui militaverunt Hierosolymnis in legione X Fretense . . .' However there are two objections to this supplement. (i) It would be odd and ambiguous Latin for 'he gave citizenship to those of the veterans with [= and to] their wives and children'. (ii) The phrase 'cum uxoribus' is balanced with 'aut si qui caelibes . . . cum is quas postea duxissent', which, in line with the language of discharge *diplomata*, should reasonably refer to marriage and a grant of *conubium*. Hence 'cum uxoribus' ought to refer to a 'grant of marriage rights with'. 'Caelibes' implies a mention in a preceding clause of *conubium* for those who were not 'caelibes'. That however would give an impossible suggestion of *conubium* with the *liberi*. The text may have been seriously distorted when it was being inscribed.

In any event, it seems clear enough from his *tria nomina* that Quadratus was a Roman citizen of long standing. If he had received his citizenship under the Flavians, we would expect him to have taken the name 'Flavius'. At the end of the tablet he makes a statement of the birth of three children to him in military service, obviously from a liaison with a *peregrina*, and the grant of Roman citizenship to them — 'testatus est . . . in militia sibi . . . omnes tres s.s. natos esse, eosque in aere incisos civitatem Romanam consecutos esse beneficio eiusdem optumi principis.' The word *beneficium* does not imply that the grant was unusual or bestowed on only a few soldiers. *Beneficium* surely refers to Domitian's recent edict extending or confirming privileges for veterans, for all military privileges were imperial *beneficia.* There is no reason to think that the *X Fretensis* or its veterans were in any way unusual. If therefore, under Domitian, legionaries were receiving citizenship for children born in service, it is difficult to see when this right can have been removed from them. After the rebellion of Saturninus, Domitian will have wished to keep the soldiers as happy as possible; Nerva was in no position to take liberties with the army, and Trajan went out of his way to extend the legal rights of soldiers. I conjecture that informally soldiers of the legions had always received the citizenship for children born in service, that for the first time since 31 BC this was formally confirmed in general terms by Domitian, and that thereafter it was one of the legionaries' regular discharge privileges.

It remains to consider why between 140 and 144 at least the *auxilia* lost the right of citizenship for those children born in military service. This problem has much vexed scholars (for a summary, see Nesselhauf, *CIL* XVI; also *Hist.* 8 (1959), 434 — arguing that the children of auxiliary decurions and centurions still received citizenship; Mommsen, *CIL* III, p. 2015; Kraft, *Rekrutierung*, 117 ff.), and there is little new to be said. Antoninus Pius, it seems, took a personal decision to reduce some of the army's privileges, and the personal decisions of autocrats are most difficult to explain. The move perhaps had a limited purpose, to reduce cohabitation and the production of illegitimate children with their troublesome legal consequences. Cohabitation was probably on the increase after the concessions made to legionaries by Trajan and Hadrian. Pius could have made marriage legal or he could have enforced the rules strictly against the offspring of illicit liaisons. He may have adopted a middle course and reduced the privileges of the *auxilia* alone, possibly as an experiment to test the reaction of the army. The *diplomata* of the Praetorians continue unchanged, but it is impossible to say if the legionaries, assuming that they did receive the citizenship for *liberi* born in service, lost this right under Pius. We do know that the sailors continued to receive citizenship for children born in service (*CIL* XVI, no. 100 — AD 152). However by 166 the formula of their *diplomata* had changed to include a reference to the wife with whom they lived 'concessa consuetudine'. This phrase must mean the practice by which emperors tacitly allowed soldiers to keep a 'wife' during service (See Campbell, *JRS* 1978, p. 165, n.89; cf. C.G. Starr, The *Roman Imperial Navy*[2] (1960), 91 ff.). The reason for this change may be that the restriction in *auxilia* privileges had occasioned the sailors some difficulty in obtaining their rights because local officials believed that the new restriction applied to them. And so the privileges of the sailors had to be stated more specifically.

Finally, it is worth emphasizing that the right of *conubium* with a *peregrina* and the grant of citizenship for existing *liberi* of such unions were privileges to which no civilian could ordinarily aspire. (For the legal privileges of veterans, see *D* 49. 18. 1-5; P. Garnsey, *Social Status and Legal Privilege in the Roman Empire* (1970), 245-51).

BIBLIOGRAPHY

This is not intended to be a general bibliography of the period 31 BC-AD 235. It lists books and articles expressly cited in the footnotes, with the exception of a few peripheral items. Standard collections of documents and evidence, and most of the works dealing with provincial *fasti*, have been excluded.

ALEXANDER, P.J., 'Letters and Speeches of the Emperor Hadrian', *HSCPh* 49 (1938), 141.

ALFÖLDI, A., 'Hasta, Summa Imperii', *AJA* 2nd series 63 (1959), 1.

——, *Die Monarchische Repräsentation im römische Kaiserreiche*, Darmstadt (1971).

ALFÖLDY, G., 'Septimius Severus und der Senat', *BJ* 168 (1968), 112.

——, 'Der römische Generälitat', *BJ* 169 (1969), 233.

——, *Noricum*, London (1974).

——, 'Consuls and Consulars under the Antonines: Prosopography and History', *Ancient Society* 7 (1976), 263.

BADIAN, E., *Imperialism in the Late Republic*, Oxford (1968).

BALSDON, J.P.V.D., *The Emperor Gaius*, Oxford (1934).

BANG, M., 'Die militärische Laufbahn des Kaisers Maximinus', *Hermes* 41 (1906), 300.

BARBIERI, G., *L'Albo Senatorio da Settimio Severo a Carino*, Rome (1952).

——, 'Aspetti della politica di Settimio Severo', *Epigraphica* 14 (1952), 1.

BARDON, H., *Les Empereurs et les Lettres Latines d'Auguste à Hadrian*, Paris (1940).

BARNES, T.D., 'Hadrian and Lucius Verus', *JRS* 57 (1967), 65.

——, 'The Family and Career of Septimius Severus', *Hist.* 16 (1967), 87.

——, 'The Victories of Augustus', *JRS* 64 (1974), 21.

BAUMAN, R.A., *Impietas in Principem, a Study of Treason against the Roman Emperor with Special Reference to the First Century AD.*, Munich (1974).

BECATTI, G., *La Colonna Coclide Istoriata*, Rome (1960).

BELL, H.I., 'A Latin Registration of Birth', *JRS* 27 (1937), 33.

BELLEZZA, A., *Massimo il Trace*, Genoa (1964).

BELOCH, K.J., *Die Bevölkerung der griechisch-römischen Welt*, Leipzig (1886).

BENGTSON, H., *Die Flavier*, Munich (1978).

BERANGER, J., *Recherches sur L'Aspect Idéologique du Principat*, Basel (1953).

Van BERCHEM, *L'Annone Militaire dans L'Empire Romain au troisième siècle*, Paris (1937).

BERGER, A., *An Encyclopedic Dictionary of Roman Law*, Philadelphia (1953).

BERSANETTI, G., *Studi sull' Imperatore Massimo il Trace*, Rome (1964).

BIRLEY, A.R., 'The Status of Moesia Superior under Marcus Aurelius', *Acta Antiqua Philippopolitana* (1963), 109.

———, 'The Duration of Provincial Commands under Antoninus Pius', *Corolla Memoriae Erich Swoboda Dedicata*, Cologne (1966), 43.

———, *Marcus Aurelius*, London (1966).

———, 'The Coup d' Etat of the Year 193', *BJ* 169 (1969), 247.

———, *Septimius Severus*, London (1971).

———, *The Fasti of Roman Britain*, Oxford (1981).

BIRLEY, E.B., 'Senators in the Emperor's Service', *PBA* 39 (1953), 197.

———, *Roman Britain and the Roman Army*, Kendal (1953).

———, 'The Epigraphy of the Roman Army', *Actes du Deuxième Congres Internationale d'Epigraphie Greque et Latine* (1953), 226.

———, 'Beforderungen und Versetzungen im römischen Heere', *Carntuntum Jahrb.* (1963-4), 21.

———, 'Alae and Cohortes Milliariae', *Corolla Memoriae Erich Swoboda Dedicata* Cologne (1966), 54.

———, 'Septimius Severus and the Roman Army', *Epig. Stud.* 8 (1969), 63.

BOSWORTH, A.B., 'Arian and the Alani', *HSCPh* 81 (1977), 217.

BOTERMANN, H., *Die Soldaten und die römishe Politik in der Zeit von Caesars Tod bis zum Begrundung des Zweiten Triumvirats*, Munich (1968).

BOWERSOCK, G.W., 'Syria Under Vespasian', *JRS* 63 (1973), 133.

BOWMAN, A.K., 'A Letter of Avidius Cassius?', *JRS* 60 (1970), 20.

BOYCE, A.A., 'Ornamenta Triumphalia', *Class. Phil.* 37 (1942), 130.

———, 'The Twelfth Imperial Acclamation of Septimius Severus, *AJA* 53 (1949), 337.

BRAND, C.E., *Roman Military Law*, Austin (1968).

BREEZE, D.J., 'Pay Grades and Ranks below the Centurionate', *JRS* 61 (1971), 130.

——, 'The Organization of the Career Structure of the Immunes and Principales of the Roman Army', *BJ* 174 (1974), 245.

BRILLIANT, R., *Gesture and Rank in Roman Art*, New Haven (1963).

——, *The Arch of Septimius Severus in the Roman Forum MAAR* 29 (1967).

BRUHL, A., 'Le Souvenir d'Alexandre le Grand et les Romains', *Mélanges d'Archéologique et d'Histoire* 47–8 (1930–1), 202.

BRUNT, P.A., 'Pay and Superannuation in the Roman Army', *PBSR* 18 (1950), 50.

——, 'The Revolt of Vindex and the Fall of Nero', *Latomus* 18 (1959), 531.

——, 'Charges of Provincial Maladministration under the Early Principate', *Hist.* 10 (1961), 189.

——, 'The Army and the Land in the Roman Revolution', *JRS* 52 (1962), 75.

——, Review of Meyer, *Die Aussenpolitik des Augustus und die Augusteische Dichtung* (1961) in *JRS* 53 (1963), 170.

——, Review of Botermann in *Gnomon* 41 (1969), 515.

——, *Italian Manpower* (1971).

——, Review of Garnsey, *Social Status and Legal Privilege in the Roman Empire* (1970), in *JRS* 62 (1972), 166.

——, 'The Fall of Perennis in Dio-Xiphilinus 72.9.2', *CQ* 23 (1973), 172.

——, 'Conscription and Volunteering in the Roman Army', *Scripta Classica Israelica* 1 (1974), 90.

——, 'C. Fabricius Tuscus and the Augustan Dilectus', *ZPE* 13 (1974), 161.

——, 'Marcus Aurelius in his *Meditations*', *JRS* 64 (1974), 1.

——, 'The Administrators of Roman Egypt', *JRS* 65 (1975), 124.

——, 'Lex de Imperio Vespasiani', *JRS* 67 (1977), 95.

——, 'Laus Imperii', in *Imperialism in the Ancient World* (P. Garnsey and C.R. Whittaker, eds.), Cambridge (1978).

——, Review of Fears, *Princeps a Diis Electus, JRS* 69 (1979), 168

BUCKLAND, W.W., *A Text-Book of Roman Law*[3], Cambridge (1975).

BURTON, G.P., 'The Issuing of Mandata to Proconsuls and a New Inscription from Cos', *ZPE* 21 (1976), 63.

CAGNAT, R., *L'Armée Romaine d'Afrique*, Paris (1913).

CAMPBELL, J.B., 'Who were the *viri militares?*', *JRS* 65 (1975), 11.

——, 'The Marriage of Roman Soldiers under the Empire', *JRS* 68 (1978), 153.

CAPRINO, C., *La Colonna di Marco Aurelio*, Rome (1955).

CHAMPLIN, E., *Fronto and Antonine Rome*, Harvard (1980).

CHARLESWORTH, M.P., 'Virtues of the Roman Emperor', *PBA* 23 (1937), 105.

————, 'Nero: Some Aspects', *JRS* 40 (1950), 69.

CHEESMAN, G.L., *The Auxilia of the Roman Imperial Army*, Oxford (1914).

CHILVER, G., 'The Army in Politics, AD 68–70', *JRS* 47 (1957), 29.

————, *A Historical Commentary on Tacitus' Histories I and II*, Oxford (1979).

CICHORIUS, C., *Die Reliefs des Trajanssäule*, Berlin (1886–1900).

COMBÈS, R., *Imperator*, Paris (1966).

CROOK, J.A., *Consilium Principis*, Cambridge (1955).

————, *Law and Life of Rome*, London (1967).

DAICOVICIU, H., 'Osservazioni intorno alla Colonna Traiana', *Dacia* 3 (1959), 311.

DARIS, S., *Documenti per la Storia dell' Esercito Romano in Egitto*, Milan (1964).

DAUBE, D., *Roman Law: Linguistic, Social, and Philosophical Aspects*, Edinburgh (1969).

DAVIES, R.W., 'The Daily Life of the Roman Soldier under the Principate', *ANRW* II.1, 299.

DEGRASSI, A., 'Il papiro 1026 della Societa Italiana e i diplomi militari Romani', *Aegyptus* 10 (1929), 242.

DEVELIN, R., 'Pay Rises under Severus and Caracalla and the Question of the Annona Militaris', *Latomus* 30 (1971), 687.

DOBSON, B., 'The Significance of the Centurion and the Primipilaris', *ANRW* II.1, 392.

————, *Die Primipilares*, Cologne (1978).

VON DOMASZEWSKI, A., *Die Fahren im römischen Heere*, Vienna (1885) = *Aufsätze*, 1.

————, *Die Religion des römischen Heeres* (1895) = *Aufsätze*, 81.

————, 'Der Truppensold der Kaiserzeit', *Neue Heidelberger Jahrb.* 90 (1899), 218 = *Aufsätze*, 210.

————, *Die Rangordung des römischen Heeres* (ed. B. Dobson), Cologne (1967).

————, *Aufsätze zur römischen Heeresgeschichte*, Darmstadt (1972).

DUDLEY, D.R., 'The Celebration of Claudius' British Victories', *Univ. of Birmingham Historical Journal* 7 (1959), 6.

DUNCAN-JONES, R.P., *The Economy of the Roman Empire*[2], Cambridge (1982).

DURRY, M., 'Juvénal et les Prétoriens', *REL* 13 (1935), 95.

————, *Les Cohortes Prétoriennes*, Paris (1938).

ECK, W., *Senatoren von Vespasian bis Hadrian*, Munich (1970).

EVANS, J.E.K., 'The Dating of Domitian's Wars against the Chatti again', *Hist.* 24 (1975), 121.

FEARS, J.R., *Princeps a Diis Electus: The Divine Election of the Emperor as a Political Concept at Rome*, Rome (1977).

450   BIBLIOGRAPHY

FINK, R.O., 'The Feriale Duranum', *YCS* 7 (1940), 1.

———, 'Feriale Duranum 1.1 and Mater Castrorum', *AJA* 48 (1944), 17.

———, *Roman Military Records on Papyrus*, Cleveland (1971).

FINK, R.O., GILLIAM, J.F., BRADFORD-WELLS, C., *Dura Final Report: The Parchments and Papyri* V. 1, New Haven (1959).

FLORESCU, F.B., *Die Siegesdenkmal von Adamklissi; Tropaeum Traiani*, Bonn (1965).

———, *Die Trajanssäule*, Bonn (1969).

FORNI, G., *Il Reclutamento delle legioni da Augusto a Diocleziano*, Rome (1953).

———, 'Estrazione etnica e sociale dei soldati delle legioni nei primi tre secoli dell' impero', *ANRW* II.1, 339.

FRANK, T., *An Economic Survey of Ancient Rome* I-V, New York (1933-40).

FRERE, S., *Britannia²*, London (1974).

GAGÉ, J., 'Victoria Augusti', *Revue Archéologique* 96-7 (1930), 1.

———, 'La Théologie de la Victoire Impériale', *Rev. Hist.* 171 (1933), 1.

GARNSEY, P., *Social Status and Legal Privilege in the Roman Empire*, Oxford (1970).

———, 'Septimius Severus and the Marriage of Soldiers', *CSCA* 3 (1970), 45.

GILLIAM, J.F., 'Paganus in B.G.U. 696', *AJP* 73 (1952), 75.

———, 'The Roman Military Feriale', *HThR* 47 (1954), 190.

———, 'The Appointment of Auxiliary Centurions', *TAPA* 88 (1958), 155.

———, 'The Governors of Syria Coele from Severus to Diocletian', *AJP* 79 (1958), 225.

GORDON, A.E., *Quintus Veranius, Consul AD 49*, California (1952).

GRAHAM, A.J., 'The Division of Britain', *JRS* 56 (1966), 92.

———, 'The Limitations of Prosopography in Roman Imperial History', *ANRW* II.1, 136.

GRANT, M., *The Army of the Caesars*, London (1975).

GRIFFIN, M., *Seneca, A Philosopher in Politics*, Oxford (1976).

GROSSO, F., *La Lotta Politica al Tempo di Commodo*, Turin (1964).

GUEY, J., *Essai sur la Guerre Parthique de Trajan (114-117)*, Bucharest (1937).

HAMBERG, P., *Studies in Roman Imperial Art*, Uppsala (1945).

HAMMOND, M., 'Corbulo and Nero's Eastern Policy', *HSCPh* 45 (1934), 81.

———, 'Septimius Severus, Roman Bureaucrat', *HSCPh* 51 (1940), 137.

———, 'The Transmission of the Powers of the Roman Emperor',

MAAR 24 (1956), 63.

————, 'The Composition of the Senate AD 68–235', *JRS* 47 (1957), 74.

————, *The Antonine Monarchy*, Rome (1959).

HARMAND, J., *L'Armée et le Soldat à Rome 105–57 BC*, Paris (1967).

HARRER, G.A., *Studies in the History of the Roman Province of Syria*, Princeton (1915).

HASEBROEK, J., *Untersuchungen zur Geschichte des Kaisers Septimius Severus*, Heidelberg (1921).

HASEL, F.J., *Der Trajansbogen in Benevent*, Mainz (1966).

HAYWOOD, R.M., 'The African Policy of Septimius Severus' *TAPA* 71 (1940), 175.

————, 'A further note on the African Policy of Septimius Severus', *Hommages à A. Grenier* (1962), 786 = *Collection Latomus*, vol. 58.

HENDERSON, M.I., Review of Lepper, *Trajan's Parthian War* in *JRS* 39 (1949), 121.

HERRMANN, P., *Der römische Kaisereid*, Göttingen (1968).

HIGHET, G., *Juvenal the Satirist*, Oxford (1954).

HIRSCHFELD, O., *Die Kaiserlichen Verwaltungsbeamten bis auf Diocletian*², Berlin (1905).

HOHL, E., 'Kaiser Commodus und Herodian', *SDAW* (1954), 1.

HOLSCHER, T., *Victoria Romana*, Mainz (1969).

HONORÉ, A.M., *Gaius*, Oxford (1962).

————, 'The Severan Jurists. A Preliminary Survey', *Studia et Documenta Historiae et Iuris* 28 (1962), 162.

————, 'Imperial Rescripts AD 193–305: Authorship and Authenticity', *JRS* 69 (1979), 51.

————, *Emperors and Lawyers*, Oxford (1981).

HOPKINS, K., *Conquerors and Slaves*, Cambridge (1978).

————, 'Taxes and Trade in the Roman Empire, 200 BC–AD 400', *JRS* 70 (1980), 101.

HOWE, L., *The Praetorian Prefect from Commodus to Diocletian*, Chicago (1942).

HÜTTL, W., *Antoninus Pius*, 2 vols., Prague (1933).

INSTINSKY, H.U., 'Wandlungen des römischen Kaisertums', *Gymnasium* 63 (1946), 260.

JOLOWICZ, H.F., *A Historical Introduction to the Study of Roman Law*³ (ed. Nicholas), Cambridge, 1972.

JONES, A.H.M., 'Numismatics and History', in *Essays in Roman Coinage Presented to Harold Mattingly* (1956), 13.

————, *Studies in Roman Government and Law*, Oxford (1960).

————, *The Later Roman Empire*, 3 vols., Oxford, (1964).

JONES, B.W., 'The Dating of Domitian's War against the Chatti', *Hist.* 22 (1973), 79.

———, *Domitian and the Senatorial Order: a prosopographical Study of Domitian's Relationship with the Senate AD 81-96*. Philadelphia (1979).

JONES, H.S., 'The Historical Interpretation of Trajan's Column' *PBSR* 5 (1910), 435.

KASER, M., *Das römische Privatrecht*, 2 vols., Munich (1959).

KEYES, C.W., *The Rise of the Equites*, Princeton (1915).

KIECHLE, F., 'Die Taktik des Flavius Arrianus', *45 Bericht der röm.-ger. Komission 1964* (1965), 85.

KIENAST, D., *Untersuchungen zu den Kriegsflotten der römischen Kaiserzeit*, Bonn (1966).

———, 'Augustus und Alexander', *Gymnasium* 76 (1969), 430.

KNEISSL, P., *Die Siegestitulatur der römischen Kaiser*, Göttingen (1969).

KOEPPEL, G., 'Profectio und Adventus', *BJ* 169 (1969), 130.

KRAAY, C.M., 'The Coinage of Vindex and Galba, AD 68, and the Continuity of the Augustan Principate', *Num. Chron.* 9 (1949), 129.

KRAFT, E., *Zur Rekrutierung von Alen und Kohorten an Rhein und Donau*, Bern (1951).

KUNKEL, W., *Herkunft und soziale Stellung der römischen Juristen:* Forschungen zum römischen Recht 4, Weimar (1952).

———, *An Introduction to Roman Legal and Constitutional History*² (translation by J.M. Kelly), Oxford (1973).

LAMBRECHTS, P., 'L'Empereur Lucius Verus: Essai de Réhabilitation', *Ant. Class.* 111 (1934), 173.

———, *La Composition du Sénat Romain de l'Accession au trône d'Hadrian à la morte de Commode (117-192)*, Antwerp (1936).

LEPPER, F.A., *Trajan's Parthian War*, Oxford (1948).

LESQUIER, J., *L'Armée Romaine d'Egypt d'Auguste à Diocletian*, Paris (1898).

LEVICK, B.M., 'Caracalla's Path', *Hommages à M. Renard*, Brussels (1969), 426.

———, *Tiberius the Politician*, London (1976).

LUTTWAK, E.N., *The Grand Strategy of the Roman Empire*, Baltimore (1976).

MANN, J.C., 'A Note on the Numeri', *Hermes* 82 (1954), 501.

———, 'The Raising of New Legions during the Principate', *Hermes* 91 (1963), 483.

MAXFIELD, V.A., *The Military Decorations of the Roman Army*, London (1981).

McCANN, A.M., *The Portraits of Septimius Severus (AD 193-211)*, *MAAR* 30 (1968).

MacMULLEN, R., *Soldier and Civilian in the Later Roman Empire*,

Harvard (1963).

——, *Enemies of the Roman Order: Treason, Unrest and Alienation in the Roman Empire*, Harvard (1967).

MILLAR, F., 'The Fiscus in the First Two Centuries', *JRS* 53 (1963), 39.

——, 'The Aerarium and its Officials under the Empire', *JRS* 54 (1964), 33.

——, *A Study of Cassius Dio*, Oxford (1964).

——, 'Epictetus and the Imperial Court', *JRS* 55 (1965), 141.

——, 'The Emperor, the Provinces, and the Senate', *JRS* 56 (1966), 156.

——, 'Emperors at Work', *JRS* 57 (1967), 9.

——, *The Roman Empire and its Neighbours* London (1967).

——, 'P. Herennius Dexipus: The Greek World and the Third Century Invasions', *JRS* 59 (1969), 12.

——, *The Emperor in the Roman World*, London (1977).

——, 'The World of the *Golden Ass*', *JRS* 71 (1981), 63.

MITCHELL, S., 'Requisitioned Transport in the Roman Empire: A New Inscription from Pisidia', *JRS* 66 (1976), 106.

MITTEIS, L., *Reichrecht und Volksrecht*, Leipzig (1891).

MITTEIS and WILCKEN, *Gründzuge und Chrestomathie der Papyruskunde I: Historischer Teil; II Juristischen Teil*, Leipzig (1912).

MOCSY, A., *Pannonia and Upper Moesia*, London (1974).

MOMIGLIANO, A.D., *Claudius: The Emperor and his Achievement*, Oxford (1934).

MOMMSEN, T., *Römische Staatsrecht*, Berlin (1887).

MORRIS, J., 'Leges Annales under the Principate', *Listy Filologické* 87 (1964), 316.

——, 'Leges Annales: Political Effects', *Listy Filologické* 88 (1965), 22.

MURPHY, G.T., *The Reign of the Emperor Septimius Severus from the Evidence of Inscriptions*, Philadelphia (1945).

NESSELHAUF, H., 'Das Bürgerrecht der Soldatenkinder', *Hist.* 8 (1959), 434.

NICHOLAS, B., *An Introduction to Roman Law*, Oxford (1962).

NICOLS, J., *Vespasian and the Partes Flavianae*, Wiesbaden (1978).

NOCK, A.D., 'The Roman Army and the Roman Religious Year', *HThR* 45 (1952), 187.

OLIVA, P., *Pannonia and the Onset of Crisis in the Roman Empire*, Prague (1962).

OLIVER, J.H., 'The Ruling Power: A Study of the Roman Empire in the Second Century after Christ through the Roman Oration of Aelius Aristides', *TAPhA* 43.4 (1953).

OPPERMANN, H., ed., *Römische Wertbegriffe*, Darmstadt (1967).

454 BIBLIOGRAPHY

PARKER, H.M.D., *The Roman Legions*, Cambridge (reprint with corrections, 1958).

——, *A History of the Roman World AD 138-337²*, London (1958).

PARSI, B., *Désignation et Investiture de L'Empereur Romain*, Paris (1963).

PASSERINI, A., *Le Coorti Pretorie*, Rome (1939).

——, 'Gli argumenti de Soldo Militare da Commodo a Massimo', *Athenaeum* 24 (1946), 145.

PEKARY, T., 'Studien zur römische Wahrungs und Finanzgeschichte von 161 bis 235 n. Chr.', *Hist.* 8 (1959), 443.

PFLAUM, H.G., *Le Marbre de Thorigny*, Paris (1948).

——, *Les Procurateurs équestres*, Paris (1950).

——, 'Les Governeurs de la Province Romaine d'Arabie de 193 à 304, *Syria* 34 (1957), 130.

——, *Les Carriéres procuratoriennes équestres sous the Haut-Empire romaine*, 3 vols., Paris (1960-1).

——, 'Comites Augusti', *Bayerische Vorgeschichtsblätter* 27 (1962), 90.

PICARD, G.C., *Les Trophées Romaines*, Paris (1957).

PISTOR, H., *Prinzeps und Patriziat*, Freiburg (1965).

PLATNAUER, M., *The Life and Reign of the Emperor Lucius Septimius Severus*, Oxford (1918).

VON PREMERSTEIN, A., *Vom Werden und Wesen des Prinzipats*, Munich (1937).

RICCOBONO, S., *Il Gnomon dell' Idios Logos*, Palermo (1950).

RICHMOND, I.A., 'Trajan's Army on Trajan's Column', *PBSR* 13 (1945), 1.

——, 'Gnaeus Iulius Agricola', *JRS* 34 (1944), 34.

ROBERT, L., 'Sur un Papyrus de Bruxelles', *Revue de Philologie* 3rd series 17 (1943), 111.

ROSSI, L., *Trajan's Column and the Dacian Wars*, London (1971).

ROSTOVTZEFF, M., *Social and Economic History of the Roman Empire,²* Oxford (1957).

RUBIN, Z., *Supernatural and Religious Sanction of the Emperor's Rule AD 193-217*, Oxford D. Phil. MSS 5317-8.

SALLER, R.P., 'Promotion and Patronage in Equestrian Careers', *JRS* 70 (1980), 44.

——, *Personal Patronage under the Early Empire*, Cambridge (1982).

SAEGER, R., *Tiberius*, London (1972).

SANDER, E., 'Das Recht des römischen Soldaten', *RhM* 101 (1958), 152.

——, 'Das römische Militarstrafrecht', *RhM* 103 (1960), 289.

SCHULZ, F., 'Roman Registers of Births and Birth Certificates, *JRS* 32 (1942), 79, and 33 (1943), 59.

SCHULZ, O., *Das Wesen des römischen Kaisertums der ersten Zwei Jahrhunderte*, Paderborn (1916).

——, *Vom Prinzipat zum Dominat*, Paderborn (1919).

SCHUR, W., 'Die Orientpolitik des Kaisers Nero', *Klio Beiheft* 15 (1923).

SCHÜRER, E., *History of the Jewish People in the Age of Jesus Christ*, vol. I (eds. G. Vermes and F. Millar), Edinburgh (1973).

SHERWIN-WHITE, A.N., *The Letters of Pliny*, Oxford (1966).

——, 'The Tabula Banasitana and the Constitutio Antoniniana', *JRS* 63 (1973), 86.

——, *The Roman Citizenship*², Oxford (1973).

SKEAT, T.C., *Two Papyri from Panopolis*, Dublin (1964).

SMALLWOOD, E.M., *The Jews under Roman Rule*, Leiden (1976).

SMITH, R.E., *Service in the Post-Marian Roman Army*, Manchester (1958).

SPEIDEL, M., *Die Equites Singulares Augusti*, Bonn (1965).

——, 'The Captor of Decebalus: a New Inscription from Philippi', *JRS* 60 (1970), 142.

——, 'The Pay of the Auxilia', *JRS* 63 (1973), 141.

——, *Guards of the Roman Armies*, Bonn (1978).

STADTER, P.A., *Arrian of Nicomedia*, University of Carolina (1980).

STARR, C.G., *The Roman Imperial Navy*², New York (1960).

STEIN, A., *Der römische Ritterstand*, Munich (1927).

——, *Die Präfekten von Ägypten in der römische Kaiserzeit*, Bern (1950).

STEINER, P., 'Die Dona Militaria', *BJ* 114 (1906), 89.

STOCKTON, D., *Cicero: A Political Biography*, Oxford (1971).

SUTHERLAND, C.H.V., 'The Intelligibility of Roman Imperial Coin Types', *JRS* 49 (1959), 46.

SYME, R., 'The Imperial Finances under Domitian, Nerva, and Trajan', *JRS* 20 (1930), 55 = Roman Papers, 1.

——, 'Some Notes on the Legions under Augustus', *JRS* 24 (1934), 14.

——, *The Roman Revolution*, Oxford (1939).

——, Review of Stein, *Die Reichsbeamten von Dazien* in *JRS* 36 (1946), 159.

——, 'Tacfarinas, the Musulamii and Thubursicu', *Studies in Honor of A.C. Johnson*, Princeton (1951), 113 = *Roman Papers*, 218.

——, 'The Jurist Neratius Priscus', *Hermes* 85 (1957), 480 = *Roman Papers*, 339.

——, 'The Friend of Tacitus', *JRS* 47 (1957), 131.

——, 'Consulates in Absence', *JRS* 48 (1958), 1 = *Roman Papers*, 378.

——, 'Imperator Caesar. A Study in Nomenclature', *Hist.* 7 (1958),

172 = *Roman Papers*, 361.

———, *Tacitus*, Oxford (1958).

———, 'The Wrong Marcius Turbo', *JRS* 52 (1962), 87 = *Roman Papers*, 541.

———, The Governors of Pannonia Inferior', *Hist.* 14 (1965), 342.

———, *Ammianus and the Historia Augusta*, Oxford (1968).

———, 'Three Roman Jurists', *Bonner Historia Augusta Colloquium 1968/69* (1970), 309 = *Roman Papers*, 790.

———, 'Domitius Corbulo', *JRS* 60 (1970), 27 = *Roman Papers*, 805.

———, *Ten Studies in Tacitus*, Oxford (1970).

———, *Emperors and Biography*, Oxford (1971).

———, *Danubian Papers*, Bucarest (1971).

———, 'Antonius Saturninus', *JRS* 68 (1978), 12.

———, *Roman Papers* (2 vols., ed. E. Badian), Oxford (1979).

———, 'Guard Prefects of Trajan and Hadrian', *JRS* 70 (1980), 64.

———, *Some Arval Brethren*, Oxford (1980).

TALBERT, R.J.A., 'Some Causes of Disorder in AD 68–69', *American Journal of Ancient History*, 1, vol. 2 (1977), 69.

———, 'Pliny the Younger as Governor of Bithynia-Pontus', *Collection Latomus*, vol. 168.

TAUBENSCHLAG, G., *The Law of Greco-Roman Egypt in the Light of the Papyri 332 BC–AD 640*[2], Warsaw (1955).

TAYLOR, L.R., 'M. Titius and the Syrian Command' *JRS* 26 (1936), 168.

TOWNEND, P.W., 'The Revolution of AD 238: the Leaders and their Aims', *YCS* 14 (1955), 49.

———, 'The Post of *ab epistulis* in the Second Century', *Hist.* 10 (1961), 375.

TOYNBEE, J.M.C., *The Hadrianic School*, Oxford (1934).

VERSNEL, H.S., *Triumphus; an Enquiry into the Origin, Development and Meaning of the Roman Triumph*, Leiden (1970).

WARMINGTON, B.H., *Nero: Reality and Legend*, London (1969).

———, *Suetonius: Nero*, Bristol (1977).

WATSON, G.R., 'The Pay of the Roman Army: Suetonius, Dio and the Quartum Stipendium', *Hist.* 5 (1956), 332.

———, 'The Pay of the Roman Army: the Auxiliary Forces', *Hist.* 8 (1959), 372.

———, *The Roman Soldier*, London (1969).

WEBSTER, G., *The Roman Imperial Army*[2], London (1979).

WELLESLEY, K., *The Histories, Book III*, Sydney (1972).

WELLS, C.M., *The German Policy of Augustus*, Oxford (1972).

WHITTAKER, C.R., ed. Herodian, 2 vols (*Loeb*), Harvard (1969).

WILLIAMS, W., 'The *Libellus* Procedure and the Severan Papyri', *JRS*

64 (1974), 86.

——, 'Individuality in the Imperial Constitutions, Hadrian and the Antonines' *JRS* 66 (1976), 67.

YAVETZ, A., *Plebs and Princeps*, Oxford (1967).

INDEX OF PASSAGES

This index cites only passages translated or specifically discussed in the text.

INDEX OF NAMES AND SUBJECTS

This index is selective and is intended to be only a general guide to the main topics and names in the book. Material in the footnotes is not included.